LIVINGSTON ON
CRIMINAL JURISPRUDENCE

PATTERSON SMITH

REPRINT SERIES IN

CRIMINOLOGY, LAW ENFORCEMENT, AND SOCIAL PROBLEMS

PUBLICATIONS

No. 1. Lewis, Orlando F. *The Development of American Prisons and Prison Customs, 1776-1845.*

No. 2. Carpenter, Mary. *Reformatory Prison Discipline.*

No. 3. Brace, Charles Loring. *The Dangerous Classes of New York.*

No. 4. Dix, Dorothea Lynde. *Remarks on Prisons and Prison Discipline in the United States.*

No. 5. Bruce, Andrew A., Albert J. Harno, Ernest W. Burgess, & John Landesco. *The Workings of the Indeterminate-Sentence Law and the Parole System in Illinois.*

No. 6. Wickersham Commission. *Complete Reports, Including the Mooney-Billings Report.* 14 Vols.

No. 7. Livingston, Edward. *Complete Works on Criminal Jurisprudence.* 2 Vols.

No. 8. Cleveland Foundation. *Criminal Justice in Cleveland.*

No. 9. Illinois Association for Criminal Justice. *The Illinois Crime Survey.*

No. 10. Missouri Association for Criminal Justice. *The Missouri Crime Survey.*

No. 11. Aschaffenburg, Gustav. *Crime and Its Repression.*

No. 12. Garofalo, Raffaele. *Criminology.*

No. 13. Gross, Hans. *Criminal Psychology.*

No. 14. Lombroso, Cesare. *Crime, Its Causes and Remedies.*

No. 15. Saleilles, Raymond. *The Individualization of Punishment.*

No. 16. Tarde, Gabriel. *Penal Philosophy.*

No. 17. McKelvey, Blake. *American Prisons.*

No. 18. Sanders, Wiley B. *Negro Child Welfare in North Carolina.*

No. 19. Pike, Luke Owen. *A History of Crime in England.* 2 Vols.

No. 20. Herring, Harriet L. *Welfare Work in Mill Villages.*

No. 21. Barnes, Harry Elmer. *The Evolution of Penology in Pennsylvania.*

No. 22. Puckett, Newbell N. *Folk Beliefs of the Southern Negro.*

No. 23. Fernald, Mabel Ruth, Mary Holmes Stevens Hayes, & Almena Dawley. *A Study of Women Delinquents in New York State.*

No. 24. Wines, Enoch Cobb. *The State of Prisons and of Child-Saving Institutions in the Civilized World.*

PUBLICATION NO. 7: PATTERSON SMITH REPRINT SERIES IN
CRIMINOLOGY, LAW ENFORCEMENT, AND SOCIAL PROBLEMS

THE COMPLETE

WORKS OF EDWARD LIVINGSTON

ON

CRIMINAL JURISPRUDENCE;

CONSISTING OF

SYSTEMS OF PENAL LAW FOR THE STATE OF LOUISIANA AND FOR THE UNITED STATES OF AMERICA;

With the Introductory Reports to the same.

TO WHICH IS PREFIXED AN INTRODUCTION

BY

SALMON P. CHASE,

CHIEF JUSTICE OF THE UNITED STATES.

IN TWO VOLUMES.

VOL. II.

Montclair, New Jersey

PATTERSON SMITH

1968

Originally published 1873 by The National Prison Association
Reprinted 1968, with the cooperation of
The American Correctional Association, by
Patterson Smith Publishing Corporation
Montclair, New Jersey

Library of Congress Catalog Card Number: 68-55775

TABLE OF CONTENTS.

VOLUME II.

A SYSTEM OF PENAL LAW.

A CODE OF EVIDENCE.

A CODE OF REFORM AND PRISON DISCIPLINE.

EXTRACTS FROM THE SYSTEM OF PENAL LAW FOR THE UNITED STATES.

A BOOK OF DEFINITIONS.

A SYSTEM OF PENAL LAW.

INTRODUCTORY TITLE.

INTRODUCTORY TITLE.

CHAPTER I.

Preamble.

No act of legislation can be or ought to be immutable. Changes are required by the alteration of circumstances ; amendments, by the imperfection of all human institutions ; but laws ought never to be changed without great deliberation, and a due consideration as well of the reasons on which they were founded, as of the circumstances under which they were enacted. It is therefore proper, in the formation of new laws, to state clearly the motives for making them, and the principles by which the framers were governed in their enactment. Without a knowledge of these, future legislatures cannot perform the task of amendment, and there can be neither consistency in legislation, nor uniformity in the interpretation of laws.

For these reasons, the general assembly of the state of Louisiana declare that their objects in establishing the following code, are—

To remove doubts relative to the authority of any parts of the penal law of the different nations by which this state, before its independence, was governed.

To embody into one law, and to arrange into system, such of the various prohibitions enacted by different statutes as are proper to be retained in the penal code.

To include in the class of offences, acts injurious to the state and its inhabitants, which are not now forbidden by law.

To abrogate the reference, which now exists, to a foreign law, for the definition of offences and the mode of prosecuting them.

To organize a connected system for the prevention as well as for the prosecution and punishment of offences.

To collect into written codes, and to express in plain language, all the rules which it may be necessary to establish for the protection of the government of the country, and the person, property, condition and reputation of individuals ; the penalties and punishments attached to a breach of those rules ; the legal means of preventing offences, and the forms of prosecuting them when committed ; the rules of evidence, by which the truth of accusations are to be tested ; and the duties of executive and judicial officers, jurors, and individuals, in preventing, prosecuting, and punishing offences : to the end that no one need be ignorant of any branch of criminal jurisprudence, which it concerns all to know.

And to change the present penal laws, in all those points in which they contravene the following principles, which the general assembly consider as fundamental truths, and which they have made the basis of their legislation on this subject, to wit :

Vengeance is unknown to the law. The only object of punishment is to prevent the commission of offences : it should be calculated to operate—

First, on the delinquent, so as by seclusion to deprive him of the present means, and, by habits of industry and temperance, of any future desire, to repeat the offence.

Secondly, on the rest of the community, so as to deter them, by the example, from a like contravention of the laws. No punishments, greater than are necessary to effect these ends, ought to be inflicted.

No acts or omissions should be declared to be offences, but such as are injurious to the state, to societies permitted by the laws, or to individuals.

But penal laws should not be multiplied without evident necessity ; therefore acts, although injurious to individuals or societies, should not be made liable to public prosecution, when they may be sufficiently repressed by private suit.

From the imperfection of all human institutions, and the inevitable errors of those who manage them, it sometimes happens that the innocent are condemned to suffer the punishment due to the guilty. Punishments should, therefore, be of such a nature that they may be remitted, and as far as possible compensated, in cases where the injustice of the sentence becomes apparent.

Where guilt is ascertained, the punishment should be speedily inflicted.

Penal laws should be written in plain language, clearly and unequivocally expressed, that they may neither be misunderstood nor perverted; they should be so concise as to be remembered with ease; and all technical phrases, or words they contain, should be clearly defined. They should be promulgated in such a manner as to force a knowledge of their provisions upon the people; to this end, they should not only be published, but taught in the schools, and publicly read on stated occasions.

The law should never command more than it can enforce. Therefore, whenever, from public opinion, or any other cause, a penal law cannot be carried into execution, it should be repealed.

The accused, in all cases, should be entitled to a public trial, conducted by known rules, before impartial judges and an unbiassed jury; to a copy of the act of accusation against him; to the delay necessary to prepare for his trial; to process to enforce the attendance of his own witnesses; and to an opportunity of seeing, hearing and examining those who are produced against him; to the assistance of counsel for his defence; to free communication with such counsel, if in confinement; and to be bailed in all cases, except those particularly specified by law. No presumption of guilt, however violent, can justify the infliction of any punishment before conviction, or of any bodily restraint greater than is necessary to prevent escape ; and the nature and extent of this restraint should be determined by law.

Perfect liberty should be secured of hearing and publishing a true account of the proceedings of criminal courts, limited only by such restrictions as morality and decency require ; and no restraint whatsoever should be imposed on the free discussion of the official conduct of the judges and other ministers of justice, in this branch of government.

Such a system of procedure, in criminal cases, should be established as to be understood without long study ; it should neither suffer the guilty to escape by formal objections, nor involve the innocent in difficulties, by errors in pleading.

For this purpose, amendments should be permitted in all cases, where neither the accused nor the public prosecutor can be surprised.

Those penal laws counteract their own effect, which, through a mistaken lenity, give greater comforts to a convict than those which he would probably have enjoyed while at liberty.

The power of pardoning should be only exercised in cases of innocence discovered, or of certain and unequivocal reformation.

Provision should be made for preventing the execution of intended offences, whenever the design to commit them is sufficiently apparent.

The remote means of preventing offences, do not form the subject of penal laws. The general assembly will provide them in their proper place. They are, the diffusion of knowledge, by the means of public education, and the promotion of industry, and consequently of ease and happiness among the people.

Religion is a source of happiness here, and the foundation of our hopes of it hereafter; but its observance can never, without the worst of oppression, form the subject of a penal code. All modes of belief, and all forms of worship, are equal in the eye of the law ; when they interfere with no private or public rights, all are entitled to equal protection in their exercise.

Whatever may be the majority of the professors of one religion or sect in the state, it is a persecution to force any one to conform to any ceremonies, or to observe any festival or day, appropriated to worship by the members of a particular religious persuasion : this does not exclude a general law, establishing civil festivals or periodical cessations from labour for civil purposes unconnected with religious worship, or the appointment of particular days on which citizens of all persuasions should join, each according to the rites of his own religion, in rendering thanks to God for any signal blessing, or imploring his assistance in any public calamity.

The innocent should never be made to participate in the punishment inflicted on the guilty ; therefore, no such effects should follow conviction as to prevent the heir from claiming an inheritance through or from the person convicted. Still less should the feelings of nature be converted into instruments of torture, by denouncing punishment against the children, to secure the good conduct of the parent.

Laws intended to suppress a temporary evil should be limited to the probable time of its duration, or carefully repealed after the reason for enacting them has ceased.

CHAPTER II.

Plan and division of the system of penal law.

Art. 1. This system comprises four distinct codes, and a Book of Definitions. The first, called the CODE OF CRIMES AND PUNISHMENTS, is divided into two books, containing :—General Principles ; and the description of all acts or omissions that are declared to be offences; with the punishment assigned to each.

Art. 2. The second is called the CODE OF CRIMINAL PROCEDURE. It is divided into two books. It contains the means provided for preventing offences that are apprehended, and for repressing those that exist; and it directs the mode of proceeding for bringing offenders to justice.

Art. 3. The third is the whole law of evidence, applicable as well to civil as to penal cases, and is called the CODE OF EVIDENCE.

Art. 4. The fourth contains a system of prison discipline, in all the stages in which imprisonment is used, either as the means of detention or punishment. It is designated as the CODE OF REFORM AND PRISON DISCIPLINE.

Art. 5. The concluding division of the system is a BOOK OF DEFINITIONS, which defines all the technical words or phrases that are used in the several codes.

CHAPTER III.

Introductory notice.

Art. 6. Whenever the office, trust, state, or relation of tutor, ward, administrator, executor, ancestor, heir, parent, child, ascendant, descendant, minor, infant, master, or servant, and the relative pronouns, he or they, as referring to them, are used, they are intended to mean as well females as males, standing in those relations, or exercising the same offices, trusts, or duties, unless the contrary be expressed.

Art. 7. The general terms—whoever; any person; any one; and the relative pronouns—he or they, when they refer to them, are intended to include females as well as males, unless there is some expression to the contrary. The word *man* is used in this system, not as a generical term, but to express a person of the male sex, of whatever age. The term woman includes females of every age.

Art. 8. Whenever anything is forbidden or directed, by using the general terms—any one ; one ; any person ; whoever ; or the relative pronoun—he ; referring to any such general term, the same prohibition or direction (if the contrary be not expressed) is extended to more persons than one, doing or omitting the same act.

Art. 9. Whenever anything is directed or forbidden with respect to one object or thing, the same direction or prohibition extends to more than one of the same objects or things, and a direction or prohibition as to more objects than one, includes the same prohibition as to a single one of the same objects.

Art. 10. All words printed in small capitals, are defined and explained in the Book of Definitions ; and in all other parts of the system are used in no other sense than that given to them by such definition or explanation.

Art. 11. Every word or phrase, other than those so printed, is to be taken and construed in the sense in which it is used in common parlance, taken in connexion with the context, and the subject relative to which it is employed.

Art. 12. It is not intended that each article should contain in itself a complete expression of legislative will, on the subject of which it treats, independent of the other articles of the same section ; the whole are to be considered together ; to avoid repetition, a provision in one article sometimes relates to something expressed in another; an example of which is found in the article immediately preceding this, where the words " so printed " relate to printing in " small capitals," provided for in the section preceding it.

Art. 13. Whenever the degrees of relationship between persons are referred to, the degrees by AFFINITY, as well as CONSANGUINITY, are intended, unless the contrary be expressed.

Art. 14. Whenever anything is forbidden or commanded for the protection of property or interest, and the general term " person," or any other general term, is used, to designate the party whose property or interest it is intended to protect by such prohibition or command; in all such cases, the state, and all public and private bodies corporate are included.

A CODE OF CRIMES AND PUNISHMENTS.

INTRODUCTORY TITLE.

This code is divided into two books, and each book into titles, chapters, sections and articles, numbered throughout the whole code.

The first book contains general provisions, applicable to prosecutions and trials; to the persons who are amenable to the penal laws of the state; to the circumstances under which all acts that would otherwise be offences may be justified or excused; to the repetition of offences; and to the case of different persons participating in the same offence, as principals, accomplices and accessaries.

The second book defines offences, and designates their punishments.

BOOK I.

CONTAINING GENERAL PROVISIONS.

CHAPTER I.

Containing general provisions relative to the operation of the penal laws of this state.

Art. 1. No act or omission done or made before the promulgation of the law which forbids it, can be punished as an OFFENCE.

Art. 2. If an act or omission be created an offence by one law, and the penalty be altered by another, no breach of the first law, committed before the promulgation of the second, can be punished by inflicting the penalty of the latter.

Art. 3. After a PENAL LAW is repealed, no person can be arrested, imprisoned, tried or condemned, for a breach of it while it was in force, unless the repealing law has an express provision to that effect.

Art. 4. The distinction between a favourable and unfavourable construction of laws is abolished. All penal laws whatever are to be construed according to the plain import of their words, taken in their usual sense, in connexion with the context, and with reference to the matter of which they treat.

Art. 5. When a second penal law shall direct a NEW PENALTY, the penalty of the first law shall be deemed to be abolished, unless the contrary be expressed.

Art. 6. A law which simply commands or forbids an act to be done, but which contains no denunciation of a penalty, can have none but civil effects; the act or omission which is forbidden cannot be punished as an offence.

Art. 7. The legislature alone has the right to declare what shall constitute an offence; therefore it is forbidden to punish any acts or omissions, not expressly prohibited, under pretence that they offend against the laws of nature, of religion, morality or any other rule, except written law.

Art. 8. Courts are expressly prohibited from punishing any acts or omissions which are not forbidden by the plain import of the words of the law, under the pretence that they are within its spirit. It is better that acts of an evil tendency should for a time be done with impunity, than that courts should assume legislative powers; which assumption is itself an act more injurious than any it may purport to repress. There are, therefore, no constructive offences. The legislature, when the necessity appears, will bring such acts as ought to be punished within the letter of the law.

Art. 9. If, however, any penal law shall be so inaccurately drawn, as to bring within its penalty an act that it could not, in the opinion of the court, have been the intention of the legislature so to punish; the accused must be acquitted, but the court shall report such case to the legislature at their next session, or within eight days if they be in session.

Art. 10. When a competent tribunal, judging in the last resort, hath rendered a final judgment, acquitting or condemning the accused, on the merits of the charge against him, he can never be again prosecuted for the same offence.

Art. 11. An accusation being an affirmation of guilt, it must be proved to the satisfaction of those whose province it is to decide.

CHAPTER II.

General provisions relative to prosecutions and trials.

Art. 12. No person accused of any offence shall be compelled by violence or menace, to answer any interrogations relative to his innocence or guilt ; nor shall his confession, unless it be given freely, without violence, menace, or promise of indemnity or favour, be produced in evidence against him.

Art. 13. No person shall be arrested to answer for any offence, but in the manner and on the evidence specially set forth in the Codes of Procedure and Evidence.

Art. 14. No SEARCH WARRANT shall issue in any case but in those provided for, and in the manner directed in the Code of Procedure.

Art. 15. The accused, in every stage of the prosecution, is entitled to have advice of such counsellor at law, or other person, as may be employed by him for his defence. If he declare himself unable to procure counsel, the court shall assign him an advocate in the manner directed by the said code.

Art. 16. No trial for any CRIME shall be had, but in the presence of the accused. No examination of witnesses shall be used on such trial, but such as is taken in the joint presence of the court, the jury, the public prosecutor and the accused; all of whom shall have leave to question the witness. Those cases in which testimony is allowed to be taken by commission, and those which are specially provided for in the Code of Procedure, are excepted from the provisions of this article.

Art. 17. All trials for offences shall be held in public. All persons under no legal disability or restraint, have a right to be present at such trials ; provided, however, that the court may, on the prayer of the prosecutor or the accused, direct witnesses to withdraw until they are called for examination; and may also, in the manner directed by the provisions of the Code of Procedure, remove such persons as shall obstruct the administration of justice.

Art. 18. The preceding article is subject to the restriction required by decency and morals, which are particularly provided for in the Code of Procedure.

Art. 19. All final judgments in trial for offences, with the reasons on which they are founded, shall be distinctly pronounced in open court, in the presence of the accused (if he be in custody), and they shall be entered at large on the minutes of the court. And in like manner all other judgments, orders or decisions, shall be pronounced and entered on the minutes, whenever either the public prosecutor or the accused shall require the same.

Art. 20. After a cause, whether civil or criminal, is decided, it shall be lawful for any one, by printing and in writing as well as by speech, to discuss the reasons of any judgment, order, or decree, given in the course of any such suit or prosecution, and to call in question the legality or propriety of the same.

Art. 21. The process to which the accused is entitled by the constitution, to compel the attendance of his witnesses, shall be granted for witnesses who may be in any part of the state, and the sheriff of any parish to whom the same may be directed, shall serve and return such process, and such witnesses shall be paid by the state whenever the accused shall be acquitted, and whenever it shall appear to the court that the accused, if convicted, is unable to pay them.

Art. 22. All witnesses summoned to attend the trial of any offence, shall be protected from arrest in any civil suit, and in any penal suit for a misdemeanor, other than a breach of the peace, while attending on the court, and for a reasonable time, while going to or returning therefrom; unless it shall appear that the witness was summoned by collusion merely to protect him from arrest. And in case of any arrest, contrary to this article, any judge of any court of this state, either of criminal or civil jurisdiction, except justices of the peace, may grant relief by discharging the person arrested, first giving notice to the person causing the arrest, or to his agent.

Art. 23. No person after being acquitted or ordered to be discharged, shall be detained for the payment of any fees or costs attending the prosecution for which he has been discharged, or for the reimbursement of the sum allowed by the law for his support, or for any sums whatever due for his maintenance, or for services or supplies while he was in prison. Nor shall any court or magistrate give judgment in any suit against a person who has been acquitted or discharged for want of prosecution, if he shall be sued for any such fees, or for any such sum as is allowed by law for the maintenance of prisoners.

Art. 24. The trial by jury, as regulated in the Code of Procedure, is declared to be the mode of trial for all offences, and it cannot be renounced.

Art. 25. There shall be no trial for any CRIME but on indictment, nor for any MISDEMEANOR but on indictment or information, in the manner directed by the Code of Procedure.

CHAPTER III.

Of persons amenable to the provisions of this code, and of the circumstances under which all acts that would otherwise be offences, may be justified or excused.

Art. 26. All persons, whether they be inhabitants of this state, or of any other of the United States of America, or aliens, are liable to be punished for any offence committed in this state against the laws thereof. Citizens or inhabitants of the state may be punished for acts committed out of the limits thereof, in those cases in which there is a special provision of law, declaring that the act forbidden shall be an offence, although done out of the state.

Art. 27. An offence is a voluntary act or omission, done or made contrary to the directions of a penal law. There can, therefore, generally be no offence, if the will do not concur with the act; but the law has established exceptions to, and modifications of, this rule: but on modifications or exceptions, other than those expressly provided, are to be allowed.

Art. 28. After the promulgation of a law, no one shall be excused for a breach of it on an alleged ignorance of its provisions.

Art. 29. No person shall be convicted of any offence committed when under nine years of age; nor of any offence when between nine and fifteen years of age, unless it shall appear by proof to the jury, that he had sufficient understanding to know the nature and illegality of the act which constituted the offence.

Art. 30. If a minor shall commit an offence by command or persuasion of any relation in the ascending line; of his tutor or curator, or any person acting as such; or of his master, if he be an apprentice or servant, then the minor shall be punished for such offence by simple imprisonment during one half of the time to which he would have been sentenced had he been of full age. Provided such minor have attained the age of fifteen years at the time of the commission of the offence; if under that age, the command or persuasion of either of the persons, standing in either of the relations to him which are above enumerated, shall excuse him from punishment, if the offence committed be a misdemeanor only; but if the offence be a crime, such minor, under fifteen years of age, shall be committed to a school of reform, for the purpose of being instructed in some trade, in the manner particularly provided for in the Code of Reform and Prison Discipline. And in all cases of crimes committed by minors, under the age of eighteen years, except those punishable by imprisonment for life, the court may direct that the offender be, either in lieu of, or in addition to, the punishment generally provided for the offence, be so committed to the school of reform.

Art. 31. In like manner, a married woman committing an offence by the command or persuasion of her husband, shall suffer no greater punishment than simple imprisonment, for one half of the time to which she would have been sentenced, if she had committed the offence without such command or persuasion. The relation of husband and wife, for the purposes of this article, need not be proved by testimony of the celebration of the marriage contract. Living together at the time, and general reputation of marriage, shall be sufficient to reduce the punishment of the reputed wife, and to increase that of the reputed husband, in the manner hereafter directed.

Art. 32. Offences punishable by imprisonment for life, are excepted from the operation of the two last preceding articles.

Art. 33. In all cases where a minor shall be AIDED in the commission of an offence, by either of the persons standing in the relation to him hereinbefore enumerated; or if the husband, or the reputed husband, shall aid the wife in the commission of the offence, or shall be PRESENT during the time of its commission, without endeavouring to prevent it, either of these circumstances shall be proof that the offence was committed by their command or persuasion.

Art. 34. If any minor or married woman shall have committed any offence, and the persons standing in the relations to such minor, which are above enumerated, or the husband of the wife, shall be convicted of having persuaded, commanded, or aided in the said offence, then said persons so convicted shall be punished as follows, that is to say :—

If the minor be under fifteen years of age at the time of committing the offence, then the duration of the punishment, if the same shall consist of imprisonment, and the amount of the fine, if any, which would otherwise have been inflicted on such persons, shall be increased one-half. And if the minor shall be above fifteen years, then one-fourth ; and in either case, if the punishment for such offence be imprisonment for life, then one month of such imprisonment, in every year, shall be in solitude.

Art. 35. No act done by a person in a state of INSANITY, can be punished as an offence. No person becoming INSANE after he has committed an offence, can be tried for the same. No person becoming insane after he has been found guilty, shall be sentenced while in that state. No person sentenced shall be punished, if he afterwards become and continue insane.

And during the continuance of the punishment, if the convict is deprived of his reason, so much of the punishment as may consist of hard labour, shall, during such insanity, cease ; and the court shall make such order with respect to the convict, as is provided in the Code of Reform and Prison Discipline.

In all the cases mentioned in this article, the court having cognizance of the offence, shall make order for securing the person of the accused. The manner of ascertaining whether insanity is feigned or real, is provided for in the Code of Procedure.

Art. 36. Private soldiers and non-commissioned officers in the army, or in the militia when in actual service, are not liable to punishment for misdemeanors committed by the order of any officer, whose legal military order they are bound to obey ; but all officers giving or transmitting the command, are liable to the penalties of the law.

Art. 37. The order of a military superior is no justification or excuse for the commission of a crime.

Art. 38. The order, warrant or writ issued by a magistrate or court, shall justify the person executing it for any act done in obedience thereto, only in cases wherein the following circumstances concur :—

1. The court or magistrate must have JURISDICTION of the cause or COGNIZANCE of the matter in which the order, warrant, or writ was issued.

2. The writ, warrant, or order, if written, must have all the substantial requisites prescribed by law for such writs as it purports to be.

3. The person executing it must be an officer bound to

execute, by virtue of his office, such writs as it purports to be; or he must be a person to whom such writ is legally directed; or he must be one legally called upon by such officer to aid in the execution of the order, warrant, or writ.

4. He must have no knowledge of any illegality in obtaining or executing the order, warrant, or writ.

Art. 39. The legal order of a COMPETENT magistrate or court, if executed by a person DULY AUTHORIZED, will justify those acts which are expressly commanded by such order, and also all those acts which are the necessary means of carrying the order into execution, but it will justify no other acts; the means allowed as necessary by law are detailed in the Code of Procedure.

Art. 40. If one be forced by threats or actual violence to do any act, which, if voluntarily done, would be an offence, he shall be exempted from punishment, by proving the following circumstances :

1. That he was threatened with the loss of life or limb, if he did not perform the act; and that he had good reason to believe that such threat would be executed.

2. That he made every endeavour which could be made by any man of common courage to resist or escape from the power of the person using the threats.

3. That the act of which he is accused was done while he was in the presence of the person using the threats or violence, and during the continuance of the same.

Art. 41. If one intending to commit an offence, and in the act of preparing for or executing the same, shall, through MISTAKE or ACCIDENT, do another act which, if voluntarily done, would be an offence, he shall incur the penalty for the act really done. Provided, that if the act intended to be done be a misdemeanor, he shall only incur the highest penalty provided by law for the offence he intended to commit, although the act done would, if he had intended it, have been a crime.

But if the intent was to commit a crime, although INFERIOR IN DEGREE, he shall incur the penalty provided by law for the act really done.

Art. 42. No event happening through MISTAKE or ACCIDENT in the performance of a lawful act, done with ORDINARY ATTENTION, is an offence.

Art. 43. An act forbidden by law, though done through MISTAKE or ACCIDENT, from the want of ORDINARY CARE AND ATTENTION, is punishable.

Art. 44. The provisions of the last preceding article are subject to modifications in the case of homicide, which are expressed in the part of the code which treats of homicide.

Art. 45. The intention to commit an offence shall be presumed whenever the means used are such as, in the common course of events, must produce the event which is forbidden.

Art. 46. The fact which constitutes an offence being proved, all facts or circumstances on which the accused relies to justify or excuse the prohibited act or omission must be proved by him.

Art. 47. If any person who shall ATTEMPT TO COMMIT an offence, fail in completing the same, or is interrupted from any cause not depending on his own will, he shall suffer ONE HALF OF THE PUNISHMENT to which he would have been sentenced if he had completed the whole.

Art. 48. Military offences are not comprehended in this code.

Art. 49. The Indian tribes residing within the boundaries of this state, being governed by their own usages, no act done within their boundaries by individuals belonging to such tribes, in their intercourse with each other, or with other tribes, and not affecting any other person, is considered as an offence against this code: in other respects they are considered in the same light with other persons in the state, both as to protection and liability to punishment.

Art. 50. Offences committed by slaves form the subject of a separate code: such offences are not included in any of the provisions of this system.

Art. 51. The Second Book of this code contains modifications of the general provisions contained in this chapter, which control them.

CHAPTER IV.

Of a repetition of offences.

Art. 52. Any person, who, having been convicted of a misdemeanor, shall afterwards repeat the same offence, or commit any other misdemeanor of the same nature, shall suffer ADDITION OF ONE HALF to the punishment he would otherwise have suffered. If the first conviction was for a crime, the punishment for the second offence of the same nature, shall also be INCREASED ONE HALF.

Art. 53. And if any person, having been twice previously convicted of crimes, no matter of what nature, shall a third time be convicted of any crime afterwards committed, he shall be considered as unfit for society, and be imprisoned at hard labour for life.

Art. 54. A previous conviction in any of the United States of America, operates the same effect as to the increase of punishment for subsequent offences, as if the same conviction had taken place in this state.

Art. 55. By offences of the SAME NATURE, in this section, are intended all such as are comprised within the same title in the Second Book of this code.

Art. 56. Where the punishment of the crime of which the offender is a second or a third time convicted, is imprisonment for life, the increased punishment must consist in seclusion, or such other privations as the judges are empowered in the Second Book to direct, with respect to offenders in general.

CHAPTER V.

Of principals, accomplices, and accessaries.

Art. 57. An offence being the doing of an act which is forbidden under a penalty imposed by law, or omitting to do some act, which, under like penalty, is directed by law to be done ; those are principal offenders who do the forbidden act, or who, being bound to do the act enjoined, are guilty of the omission.

Art. 58. If the forbidden act be done by several, all are principal offenders. If several are bound to perform the act which is enjoined, all who omit it are principal offenders.

Art. 59. When the act constituting the offence is actually done by only one or more persons, but others are present, and knowing the unlawful intent, aid them by acts, or encourage them by words or gestures ; or if not being actually present, others shall keep watch to give notice of the approach of any one who might interrupt the commission of the offence ; or shall be employed in procuring aid, or arms, or instruments for the performance of the act, while it is executing ; or shall do any other act at the time of executing the offence, to secure the safety or concealment of those who perform the offence, or to aid them in its execution : all such persons are also principal offenders, and may be prosecuted and convicted as such.

Art. 60. When the offence is committed by SECONDARY MEANS, without employing the agency of a person who may be convicted as a principal offender, the person employing and preparing those secondary means is a principal offender, although he may not be present when the means he had prepared took their effect.

Art. 61. Laying poison where the person whom it is intended to murder may take it himself; employing a child, or other innocent person, to give it; setting a spring-gun, so that the party may fire it himself; are examples of the secondary means intended by the last preceding article.

Art. 62. Those persons are also principals who, having counselled or agreed to the performance of the act, shall be present when it is done, whether they aid in the execution or not.

Art. 63. There may be accessaries to all offences committed with premeditation, and accomplices to all except manslaughter, and offences occasioned by neglect.

Art. 64. There can be neither accomplice nor accessary, except in cases where an offence has been committed.

Art. 65. All those are accomplices who are not present at the commission of an offence, but who, before the act is done, verbally or in writing, shall advise or command, or encourage another to commit it :

Those who agree with the principal offender to aid him in committing the offence, although such aid may not have been given :

Those who shall promise money, or other reward, who shall offer any place or particular favour, or any other inducement ; or shall menace any injury or loss of favour, in order to procure the commission of an offence :

Those who shall prepare arms or instruments, men, money, or aid of any kind, or do any other act prior to the commission of the offence, to facilitate its execution, and knowing that it is intended : all these persons are accomplices.

Art. 66. No person can be found guilty as an accomplice to any offence, other than such as have aided, promoted, advised, or encouraged it by some of the means set forth in the last preceding article ; but it is not necessary that the advice should be strictly pursued : it is sufficient if the offence be of the SAME NATURE and for the same object as the offence advised or encouraged.

Art 67. If, in the attempt to commit an offence, the principal offender shall make himself liable to punishment for any other act committed by mistake or accident, according to the provisions for that purpose hereinbefore contained, his accomplices shall be punished only as they would have been had the offence been committed which he intended to commit.

Art. 68. The punishment of an accomplice is the same as that designated for the principal offender, excepting the increase of such punishment provided for in the next article.

Art. 69. If the principal offender be under fifteen years of age, whether he be found of sufficient intelligence to understand the nature and illegality of the act or not, and there be an accomplice of full age, the punishment of such accomplice shall be INCREASED ONE HALF, and if the principal offender be a minor, above fifteen, then the punishment of the accomplice shall be INCREASED ONE QUARTER.

Art. 70. Accessaries are those who, knowing that an offence has been committed, conceal the offender, or give him any other aid, in order that he may effect his escape from arrest or trial, or the execution of his sentence ; he who aids the offender in preparing and making his defence at law ; or who procures him to be bailed, although he may afterwards abscond, shall not be considered as an accessary.

Art. 71. The following persons cannot be punished as accessaries :

1. The husband or wife of the offender.

2. His relations in the ascending or descending line, either by affinity or consanguinity.

3. His brothers or sisters.

4. His domestic servants.

Art. 72. The accessary shall be punished by fine and simple imprisonment in the manner directed by the Second Book.

Art. 73. The accomplice may be arrested, tried and punished before the conviction of the principal offender, and the acquittal of the principal shall be no bar to the prosecution of the accomplice ; but on the trial of such accomplice, the commission of the offence must be clearly proved, or the accomplice cannot be convicted.

Art. 74. The accessary may be arrested, but not tried, without his consent, before the conviction of the principal, and the acquittal of the principal shall discharge the person named as accessary.

BOOK II.

OF OFFENCES AND PUNISHMENTS.

TITLE I.

OF THE GENERAL DIVISIONS AND DESCRIPTIONS OF OFFENCES AND PUNISHMENTS.

CHAPTER I.

Definition and divisions of offences.

Art. 75. Offences are those acts and omissions which are forbidden by positive law, under the sanction of a penalty.

Art. 76. There are two divisions of offences, establishing distinctions drawn, the one from the degree of the offence, the other from its object.

By the first division, all offences are either CRIMES OR MISDEMEANORS.

By the second, they are PUBLIC OR PRIVATE OFFENCES.

Art. 77. All offences punishable by confinement and hard labour, or by a forfeiture of any civil or political right, are crimes; all other offences are misdemeanors.

All offences to which either of the punishments enumerated in the last preceding article are expressly assigned, or to which the court have a discretionary power to apply them, are punishable in that manner within the meaning of that article.

Art. 78. Offences, in relation to their object, are public or private offences.

Art 79. These are public offences which principally affect the state or its government in any of its branches, or any of its institutions, or operations for the benefit of the citizens.   Those are public offences which affect :

1, The sovereign power of the state.

2. The legislative power.

3. The executive power.

4. The judiciary power.

5. The public tranquillity.

6. The right of suffrage.

7. The freedom of the press.

8. The public records.

9. The current coin and public securities.

10. The public revenue.

11. The commerce and manufactures.

12. The public property.

13. The public roads, embankments, navigable waters, and other property held by the sovereign power for the common use of the people.

14. The public health.

15. The morals of the people.

Art. 80. Those are private offences which principally affect individuals, or such societies as are either established or permitted by law ; they are such as affect them :

1. In the exercise of their religion.

2. In their honour and reputation.

3. In their persons.

4. In their profession and trade.

5. In their civil and political rights and conditions.

6. In their property.

Art. 81. The division of offences marked out by this chapter, is intended only for the establishment of order in the arrangement of the code ; each offence will be hereinafter particularly defined and illustrated ; and no act or omission is an offence, which does not come within some one of those definitions as they are explained and illustrated.

CHAPTER II.

Of punishments.

Art. 82. To enforce the performance of a duty, or to give compensation for or prevent the infraction of a right, is the province of civil law. Penal law designates such infractions as require coercion or punishment to prevent or repress them; and it provides for each wrong thus designated, the requisite remedy of prevention, removal of the evil, or penalty for its commission. This code is strictly penal : compensation forms no part of its sanction. But no punishment deprives the party who is injured by an offence of his civil remedy ; the reservation of such right to civil redress is no where expressly made, but is in all cases understood.

Art. 83. The claim of the party injured by an offence, when it becomes liquidated by a judgment, is preferred in cases of insolvency, to the claim of the state for a fine imposed for the same offence. And if the fine be levied, and there is no property sufficient to satisfy the execution on the private suit, the amount of the fine, or as much of it as may be necessary, shall, on petition against the officer of government in whose hands it may be, be paid over to satisfy the judgment obtained by the party injured.

Art. 84. The civil remedy for the wrong occasioned by an offence may be pursued, either against the offender (when he is not confined at hard labour), or against the curators of his estate, when they are appointed according to the directions hereinafter contained.

Art. 85. The punishments and penalties to be incurred for offences under this code are :

1. Pecuniary fines.
2. Simple imprisonment.
3. Imprisonment in close custody.
4. Deprivation of office.
5. The suspension of some one or more political or civil rights for a limited period.
6. The forfeiture of some one or more political or civil rights.
7. Imprisonment and hard labour for a limited time.
8. Imprisonment at hard labour for life. Both these last punishments, with or without the addition of solitary confinement and other privations, as are directed in different parts of this code.

Art. 86. In addition to these punishments, where the offence is of a continuous nature, there must be judgment for its discontinuance.

Art. 87. In conviction for offences that affect honour or reputation, the judgment may, in addition to, or as an alternative for the punishment assigned, grant an honorary reparation, in the manner designated in that class of offences.

Art. 88. Pecuniary fines imposed for offences shall be levied by execution in the name of the state ; in the same manner as is directed by the practice in civil cases, for enforcing the execution of a judgment for debt, in the highest court of original jurisdiction in the state ; and the fine shall be a lien upon real property, from the time it is registered in the office of the register of mortgages, in the manner directed by law for the registry of judicial mortgages.

Art. 89. The death of the offender operates as a discharge of all pecuniary fines imposed upon him : even if execution be issued, the officer shall proceed no further therein. If the offender die before a sale on such execution, the lien created by the registry of such fine shall, by order of the court, be taken off, on proving the death of the offender ; unless real property shall have been sold, subject to such lien, and the amount thereof shall have formed part of the price ; in which case, the amount of such fine shall be levied by sale of the said real property, notwithstanding the death of the person on whom the fine was imposed.

Art. 90. A pecuniary fine shall in no case exceed one fourth part of the value of the property, real and personal, of the person on whom it is imposed ; and such person may, in all cases, have any pecuniary fine reduced to that amount, on showing the true value of his property, to the satisfaction of the court ; in which case the court must commute the part of the fine that is deducted into imprisonment ; calculating one day's imprisonment for every two dollars deducted from the fine, and the imprisonment, or any part of it, may be in close custody, with the limitation contained in the next article.

Art. 91. The wearing apparel, implements of trade, and household furniture of the delinquent, shall not be seized on an execution to satisfy a pecuniary fine, nor shall his arms or accoutrements, as an officer or private in the militia. If no other property be found, the court imposing the fine may, on such return being made on the execution, direct that the offender be imprisoned (either in close custody or in simple imprisonment, for the whole or a part of the time, at their discretion) one day for every two dollars contained in the amount of the fine imposed ; provided that such imprisonment do not exceed the term of ninety days, whatever be the amount of such fine ; and such imprisonment shall operate as full satisfaction of such fine.

Art. 92. Simple imprisonment is inflicted by the mere confinement of the offender in the common prison, appointed for that purpose by law, which shall be in a building or apartment distinct from the penitentiary. This punishment consists simply in the confinement of the person within the walls of such a prison, the prisoner being debarred neither the use of books nor the means of writing, nor the society of such persons as may desire

to see him during the hours established by the general
regulations for the prison.

Imprisonment in close custody is an imprisonment
within a single chamber of the common prison, during
which the prisoner is to be allowed no other sustenance
than the common prison allowance, and is debarred all
visits, except such as may be specially allowed by the
judge in particular cases of business or sickness.

Art. 93. The civil rights, which may be forfeited or
suspended by virtue of any sentence importing such
forfeiture or suspension, are divided into three classes :

1. The right of exercising the duties of executor,
administrator, curator, attorney at law, attorney in fact,
or being appointed to any PRIVATE OFFICE, which is now,
or may hereafter, be established by law.

2. The right of appearing in person, or by attorney,
in any court, as party to a suit, either as plaintiff or
defendant.

3. The right of bearing arms in defence of the country,
and of serving on juries.

Art. 94. All political rights are suspended by a sentence of imprisonment at hard labour, during the period
for which such imprisonment is directed; if such sentence
be for life, all those rights are forfeited.

Art. 95. A sentence of imprisonment at hard labour
suspends, during the term of such imprisonment, all civil
rights. If such sentence be for life, all civil rights are
forfeited. Forfeiture or suspension of civil rights is
directed in certain cases, which are specially provided
for.

Art. 96. A suspension or forfeiture of political rights,
whether expressly pronounced or implied, by the operation of the two last preceding articles, deprives the
offender of any PUBLIC OFFICE he may hold at the time.

Art. 97. When sentence of forfeiture or suspension of
civil rights, or of those of the first class only, has been
expressly pronounced or implied by a sentence of imprisonment at hard labour, all the duties, trusts, or
PRIVATE OFFICES, coming within the first class of civil

rights, are vacated by the sentence : and some other person shall be appointed to fulfil the same, in the same manner as if the vacancy had been occasioned by death.

Art. 98. During the term of imprisonment at hard labour, the administration of the affairs of the convict is committed to a curator, named in the manner directed by the Code of Procedure.

Art. 99. Imprisonment at hard labour is inflicted in the following degrees :

1. At labour in classes of convicts, in the manner directed by the Code of Reform and Prison Discipline.

2. At labour in solitude.

3. In solitude, with occasional labour.

Art. 100. When any one convicted of murder under trust, assassination or parricide, shall die in prison, his body shall be delivered for dissection; and the court may, at their discretion, add the same provision to their judgment in the case of simple murder or rape.

Art. 101. The punishment of imprisonment at hard labour admits of aggravation and alleviation, in different offences, as to food, dress, hours of labour, solitude, and other particulars which are described in this code, and in the Code of Reform and Prison Discipline.

Art. 102. For different modifications of the same offence, aggravations and alleviations of punishment are directed in this code, by a reference to the punishment assigned to the principal offence ; which it orders to be increased or diminished in a certain proportion. To apply this proportion, the following rules are to be observed :

1. If the direction be to diminish the punishment of imprisonment for life, the proportion shall be taken on a period of twenty-four years.

2. If the punishment directed to be increased or diminished leave a discretion to the court between a longer and a shorter term of time, or a greater or a smaller fine, the highest and the lowest terms or sums shall be diminished or increased in the proportion directed.

3. When no lower term or sum is fixed, the highest term or sum must be increased or diminished in the proportion directed, as the highest limit. The court must determine what judgment they would have probably rendered for the simple offence, and take that as the sum or term on which to calculate the proportion of punishment for the modified offence.

4. In all cases where a discretion is given to the court, they must observe the last preceding rule ; and within the increased or diminished limits, calculate the increase or diminution of punishment for the modified offence, upon the term or sum they would have assigned to the simple offence.

5. Where the punishment is a forfeiture of civil or political rights, and a diminution is directed, the proportion shall be determined by a suspension of those rights, calculated on a number of twenty-four years as the whole.

6. When the judgment is a suspension of such rights for a definite time, the proportion shall be calculated on that time.

All the other incidents of the whole punishment are annexed to the proportion during the period it lasts.

Art. 103. Fines for certain offences are directed to bear a certain proportion to the income or emoluments of the office held by the offender. To determine the amount of these fines, the court may examine witnesses as to the reputed emoluments, which may be reduced, if higher than the truth, by the oath of the defendant, which it is optional with him to give.

Art. 104. Where for the offence of bribery a fine is directed to be imposed, bearing a certain proportion to the value of the bribe offered or received, and such value cannot be ascertained, or if the bribe is something which cannot be appreciated in money, the fine imposed shall not be less than five hundred dollars, nor more than three thousand dollars, unless there be a special provision to the contrary.

Art. 105. No other punishments can be inflicted for

any offence than those enumerated in this chapter, and only in the cases provided for by this code.

Art. 106. Where one person shall be guilty of several offences before he has been convicted of any, the punishment for each successive offence is cumulative; but the augmented punishment prescribed for the repetition of offences is not thereby incurred; and where the punishment for a former offence is less than imprisonment for life, the imprisonment incurred for the second conviction shall commence at the expiration of the first imprisonment.

Art. 107. The person of a convict who is condemned to imprisonment, which brings with it a forfeiture of his civil rights, is under the protection of the law, as well as in its custody. Any restraint or violence to his person, beyond that necessary to the execution of the sentence of the law, is punishable in the same manner as it would be if he were not convicted.

Art. 108. The privation of the right to bear arms in defence of the country, does not give an exemption from military duty. Persons under this disability are forced to serve, but without arms, on working parties, and in the drudgery of the service.

TITLE II.

OF OFFENCES AGAINST THE SOVEREIGN POWER OF THE STATE.

CHAPTER I.

Of treason.

Art. 109. Treason is defined by the constitution of the state. It consists in levying war against the state, or in adhering to its enemies, giving them aid and comfort; but as, by the nature of the union between the different states, the levying war against one state is a levy of war against the whole, and the constitution of the United States having made that act treason, and vested the cognizance of the crime in the courts of the United States, no provisions are deemed proper to be made respecting that offence.

CHAPTER II.

Of sedition.

Art. 110. Whoever shall, by FORCE OF ARMS, attempt to DISMEMBER the state, or to SUBVERT OR CHANGE the constitution thereof, shall be imprisoned at hard labour in solitude for life, and after death his body shall be delivered for dissection.

Art. 111. To constitute this offence, there must be not only a design to dismember the state, or to subvert or change its constitution, but an attempt must be made to do it by FORCE.

Art. 112. The attempt consists in enlisting men, preparing arms, or making an assemblage of men, armed or otherwise arrayed, in such a manner as to show the design to effect their object by force. This is sufficient evidence of the attempt, whether any actual violence be committed or not.

Art. 113. If any one shall, by writing, printing, or verbally, counsel or EXCITE the people of this state, or of any part thereof, to commit either of the offences described in the preceding part of this chapter, or to resist by force the legal execution of any constitutional law of the state, he shall be fined not less than five hundred dollars, nor more than two thousand dollars ; shall be imprisoned in close custody not less than three nor more than twelve months, and be suspended from his political rights for four years.

Art. 114. It is not necessary, to constitute this offence, that the crime advised should be committed.*

TITLE III.

OF OFFENCES AGAINST THE LEGISLATIVE POWER.

Art. 118. If any one shall designedly, and by FORCE, prevent the general assembly of this state, or either of the houses composing it, from meeting, or shall, with intent to prevent such meeting, by the use of personal violence or threats thereof, prevent any of the members of the general assembly from attending the house to which they may belong, or shall, by force or threats thereof, force either of the said branches of the general assembly to adjourn or disperse, or to pass any resolution or law, or do any other act; or to reject any resolution or law which they constitutionally might pass; he shall be fined not less than five hundred dollars, nor more than two thousand dollars; be confined not less than five, nor more than ten years at hard labour, and shall forfeit his political rights.

Art. 119. Whoever shall use any threats of violence to any member of the general assembly, with intent to influence his official conduct, or shall make any assault on him in consequence of any thing he may have said or done, as a member of the assembly, or of his conduct as a member thereof, shall be fined not less than one hundred dollars, nor more than five hundred dollars; and be imprisoned in close custody, not less than one, nor more than six months.

Art. 120. Whoever shall BRIBE or offer to BRIBE any

---

* Chapter III. of this title—providing for the punishment of those who promote or participate in slave insurrections,—has been omitted; there being, happily, no longer any necessity, in the United States, for legislative enactment on this subject.

member of the general assembly, shall be fined in a sum equal to four times the value of the bribe, and if the amount thereof cannot be ascertained, or cannot be appreciated in money, then in a sum not less than one thousand, nor more than two thousand dollars ; shall suffer imprisonment at hard labour, not less than six months, nor more than one year, and be suspended from all political rights for five years.

Art. 121. If any member of the general assembly shall receive or agree to receive a BRIBE, he shall be fined in a sum equal to five times the value of the bribe, and if the value thereof cannot be ascertained, or cannot be appreciated in money, then in a sum not less than two thousand, nor more than five thousand dollars ; shall forfeit his political rights, and be imprisoned in solitude and at hard labour, not less than one, nor more than two years.

TITLE IV.

OF OFFENCES AGAINST THE EXECUTIVE POWER.

CHAPTER I.

Art. 122. If any person elected or appointed to any EXECUTIVE OFFICE, shall do any official act, before he shall have given security, if any is required by law, or before he shall have taken the oaths of the office, when they are required by law, he shall pay a fine equal to one half year's emolument of his office.

Art. 123. Any person who shall BRIBE, or offer to BRIBE AN EXECUTIVE OFFICER, shall be suspended from the enjoyment of his political rights, for not less than four, nor more than six years, be fined not less than three times the value of the bribe offered, and be imprisoned in close custody, not less than two, nor more than six months.

Art. 124. If any one by VIOLENCE OFFERED TO THE PERSON of any executive officer, or by threats of violence, shall induce, or force him to do any official act, in an illegal manner, or to do under colour of his office any other act, which he is not authorized to do, or to omit the performance of any official act, which he is bound to perform, the offender shall be imprisoned in close custody, not less than three, nor more than twelve months, and shall be fined in a sum not less than fifty, nor more than two hundred dollars; in addition to the punishment provided by law for the act or omission, to which he compelled the officer, if it be an offence, and in addition also to the punishment directed by law for the violence itself, considered as unconnected with the motive for offering it.

Art. 125. If any one shall by force resist any executive officer in the performance of his office, or attempt by force to commit either of the acts made punishable by the last preceding article, without succeeding in such resistance or attempt, he shall suffer one half the punishment directed by the said article.

CHAPTER II.

Of offences committed by executive officers.

Art. 126. Any EXECUTIVE OFFICER who shall receive a BRIBE, shall forfeit his political rights, and be imprisoned, not less than one, nor more than two years; one-fourth of the time in close custody; and shall be fined not less than four times the value of the bribe received.

Art. 127. If any executive officer shall corruptly agree to make any appointment, or do any other official act in consideration of some ADVANTAGE (which is not incident to the act) given or promised to him for such act, but which ADVANTAGE does not come within the definition of an EMOLUMENT, he shall forfeit the amount of the emoluments of his office for not less than six months, nor more than two years.

Art. 128. If any executive officer shall EXTORT money, or OTHER REWARD, for the performance of acts he was obliged by law to perform, and for which no remuneration is given by law, or shall extort more than is allowed by law for the performance of any service, or shall EXTORT money or other REWARD from any one, under the pretence that he has performed services for which a remuneration is given by law, when, in fact, no such services have been rendered, he shall be imprisoned in close confinement, not less than two months, nor more than one year, and shall moreover forfeit the office he holds, and be fined in a sum equal to one year's salary or emoluments of the said office.

Art. 129. If any executive officer shall RECEIVE, or agree to RECEIVE, any EMOLUMENT whatever, though voluntarily given, for doing any act required to be done by virtue of his office, or for refraining from doing any thing, which he is not authorized to do, if the law does not expressly authorize the receipt of such emolument; or shall receive any emolument greater in value than the sum determined by law for any services rendered by virtue of his office, although such emolument be voluntarily given, he shall forfeit the amount of one half year's salary or emoluments of his office.

Art. 130. If any executive officer shall, under pretence of performing the duties of his office, do any act which amounts to an offence, he shall suffer an additional punishment of one half, to that which is by law provided for the offence when committed by another.

Art. 131. If any executive officer shall undesignedly do any act, under colour of his office, which he is not authorized by his office to perform, or shall negligently omit to do any act which he ought by virtue of his office to perform, by which act or omission any individual or society receives such injury as would entitle them to a civil action, such officer shall be fined, in a sum not less than two months, and not more than six months, of the emoluments of his office. This article does not extend to any other such act or omission, as by any other part of this code is created an offence.

Art. 132. If any of the acts or omissions described in the last preceding section shall be intentionally done or made, the party guilty thereof shall, in addition to the fine, be suspended from his political rights, for not less than two, nor more than four years.

Art. 133. All the articles of this title, which impose penalties upon executive officers for offences, extend to the deputies and clerks of such officers who shall commit the same offences.

Art. 134. Every person entrusted by the officer with the performance of his official duties, is considered as a deputy for the purpose of this section, whether the officer had a right to appoint a deputy or not.

Art. 135. Every person who publicly exercises the duties of any office, is subject to the penalties imposed by this section; although there be such defect or informality on his appointment or election, or any such omission to comply with the formalities required by law, as would render his official acts invalid.

Art. 136. The principal officer is considered as himself guilty of all such offences committed by his deputy, in relation to his office, as are committed with his knowledge or consent; and he shall be presumed to have known and consented to such offence, if it can be shown that the deputy had, before the act complained of, committed a similar official offence, while in his service, to the knowledge of the officer; and that, after such knowledge, he continued to employ him in the performance of his official duties.

Art. 137. The provisions of this and of the last preceding chapter, relating to bribery, extend to those who exercise any CORPORATE or PRIVATE office, and to those who may bribe or attempt to bribe them.

TITLE V.

OF OFFENCES AFFECTING THE JUDICIARY POWER.

CHAPTER I.

Of offences committed by and against judges or jurors in their official capacity.

SECTION I.

Of offences committed by judges and jurors.

Art. 138. If any judge or juror shall take a bribe, he shall be fined five times the value of the bribe received, shall suffer imprisonment, in close confinement, not less than six, nor more than twelve months ; and shall forfeit his political rights.

Art. 139. If any judge shall maliciously, but without being bribed, do any official act, or render any judgment, which he is not by law authorized to do or render, or shall maliciously omit to do any act which he ought, by virtue of his office, to perform, he shall forfeit his political rights, and be fined to the amount of his income of office for one year.

Art. 140. If any judge shall corruptly agree to give any judgment or to do any other official act, in consideration of some advantage (which is not incident to the official act) given or promised to him for rendering such judgment or doing such act, which advantage shall not come within the definition of an emolument, he shall forfeit his office and be fined in the amount of the income thereof for one year.

Art. 141. If any judge shall receive from any person

whatever, unless he be a relation in the ascending or descending line, or a collateral relation within the second degree, any gift or donation whatever, of any assigned value, unless it be made by last will and testament or codicil, he shall be fined in a sum equal to six months' income of his office.

Art. 142. If any judge, whose duty it shall or may be to assist at the drawing of jurors to form the panel for the grand jury or the petit jury in any court in this state, shall designedly put, or consent to the putting of any name on the said panel not drawn according to law, or shall omit to put on any such panel any name which shall be legally drawn, or shall sign or certify any panel of names not drawn according to law, such judge, or any other person who shall designedly aid therein, shall be fined not less than two hundred dollars, nor more than one thousand dollars, and shall be imprisoned not less than one, nor more than six months; and if the offence shall be committed at the solicitation of any person accused of an offence, or of the prosecutor, or any party in a civil suit, the offender shall also be suspended from the exercise of his political rights for five years.

Art. 143. If any juror shall (except in the deliberation with his fellow jurors) make any promise or agreement to give a verdict for or against any one accused of any offence or for or against any party to a civil suit; or shall receive any papers or evidence from the prosecutor or the accused in any criminal suit, or either of the parties in any civil suit, other than such as shall be delivered in open court, he shall be fined not less than fifty, nor more than four hundred dollars, or may be imprisoned not exceeding thirty days, or both.

Art. 144. If any judge, who is allowed to take fees or compensation for any official act that he is authorized to do, whether of a judicial or executive nature, shall exact and receive more for each service than by law he is authorized to receive, he shall pay a fine equal to one year's income of his office and shall forfeit his political rights.

Art. 145. If any judge, even with the consent of the party paying the same for any official act, whether of a judicial nature or executive nature, for which he is authorized to take any fees or compensation, shall receive any greater sum than that allowed by law for such service he shall be fined in a sum equal to six months' income of his office.

Art. 146. No judge shall take any part, either by sitting as a judge, or deciding any point, or advising with the other judges, either in or out of court, in the trial or hearing of any cause in which or in the controversy out of which it has arisen he shall have been employed either as counsellor or attorney, or in which or in the controversy out of which it shall have arisen he shall have acted as ARBITRATOR, or on any former trial of which he shall have been sworn as a juror, or in which he has any interest, or to which any of his ascendants or descendants, or any collateral relation, either by consanguinity or affinity, within the third degree, are parties, or are anywise interested ; nor shall any of the other judges of the same court consult with, or take the opinion of such other, in or out of court, in any such cause as is above described. And any judge who shall designedly offend against any provision of this article, shall be fined in a sum equal to his salary and emoluments for six months.

Art. 147. The first article of this chapter relates to ARBITRATORS as well as judges ; and all the preceding articles of this chapter, except the fourth, relate to justices of the peace as well as judges.

SECTION II.

Of offences against judges or jurors in their official capacity.

Art. 148. If any one shall bribe or offer to bribe any judge, justice of the peace or arbitrator or juror, either of the grand jury or trial jury, he shall be confined in close custody, not less than two, nor more than six months, and shall be fined in a sum equal to four times the value of the bribe offered or given.

Art. 149. If any one by violence or threats of bodily harm, or illegal injury to property or reputation, shall attempt to oppose or influence any judge or justice of the peace in the execution of any official act, or shall in like manner attempt to force or influence any judge, justice of the peace or ABBITRATOR or juror to render or find any judgment, order, verdict, or indictment, or to do any other official act, he shall be fined not less than fifty, nor more than four hundred dollars ; or be imprisoned, not less than twenty days, nor more than six months, or both ; and the imprisonment, or any part of it, may be in close custody, in addition to any punishment that may be incurred by the violence used.

Art 150. If any one, with intent to influence the verdict of a jury in a criminal or civil suit, shall anywhere but in open court, or by leave of the court, exhibit to any person drawn or summoned to serve as a grand juror or petit juror during the term at which such suit is to be tried, knowing or believing him to be so summoned or drawn, any evidence in such suit, or use any arguments in favour of, or against either of the parties in such suit, he shall be fined not less than twenty, nor more than one hundred dollars, and shall be imprisoned not less than five, nor more than thirty days ; and if the offender be an officer of justice, or an attorney or counsellor, or an officer of the court, the punishment shall be double.

Art. 151. If any one shall, during the pendency of any civil suit, or criminal prosecution, publish or print any argument, statement or observations relating to such cause, of such a nature as to influence the verdict of a jury, or to excite any public prejudice for or against either of the parties in such cause, he shall be imprisoned, not exceeding thirty days, or fined, not exceeding two hundred dollars.

Art. 152. But nothing in the preceding article contained, shall prohibit in any stage of a criminal prosecution, the publication of a true statement of any judicial proceeding, or the examination of witnesses judicially taken, with the exceptions contained in the Code of Procedure, in cases affecting decency and morals.

CHAPTER II.

Of offences against officers of justice and officers of courts.

Art. 153. Whoever shall BRIBE or offer to BRIBE any officer of justice, or any clerk, translator, or other officer of a court of justice, he shall be imprisoned not less than one, nor more than six months, shall be fined not less than one hundred, nor more than five hundred dollars, and be suspended from his political rights for five years.

Art. 154. Whoever shall forcibly oppose any officer of justice, knowing him to be such, in the lawful execution of an official act, he shall be imprisoned not less than ten days, nor more than six months ; and shall be fined not less than fifty, nor more than five hundred dollars ; and the whole or any part of the imprisonment may be close custody.

Art. 155. Persons to whom a special warrant is directed in the manner prescribed in the Code of Procedure, and those who are, by the provisions of the same code, authorized to make arrests, without warrant in the cases allowed by law, are officers of justice within the purview of this title, while actually employed in executing such warrant or making such arrest.

Art. 156. To constitute this offence, it must be known not only that the person opposed is an officer of justice, but that the act he is doing is an official one ; this knowledge may be proved by other circumstances, but no other proof is necessary than that the officer (if he were one) at the time gave notice of his official character, and of the purpose of this act.

Art. 157. The offence is not committed by an opposition to any other than official acts, therefore the penalty is not incurred by opposing an officer of justice, when he attempts to do any act that is not authorized by his legal powers, or to do an authorized act by illegal means; the opposition, if confined in purpose to that part of the act which is illegal, and in degree to the force necessary to prevent its execution, does not amount to this offence.

Art. 158. No other error in a warrant, or order, will justify an opposition to it than the following :

1. That it was not issued by either a court or magistrate.

2. That the person named or described in the warrant is not the person against whom the warrant or order is attempted to be executed.

3. That the person executing it is neither the one to whom it is directed, nor an officer of justice ; if he be an officer of justice, he may execute the warrant to whomsoever it may be directed.

4. That the warrant or order is issued or allowed by a magistrate, whose authority does not extend to the place in which it is attempted to be executed.

Art. 159. Force used against an officer of justice while in the legal execution of his duty, does not amount to this offence, unless the intent be to prevent the execution of his duty, although the force should have that effect.

Art. 160. In making an arrest under a warrant, a forcible opposition to it is not justified by a refusal to deliver the warrant out of the officer's hands, provided he show it when required.

Art. 161. If by reason of the opposition the officer of justice is prevented from executing his duty, the punishment shall be increased one half.

Art. 162. This offence may be committed as well by a person not concerned in the official act which is opposed, as by the party against whom it is directed.

Art. 163. All official acts that can be lawfully done by an officer of justice, either in obedience to the lawful order of a court or magistrate, whether of a civil or criminal jurisdiction; or such as he is required to do as conservator of the peace, or for the prevention of offences, or securing the persons of offenders, come within the purview of this chapter.

Art. 164. Threats of such violence as the party has it in his power to execute, and as would be sufficient to intimidate a man of common firmness, amount to a forcible opposition within the meaning of this and the next chapter, as to rescue.

CHAPTER IV.

Of rescue.

Art. 165. Whoever shall by force set any one at liberty who is in custody on a lawful arrest for any offence, shall suffer one half of the punishment assigned by law to the offence for which the person rescued was charged. If the arrest was on a civil suit, the punishment shall be fine, not less than fifty nor more than five hundred dollars, or imprisonment in close custody not less than thirty days nor more than six months, or both; provided that, whatever may be the punishment assigned to any offence for which the person rescued shall have been arrested, no judgment, on a conviction for rescuing one who was arrested for an offence, shall be less than that assigned for the rescue of one arrested in a civil suit.

Art. 166. If the warrant, under which the arrest was made, be so defective as to justify the party arrested in resisting it, according to the previous disposition of this code, and he does so resist, those who aid him in a legal manner are not guilty of a rescue.

Art. 167. In like manner, those who aid a person in resisting an arrest made without warrant, under circumstances which do not legally justify such arrest, are not guilty of a rescue.

Art. 168. There can be no rescue, unless there has been an arrest; any forcible opposition to making a lawful arrest is another offence already provided for.

Art. 169. If the party arrested make no opposition, and the officer or other person making the arrest is proceeding with the prisoner to a magistrate for examination, when he is forcibly set at liberty, it is a rescue, although the original arrest were unlawful.

Art. 170. If the rescue be after a commitment is made out, and before the prisoner is actually received in prison, no defect whatever in the commitment can justify the rescue.

CHAPTER V.

Of escape.

Art. 171. If any one lawfully arrested for whatever cause, shall escape from custody, without being legally discharged, he shall be fined not exceeding one hundred dollars, or imprisoned not exceeding sixty days; provided such escape be not effected by breach of prison or by violence.

If the escape be effected by violence, it shall be punished in the manner hereinbefore directed with respect to those who oppose executive officers of justice in the performance of their duty.

Art. 172. Any executive officer of justice, or other person having the legal custody of any one who has been lawfully arrested for any offence, who shall voluntarily suffer such person to escape or to be rescued, shall suffer one half of the punishment of the offence with which the person was charged; and, if an officer, he shall be suspended from his political rights for four years.

Art. 173. If the escape or rescue be owing to negligence, the punishment shall be one fourth of that which would have been incurred by the person escaping, had he been found guilty.

Art. 174. Offenders against the provisions of either of the two last preceding articles may be convicted, although the person escaping should not be retaken or should be acquitted on trial.

CHAPTER VI.

Of breach of prison.

Art. 175. If any one legally committed to any PUBLIC PRISON, either before or after conviction, for any offence or in any civil suit, shall, by breaking the prison or by violence offered to any person employed to keep or guard such prison, escape or attempt to escape from such prison, he shall be imprisoned in close custody, not less than six months nor more than two years, to commence after the expiration of his original imprisonment.

Art. 176. If any one shall rescue or attempt to rescue any other person who is confined in any public prison, by breaking such prison, he shall be imprisoned at hard labour, not less than two nor more than five years, in addition to the punishment assigned for the offence of rescuing such prisoners, should the rescue be effected.

Art. 177. The penalty of the last preceding article is incurred whether the prisoner be legally or illegally committed.

Art. 178. If any one shall, by any means not amounting to breach of prison, aid any prisoner legally confined in a public prison to escape, or shall supply instruments for breaking the prison, or other means of escape, for the purpose of attempting it, whether the escape be effected or not, he shall be fined not less than one hundred nor more than five hundred dollars, and be imprisoned not less than one nor more than six months in close custody, or by simple imprisonment for the whole or part of the time.

Art. 179. If the breach of prison be effected by the means set forth in the last preceding article, the person aiding or providing the means may also be punished as an accomplice in that offence.

CHAPTER VII.

Of offences committed by officers of justice and officers of courts in their official capacity.

Art. 180. All the articles of the first and second chapters of the fourth title of this book, entitled, "of offences committed by executive officers," apply to officers of justice and officers of courts, they being comprehended in the definition of executive officers.

CHAPTER VIII.

Of counsellors and attorneys at law.

Art. 181. If any of the offences enumerated in the other chapters of this title, and not provided for in this chapter, shall be committed by an attorney at law or a counsellor at law, the punishment assigned to such offence shall be increased one half.

Art. 182. Any counsellor at law, or attorney at law, or any attorney in fact, charged with the prosecution or defence of a civil suit, who shall receive a bribe, shall be fined a sum equal to five times the value of the bribe received, shall be imprisoned not less than six nor more than twelve months, and shall forfeit his political rights, and his civil rights of the first class.

Art. 183. If any attorney at law, or counsellor at law, or any attorney in fact, who is charged in any prosecution or defence of a civil suit, or the defence of any one accused of an offence, shall designedly divulge any circumstance which came to his knowledge in virtue of his trust, to the injury of his client; or shall give counsel to the opposite party, to the injury of his client; or after having engaged to prosecute or defend any civil suit, and been consulted on the merits of the case, for any one, shall, on account of the non-payment of fees, or for any other cause or pretext, appear for the opposite party, either as his attorney or counsellor in court, or secretly as his adviser; or shall, with intent to injure the party for whom he is employed, do any other act which he is not legally required to do, that is injurious to the interest of such party, or omit to do any other lawful official act, whereby his client shall suffer in his interest or reputation; he shall, for either of these offences, be imprisoned not less than twenty days, nor more than six months; and if an attorney or counsellor at law, be suspended from the exercise of his profession not less than three nor more than twelve months; and if an attorney in fact, in addition to the imprisonment, be fined not less than one hundred, nor more than five hundred dollars.

Art. 184. If any attorney at law, or counsellor at law, or any attorney in fact, employed to conduct a suit or defence in court, shall, within five days after demand in writing, by a person legally authorized to make such demand, refuse or neglect to pay the balance due on any sum of money, or deliver any notes or other securities he may have received for the person by whom he was employed, on any suit in court, or on any demand he was professionally employed to make, or any papers with which he was intrusted in his official capacity, he shall, if an attorney in fact, be fined not less than one hundred, nor more than three hundred dollars ; and if a counsellor at law, or attorney at law, shall be suspended from the exercise of his profession, not less than six, nor more than twelve months, and until he shall have paid the sum due, with interest.

Art. 185. No attorney or counsellor at law, or attorney in fact, shall be liable, under the preceding article, for retaining out of the moneys by him received, any sum due to him by his employer, for any liquidated debt due to him, or for legal or customary and reasonable fees and costs or commissions ; nor shall he be guilty of any offence in retaining any papers or securities he may have received until such sums be paid, as may be due for costs or fees in any suit or controversy, for the defence or prosecution of which the papers were delivered to him ; nor for not delivering papers that have been casually lost or destroyed.

Art. 186. If any attorney or counsellor at law shall fraudulently commence, prosecute or defend any suit in any court in this state, in the name of any person by whom he has not been authorized to prosecute or defend such suit, he shall be suspended from the exercise of his profession, not less than six months, nor more than two years.

Art. 187. Whoever shall bribe or offer to bribe any attorney or counsellor at law, or any attorney in fact, who is charged with the conducting a suit in court, shall be imprisoned in close custody, not less than one nor more than six months, and shall pay a fine equal to four times the amount of the bribe given or offered.

Art. 188. All offences committed by counsellors or attorneys at law, shall be tried in the same manner as other offences, except as is hereinafter provided, in the case of offences committed in the courts of justice.

CHAPTER IX.

Of offences by falsely personating another in judiciary proceedings.

Art. 189. If any one, not being an officer of justice, shall fraudulently pretend to be such, and in such assumed character shall commit any assault, or false imprisonment, or receive or attempt to receive property, he shall be imprisoned at hard labour not less than three, nor more than six years, in addition to the punishment incurred by the other offence he may commit.

Art. 190. If any one shall falsely PERSONATE ANOTHER, and in such assumed character shall become bail, confess judgment, or do any other act in the course of any proceeding in any suit or prosecution, he shall be imprisoned at hard labour not less than two nor more than five years, in addition to the punishment he may incur by any other offence he may commit in such assumed character.

CHAPTER X.

Of perjury and false swearing.

Art. 191. Perjury is a falsehood, asserted verbally or in writing, deliberately and wilfully, relating to something present or past, under the sanction of an oath, or such other affirmation as is or may be by law made equivalent to an oath, legally administered, under circumstances in which an oath or affirmation is required by law, or is necessary for the prosecution or defence of private right, or for the ends of public justice. Perjury is punished by penitentiary imprisonment, not less than three, nor more than seven years ; by a forfeiture of all political rights, and of civil rights of the first and third class. But if any one by means of perjury shall cause another to be convicted of a crime, he shall suffer the same punishment that is incurred by the commission of the crime of which such person has been convicted by means of the perjury.

Art. 192. Falsehood in this definition refers to the belief of the party attesting ; therefore, if he believes what he swears to be false, and it should happen to be true, he is as guilty of the offence as if he had sworn that to be true which he knew to be false.

Art. 193. The declaration must be deliberate ; a false statement made inadvertently, or under agitation, or by mistake, is not perjury.

Art. 194. It must be with design to make the falsehood believed by another, the party taking the oath knowing or believing it to be false ; and this design is presumed whenever the falsehood of the declaration is proved.

Art. 195. The oath or affirmation must be administered in the manner required by law, and by a magistrate, or other person duly authorized to administer oaths in the matter or cause in which the oath was taken.

Art. 196. The declaration, to constitute perjury, must be of something present or past; a promissory oath, although broken, is not perjury. An oath of office is one of this last description.

Art. 197. The occasion of taking the oath, in the description of the offence, includes those taken in every stage of a judicial proceeding, either civil or criminal, either in or out of court ; and all declaratory oaths required by special laws, whether they impose the penalty of perjury or not.

Art. 198. As the falsehood must be wilful and deliberate to constitute the crime ; the assertion of any circumstance, so immaterial to the matter in relation to which the declaration is made, as reasonably to induce a belief that it was not intended to conceal the truth or assert a falsehood, is not perjury; although the circumstance be not true.

Art. 199. It is not necessary, to complete this offence, that any credit should be given to the false declaration.

Art. 200. Whoever shall deliberately and wilfully, under oath, or affirmation (in cases where it is by law equivalent to an oath), legally administered, declare a falsehood, by a voluntary declaration or affidavit, which is neither required by law nor made in the course of any judicial proceeding, is guilty of false swearing, and shall be confined in close custody not less than one nor more than six months; and the conviction of such an offence may be produced as evidence against his CREDIT in any court where he may be offered as a witness.

Art. 201. The punishment for the offence mentioned in the last preceding article is independent of any that may be inflicted for the publication of the affidavit, should it be a libel.

Art. 202. The term declaratory oath, or declaratory affidavit, in this section, means an oath made to the truth of something present or past, and is used in contradistinction to promissory oath, which is a stipulation confirmed by oath, that some act shall be done or omitted, or some event take place in future. The breach of this last description of oaths, does not amount either to perjury or to false swearing, except as will be hereafter provided in the case of officers of justice for duties done in court.

Art. 203. Whoever shall designedly, by any MEANS whatever, induce another to commit perjury, or to be guilty of false swearing, shall undergo the same punishment as if he had committed the crime himself.

Art. 204. Whoever shall endeavour, by offering any INDUCEMENT or persuasion whatever, to procure another to commit perjury, or to be guilty of false swearing, shall be fined not less than fifty nor more than three hundred dollars, and imprisoned in close custody not less than thirty days, nor more than six months.

CHAPTER XI.

Offences against the judiciary power committed in a court of justice.

Art. 205. If any one shall, during the session of any COURT OF JUSTICE, in the presence of the court, by words or by making a clamour or noise, wilfully obstruct the proceedings of such court, or shall refuse to obey any legal order of such court made for the maintenance of order or to preserve regularity of proceedings in court, it shall be lawful for the said court to cause the offender to be removed by the proper officer of justice from the building in which the sessions of such court are held ; and if such offender shall persevere in returning to and disturbing said court, it shall also be lawful for them to cause him to be imprisoned during the time the court shall be in session during the same day ; and the party offending against this article is guilty of a misdemeanor, and shall be punished by fine not exceeding twenty dollars, and by imprisonment not exceeding three days.

Art. 206. If any person shall, either verbally in court, or in any pleading or other writing addressed to the judges in any cause pending in any court of justice, use any indecorous, contemptuous or insulting expressions, to or of the court or the judges thereof, with intent to insult the said court or any of the said judges, he shall be punished by simple imprisonment not more than fifteen days, and by fine not exceeding fifty dollars ; and the fact of the intent with which the words were used, and also whether they were indecorous, contemptuous and insulting, shall be decided by the jury who shall try the cause. The said punishment shall be doubled on a second conviction for an offence under this article ; and for a third, the party shall, in addition to the said punishment, if an attorney or counsellor, be suspended for not less than one nor more than four years from practising in the said court as attorney or counsellor at law, or as attorney in fact.

Art. 207. If any one shall obstruct the proceedings of a court of justice by violence, or threats of violence, offered either to the judges, jurors, witnesses, parties, or attorneys or counsellors, he shall be fined in a sum not less than one hundred and not exceeding five hundred dollars, and by imprisonment, in close custody, not less than ten days nor more than six months; and if the offender be an attorney or counsellor at law, he shall be suspended from practising in such court for not less than one nor more than three years, either as attorney or counsellor at law, or as attorney in fact.

Art. 208. Courts of justice have no power to inflict any punishment for offences committed against their authority, other than those specially provided for by this Code and the Code of Procedure. All proceedings for offences, heretofore denominated contempts, are abolished. All offences created by this chapter, shall be tried on indictment, or information, in the usual form.

TITLE VI.

OF OFFENCES AGAINST PUBLIC TRANQUILLITY.

CHAPTER I.

Of unlawful assemblies and riots.

Art. 209. If any three or more persons shall ASSEMBLE with intent to aid each other by violence, either to commit an offence, or illegally to deprive any person of the enjoyment of a right, such assembly shall be called an unlawful assembly, and those guilty thereof shall be fined not less than fifty nor more than three hundred dollars, and shall be imprisoned not less than three nor more than twelve months, in close custody.

Art. 210. If persons, assembled for either of the purposes mentioned in the last preceding article, shall, by VIOLENCE, commit any illegal act, they are guilty of a riot, and in addition to the punishment to which they may be liable by reason of the illegal act they may commit, if it be an offence, they may be suspended from their political rights for three years, shall be fined not less than fifty nor more than five hundred dollars, and imprisoned not less than three nor more than eighteen months, in close custody for at least one half the time, or more, at the discretion of the court.

Art. 211. If the purpose of the unlawful assembly be illegally to oppose the collection of any taxes, tolls, imposts, or excises legally imposed, or the execution of any law of the state, or any lawful sentence of a court, or to effect the rescue of a prisoner legally arrested for any crime, the punishment for that offence shall be increased one half.

Art. 212. If a riot be committed for either of the purposes set forth in the last preceding article, the punishment hereinbefore imposed for that offence shall be doubled.

Art. 213. If any person engaged in an unlawful assembly, before the unlawful object of such meeting, or any other offence except such unlawful meeting, has been committed by them, or those with whom they are combined, shall either voluntarily, or on being warned by a magistrate, retire therefrom, without the intent to return, he shall not be prosecuted for being concerned in the unlawful assembly, or for any riot or other offence of which any persons concerned in it may afterwards be guilty, provided he do not return to the said assembly.

Art. 214. Any one person concerned in an unlawful assembly, may be indicted and convicted before the others are arrested ; but it is necessary to state in the indictment, and prove on the trial, that three or more persons were assembled ; if known, they must be described or named ; if unknown, it must be so alleged.

It is necessary to state, in an indictment for either of those offences, the illegal act which was the object of the meeting, or which they proceeded to do if the assembly was originally for a lawful purpose.

Art. 215. If three or more persons assemble for a lawful purpose, and they afterwards proceed to commit any act that would amount to a riot, if it had been the original purpose of the meeting, all those who do not retire when the change of purpose is known, are guilty of a riot.

Art. 216. If two or more persons engaged in an unlawful assembly or riot are ARMED, the punishment of the person so armed shall be doubled ; and of those who assisted in such assembly, when part were armed, although they themselves were unarmed, shall be increased one-half.

Art. 217. If any judge, military officer or executive officer, or officer of justice, shall be engaged in an unlawful assembly or riot, his punishment shall be doubled.

Art. 218. When proof shall be made to any magistrate, by the oath of two or more credible witnesses, of the existence of any unlawful assembly or riot, consisting of more than twenty persons, it shall be the duty of such magistrate to go to the place where the unlawful assembly is, and he shall there proclaim the office which he holds, and order such unlawful assembly to disperse ; and that he may be the better known and distinguished, he shall display a white flag ; and if the offenders shall, after being so warned, proceed to commit a riot, they shall be imprisoned at hard labour, not less than one, nor more than three years, in addition to the other punishment for any other offence of which they may be guilty by such riot or illegal assembly.

Art. 219. Any one being in the said assembly at the time such order was given, or having joined it afterwards, (provided this last have notice of such order), who shall be found therein after the expiration of half an hour, shall, if no other offence be committed, be imprisoned, in close custody, not less than one nor more than six months, or fined not less than fifty, nor more than three hundred dollars. And immediately after the expiration of the said half-hour, or before, if any other illegal act be committed, it shall be lawful for any magistrate, or minister of justice, to arrest any of those composing the said assembly who shall disobey such order, or to cause them to be arrested with or without warrant ; and for that purpose, any magistrate may call for the assistance of any person who may be within three miles of the place where the said unlawful assembly shall be, to aid him in the arrest of the said offenders ; and such arrest shall be made in the manner directed by the Code of Procedure, in the chapter relative to arrests.

Art. 220. If any free, able-bodied male person, above eighteen years of age and under fifty, shall be called on to aid in arresting the offenders in the manner directed by the last preceding article, and shall refuse or neglect so to do, such person shall be fined fifty dollars.

Art. 221. Any assembly for the purpose of witnessing a boxing match is an unlawful assembly.

If any boxing match takes place at such assembly, it is a riot, for which the combatants, and each of those who lay a wager on the event of such combat, shall be fined not less than ten, nor more than one hundred dollars, or may be imprisoned not less than ten, nor more than twenty days, in close custody, or both ; and those who are guilty of the riot, without laying a wager on the combat, shall be fined not less than five, nor more than fifty dollars ; or may be imprisoned ten days in close custody.

CHAPTER II.

Of public disturbance.

Art. 222. Those are guilty of making a public disturbance, who, without any such intent as would give to a meeting the character of an unlawful assembly, shall, to the number of two or more, meet or assemble in a tumultuous manner, in a public place, and by vociferation, quarrelling, or fighting, disturb the inhabitants of the place in the prosecution of their lawful business, or in their necessary repose. Public disturbers shall be fined not exceeding twenty dollars, or imprisoned not exceeding ten days, or both.

Art. 223. All magistrates and officers of justice are required to arrest, or cause to be arrested, persons guilty of this offence, on their own view, or on complaint, with or without warrant.

Art. 224. No public meeting, for the purpose of exercising any political or private right; no assembly for the purpose of legal recreation, or the expression of dissatisfaction or approbation made in such assembly in the usual manner, although it may disturb those in the vicinity, is an offence under this chapter.

Art. 225. The police of places of public amusement continues under the superintendence of the mayors, or other first magistrates of cities and towns.

TITLE VII.

OF OFFENCES AGAINST THE RIGHT OF SUFFRAGE.

CHAPTER I.

Of bribery and undue influence.

Art. 226. Whoever shall offer or give a BRIBE to any elector, for the purpose of influencing his vote at any PUBLIC ELECTION, and any elector entitled to vote at such election who shall receive such bribe, shall be fined not less than one hundred, nor more than five hundred dollars, shall forfeit all his political rights, and be confined in close custody not less than six months, nor more than one year.

Art. 227. Whoever shall give or offer a bribe to any JUDGE or CLERK of any public election, or any executive officer attending the same, as a consideration for some act done, or omitted to be done, or to be done or omitted contrary to his official duty in relation to such election, shall pay a fine not less than one hundred, nor more than five hundred dollars, shall forfeit all political rights, and shall be confined in close custody, not less than one, nor more than two years.

Art. 228. If any one shall offer or give a reward to any person whatever, for the purpose of inducing him to persuade, or by any other means not amounting to bribery, to procure persons to vote at any PUBLIC ELECTION, for or against any person, the person so giving or offering, and he who shall receive such reward, shall forfeit not less than fifty, nor more than one hundred dollars.

Art. 229. Whoever shall procure or endeavour to procure the vote of any elector, or the influence of any person over other electors at any public election, for himself or any candidate, by means of VIOLENCE, threats of violence, or threats of withdrawing custom or dealing in business or trade, or of enforcing the payment of a debt, or bringing a suit or criminal prosecution, or any other threat of injury to be inflicted by him or by his means, the person so offending shall forfeit not less than fifty, nor more than three hundred dollars, and be confined in close custody not less than one, nor more than six months, and shall be suspended from the exercise of his political rights for four years.

CHAPTER II.

Of offences committed by the judges or other officers of elections.

Art. 230. If any judge or clerk of any public election, or executive officer attending the same, shall knowingly make or consent to any false entry on the list of voters ; but into the ballot box, or permit to be so put in, any ballot not given by a voter ; or take out of such box, or permit to be so taken out, any ballot deposited therein, except in the manner prescribed by law ; or by any other act or omission, designedly destroy, or change the ballots given by the electors ; the offender shall pay a fine of not less than five hundred, nor more than one thousand dollars, forfeit his political rights, and be imprisoned in close confinement, not less than six months nor more than one year.

Art. 231. Any such judge who shall proceed to any such election, without having the ballot box locked and secured in the manner directed by law ; or who shall open and read, or consent to any other person opening and reading any ballot given to him to deposit in the box at such election, before it is put into the box, without the consent of the voter giving the same, shall be fined one hundred dollars.

Art. 232. Any judge of a public election, who, before the votes are counted, shall dispose of, or deposit the ballot box in a manner not authorized by law ; or shall at any time after the election has begun, and before the ballots are counted, give the key of the ballot box with which he is intrusted to any other, the person so offending shall pay a fine of five hundred dollars.

Art. 233. When any one who offers to vote at any such election, shall be objected to by an elector, as a person unqualified to vote, if any judge of such election shall permit him to vote without producing proof of such qualification, in the manner directed by law ; or if any such judge shall refuse the vote of any person, who shall comply with the requisites prescribed by law to prove his qualifications, knowing him to be entitled to vote, he shall forfeit for such offence one hundred dollars, and if the offence be committed for the purpose of favouring or injuring the election of any candidate, shall moreover be suspended from the exercise of his political rights for five years.

Art. 234. If any judge, or clerk, or executive officer, shall designedly omit to do any official act required by the law, or designedly do any illegal act, in relation to any public election, by which act or omission the votes taken at any such election in any city, parish or district, shall be lost, or the electors thereof shall be deprived of their suffrages at such election, or shall designedly do any act which shall render such election void, he shall be fined not less than one hundred nor more than five hundred dollars, shall forfeit his political rights, and shall be confined in close custody not less than six months nor more than one year.

CHAPTER III.

Of violence and riots at elections, and of the protection of electors from arrest.

Art. 235. It shall not be lawful for any military officer, or other person, to order or bring, or keep any troops or armed men, at any place within a mile of the place where any public election is held, on any day during which the same shall be held, under the penalty of five hundred dollars ; unless it be for the purpose of quelling a riot or insurrection, in the manner provided by law, or for the purpose of defence in time of war, and if the offence shall be committed with intent to influence such election, he shall moreover be imprisoned not less than thirty nor more than sixty days in close custody, and shall forfeit his political rights. This article does not apply to troops of the United States, usually stationed within a mile of the place of election, and kept there during the same.

Art. 236. If any one shall, by illegal force, or threats of such force, prevent or endeavour to prevent any elector from giving his vote ; or shall, at the place of election, commit any assault or battery on any elector, he shall be fined not less than fifty nor more than two hundred dollars, shall be imprisoned in close custody not less than thirty days nor more than six months, and shall be suspended from his right of suffrage for two years.

Art. 237. If any riot be committed at any place of any public election, or within half a mile of such place, during the time that the polls are open, the offender shall, in addition to the punishment imposed by law for a riot, also suffer imprisonment, in close custody, for not less than thirty nor more than sixty days ; and if the riot shall have been made for the purpose of influencing the election, shall be suspended from the right of suffrage for two years.

Art. 238. No elector shall be arrested at any civil suit, or on any warrant, except for a crime or a breach of the peace, or in order to obtain surety of the peace, during any day on which a public election is held, or while going to or returning from such election; and any executive officer of justice, or other person, making or causing such arrest, contrary to this article, knowing the person arrested to be an elector, shall be fined not less than fifty nor more than two hundred dollars.

TITLE VIII.

OF OFFENCES AGAINST THE LIBERTY OF THE PRESS.

Art. 239. The constitution of this state having declared, that "printing presses shall be free to every person who undertakes to examine the proceedings of the legislature or any branch of the government," and that "the free communication of thought and opinions is one of the invaluable rights of man," and that "every citizen may freely speak, write, and print, on any subject, being responsible for the abuse of that liberty," it is declared to be a misdemeanor for any one by violence, or threats of violence, or threats of any injury to person, property or credit, to prevent, or endeavour to prevent any person from exercising any of the rights asserted in the parts of the constitution above recited, and the offender shall pay a fine of not less than fifty nor more than five hundred dollars.

Art. 240. If any member of the general assembly, or any judge or judicial or executive officer, shall be guilty of the offences created by the last preceding article, in order to prevent an investigation of his official conduct, or that of the branch of government to which he belongs :

Or, if any judge or judicial or executive officer shall, by the exercise of any act of his office or the threat thereof, prevent, or endeavour to prevent any person from exercising any of the rights declared in the parts of the constitution above recited, he shall be fined not less than three hundred nor more than one thousand dollars, shall suffer imprisonment not less than sixty days nor more than six months, in simple imprisonment or close custody, at the discretion of the court, and be suspended for four years from the exercise of his political rights.

Art. 241. Nothing in this chapter contained shall render it unlawful for any person, who is apprehensive that a libel is about to be published, or that any literary property is about to be invaded by any publication, to endeavour to prevent it by threats of a suit or prosecution, or to commence such suit or prosecution for any such libel, should it be published, or for any such invasion of literary property, should it be made.

Art. 242. The constitution having declared, that no law shall ever be made to restrain the right to examine the proceedings of the legislature, or any branch of the government, any judicial or executive officer or other person, who, under pretence or colour of any existing law, or laws that may hereafter be passed, shall prevent, restrain, or attempt to restrain or prevent the exercise of the right asserted in that part of the constitution above recited in this article, shall be fined not less than three hundred nor more than one thousand dollars.

Art. 243. If any court, judge or other officer, shall enjoin, restrain or prevent the printing and publishing of any WRITING whatever, under the allegation, whether true or false, that such writing contains a libel or seditious words, or under any other pretext, or for any other reason than is contained in the next article, the judges of such court assenting to such order, and the judge (if done out of court) or other officer, offending against this article shall severally be fined not less than five hundred nor more than one thousand dollars, and shall be suspended from their political rights for two years.

Art. 244. It is no infringement of the last article to grant an injunction against the publication of any literary work, on the application of a person who shall satisfy the court or judge granting the injunction, that he is the author or proprietor of the work intended to be published, and that the publication will be injurious to his rights ; nor shall it be considered as a breach of the said article for a court of justice, in which any one shall be convicted of publishing a libel, to require security in the manner directed by the chapter of this code concerning libels, nor for a magistrate to make an admonition in the manner provided by the Code of Procedure against the publication of a libel or publication against decency.

TITLE IX.

OF OFFENCES AFFECTING PUBLIC RECORDS.

Art. 245. If any one shall FORGE, or FRAUDULENTLY carry away, deface or destroy any PUBLIC RECORD, or shall FORGE any official CERTIFICATE of any OFFICER having the custody of any public records of registry, he shall be imprisoned at hard labour, not less than seven nor more than fifteen years, and shall forfeit his political rights.

Art. 246. To FORGE, in the sense in which that word is employed in this chapter, is to make a false record or official certificate, or without authority to alter a true one in such a manner as that, if such false record were true or such alteration were legally made, some public or private right, or the condition of some individual, or the rights or immunities of some society, corporation, or general description of individuals, or some purpose of public utility, would be injured, altered or destroyed, or some right, immunity, privilege, condition or property would be vested, by such false or altered record.

Art. 247. The public and private rights mentioned in the last preceding article, are all those that are protected by the penal code, or for an injury to which a private suit is given by the civil code.

Art. 248. If any officer intrusted with the custody of PUBLIC RECORDS, shall commit any FORGERY of or upon such records, shall intentionally destroy or deface them, or conceal or carry them away, so that persons interested therein cannot have access to them, or shall advise or consent to such forgery, destruction, concealment or carrying away : or,

Shall fraudulently make and certify any entry or other act on such records in the name of one who was not present, or did not consent to such act : or,

Shall place any ACT, either AUTHENTIC or under PRIVATE SIGNATURE, on such register or record, under a date at which it was not registered or recorded, with intent to take away a right, give an illegal advantage to any one : or,

Shall knowingly permit any one falsely to PERSONATE another in the execution of any act entered or to be entered on any such register or record ; he shall be imprisoned at hard labour not less than seven nor more than fifteen years.

Art. 249. If any such officer as is described in the last preceding article shall, undesignedly, but through want of proper care, suffer the records intrusted to him, or any part of them, to be altered, defaced, taken away or lost ; or shall negligently do any act, by virtue or under colour of his office, which he is not authorized to do, or omit to do some official act which he ought to do, by either of which acts or omissions any one is INJURED in his property, condition or reputation, he shall be fined not less than one hundred nor more than four hundred dollars.

Art. 250. If any notary or other officer, authorized by law to reduce to writing any authentic acts, or receive and record any acts under private signature, shall falsely, in his official capacity, certify any thing to be true which is false, whereby any one is injured in his property, condition or reputation, he shall be fined not less than one hundred nor more than four hundred dollars, shall be imprisoned in close custody not less than sixty days nor more than one year.

Art. 251. If the offence described in the last preceding article be FRAUDULENTLY committed, the punishment, in addition to the fine, shall be imprisonment at hard labour not less than seven nor more than fifteen years.

Art. 252. If any one shall use any record of any act, so forged, or fraudulently entered, made, registered or recorded, or any such false declaration, as is described in this chapter, either by offering the same in a court of justice, or endeavouring by any other means to procure any advantage therefrom, knowing such act to be forged, or fraudulently entered or recorded, or such certificate to be false ; he shall be fined not less than six hundred nor more than two thousand dollars, and imprisoned at hard labour not less than seven nor more than fifteen years.

TITLE X.

OF OFFENCES AGAINST THE CURRENT COIN AND PUBLIC SECURITIES.

CHAPTER I.

Of offences against the current coin of the state.

Art. 253. Whoever shall counterfeit any GOLD OR SILVER COIN, whether such coin be of the United States, or of any other government ; or,

Whoever shall PASS, or offer to pass any such counterfeit coin, knowing it to be counterfeit ;

Shall be imprisoned at hard labour not less than seven nor more than fifteen years.

Art. 254. Whoever, with the intention of committing the crime of counterfeiting, or of aiding therein, shall have in his possession any die, or other instrument, such as is usually employed solely for the coinage of money, or shall make or repair any such die or other instrument, or shall prepare, or have in his possession and conceal any base metal prepared for coinage, shall be imprisoned at hard labour not less than two nor more than four years ; provided, that if any of the acts specified in this article shall be accompanied by circumstances which would render the accused liable, as an accomplice, for either of the crimes designated in the first article of this chapter, he may be prosecuted for such offence.

Art. 255. To counterfeit, under the provisions of this section, means, to make in the semblance of true gold or silver coin, one having in its composition a less proportion of the precious metal, of which the true coin intended to be imitated is composed, than is contained in such true coin, with intent that the same should be passed as true, either in the United States or elsewhere. To alter any coin of a lower value, with the like intent, so as to make it resemble one of a higher value, is also a counterfeit. It is not necessary, to constitute the offence, that the resemblance should be perfect.

Art. 256. The gold or silver coins mentioned in this chapter mean any pieces of gold or silver, or of which gold or silver is the principal component part, and which pass as money in the United States, or in any foreign nation, although such pieces may not be made current by any law of the United States.

Art. 257. Whoever shall have in his possession any counterfeited gold or silver coins, with intent to pass them as true, or to cause them to be passed either in the United States or any other nation, he shall be imprisoned at hard labour not less than two nor more than four years.

Art. 258. If any one shall, with intent to profit, diminish the weight of any gold or silver coin, and shall afterwards pass it for the same value it had before it was so diminished, or shall send or carry it to be so passed to any other place, whether in the United States or elsewhere, he shall be fined not less than two hundred, nor more than five hundred dollars, and be imprisoned not less than one nor more than three years.

Art. 259. To constitute the crime of PASSING, under the provisions of this section, it is not necessary that the counterfeit coin should have been given at the full value of the true coin of the same denomination; the crime is complete by delivering the counterfeit coin, knowing it to be counterfeit, to another, if such delivery is made either for the purpose of defrauding the person to whom it is delivered, or for the purpose of enabling him to deceive others.

Art. 260. The general provisions in this code, relative to attempts to commit offences, and to accomplices, and accessaries, apply to the offences mentioned in this chapter.

CHAPTER II.

Of offences against the public securities.

Art. 261. All offences coming under this head are provided for in the chapter concerning offences against the public revenue, or in that concerning offences affecting written contracts.

TITLE XI.

OF OFFENCES AFFECTING THE PUBLIC REVENUE.

Art. 262. If any OFFICER, or other person legally empowered to receive any money, or SECURITY FOR MONEY, for the state, or for any public corporation, shall illegally appropriate any such moneys or securities for money to his own use, or to the use of any other person, and shall, by rendering false accounts, or producing false vouchers, or in any other manner endeavour to conceal such illegal appropriation, with intent to defraud the state or the public corporation, to whom the said moneys belonged, of the same, or any part thereof, he shall pay a fine equal to double the yearly emolument of his office, shall be imprisoned not less than two nor more than six months, and shall forfeit his political rights.

Art. 263. No public officer or other person who is or shall be authorized to collect or receive moneys, or securities for the payment of money, for the state or any public corporation, shall appropriate the same, or any part thereof, to his own use, or to the use of any other person, even although he may intend to restore the same ; and whoever shall offend against this article, if he do not pay the sum so illegally appropriated within three days after demand made by a person legally authorized for that purpose, shall pay a fine equal to double the amount which he shall neglect to pay, and be suspended from his political rights for not less than two nor more than four years.

Art. 264. Although any person who may offend against the provisions of the last preceding article shall, before the expiration of the three days after demand, or even before any demand, replace or repay the money or security so illegally appropriated, he shall pay a fine equal to the amount of the said money, or the value of the said security.

Art. 265. In order to render offences against the preceding articles more difficult, and to detect them when they occur, every such receiver of moneys or public securities, who shall receive any sum or sums of money, or any such security, whenever and as often as they in the whole shall amount to the value of three hundred dollars, shall, within three days after such receipt, either pay or deliver the same to the officer appointed by law to receive the same, or deposit the same in some incorporated bank, if any be within three leagues of the place of such receiver's abode, to his credit, in the capacity or office in which he shall receive the same : and such money or security shall not be drawn out but by a draft or order specifying to whom and for what purpose it is to be paid. And any such officer or other person shall, for any offence against this article, pay a fine not less than two hundred nor more than six hundred dollars.

Art. 266. If the receiver of any such moneys or securities reside more than three leagues from the place where such bank is kept, he shall have fifteen days to make the deposit, payment, or delivery mentioned in the last preceding article ; and in cases where greater distance than twenty leagues, or difficulty of travelling may render it necessary, in the opinion of the treasurer of the state, to enlarge such time in any particular case, he may at his discretion extend it so as not to exceed thirty days.

Art. 267. If any person, employed to receive taxes or other moneys due to the state or any public corporation, shall EXTORT or attempt to extort from any one a larger sum than is due, or shall demand or receive any sum of money, emolument, service, or favour as a consideration for granting any delay in the collection of such dues, or for doing or omitting to do any act whatever in relation to the collection of such money, other than such emolument as may be allowed by law, he shall pay a fine not less than one half nor more than the whole of the amount of his yearly emoluments, be dismissed from his office, and rendered incapable of being re-appointed or re-elected to any public office for not less than one nor more than two years.

Art. 268. If any one shall by force attempt to prevent any officer or other person, authorized to enforce the payment of any tax or other debt due to the state, or to any public corporation, from performing the duties required of him by law, relative to the collection of such tax or debt, or shall by force, or threats of force, actually prevent any such officer or person above described from performing such duties, he shall be fined in a sum double to that of which he prevented or attempted to prevent the collection, and shall be imprisoned not less than ten nor more than sixty days, in addition to the other penalties which may be incurred for any act of violence committed in the course of the opposition forbidden by this article.

TITLE XII.

OF OFFENCES WHICH AFFECT COMMERCE AND MANUFACTURES.

CHAPTER I.

Of offences which affect foreign commerce.

Art. 269. If any one shall export from this state, or ship for the purpose of exportation, any article of commerce which, by the laws now in force, are, or by any laws hereafter passed may be, required to be inspected by a public inspector, without having caused such article to be inspected, according to the direction of such laws, he shall be fined one hundred dollars.

Art. 270. If any one shall counterfeit the mark, or brand, or stamp, directed by any such law to be put on any article of commerce, or on the cask or package containing the same, he shall be fined not less than one hundred nor more than three hundred dollars, and be imprisoned at hard labour not less than one nor more than three years.

Art. 271. If any one shall, with intent to defraud, put into any hogshead, barrel, or other cask, or in any bale, box, or package, containing merchandise usually sold by weight, any article whatever of less value than the merchandise with which such cask, bale, box, or package is apparently filled, or shall sell or barter, or give in payment, or expose for sale, or ship for exportation, such cask or bale, or package of merchandise, with any such article of inferior value concealed therein, with intent to DEFRAUD ; he shall pay a fine not less than five hundred nor more than one thousand dollars, and be imprisoned at hard labour not less than one nor more than three years.

Art. 272. If any one, being a citizen of or a person DOMESTICATED in this state, shall, on the high seas, or if any person whatever shall, within the limits of this state, injure or DESTROY any VESSEL of which such person is the owner, part owner, or freighter, or on board of which he shall be employed as master, supercargo, under officer, seaman, or in any other capacity whatsoever, with intent to defraud or injure the owner of such vessel, or of the cargo on board, or the underwriters on such vessel or cargo, or any part thereof, or any other person interested in such vessel or cargo, or in the voyage, or the freight or other profits of such ship or vessel, he shall be imprisoned at hard labour not less than six nor more than fourteen years.

Nothing in this article applies to any act that would be piracy by the laws of the United States.

Art. 273. If any one shall cause insurance to be made in this state on any merchandise, represented as shipped, or about to be shipped, at any place, whether within this state or elsewhere, or shall cause such insurance to be made at some place not within this state, on goods said to be shipped or about to be shipped within this state, and shall, with intent to defraud the insurer, ship articles of less value and different from those insured, or, if of the same kind, being less than one-half of the value of the articles insured, pretending that the articles so shipped are of the kind or of the quality with those insured, he shall be fined not less than one hundred nor more than five hundred dollars, and shall be imprisoned not less than sixty days nor more than six months in close custody.

Art. 274. Any person, not a citizen of or resident in this state, is guilty of an attempt to commit either of the offences described in the preceding articles, who shall make any agreement for the commission thereof within this state, and shall DO any ACT PREPARATORY thereto, whether the act be done in this state or elsewhere ; or who shall make such agreement out of the state, and do the preparatory act within this state. A citizen of or a resident in this state is guilty of such attempt, if he make the agreement or does the preparatory act, above described, any where.

Art. 275. No person shall be punished under either of the two last preceding articles who shall have been tried and acquitted, or punished, on an accusation for the same offence either in any court of the United States, of either of the United States, or of any foreign country having cognizance of the offence.

CHAPTER II.

Of offences against the laws regulating seamen in the merchant service, and the police of the port.

Art. 276. If any keeper of a tavern, or lodging or boarding-house, shall lodge, entertain, or conceal any seaman who has deserted from any merchant vessel, in any port of this state, within one month after such desertion, and knowing that he had so deserted, he shall forfeit one hundred dollars ; and for a second offence, in addition to such fine, be imprisoned for thirty days.

Art. 277. Any master of any ship or vessel who shall, in or at any port of this state, ship any seaman who has not produced a discharge, in the form required by law, from the master of the vessel with whom he last sailed, in the cases in which such discharge is by law required, shall pay a fine of fifty dollars.

Art. 278. The police of the ports of this state is regulated by ordinances, passed by the corporations of the cities and places where such ports are situated.

CHAPTER III.

Of false weights and measures.

Art. 279. Whoever shall use a false balance, weight or measure, in the weighing or measuring of any thing whatever that shall be purchased, sold, bartered, or shipped or delivered for sale or barter, or that shall be pledged or given in payment, knowing such balance, weight or measure to be false, and with intent to defraud, shall be fined not less than twenty nor more than two hundred dollars, and shall be imprisoned in close custody not less than ten nor more than ninety days.

Art. 280. The false weights and measures intended by the last preceding article, are such as shall not be conformable to the standard of weights and measures of length or capacity which are or may be established by law; the false balance thereby intended is any machine whatever used for ascertaining the weight of any personal property, which is so constructed as to make the article weighed appear to have more or less than the real weight.

Art. 281. Any person who shall sell bread or meat by a false weight or balance, shall incur double the punishment directed by the first article of this chapter.

Art. 282. The magistrate granting the warrant or arrest for this offence, shall also direct the seizure of the false weights, balances or measures; and if the party be convicted, or they be found to be false, they shall be broken or otherwise destroyed.

CHAPTER IV.

Of false marks.

Art. 283. If any one shall falsely alter any stamp, brand or mark on any cask, package, box or bale containing merchandise or produce, made by a public officer appointed for that purpose, in order to denote the quality, weight or quantity of the contents thereof, with intent to DEFRAUD, he shall be fined not less than two hundred nor more than five hundred dollars, and shall be imprisoned at hard labour not less than one nor more than three years.

Art. 284. Any one who shall counterfeit any mark, stamp or brand, intended to imitate one such as is described in the last preceding article, with intent to defraud, shall incur the same punishment as is directed by the said article.

Art. 285. Any one who, with a fraudulent intent, shall use any cask, package, box or bale, so marked, stamped or branded, for the sale of merchandise, of inferior quality, or less in quantity or weight, than is denoted by such mark, stamp or brand, shall incur one-half the punishment designated by the last preceding article.

CHAPTER V.

Of offences affecting the credit of written instruments.

Art. 286. Whoever shall be guilty of the crime of forgery, shall be imprisoned at hard labour not less than seven nor more than fifteen years, and shall forfeit his political and civil rights.

Art. 287. He is guilty of forgery, who, without lawful authority, and with intent to injure or defraud, shall either make a false INSTRUMENT in writing, purporting to be the ACT of another, or alter an instrument in writing then already in existence, by whomsoever made, in such a manner that the false instrument so made (if the same were true), or the alteration in the true instrument (if such alteration had been legally made), would have created, increased, defeated, discharged, or diminished, any PECUNIARY OBLIGATION, or would have transferred or in any manner have affected any PROPERTY whatever.

Art. 288. He is guilty of making, under the last preceding article, who, knowing the illegal purpose for which it is intended, shall write, or cause to be written, the SIGNATURE, or the whole or any part of the forged instrument. Therefore several persons may be each guilty of making the same forged instrument.

Art. 289. He who, under a void authority, but which he shall suppose good, shall make an instrument in writing in the name of another, is not guilty of making a false instrument, although it may be made without lawful authority. But if any one, without a legal authority, or without an authority which he shall have good reason to believe to be a legal one, shall make any writing over a blank signature, or on the back of a paper containing a blank signature of another person, such writing is a false instrument in writing, and if the other parts of the definition concur, is forgery.

Art. 290. The words, "instrument in writing," comprehend every writing purporting to testify the will or intent of the party whose act it purports to be, whether of RECORD by AUTHENTIC ACT, under seal, or PRIVATE SIGNATURE, or in whatever form it may be couched. It must be on paper, vellum, or parchment, or on some substance made to resemble one of them, and it comes within the definition, whether the words be traced with a pen, or stamped, or made by any other device to resemble a manuscript. An instrument, partly printed and partly written, is a written instrument. But if the whole, including the signature, be printed with types or plates, not made to resemble manuscript, it is not a written instrument, as that term is used in this chapter.

Art. 291. A name, or commercial firm, or the style of a corporation, without any other writing, is an instrument, when made for the purpose of conveying, creating, or destroying an interest.

Art. 292. In order to constitute the making a false instrument, it must purport to be the act of another. Therefore no one can be found guilty of forgery for making an instrument signed by himself, or by his authority, in his true name. Such act, when done with a fraudulent intent, is a different offence, hereinafter provided for.

Art. 293. The word " another," in the definition of the crime of forgery, includes the United States, each of the states and territories of the union, and all the several branches of the governments of either of them, including this state ; all public or private bodies, politic and corporate ; all partnerships in trade ; all courts ; all officers, public or private, in their official capacities ; and all persons whatever, whether real or fictitious, except the person making the forgery, as is provided in the last preceding article.

Art. 294. The word " whomsoever," in the said definition, as applied to the person by whom the altered instrument was originally made, is used in its most extensive sense, and includes not only all those mentioned in the last preceding article, but (in cases where the instrument at the time of making the alteration was the property of another) it includes also the person whose act it purports to be.

Art. 295. The word "alter," in the said definition, signifies not only erasing or obliterating some words, letters or figures, or extracting the writing altogether, but the substituting other words, letters, or figures, for those erased, obliterated, or extracted, and also the adding any other words, letters, or figures, to the original instrument, or making any change therein that shall have any of the effects pointed out in the said definition.

Art. 296. The words, "if the same were true," in the said definition, in describing the effect of an instrument falsely made, apply as well to the person whose act the instrument purports to be, as to the instrument itself; therefore, although the writing be made in a fictitious name, it is forgery, if the instrument would have had any of the effects detailed in the said definition, in case it had been made by a real person of the same name, or description, and if the act be done with a fraudulent intent.

Art. 297. The words " PECUNIARY OBLIGATION," used in the said definition there, and throughout this system, mean not only such as have money for their object, but every obligation for the breach of which damages might be legally, equitably, or justly demanded.

Art. 298. The words, "which would have transferred, or in any manner have affected any property whatever," are used in the most extensive sense. All property, REAL or PERSONAL, is included, as those terms are defined in this system; and the transfer or affecting such property, includes every species of disposition, whether to take effect immediately, or in future, on condition, or absolutely, by sale, delivery, will, donation, exchange, pledge, mortgage, release, discharge, or any other act that supposes a right to dispose of, or change the condition of said property.

Art. 299. The limitation, at the beginning of the said definition, is strictly to be adhered to : no act is a forgery, unless done with an intent either to injure or defraud.

Art. 300. The injury mentioned in the last preceding article, means injury affecting one in his PROPERTY, REAL, PERSONAL or mixed, corporeal or incorporeal, not an injury to person or reputation ; false writings, having the latter tendency, are provided for in another part of this code.

Art. 301. No design of refunding the money, or restoring the property received, or of preventing or compensating any damage or loss that might be occasioned by any of the offences described in this chapter, shall avoid the presumption of fraud created by the acts constituting those offences : but such design, if actually executed before any discovery of the crime, shall diminish its punishment one-half.

Art. 302. If any one shall make any written instrument in his own name, intended to create, increase, discharge, defeat or diminish any pecuniary obligation or transfer, or affect any property whatever, and shall put a false date to the same, with intent to injure or defraud—he shall be fined not less than two hundred nor more than five hundred dollars, and shall suffer imprisonment at hard labour not less than two nor more than six years.

Art. 303. If any one shall, with intent to injure or DEFRAUD, make any instrument in his own name, intended to create, increase, discharge or diminish any pecuniary obligation, or to transfer or affect any property whatsoever, and shall UTTER cr PASS it, under the pretence that it is the act of another who bears the same name—he shall be fined not less than two hundred nor more than five hundred dollars, and confined at hard labour not less than three nor more than six years.

Art. 304. All the terms of the two last preceding articles, which are contained in the definition of forgery in the second article of this chapter, are to be understood in the same sense in which they are used in the said definition.

Art. 305. If any one, having in his power a paper containing the true signature of another, shall, on the other side of the same, make a promissory note or bill of exchange in his own name, so as to make the said signature appear as an indorsement on such bill or note, with intent to defraud—he shall suffer the punishment assigned to such as are guilty of forgery.

Art. 306. Any one who shall, with intent to DEFRAUD, UTTER as TRUE, or PASS, any forged instrument in writing, or any other instrument in writing, the making of which is by this section made an offence, knowing such instrument to be forged, or made contrary to the provisions of this section, shall suffer the same punishment that is assigned to the offence of forging or making the same.

Art. 307. Whoever shall, in this state, engrave any plate, or prepare any implements, or materials, for the purpose of their being employed in the forging any notes of any bank, whether such bank be in or out of this state, or whether such bank be incorporated or not, and knowing such purpose, and with intent to defraud; or shall have in his possession any such plate, implements or materials made or prepared for such purpose, knowing the same, and with intent that they shall be used in the forging of any such notes—he shall be imprisoned at hard labour not less than one nor more than three years.

Art. 308. Whoever shall have in his possession any forged instrument in writing, or any instrument, the making of which is created an offence by this code, knowing the same to be forged, or made contrary to the provisions of this code, with intent fraudulently to utter or to pass the same—shall be imprisoned at hard labour not less than one nor more than three years.

Art. 309. If any one shall, with intent to defraud, either by falsely reading, or falsely interpreting any instrument in writing; or by misrepresenting its contents, induce any one, who, either from ignorance or infirmity, is incapable of reading an instrument in writing, or who, if he can read, does not understand the language in which it is written, to sign such instrument as his act, or give such assent to it as would, if there had been no error, make it his act; by the means of which false reading, false interpretation or misrepresenting, any PECUNIARY OBLIGATION purports to be created, increased, discharged or diminished, on the part of the person signing the same, or any of his property whatever purports to be transferred or in any manner affected—the person so offending shall be imprisoned at hard labour not less than one nor more than three years.

Art. 310. If any one, with intent to defraud, shall

induce another to sign any such instrument as is described in the last preceding article, by falsely and without the knowledge of such other, substituting it for another instrument, materially different therefrom, which the said person intended to sign—the person so offending shall be imprisoned at hard labour not less than one nor more than three years.

Art. 311. If either of the offences described in the two last preceding articles shall be committed by a public officer, whose duty it is to take or to record public acts, or by any counsellor or attorney at law, the term of imprisonment shall be doubled, and he shall forfeit his political rights.

Art. 312. If any one shall falsely personate another, whether bearing the same name or not, and in such assumed character or name shall give authority to a notary or any other person to sign such assumed name to any act, or to insert it therein, or to do any other thing implying a legal assent to any act, which, if it were the act of the party so personated, would have created, or increased, diminished or discharged, any pecuniary obligation, or transferred, or in any wise affected any property —he shall be imprisoned at hard labour not less than seven nor more than fifteen years.

CHAPTER VI.

Of fraudulent insolvencies.

Art. 313. Whoever shall institute any proceedings in any court of justice for the purpose of obtaining relief, under the laws now in force for giving relief in case of insolvency, for granting a respite, for making a cession of goods, or for giving relief from imprisonment for debt : or under any other laws that may be passed for any of the purposes above mentioned, and shall, in the course of such proceeding, with intent to defraud, make a false schedule or account of his credits, property or debts, and exhibit the same in such court as true, or shall fraudulently conceal or destroy his books of accounts, or papers relative to his estate, in cases where by law he is bound to produce the same for the use or inspection of his creditors, he shall suffer imprisonment for not less than two nor more than four years at hard labour.

Art. 314. The filing of the said schedule or account with the clerk of a court of justice, is exhibiting the same under the above article.

Art. 315. It is a false schedule or account under the said article,

1. If the party making the same shall fraudulently omit to insert on the said schedule any property, REAL or PERSONAL, to which he is entitled, and which by law ought to be placed on the said schedule or account, of the value of ten dollars or upwards.

2. If he shall place on the account of his debts any sum as due from him which he does not owe, for the purpose of defrauding his true creditors.

But the mere omission of any property on the schedule shall not make the party liable, unless from the circumstances of the case it appear that it was done with design and in order to defraud.

Art. 316. Any one who, not having property of sufficient value to pay his debts, shall make any simulated conveyance, mortgage or other disposition of any part of his property for his own use or the use of his family, and in order to prevent the same from becoming liable to the payment of his debts, shall be imprisoned for not less than sixty days nor more than six months, and shall be suspended from the exercise of his civil rights of the first class, and of his political rights for four years; and the imprisonment, or any part of it, may be in close custody.

Art. 317. A simulated conveyance, mortgage or disposition, is one sufficient in form for the alienation or affecting of the property, but made without consideration, or for an inadequate consideration, and under a secret understanding between the parties that it shall operate for the benefit of the person making the same, either by a reconveyance afterwards to be made, or by a destruction or redelivery of the instrument by which it was conveyed or affected, if it be property requiring a written conveyance, or of the property itself, or by holding or conveying the same to his use, or that of his wife or any relation in the ascending or descending line.

Art. 318. Any person who shall receive any such simulated conveyance, mortgage or disposition for the purposes aforesaid, knowing the said purpose, shall pay a fine equal to the full value of the property so intended to be conveyed, or the amount for which it was intended to be affected, to be ascertained by three appraisers appointed by the court, and sworn to make a true appraisement.

Art. 319. The word "disposition," in the three last articles, means every species of contract by which property may be subjected to any alien or onerous condition, whether by mortgage, pledge or otherwise.

Art. 320. Any one who, not having sufficient property to pay his just debts, shall voluntarily suffer a judgment to be entered in favour of any one, that shall bind or encumber any real property, or on which any personal property shall be seized, for a sum not due, or without consideration, or for an inadequate consideration shall convey, or mortgage or affect by any onerous condition any of his property, or for a larger sum than is really due, with intent to defraud his creditors, or some one or more of them, shall be imprisoned not less than sixty days nor more than six months, shall be suspended from the exercise of his political and of his civil rights of the first class for four years, and the imprisonment may in the whole or in part be in close custody.

Art. 321. The person who shall, collusively with such debtor, recover such judgment, shall be fined in a sum equal to the amount of such judgment, and he who, knowing the intent of such conveyance, mortgage or onerous disposition, shall receive the same, shall be fined in a sum equal to the value of the property if conveyed, or the amount of the incumbrance if only mortgaged or burthened.

Art. 322. All the dispositions of the six last preceding articles take effect only in cases where the inability to pay debts appears by a forced or voluntary cession of property, or petition for a respite, or a discussion of all the property of the debtor.

TITLE XIII.

OF OFFENCES AFFECTING PUBLIC PROPERTY.

Art. 323. All the provisions for the protection of the property of individuals against fraudulent or malicious injury, apply to the property of the state, and of public and private corporations.

TITLE XIV.

OF OFFENCES AFFECTING THE PUBLIC ROADS, EMBANKMENTS, BRIDGES, NAVIGABLE WATERS, AND OTHER PROPERTY HELD BY THE SOVEREIGN POWER FOR THE COMMON USE.

GENERAL PROVISION.

Art. 324. The ordinances which the juries of police in the different parishes and the public corporations in the cities and towns are authorized to make, contain the regulations of police for the making and enlarging the embankments or levees, roads, bridges, streets, and public squares, and the penalties which are incurred by disobeying them.

CHAPTER I.

Of the levees and embankments of rivers.

Art. 325. If any one shall maliciously break down any levee or embankment made to confine the waters of any river or bayou, he shall be fined not less than fifty nor more than five hundred dollars, or imprisoned not less than one month nor more than one year, or both.

Art. 326. Every breach in such levee or embankment shall be deemed to be maliciously made, if it shall be attended with any injury to the property of another, and if it be done in a manner or for a purpose forbidden by the ordinances of police.

CHAPTER II.

Of the roads, bridges, and navigable waters.

Art. 327. Whoever shall make any embankment, wharf, or other construction in the bed of any navigable river, bayou, or lake, that shall impede the navigation thereof, or that shall not be allowed by the legal ordinances of police, of the police juries in the parish in which it is made, shall be fined not less than fifty nor more than five hundred dollars.

Art. 328. Whoever shall erect any fence or building, or dig any ditch, or throw up any mound of earth in any street or public road or square, or do any other act that shall obstruct the public use thereof, or shall unlawfully destroy any bridge erected thereon, shall be fined not less than five, nor more than one hundred dollars.

Art. 329. Whoever shall erect on the space set apart by the police regulations for a tow path, along any navigable waters, or on the levee or embankment of the same, or on its banks, any building, enclosure, or other construction, or any other works whatever, that shall prevent the public use thereof, or render it less convenient, unless thereunto authorized in the manner directed by the law, or by the ordinances of police, shall be fined not less than fifty nor more than five hundred dollars.

Art. 330. All persons guilty of any of the offences designated in this chapter shall also be subject to such regulations as are or shall be lawfully made by the police ordinances, for the repair of any damages that may be occasioned by such offences, and the removal of the works that are forbidden by this chapter.

TITLE XV.

OF OFFENCES INJURIOUS TO PUBLIC HEALTH.

CHAPTER I.

Of acts injurious to public health or safety.

Art. 331. No one shall carry on a manufactory of gunpowder, or shall keep more than ten pounds of gunpowder at one time, in any building within three hundred yards of any dwelling-house, or of any public road, or of any land belonging to any other person than the proprietor of the land on which such manufactory or building is erected, unless the owner of such adjacent land shall permit such manufactory to be carried on, and will agree not to build any dwelling-house within three hundred yards of such manufactory or building in which such gunpowder is stored. Any one offending against the provisions of this article, shall be fined five hundred dollars; and on conviction may be enjoined by the court from carrying on such business.

Art. 332. Whoever shall carry on any trade, or business, or do any act that is injurious to the health of those who reside in the vicinity, or shall suffer any substance which shall have that effect, to remain on any real property possessed by him, shall be fined not exceeding three hundred dollars, and the party may be enjoined proceeding in the operations that are offensive to health, and ordered to remove such substances.

Art. 333. Whoever shall wilfully ADULTERATE for the purpose of sale, or shall sell, knowing it to be adulterated, any wine, beer, spirits of any kind, or other liquor intended for drinking, with any substance that renders them injurious to the health of those who drink them, shall be fined not exceeding three hundred dollars, and the liquor so adulterated shall be forfeited and destroyed.

Art. 334. If any person shall fraudulently adulterate for sale, or shall sell, knowing them to be so adulterated, any drugs or medicines in such a manner as to lessen the efficacy or change the operation of such drugs or medicines, or to make them injurious to health, he shall be fined not less than one hundred nor more than five hundred dollars, and imprisoned not less than ten days nor more than six months, and the imprisonment may be in close custody.

TITLE XVI.

OF OFFENCES AGAINST MORALS.

CHAPTER I.

Of disorderly houses.

Art. 335. If any one shall keep a disorderly house, he shall be punished by fine not exceeding two hundred dollars, or by imprisonment in close custody not more than sixty days.

Art. 336. The houses that are punishable as disorderly, are :

1. Houses kept for the purpose of public prostitution, and DISTURBANCE.

2. Houses kept as taverns, or for the sale of spirituous liquors by retail, without license.

3. Licensed houses of the description last above mentioned, in which any act forbidden by the license, is permitted to be done.

4. Houses in which gambling is permitted in a manner contrary to some express law.

Art. 337. Any part of a building, appropriated to either of the purposes above enumerated, is a house within the meaning of this chapter.

Art. 338. There must be more than one act of the kinds that are above forbidden, done in a house, to constitute it a disorderly house.

Art. 339. The wife may be punished with the husband, for keeping a disorderly house of the first description ; but no house shall be comprehended in that term unless such acts are habitually permitted therein, as come within the description of those public exhibitions of person, which are made punishable by the next chapter, or unless acts are habitually done therein, which, if done in a public place, would amount to the offence of PUBLIC DISTURB-ANCE.

CHAPTER II.

Of offences against decency.

Art. 340. If any one shall make, publish or print any obscene print, picture or written or printed composition, manifestly designed to corrupt the morals of youth, or shall designedly make any indecent or obscene exhibitions of their persons or of those of another, in public, by which pudicity is offended ; he shall be imprisoned not more than six months, or fined not more than one thousand dollars, or both ; and the imprisonment, or part of it, shall be in close custody.

Art. 341. If any one shall, with design to insult, in the hearing of any person of the female sex, utter any obscene or lascivious expressions, such as must shock the natural pudicity of that sex ; he shall be imprisoned in close custody not less than five nor more than thirty days, or fined not exceeding fifty dollars, or both.

Art. 342. Whoever shall be guilty of SEDUCING a woman of good reputation under a promise of marriage, and shall violate his promise, shall be fined not less than one hundred nor more than one thousand dollars, or shall be imprisoned in close custody not less than one nor more than six months.

Art. 343. Whoever shall, for hire, procure the means of illicit connexion between persons of different sexes, or shall solicit or procure a woman to prostitute her person to another, shall be imprisoned not exceeding three months in close custody.

CHAPTER III.

Of adultery.

Art. 344. Adultery is a term of which the meaning, as affixed by this code, is precisely that which it bears in common parlance ; it therefore needs no other description. When committed by the wife, it is an offence for which she forfeits all matrimonial gains, to which she would otherwise be entitled ; which immediately, on the conviction, are vested in those who would have been her legal heirs had she died on the day of conviction ; she also forfeits her civil rights of the first class.

Art. 345. The person with whom a woman commits adultery shall suffer fine not less than one hundred and not exceeding two thousand dollars, or imprisonment not more than six months, or both.

Art. 346. The husband who commits adultery, by keeping a concubine in the house with his wife, or by forcing her by ill-treatment to abandon his house, and keeping his concubine in it, shall be fined not less than one hundred nor more than two thousand dollars ; and his civil right of being tutor or curator to any minor, including his own children, is suspended from the time of conviction, for one year, and as much longer as he shall live with his concubine in the same house.

Art. 347. No prosecution for aduitery shall be commenced, but on the complaint of the husband or wife ; and the prosecution shall cease if the parties are reconciled before judgment.

Art. 348. A sentence of separation, in person and estate, for cause of adultery, must always be preceded by a conviction for that offence.

Art. 349. The indictment or information for adultery

against the wife must be a joint one, against the woman and the man with whom the adultery is said to have been committed, if he be alive, and the one cannot be found guilty without the other—subject to the modifications contained in the Code of Procedure.

CHAPTER IV.

Of the violation of places of interment.

Art. 350. Whoever shall open a grave, or other place of interment, for the purpose of stealing the coffin, or any part thereof, or the vestments, or other articles, interred with any dead body which is deposited in such place of interment; shall be imprisoned at hard labour not less than one nor more than three years.

Art. 351. Whoever, for the purpose of sale, exposure or dissection, shall remove any dead body from the grave, or other place of interment—shall be fined not less than fifty nor more than three hundred dollars, or imprisoned not less than thirty nor more than ninety days.

Art. 352. The last preceding article does not extend to cases where a dead body shall be disinterred in the manner directed by the Code of Procedure, for the purpose of examination into the means by which the deceased lost his life.

Art. 353. Whoever shall purchase, or sell, or otherwise than is hereinafter provided, shall dissect any dead body before its interment—shall be fined not less than fifty nor more than two hundred dollars, or shall be imprisoned not more than ninety days.

Art. 354. The last preceding article does not extend to cases where a dissection is ordered in case of suspicion of murder, according to the provisions of the Code of Procedure :

To cases where the deceased has himself directed it :

To cases where it is performed by the permission of the next of kin to the deceased:

Or, to cases where dissection is ordered by law to be performed upon the bodies of those who die in prison, under conviction of certain offences.

Art. 355. The dead body, intended by this chapter, is that of a human being.

TITLE XVII.

OF OFFENCES WHICH AFFECT PERSONS IN THE EXERCISE OF THEIR RELIGION.

Art. 356. If any one shall MALICIOUSLY prevent any person from doing any lawful act that is required by the religion he professes ; or shall, by force or threats of force, or of injury to person or property, oblige or endeavour to oblige, any one to follow any forms of worship, or to profess any mode of religious belief, or to perform any religious rites or ceremonies ; he shall be fined not less than twenty nor more than two hundred dollars, or imprisoned in close custody not exceeding forty days, or both.

Art. 357. If the offence, described in the last preceding article, shall be committed by a judicial or executive officer, under COLOUR of authority derived from his office, or by any priest or minister, or preacher of any religious congregation or sect, the punishment shall be doubled.

Art. 358. Nothing in this chapter contained shall prevent a parent or tutor, or curator, or master, from obliging his child, or ward, or apprentice, being a minor, by all such means as are permitted by law for the enforcement of his other legal commands, to conform to the forms of worship in which such minor was educated.

Art. 359. Nor do the provisions of this chapter prevent the enforcement of the rules, canons, or ordinances made by different churches, or religious congregations or societies, for the preservation of discipline or order among their members : provided, that such enforcement shall not be made by the infringement of any civil or political right, or by any act declared by this code to be an offence.

Art. 360. If any act which by this code is made an offence, shall be committed in a place of public worship during the celebration thereof, so as to disturb any religious society in the legal performance of their worship, or their religious rites and ceremonies, the punishment for such offence shall be doubled, and shall not in any case be less than a fine of fifty dollars or imprisonment in close custody for fifteen days.

Art. 361. If such disturbance be intentionally made by any act which is not otherwise created an offence, the punishment shall be fine not exceeding fifty dollars or imprisonment not exceeding thirty days.

TITLE XVIII.

OF OFFENCES AFFECTING REPUTATION.

CHAPTER I.

Of defamation.

Art. 362. Whoever shall defame another, shall be punished by fine or imprisonment, or both.

If the defamation impute a CRIME, it shall be punished by fine not exceeding three thousand dollars, or by imprisonment not more than twelve months, or both ; and the imprisonment may, for the whole or a part of the time, be in close custody.

If the defamation do not impute a CRIME, the punishment shall be lessened one-fourth.

If the defamation be by libel, imprisonment in close custody shall always form a part of the punishment.

Art. 363. Defamation is an injury offered to the reputation of another, by an allegation which is either untrue, or, if true, is not made with a justifiable intent.

Art. 364. Defamation may be made verbally or by signs, which is called slander; or by writing or painting, which is called libel.

Art. 365. This offence consists in the injury offered to reputation, not in any probable breach of the peace or other consequence that may result from it.

Art. 366. There must be some injury offered in order to constitute the offence; therefore, the words used, or the figures represented, must convey the idea, either—

1. That the person to whom they refer has been guilty of some crime:

2. That he has done some act, or been guilty of some omission, which, although not a crime, is of a nature to make people in general avoid social intercourse with him, or lessen their confidence in his integrity:

3. That he has some moral vice, or physical or mental defect or disease, that would cause his society to be generally avoided: or,

4. That his general character is such as to produce either of the effects mentioned in this article.

Art. 367. It is also an injury, coming within the definition, if the natural tendency of the words or representations used is to bring upon the person to whom they refer, the hatred, ridicule, or contempt of the public, or to deprive him of the benefits of social intercourse.

Art. 368. To make false representations, importing that the party referred to wants the necessary talents, or is otherwise incompetent to perform or conduct the office, business, profession, or trade in which he is engaged, or is dishonest in his conduct therein, is also an injury within this part of the definition.

Art. 369. But it is not an offence to make true statements of fact, or express any opinion, whether such opinion be correctly formed or not, as to the qualifications of any person for any public office, with a bonâ fide intent to give information to those who have the power of making the appointment or election to such office.

Art. 370. Nor is it an offence to make true statements of fact, or express the opinion which he who gives it entertains relative to the integrity or other qualifications to perform the duties of any station, profession, or trade, when it is done by way of advice to those who have asked it, or to those whom it was a duty, arising either from legal or social connexion, or from motives of humanity, to give such advice.

Art. 371. Nor shall it be deemed an offence to make or publish any criticism or examination of any work of literature, science, or art ; or to express any opinion on the qualifications, merits, or competency of the author of such work, in relation thereto ; although such criticism, examination, or opinion shall be ill-founded and prove injurious to the party to whom it refers : provided such criticism or expression of opinion be not intended to cover a malicious design to injure the party to whom it refers.

Art. 372. If the injury spoken of in the definition be OFFERED, it is sufficient to constitute the offence ; by which is not meant that the injury must be actually suffered, but that the words or representations are such as, in the ordinary course of affairs, tend to cause such injury, according to the definition and explanation of that word in this chapter.

Art. 373. All those who make, publish, or circulate a libel, are severally guilty of the offence of defamation.

Art. 374. He is the maker of a libel, who originally contrived, and either gave it form himself, by writing, printing, engraving, painting, or any other of the modes which may constitute a libel, or caused it to be so done by others.

Art. 375. He is the PUBLISHER, who executes the mechanical labour of writing it when dictated by the maker, or who paints or engraves, or in any other manner gives it form under his direction, who copies, or prints it.

Art. 376. He circulates, who sells a libel, or who, knowing the contents, gives or distributes, or reads, or exhibits it to others.

Art. 377. If the libel be in a printed form, and is printed or sold in an office, or shop, where books or other printed works are usually printed or sold, the person on whose account the business of such office or shop is carried on, is presumed to be the person who published or circulated it, until he remove that presumption by contrary proof.

Art. 378. In like manner, if the libel be an engraving, or painting, and is made and sold in an office or shop in which paintings or engravings are usually made or sold, the person on whose account the business of such office or shop is carried on, is presumed to be the person who published or circulated it.

Art. 379. No one shall be convicted merely on evidence of his having made a manuscript copy of a libel, or of having performed the mechanical labour of printing it, who can prove that he made such printed or written copy without any intent to injure the person to whom it refers ; but he, for whose account, or by whose order it is printed, shall be presumed to have known the intent of publication, and shall be liable for the offence.

Art. 380. He is not guilty of the offence who only lends or gives a book or paper containing a libel, or reads it to another after it is already in general circulation, unless some circumstances are proved to show that it was done with design to injure.

Art. 381. The injury, to constitute the offence, must be offered to the REPUTATION. Words, or representations which injure the party in his title to property only, form a different offence, provided for under its proper head.

Art. 382. The words " of another," in the definition of this offence, comprehends every person in possession of his CIVIL RIGHTS, as also aliens, whether resident within the state or not.

Art. 383. The dead are also included in this term, but subject to the following formality or proviso :

1. No prosecution shall be commenced, but on the complaint of a family meeting, called at the request of a descendant, collateral relation, or friend of the deceased, in the manner directed by the Code of Civil Procedure.

2. No prosecution can be supported, for the statement of any historical facts, or delineations of character in any literary work, whether the party to whom they refer be dead or alive, provided such statements be made in the fair prosecution of historical or other literary disquisition, and not for the purpose of defamation.

Art. 384. The word "allegation," as used in the definition, comprehends not only the direct assertion of a fact, but every mode of speech or device, by which the hearers or spectators may understand what is intended.

Art. 385. The words or representations by which the allegation is expressed, are to be understood in the sense in which they were intended by the person using them : intent and signification are matters of fact to be determined from a consideration of all the evidence in the case.

Art. 386. An important part of the definition is that which determines that the uttering of truth may sometimes constitute defamation. The truth may be expressed in all cases in which it is not forbidden by law, but the allegation of falsehood is not always an OFFENCE ; it is sometimes made the cause of private suit, sometimes left to the sanction of the moral sense, or of public opinion. For the development of this branch of the definition, the following rules are established :

1. True statements of the OFFICIAL conduct of members of the general assembly, or of public officers, and of the proceedings of all legislative bodies, PUBLIC CORPORATIONS, and courts of justice, may be legally made.

2. Observations on the tendency of the official acts of members of the legislature, and of public officers, and on

their motives in performing them, are permitted, even if the author should mistake such tendency or motives; but a false allegation or suggestion of such motives, as would, connected with the act, constitute a crime, is defamation.

3. Allegations, having no natural connexion with the case, provided for by the two last preceding articles, which would amount to defamation, if made or exhibited alone, are offences, although they may be contained in publications which treat or propose to treat of the conduct of public measures and public officers.

Art. 387. Allegations, in writing, made with respect to all other than the official acts above provided for, which would, if they were false, be defamation, shall, although true, constitute that offence, if they are made from motives of revenge, hatred, envy, or ill-will of any other kind, entertained by the party making them, or to gratify either of those passions in any other; and they shall be deemed to have been made from such motive in all cases in which the defendant cannot show that he was actuated by some motive of public good, or private duty, in making the allegation.

5. No true allegations but such as are described in the last preceding rule, and no false allegations but such as are declared to be offences by this code, are declared punishable by law.

6. No prosecution can be maintained for defamation, on account of any thing said or written, either as judge, attorney, counsel, party or witness, in a court of justice in the course of a legal proceeding, provided that what is said or written be relevant to the matter before such court, and is not introduced for the sole purpose of injuring the party to whom it refers.

7. Inquiries and suggestions, made even out of court, if done with a bonâ fide view of investigating a fact, necessary for the party's interest in a civil, or defence in a criminal prosecution, and not from malice towards the party to whom they refer, are not an offence, although they may injure such party.

8. Nothing said by a party to a civil suit or criminal prosecution, in confidence to his attorney, solicitor or counsel, relative to such suit or prosecution, while it is pending, or with a view to its commencement or defence, is an offence under this chapter.

9. The constitutions of the United States and of this state severally protect members of Congress and of the general assembly from prosecutions for anything said in either of those bodies. The same rule is to be observed with respect to members of the legislatures of the different states, and those who may publish their proceedings.

Art. 388. The word " verbally," used in the definition of slander, means the utterance of words by the voice; and the words " by signs," comprehend every motion of the fingers or other gesture, that is understood by the party using it, and by them to whom it is addressed, to signify words, or otherwise to communicate ideas.

Art. 389. It is slander to repeat the contents of any libel, or the words of any slander, unless the defendant show that he was not actuated in doing so by any desire to injure the person defamed.

Art. 390. The word " writing," in the definition of libel, comprehends not only manuscript, but printing, engraving, etching, or any other means now known, or which may hereafter be discovered or invented, to make words visible. The word " painting," in the same definition, includes not only the art usually so called, but drawing, engraving, or representing figures in any other way. It also comprehends hieroglyphics, or the representation of words by objects which they signify.

Art. 391. Offences enumerated in this chapter can only be punished by indictment, and never but on complaint of the party injured, or his legal representative, if he be alive; or if the defamation be against the reputation of the person deceased, then in the manner hereinbefore provided.

Art. 392. In all the offences created by this chapter, the jury decide not only all the facts that are in question, but the intent, when it is material, subject to the general powers given to the court in the Code of Procedure.

Art. 393. Nothing in this chapter contained shall be so construed as to prevent or punish the free discussion of the proceedings of the legislature, or any other branch of the government, which is secured by the constitution ; and nothing shall be considered as an abuse of the liberty to speak, write and print on any subject which is referred to in the constitution, but such acts of that nature as are specially constituted offences by this code.

Art. 394. There is no such offence known to our law as defamation of the government, or either of its branches, either under the name of libel, slander, seditious writing, or other appellation. When such allegations amount to defamation of the representatives of the people, or public officers, they are provided for by the preceding articles. When they amount to the crime of complicity in sedition, or in opposition to law, they are made punishable by the general provisions respecting accomplices.

Art. 395. There is no such offence as defamation of a body corporate or politic, of public justice, or religion, or good morals, either by libel or otherwise.

Art. 396. In all cases of prosecution under this chapter, the court may, at its discretion, make it a condition that the whole or any part of the punishment which is awarded, may be remitted on the offender's making apology and amends to the person injured in such a form and manner as the court shall by its sentence declare ; and if the person injured shall accept of any pecuniary amends, it shall be a bar to any private suit for defamation, founded on the same offence.

Art. 397. On the trial of any prosecution for a defamation, if the jury find that the defendant is the author of the libel, or the speaker of the defamatory words, and that the matter which constitutes the libel is false in the whole or in part, they shall specially so declare it in their verdict; declaring the allegations of the defendant to have been unfounded, and, where the case requires it, malicious; and the charge made by the defendant, the verdict and the judgment of the court, shall, when required by the prosecutor, be published at the expense of the defendant.

Art. 398. Whenever the defendant, in any prosecution for defamation, shall avow himself the author or speaker of the words alleged, and shall acknowledge that the charge they import is unfounded; or that they were not intended to apply to the prosecutor; or, in cases where there is either ambiguity in the expression, or uncertainty as to their application, that they were not used in the sense in which they were understood by him, but in another sense, stating it—in either of these cases, the punishment shall be confined to the payment of costs, and of the publication of the proceedings; unless the defendant shall make it appear that the words, according to their true import, did not imply any defamation, or did not apply to the prosecutor; in which case he shall be exempt from any costs; but the proceedings may, in like manner, be published.

CHAPTER II.

Of other injuries to reputation by effigies or dramatic representations.

Art. 399. Whoever, with intent to bring another into contempt, or to excite ridicule or indignation against him, shall exhibit, or shall make, with intent that it shall be exhibited, any effigy or figure, intended to represent such other person, shall be fined not exceeding one thousand dollars, or imprisoned not exceeding ninety days, or both; and part or whole of the imprisonment may be in close custody. And if more than twelve persons are collected to witness such exhibition, it shall be deemed an unlawful assembly, and a riot, if they refuse to disperse when thereto legally required.

Art. 400. If any one, with intent to bring another into contempt, or to excite ridicule or indignation against him, shall perform, or cause any dramatic work to be performed, in which such person is represented and personated, either by an imitation of his person, or of any peculiarity in his manner, gesture, language, or otherwise, so as to make it apparent to those who know him that he is the person intended by such personification, the offender shall be fined not exceeding one thousand dollars, or imprisoned not exceeding ninety days, or both ; and part or the whole of the imprisonment may be in close custody.

CHAPTER III.

Of false accusation, and threats of prosecution.

Art. 401. If any two or more persons shall combine falsely to accuse another of crime, and in consequence of such combination shall either verbally or in writing make such accusation, whether judicially or not, they shall be fined not less than one hundred nor more than three thousand dollars, and imprisoned at hard labour not less than one nor more than four years, besides incurring the penalty of perjury, if that crime should be committed in the prosecution of their design.

Art. 402. If the intent of such combination be to extort any pecuniary advantage by such false accusation, or the threat thereof, the punishment shall be doubled.

Art. 403. If any one, with intent to extort money or procure other profit, shall falsely accuse, or threaten to accuse, another of any crime, or of the doing of any act which, if the accusation were true, would bring him into contempt, or excite public indignation against him, the person making such threat or accusation, knowing the same to be false, shall suffer the same punishment as is set forth in the last preceding article.

CHAPTER IV.

Of fabricating defamatory papers.

Art. 404. Whoever, with intent to injure the reputation of another, shall, without any lawful authority, publish or circulate, or make, with the intent to publish or circulate, any false writing, purporting to be the act or work of such other person, which does not constitute the crime of forgery, but which would, if the same were true, bring the person, whose act or work it purports to be, into contempt, cause his society to be generally avoided, excite public ridicule or indignation against him, or injure him in his office, profession, or trade, the offender shall be fined not exceeding four thousand dollars, and shall be imprisoned not exceeding one year in close confinement.

Art. 405. The words used in the last preceding article, which occur in the first of this title, are used in the same sense in which they were explained in that, and are subject to the same limitation.

TITLE XIX.

OF OFFENCES AFFECTING THE PERSONS OF INDIVIDUALS.

CHAPTER 1.

Of assault and of battery.

SECTION I.

Of simple assault, or simple assault and battery.

Art. 406. No one has a right to use any VIOLENCE on the person of another, except in the cases and to the degree allowed by law ; such violence used in any other case or to a greater degree, with intent to inflict an injury, is an offence called a battery ; it may be a misdemeanor, or a crime, according to the measure of violence or the intent with which it is offered.

Art. 407. By the term " violence," in the above definition, is meant any physical force applied either immediately, by any part of the body of the person using it, or by the instrumentality or intervention of any other matter, whether animate or inanimate, and it comes within the definition whether the violence be produced by SECONDARY MEANS, intentionally prepared by the offender, or be caused by his immediate act.

Art. 408. The explanation in the last article may be illustrated thus : a blow with the hand is an example of physical force applied immediately by the body of the person using it ; a bullet shot from a gun, a stroke given with a cudgel, water thrown from a bowl, are examples of the employment of inanimate matter ; and one man injured by pushing another against him, or by beating or assaulting the horse which draws or carries him, are instances of battery committed by the intervention of animated matter, and a wound given by a spring-gun or trap purposely set, or an injury caused by falling into a pit or over an obstruction intentionally dug or placed in a highway, are illustrations of what is meant by the words of SECONDARY MEANS.

Art. 409. A menacing gesture, showing, either in itself or by words which accompany it, an immediate design coupled with the ability to commit a battery, is an assault; which is a misdemeanor, whether followed by a battery or not.

Art. 410. The person of every free person being entitled to perfect protection from the exercise of illegal force, the degree of such force applied to it does not enter into the definition; it is a battery, however slight, if done with intent to injure.

Art. 411. The injury meant by the definition is not only bodily pain, constraint, or inconvenience, but alarm, a sense of degradation, or other disagreeable emotion of the mind.

Art. 412. Whenever injury is caused by violence to the person, the intent to injure is presumed, and the burthen of proving accident, or another intent, is thrown on him who alleges it.

Art. 413. It is sufficient to constitute the offence if the intent be to injure any one, although not the person to whom the violence was actually offered.

Art. 414. When an injury has been done to the person, by an act, which, although not intended to injure, was such as, in the usual course of things, might be expected to produce such injury to some one, it is an offence which shall be punished by fine, not exceeding two hundred dollars, or imprisonment not exceeding sixty days, or both.

Art. 415. Violence offered to the person does not amount to the offence of battery, where it is done in either of the cases, or for either of the purposes hereafter enumerated in this article ; that is to say,

1. In the execution of that right of moderate restraint or correction which is given by law to the parent over the child : the tutor or curator over his minor ward : the master over the apprentice or servant : the schoolmaster over the scholar : or by persons duly authorized to use such restraint or correction towards minors, by persons standing in either of the above relations to them ;

2. By the curator of a person insane, for the necessary restraint of the ward, although such ward be of full age ;

3. For the preservation of order in any meeting, either for religious, political, literary, social or any other lawful purposes ;

4. For the necessary preservation of the peace, or to prevent the commission of any crime ;

5. To prevent or put an end to an intrusion on a legal possession ;

6. To make a lawful arrest, and to detain the party arrested in lawful custody, in cases where, by the Code of Procedure, arrests are permitted without warrant ;

7. In obedience to the lawful order of a magistrate, or court of competent authority ;

8. To overcome resistance to the execution of any such lawful order ;

9. In self defence, or the defence of another, against unlawful violence, offered to his person or property.

In each of the preceding cases, the force used, to effect either of the purposes thereby declared to be lawful, must be such as does not exceed what is necessary for the purpose, otherwise it will amount to the offence of battery. That degree of force shall be esteemed to have been necessary, which would have appeared so to one of ordinary prudence and firmness, placed in the situation in which the accused was.

Art. 416. An assault or battery cannot be justified by any verbal provocation ; but under certain circumstances, such provocation may be submitted to the court in the manner directed in the Code of Procedure, in mitigation of the punishment.

Art. 417. No prosecution shall be commenced for

simple assault or battery, but on the complaint of the party injured, or some one representing, or duly authorized by him: when attended with any other circumstance or intent which aggravates the offence, it may, with the exceptions hereinafter contained, be prosecuted on the complaint of any person whatever.

Art. 418. The punishment for simple assault or battery is fine, not exceeding one thousand dollars, or imprisonment not exceeding six months, or both, and the imprisonment may be in the whole, or in part, in close custody.

Art. 419. The terms, " degree of force," mean as well the instrument, or other secondary means employed, as physical or bodily power.

SECTION II.

Of assault and battery in relation to the person on whom, or by whom it is committed.

Art. 420. The law gives protection to all persons against illegal violence, but different remedies are applied according to the effect of the offence upon society, when committed by, or upon particular persons who are either appointed to preserve order, or on those who are particularly exposed to violence.

Art. 421. If assault or battery be committed on any public officer while in the legal execution of his office, the punishment assigned to the species of assault or battery that is committed, shall be doubled.

Art. 422. No act is an offence under this section, unless it was known to the party accused, that the person assaulted was a public officer, and was in the execution of his office; and he shall be deemed to have known it when it was so openly declared in his presence, or when, from the circumstances of the case, he could not have been ignorant both of the character of the officer, and of the nature of the duty he was performing.

Art. 423. If any public officer shall, under pretence of executing his office, exercise any violence against any other person, in cases where no force is permitted to be used, or shall exceed, in cases where force is permitted, that degree thereof which is allowed by law, the punishment assigned to the species of assault and battery that is committed, shall be doubled.

Art. 424. If assault or battery be committed by a relation in the descending line against his ascendant ; or by a man against a woman ; or by a ward against his tutor, the punishment assigned to the species of assault or battery that is committed, shall be doubled.

SECTION III.

Of assault and battery, aggravated by its commission in a particular place.

Art. 425. If an assault or battery be committed in a court of justice, the punishment assigned to the species of assault and battery that is committed shall be doubled; but the fine shall not be less than one hundred dollars, nor the imprisonment less than sixty days, in close custody.

Art. 426. If any one shall go into a house occupied by another, with the intent of committing an assault or battery on him, or on any one of his family, or any sojourner in such house, and shall there commit such assault, or assault and battery, the punishment assigned to the species of assault and battery that is committed shall be doubled ; but the fine shall not be less than one hundred dollars, nor the imprisonment less than sixty days, in close custody.

Art. 427. The word, "family," in the last article, comprehends all persons who habitually reside, or are guests in such house. By the term, "house," is intended, not only the dwelling-house, but shops, stores, and other buildings, which are used for carrying on business, or for domestic purposes. By "sojourners," is meant any person who lodges in, boards in, or occupies any part of such house.

Art. 428. In all cases of offences, under this and the last preceding section, imprisonment in close custody shall form a part of the punishment.

SECTION IV.

Of assault and battery aggravated by the intent.

Art. 429. If an assault or battery be made with an intent to commit murder or rape, the offender shall be imprisoned at hard labour not less than six nor more than ten years.

Art. 430. If the assault or battery be made with design to DISMEMBER, DISFIGURE, or inflict a PERMANENT INJURY, the offender shall be fined not less than two hundred nor more than two thousand dollars, and imprisoned in close custody not less than sixty days nor more than one year.

Art. 431. If any one shall commit an assault or battery, with intent to commit any other crime than murder and rape, he shall be imprisoned at hard labour not less than two nor more than six years.

Art. 432. An assault or battery, with intent to force the party injured to commit an offence, shall be punished by one-half of the punishment assigned to the offence intended to be committed.

Art. 433. If the assault or battery be committed against a woman, attended with any circumstances, either of words or action, that are calculated to wound the modesty of her sex, not amounting to an attempt to ravish ; the offender shall be fined not less than two hundred, nor more than two thousand dollars, and imprisoned in close custody not less than one month nor more than one year. If the offence, designated by this article, be committed by a tutor or curator against his

ward, or a SCHOOLMASTER against his scholar, the imprisonment shall be at hard labour, and for a term not less
than one nor more than two years.

Art. 434. If an assault or battery be committed, with
intent to DISHONOUR; or in consequence of a refusal to
fight a duel, or to provoke another to fight a duel, or to
give a challenge; the punishment, assigned to the species
of assault or assault and battery, that is committed, shall
be doubled; but the fine shall not be less than two
hundred dollars, nor the imprisonment less than sixty
days, in close custody.

SECTION V.

*Of assault and battery, aggravated by the manner and degree in which
it is inflicted.*

Art. 435. If assault and battery be committed with a
DEADLY WEAPON, and in consequence of a premeditated
design, although there be no design to kill actually
proved; the punishment shall be fine, not less than twc
hundred nor exceeding two thousand dollars, and imprisonment in close custody, not less than sixty days nor
more than one year, in addition to the punishment
assigned to the species of assault or assault and battery
that is committed.

Art. 436. If the offence be committed in the execution
of a premeditated design, but not with a deadly weapon;
the punishment shall be fine, not less than fifty dollars,
and imprisonment not less than twenty days, in addition
to the punishment assigned to the species of assault and
battery which is committed.

Art. 437. If the premeditated design be shown by
LYING IN WAIT; the punishment, assigned to the species of
assault or assault and battery which is committed, shall
be doubled; but shall not be less than a fine of one
hundred dollars, and imprisonment in close custody, for
thirty days.

Art. 438. If, in consequence of any assault or battery, the person against whom it is committed shall be DIS-FIGURED, or shall be deprived of or lose the use of any MEMBER OF HIS BODY, or receive such other injury as shall render it certain or probable that he will for the rest of his life labour under some bodily infirmity, although there be no design proved of doing such particular injury —the punishment shall be fine, not less than one hundred nor more than two thousand dollars, and imprisonment in close custody, or at hard labour, not less than three months nor more than two years.

Art. 439. If either of the injuries, mentioned in the last preceding article, shall be committed by premeditated design to do that particular injury, or by LYING IN WAIT, although no design to do that particular injury shall be proved—the punishment shall be fine, not less than five hundred nor more than three thousand dollars, and imprisonment, in close custody, not less than three months nor more than two years.

SECTION VI.

General provisions.

Art. 440. All the punishments assigned for the offences described in the second, third, fourth and fifth sections of this chapter, are CUMULATIVE in cases where the different circumstances, constituting such offences, concur in the same offence, and the lighter species of imprisonment shall be made to commence after the expiration of the heavier.

Art. 441. No prosecution for simple assault and battery, as described in the first section ; or for assault, with intent to ravish ; or for the offence described in the two last articles of the fourth section—shall be commenced but on the complaint of the party injured, or his legal representative, or some one duly authorized by him ; unless such offence was committed in public, that is to say, in the presence of six or more persons, or in any dwelling-house, shop or store—in the first of which cases, any person—in the latter, the occupant of the house, shop or store, may make the complaint.

Art. 442. Where two persons agree to fight, unless it be with deadly weapons, no prosecution shall be commenced for assault and battery committed in consequence of such agreement, on the complaint of either of the parties, or any other person, unless the assault and battery took place in public, or in a dwelling-house, shop or store ; in which cases the prosecution may be commenced as is directed in the last preceding article.

CHAPTER II.

Of false imprisonment.

SECTION. I.

Of simple false imprisonment.

Art. 443. Any intentional detention of the person of another, not expressly authorized by law, is false imprisonment.

Art. 444. The detention, to constitute this offence, may be either—

By assault.

By actual violence to the person.

By some impediment opposed to the power of locomotion.

By threats.

Art. 445. The assault and violence mentioned in the preceding article, are such as are defined in the last chapter ; but to constitute this offence, they must be such as to show the intent, and to have the effect of detaining the party against his will.

Art. 446. The material impediment must be such as is not applied immediately to the person, in which case it would be actual violence ; but it must be of such a nature as to prevent the free exercise of the right of locomotion, without having recourse to extraordinary means.   A door merely closed with a latch, or in any other usual mode, so that the party complaining might, without any unusual effort, open it, would not be such an impediment ; but if bolted or locked on the outside, it would come within the definition, although the party imprisoned might escape by the window, or was strong enough to break the door.

Art. 447. Threats, to constitute the means of false imprisonment, must be such as would materially operate on a person of ordinary firmness, and inspire a just fear of great injury to person, reputation or fortune.   The age, sex, state of health, temper, and disposition of the party complaining, and all other circumstances that may be calculated to give greater or less effect to the violence or threats, must be taken into consideration ; and the threat must be to inflict the injury if the person departs from the bounds prescribed.

Art. 448. A detention of the person shall not be deemed illegal, if made in any of the nine cases set forth in the first section of the first chapter, and nineteenth title of this book ; provided, under the circumstances of such a case, a detention of the person was necessary to effect the object relied on as a justification, and was not continued longer than was so necessary.   The rule for determining the necessity established by the said section, also applies to this.

Art. 449. The punishment for this offence is fine not exceeding five thousand dollars, or imprisonment not exceeding two years, or both, and the whole or part of the imprisonment may be in close custody.

SECTION II.

Of false imprisonment aggravated by the purpose or the degree.

Art. 450. If the party falsely imprisoned be conveyed, whilst so imprisoned, out of the state, the punishment shall be doubled, but shall not be less than five hundred dollars fine, and six months imprisonment, one-half in close custody.

Art. 451. If the offence be committed with intent to convey the person imprisoned out of the state, although the purpose be not actually effected, the punishment shall not be less than three hundred dollars fine, and three months imprisonment in close custody.

Art. 452. If the offence be committed against a free person for the purpose of detaining or disposing of him as a slave, knowing such person to be free, the punishment shall be fine, not less than five hundred dollars nor more than five thousand dollars, and imprisonment at hard labour, not less than two nor more than four years.

Art. 453. If false imprisonment be used as the means of forcing one to do an act which, if voluntarily done, would be an offence, the punishment shall be the one-half of that designated in this code for the offence which it was intended to force the party to commit.

Art. 454. If this offence be committed with intent to commit a crime or misdemeanor, the punishment shall be one-half of that designated by this code for the offence intended to be committed.

Art. 455. If false imprisonment be used as the means of forcing a woman to do an act or submit to treatment injurious to the modesty of her sex, the punishment, besides the fine, shall be confinement at hard labour not less than one and not exceeding three years ; and if the offence described in this article be committed by the tutor or curator against his ward, or a schoolmaster against his scholar, the confinement at hard labour shall not be less than three nor more than six years.

Art. 456. If an imprisonment, otherwise legal, shall be used for the purpose expressed in the preceding article, it shall be deemed a false imprisonment.

SECTION III.

Of abduction.

Art. 457. Abduction is false imprisoment of a woman with the intent to force her into a marriage, either with the offender or some other, and that whether the marriage takes place or not.

Art. 458. If any female, under the age of fourteen years, be taken away from her father, mother, tutor, or other person having legal charge of her person, without their consent, either for the purpose of marriage, concubinage or prostitution, it is an abduction, although the female should consent, and although a marriage should afterwards take place between the parties.

Art. 459. The punishment for this offence is a fine not less than one hundred nor more than two thousand dollars, or imprisonment not less than sixty days nor more than two years, or both ; and the imprisonment may be, in the whole or in part, in close custody, and in case the abduction be for the purpose of prostitution, the imprisonment may be at hard labour.

CHAPTER III.

Of rape.

Art. 460. Rape is the carnal knowledge of a woman, obtained against her consent, by force, menace or fraud.

Art. 461. The force used to constitute this crime must

be such in kind as would constitute a battery, and in degree such as may reasonably be supposed sufficient to overcome resistance, taking into consideration the relative strength of the parties, and other circumstances of the case.

Art. 462. The menace must be such as may reasonably be supposed to inspire a just fear of death, or great bodily harm, taking into consideration the age and strength of the parties ; the state of health, temper and disposition of the party injured, and all other circumstances that may have increased or diminished her fears, into consideration.

Art. 463. A carnal knowledge obtained by fraud, does not amount to the crime of rape, unless the fraud consist,

1. In causing the woman, against whom the offence is committed, to believe during its commission, that the offender is her husband.

2. In forcibly, or without her knowledge, administering to the woman who is injured, any substance that produces an unnatural sexual desire, or such stupor as to prevent or weaken resistance, and committing the crime while she is under the operation of that which is so administered.

Art. 464. Consent cannot be presumed to have been given, from an acquiescence in the sexual connexion, when produced by either of the means mentioned in the definition.

Art. 465. Carnal knowledge is accomplished by the commencement of a sexual connexion ; proof of the circumstance that usually terminates it is not required.

Art. 466. No person can be convicted of this offence, or of an assault with intent to commit it, who had not, at the time the offence is said to have been committed, attained the age of fourteen years.

Art. 467. Carnal knowledge of a female under the age of eleven years, is in itself a rape, without any evidence of force, menace, imprisonment or fraud.

Art. 468. The punishment of rape is imprisonment in the penitentiary for life.

CHAPTER IV.

Of abortion.

Art. 469. Whoever, by violence, or by any means, externally or internally applied to any pregnant woman, with her consent, shall designedly procure an abortion, shall be imprisoned in the penitentiary not less than three nor more than six years. If it be done without her consent, the punishment shall be doubled.

Art. 470. He who furnishes such means, knowing the purpose to which they are intended to be applied, is guilty of this offence.

Art. 471. He who designedly furnishes or administers the means intended to produce abortion, when they are administered, but fail in their effect, shall suffer one half the punishment that the crime would have incurred, had it been completed.

Art. 472. If the offender be a physician or surgeon, or practising as such, he shall suffer the highest punishment that can be inflicted for the offence.

Art. 473. Nothing herein contained shall extend to the case of an abortion procured by medical advice, for the purpose of saving the life of the mother.

Art. 474. If death ensues, by reason of the attempt to procure abortion, it is murder, except in the case provided for in the last article.

CHAPTER V.

Of injury to the person by malicious potions.

Art. 475. If any one shall maliciously cause another, without his knowledge, or against his will, to swallow or inhale any substance which causes any interruption or violent change in the usual functions of his body, or injures his health, he shall be fined not less than one hundred dollars nor more than one thousand dollars, and imprisoned in close custody not less than ten days nor more than three months ; and if such substance was given with intent to murder, he shall be punished in the manner hereinafter directed in the chapter concerning murder.

Art. 476. If such substance, so maliciously administered, causes any malady of which the party to whom it is administered shall die within one year, although there was no intent to kill, the offender shall be punished by imprisonment at hard labour not less than four nor more than ten years.

Art. 477. If the malicious intent was not to kill, and the substance so administered shall be the immediate cause of the death of the person to whom it is given, the offender shall be punished by imprisonment at hard labour not less than seven nor more than fifteen years.

Art. 478. If such substance, although not coming within the definition of POISON, be given with intent to kill, and it shall have that effect, it is murder.

CHAPTER VI.

Of homicide.

SECTION I.

Of homicide in general, and of its different divisions.

Art. 479. Homicide is the destruction of the life of one human being, by the act, procurement or culpable omission of another.

Art. 480. The life which is destroyed must have been complete by the birth of the being who is deprived of it. The destruction of a child before its birth is an offence specially defined.

Art. 481. The destruction of human life at any period of its existence after birth, is homicide, however near it may be extinction from any other cause.

Art. 482. The destruction must be by the act of ANOTHER; therefore self-destruction is excluded from this definition.

Art. 483. It must be operated by some act; therefore death, although produced by the operation of words on the imagination, or the passions, is not homicide. But if words are used, which are calculated to produce, and do produce, some act which is the immediate cause of death, it is homicide. A blind man, or a stranger in the dark, directed by words only to a precipice, where he falls and is killed; a direction verbally given to take a drug that it is known will prove fatal, and which has that effect; are instances of this modification of the rule.

Art. 484. Homicide by omission only, is committed by voluntarily permitting another to do an act that must, in the natural course of things, cause his death, without apprizing him of his danger, if the act be involuntary, or endeavouring to prevent it if it be voluntary. He shall be presumed to have permitted it voluntarily, who omits the necessary means of preventing the death, when he knows the danger, and can cause it to be avoided, without danger of personal injury or pecuniary loss. This rule may be illustrated by the examples put in the last preceding article : if the blind man is seen walking to the precipice by one who knows the danger, can easily apprize him of it, but does not ; or if one who knows that a glass contains poison, sees him about to drink it, either by mistake or with intent to destroy himself, and makes no attempt to prevent him : in these cases the omission amounts to homicide.

Art. 485. The exposing another to causes either natural or adventitious, which, in the natural course of things, must probably produce and do actually produce death, is homicide ; and this may be either by act, or by omission : the placing an infant or other helpless person in the open air during a winter's night by which he is frozen to death, or in the midst of a frequented highway where he is killed by the wheel of a carriage, is an illustration of this species of homicide by act.

He who shall with the knowledge of the danger leave a person of such description to perish in either of those situations, when he could have been removed without personal danger or pecuniary loss, commits this kind of homicide by omission.

Art. 486. Every being of the human species, of whatever age or condition, is included in the relative terms, " one human being" and " another," in the definition of this article. Therefore no death is homicide that is not caused by human agency. If the agent or sufferer have never attained, or have been deprived of reason, it is still homicide.

Art. 487. Human agency must be the cause of the death ; therefore, he who gives a slight wound, which from neglect becomes a mortification, and proves fatal, is not guilty of homicide. If the same kind of injury proves fatal by the administration of improper remedies, the homicide is not the act of him who inflicted the wound, but of the one who applied the remedy, and may be criminal or not, according to the intent and other circumstances.

Art. 488. Although the injury that caused the death might not, under other circumstances, have proved fatal, yet if, without any evident neglect, or treatment manifestly improper, it causes death, it is homicide. Thus, if an artery be cut, and the party bleed to death for want of aid, it is homicide, although, if proper assistance had been obtained, the artery might have been secured. What shall be proper or conclusive evidence of the cause of death in questions of homicide, is found in the Code of Evidence.

Art. 489. Death, or the total extinction of life, is a necessary part of the definition. If the act produce disability of any kind, or even the extinction of any or all of the senses, it is not homicide, while life remains.

Art. 490. The nature of the means or instrument by which death is caused or inflicted, is not essential to constitute homicide. All means by which life is destroyed, are within the definition.

Art. 491. Homicide is justifiable, excusable, or culpable.

SECTION II.

Of justifiable homicide.

Art. 492. That is justifiable homicide which, although committed voluntarily, is inflicted in cases where it is required or permitted by law. These cases are enumerated in the following section.

SECTION III.

Of homicide justified by the requisition of law.

Art. 493. Homicide of a public enemy in the prosecution of war, is justified by the laws of nations. An enemy in the act of hostile invasion or occupation of any part of this state, is not within the protection of its laws; but an enemy, although one of an invading force, who is within the state as a prisoner of war, as a deserter, as the bearer of a flag of truce, or in any other character which does not show a design to commit hostilities, and all enemies' subjects, brought within the state by force, coming there without any hostile intent, or found there at the commencement of the war, are entitled to the same personal protection of the laws as citizens are, excepting only the degree of personal restraint that may be imposed by the laws of the United States, or the rules and usages of war.

Art. 494. Neither the laws of the United States, nor the laws of nations, justify the homicide even of an invading enemy, by poison, by assassination, or by the use of poisoned weapons.

Art. 495. By assassination, in the preceding article, is meant homicide, committed on a public enemy by one who has come under an express or implicit obligation to refrain from any hostile act ; if one who should be received as a deserter in the enemy's camp, or should go there in the disguise of a person bringing provisions, or who being a prisoner should be suffered to go at large on his parole, and should, under such circumstances, put an enemy to death, afford an example of what is meant by the term as here employed.

Art. 496. Those are PUBLIC ENEMIES, who are declared such by the constitutional authority, and those who have declared themselves such, either in the manner usual among nations, or by a hostile invasion of the territory of the nation.

Art. 497. It may also be required by law, that persons convicted of certain offences be punished by death. Whenever such laws, either of the United States or of this state, exist, the execution of a criminal, in pursuance of the unreserved sentence passed by a competent court, in the manner, at the time, and by the officer, prescribed by the law and the sentence, is justifiable homicide.

Art. 498. The preceding articles of this section describe the only cases in which homicide can be justified, as being required by law. It is permitted, as a necessary alternative, to avoid a greater evil in the following cases: that is to say, in the execution of certain public duties, specially designated; to prevent the commission of certain enumerated crimes, and in defence of person or property, against the injuries, and in the manner designated by law. The circumstances under which homicide will be justified in each of the above cases, is more fully developed in the following sections.

SECTION IV.

Of homicide, permitted in the performance of a duty to the state.

Art. 499. There are certain public duties of such importance to society, that those upon whom the obligation to perform them devolves, are bound to it at the risk of their lives. Justice, therefore, requires that the law should permit all proper means of defence against the dangers to which they are exposed. On this principle is founded the impunity allowed by law to the class of homicides, treated of in this section, which designates what public duties come within its purview, and under what circumstances homicide, done in the performance of them, shall be justified.

Art. 500. The first of these duties is the execution of the lawful orders of MAGISTRATES and courts ; and in such cases, homicide, by the person legally charged with that duty, is justifiable where it is violently resisted, and he has a JUST REASON to fear, that his own life will be in danger if he persevere in executing the order; subject, however, to the modifications and restrictions contained in the following rule :

§ 1.

As to the order itself.

1. The order must be that of a MAGISTRATE or court, having legal power to issue it.

2. It must have so much of the form prescribed by law as is declared necessary to give it validity.

3. Whether the court or magistrate have judged erroneously or not in making the order : it is a justification to the person executing it, if it emanate from a proper authority, and is made in legal form, or with all essential requisites.

§ 2.

As to the person executing the order, and his conduct in performing that duty.

4. The person must be an OFFICER OF JUSTICE, or some other legally authorized to perform the duty in question, according to the provisions contained in the Code of Procedure.

5. If an officer of justice, and performing an act which none but an officer could do, he must have taken the oath of office, and given security, when they are required by law.

6. He must execute the order in the manner prescribed by law, and must in all cases, whether it be elsewhere prescribed or not, at the time of performing the duty, and before doing the act which caused the homicide, have declared to the person making opposition that he was an

executive officer of justice, or had other authority (designating it) to perform the duty.

7. If the order be by written warrant, and the party against whom it is issued submits, but desires to see it, or hear it read, the person charged with its execution is bound to produce and show, or read it, according to the request; and if he refuse such request, and persevere in executing the order, it shall be no justification to him for any homicide committed after such refusal.

8. If the order be to make an arrest, the person executing it is bound not only to show the order where it is in writing, and is required, in the manner prescribed in the last preceding rule, but to declare in all cases, at least to the person he is about to arrest, for what offence, or at whose suit (if in a civil suit) the arrest is made.

9. At or after the arrest, if any resistance be made by force, the officer, or other person making the arrest, is bound to oppose to such resistance a force sufficient so to overcome it, as to be enabled to perform the duty required of him by the writ, and no greater force; but if the resistance be of such a nature as to give him JUST REASON TO FEAR THE LOSS OF LIFE if he persevere, he may then use such force as is necessary for his own defence, and if homicide ensues, he is justified.

10. An endeavour to escape before or after an arrest, by flight only, will not justify the infliction of death, or the use of DEADLY WEAPONS to prevent it; but if the fugitive be armed with a deadly weapon, and the pursuer has JUST REASON TO FEAR, from the threats or gestures of the person pursued, that his own life will be endangered by continuing the pursuit, he may then use deadly weapons to stop the flight; and if they produce death, he is justifiable.

11. The case of prisoners attempting to escape from a public prison, is an exception to the last preceding rule. Deadly weapons may be used, and death inflicted on any prisoners legally committed, who shall endeavour, BY BREACH OF PRISON, to escape; but not until previous

warning has been given, and the prisoners persevere in their attempt.

12. These rules apply as well to the justification of those who are legally aiding an executive officer of justice in the execution of a legal order, as to that of the officer, or other person, specially charged with the duty. They also apply to the homicide of any other person opposing the execution of the order, as well as to him against whom the order is directed.

13. They apply also to orders in civil suits, as well as in criminal prosecutions, and to courts and magistrates of the United States, lawfully acting in this state, as well as to the state magistrates and courts.

14. The words, "just reason," as used in this section, mean such reasons as would impress a man of ordinary understanding and firmness, if placed in the same circumstances, with a belief that he was in great hazard of losing his life.

Art. 501. Another duty to the state, which justifies homicide when necessary to its performance, is the opposition to rebellions, insurrections and riots. Death inflicted by any one acting in pursuance to the provisions of this code, or to those of any other law of the state that may be made for the suppression of riots, is justifiable homicide.

Art. 502. Whenever any law of this state, or of the United States, shall require an officer or any other person to perform a public duty, and, from the law, or the nature of the duty, the legislative will plainly appears to be that the duty should be performed, notwithstanding any forcible opposition, then homicide in the performance of the duty is justifiable, provided the directions of such law be strictly pursued and subject to such of the rules laid down in this section for the execution of judicial orders as can be applied to the case, although it may not be a judicial order; but if it be a case of judicial order, then subject to all those rules; and all those which designate the nature of the opposition, and to limit the lawful resistance that may be applied to overcome it, are hereby declared to apply to all cases provided for by this article.

Art. 503. Whenever any law of the state, or of the United States, shall give authority to any officer or other person to call for the aid of the country or the military power, to enforce its execution, it shall be deemed, without any other indication, such a case as is contemplated by the last preceding article.

Art. 504. Homicide by a military or a naval officer, or by any one under the command of either of them, or by an officer or soldier of the militia on actual service, is justifiable if it happen in the lawful arrest of a deserter or other person amenable to the military laws to answer for a military offence; but in such case the rules laid down in this section with respect to judicial arrest must be observed.

SECTION V.

Of homicide permitted in defence of person or property.

Art. 505. Homicide is permitted in the necessary defence of person or property under the circumstances and restrictions set forth in the following articles.

Art. 506. For the prevention of the crimes of murder by violence, rape, robbery, arson, burglary and nocturnal theft; the necessity of the case permits the infliction of death on those who have begun to commit either of them, subject, to the following rules, that is to say,

1. The intent to commit the crime must be unequivocal, and apparent by acts, or by acts coupled with words.

2. The homicide for this cause cannot be justified, unless it be done before the crime is completed, and after it is begun to be executed, that is to say, after some act is done showing unequivocally either by itself, or by words coupled with it, an intent immediately to commit the crime.

3. The crime is not completed in the sense of the last

preceding article, while the offender, in the case of murder, is still committing violence, although the mortal stroke may have been given ; in the case of rape, while the ravisher is continuing his violence, although he may have done enough to make himself guilty of the crime ; in the case of robbery, while the robber is still in the presence of the party robbed, or is flying with his booty ; and in the cases of arson, burglary, and nocturnal theft, while the offender is still in the building where the crime has been committed.

4. The beginning to commit either of the crimes above mentioned, is primâ facie evidence of the necessity of inflicting death, to prevent the completion of it ; but if the crime would have been prevented, or the persons of offenders secured by means within the knowledge and power of the person doing the homicide, without resorting to that act, and without danger of life, it is not justifiable homicide ; but receives its designation from the circumstances of extenuation or criminality attending it, according to the rules hereafter established in this code.

5. The rules contained in this article relate to death inflicted by design ; the use of weapons or other means calculated to produce death, is presumptive evidence of the design to inflict it.

Art. 507. When any other crime, but one of those enumerated in the last preceding article, is attempted, it is not lawful to inflict death for its prevention, until all reasonable endeavours have been made to avoid the danger, if the crime be one of those which endanger the person, or to prevent it by other means, if it affect property.

Art. 508. The endeavour to avoid the danger, in the case of a crime attempted against the person, which are mentioned in the preceding article, are,

1. The use of such means as are in the party's power to repel the assault, short of such as are of a nature to produce death, if the nature of the attack, the weapons with which it is made, the relative weakness of the assailant, or other circumstances, enable the person

assailed to secure himself without resorting to the infliction of death, or the use of such means as will probably produce it.

2. If he have not the means to repel the attack without endangering the life of the assailant, or do not think proper to use those means, if he have them, he must retire from the assailant; the idea of dishonour being attached to such means of avoidance will not excuse the neglect of it; the laws can acknowledge no dishonour in obedience to what they command. This retiring must be with a bonâ fide intent to avoid the danger : it must be continued until it is stopped by some material obstacle, or the want of physical power to continue it. But in cases where retreat would expose to greater danger than facing the attack, it is not required.

Art. 509. Even after using the endeavours above mentioned to avoid personal dangers without effect, it is not lawful to inflict death in order to repel every attack, or avoid every species of personal danger : it must be such an attack as gives a JUST FEAR of death, or of permanent bodily injury.

Art. 510. Whatever circumstances are by this section declared to be a justification for homicide, in the party against whom the crime is committed or intended, will be a justification for others interfering with a bonâ fide intention to prevent the commission of a crime.

Art. 511. Homicide is also justifiable in the necessary defence of property, although the attempt to take it do not amount to the crimes above provided for, of murder by violence, robbery, rape, burglary, and nocturnal theft. Every man has a right to his legal possession of property ; he is not bound to yield it to the force of any invaders. If, therefore, any one attempt by illegal force to deprive another of property, either real or personal, in his actual, corporal and legal possession : the legal and actual possessor may defend his possession by a force proportioned to that with which it is attacked, and if the aggressor persist in his unlawful attempt in a manner that gives the party attacked a JUST FEAR of death, he is justified in defending himself and his possession by killing the invader.

This article is to be construed by the following rules, and modified as follows, that is to say,

1. The possession must be of a corporal property, not a mere right; and must be an ACTUAL not a mere CONSTRUCTIVE possession.

2. The possession must be a legal one; but it is not necessary that the actual property be vested in the possessor, but he must have acquired the right of possession.

3. The resistance must be made to the illegal force during its exercise; if the actual possession be once lost, it will be no justification of a homicide that it was inflicted in an attempt to regain it.

4. No resistance that would probably produce death, can be justified in this case, unless the attack is made in such a manner as to create in the possessor a JUST FEAR of death, in case he should persevere in the defence of his possession.

5. Every endeavour in the power of the possessor must have been used to induce the aggressor to desist, both by words and such physical means as were in his power, before resorting to the means that produced death.

6. Everything in this article which relates to the nature of the possession, or the degree of force that may be justifiably used, applies to any person aiding the possessor to maintain his possession.

7. Nothing in this article contained, relates to the defence of property against an attempt to rob, which is heretofore provided for.

Art. 512. Except in the instance provided for by the last preceding article, homicide is not permitted by law for the prevention of any offence that is not a crime; thus, neither simple assault and battery, nor trespass, will justify homicide, nor will any crime not accompanied by force; thus, neither private stealing, nor even poisoning, can be lawfully prevented by homicide.

SECTION VI.

Of excusable homicide.

Art. 513. Homicide is excusable, and consequently not criminal, whenever the death of one human being, though caused by the act of another, can be attributed neither to negligence nor design, but happens in the prosecution of a lawful act by lawful means ; and is caused by some accident which ordinary human prudence could not foresee nor avoid. If in shooting at game on his own grounds, a man kill another who is hid unknown to him in the wood, he commits homicide, for it comes within the definition of that act ; but it is excusable, for it was involuntary, and was not caused by negligence ; but if the shot is fired across a highway, and one travelling thereon is killed, there is negligence, and the homicide is not excusable.

Art. 514. The lawful act which causes the death must be done by lawful means, used in a lawful degree. It is lawful to correct a scholar, or an apprentice ; but if this be done with an instrument likely to produce death, or if with a proper instrument the chastisement be cruelly inflicted, and death ensue, it is not excusable homicide.

SECTION VII.

Of culpable homicide.

Art. 515. Every homicide that is neither justifiable nor excusable, according to the foregoing definitions and illustrations, is a culpable homicide.

They are negligent or voluntary.

§ 1.

Of negligent homicide.

Art. 516. The species of homicide thus called, is that which is inflicted without design to kill either the person actually killed or any other.

Art. 517. This is an offence, of which the several grades are distinguished by the degree of negligence and the nature of the act, in the performance of which the homicide happens; each degree forming a separate class of offences.

§ 2.

Of negligent homicide in the first degree.

Art. 518. The first degree of this offence, is homicide involuntarily inflicted in the performance of a LAWFUL ACT, in which there is no apparent risk of life, by ordinary means, but without that care and precaution which a prudent man would take to avoid the risk of destroying human life.

Whoever is guilty of this offence, in this degree, shall suffer imprisonment, not less than two months nor more than one year, of which such party may be in close custody as the court may direct.

Art. 519. The following rules, derived from the foregoing definition, are to be observed :

1. The act, in the performance of which the homicide happens, must be lawful ; by which is meant, any thing that is not forbidden by the penal law, or which would not give just cause for a civil suit.

2. It is an essential part of this definition, that the danger of causing death, in doing the act, should not be apparent. Where there is such apparent danger, the offence becomes a crime.

3. The terms, "ordinary means," in the definition, are not confined strictly to such as are usually employed; they are intended to admit the employment of means different from those ordinarily used, provided they are not more dangerous.

4. The want of care and precaution distinguishes this from excusable homicide, and places it in the first or incipient degree of culpability. In all that regards the preservation of human life, a greater degree of caution is required, by law, than it demands in other cases. By "caution," is meant a consideration of probable consequences, and the use of means to avoid them, if they appear injurious. Therefore, in order to avoid the guilt of this offence, it is not enough to abstain from acts, or from the use of such means, in performing them, in which a risk of homicide is known or apparent; but where, from the nature of the case, it is as reasonable to believe, that danger of destroying life may exist, as that it may not exist, the law requires a previous examination.

5. The degree of caution described, as that which a prudent man would use, must be determined by a consideration of the circumstances as they appeared before the event; if the event alone were sufficient to prove want of caution, all casual homicide would be culpable.

1st Example. When death is casually inflicted, by the discharge of fire-arms which are believed not to be loaded, without examining whether they are so or not, it constitutes this offence. If the examination be made, and owing to some unknown cause, although loaded, they appear to be empty; or, if unknown to the person using them, they have been loaded immediately after the examination, due caution has been used, and there is no offence.

2nd Example. If one, in blasting a quarry, although at a distance from a public way, makes the explosion without examining whether any persons are so near as to be injured by it, the offence is incurred. If he make the examination and discover no one, he is innocent, although a person concealed from his view, or one who came suddenly on the spot, should be killed. If the quarry be in a frequented place, or he knew there were bystanders, another offence would be incurred.

Art. 520. Death caused by any kind of fire-arms, purposely directed against any one, without intention to kill or injure, but merely in sport, is negligent homicide of the first grade, whether any examination of the arms have been previously made or not.

§ 3.

Of negligent homicide in the second grade.

Art. 521. Homicide of the second grade, is that which is involuntarily committed in the performance of a lawful act, but under circumstances, in a manner, or by means, which cause an apparent danger of inflicting death, without due precaution to avoid such danger. It is punishable by imprisonment, not less than two nor more than four years, in the penitentiary, or in close custody, at the discretion of the court.

Art. 522. An important distinction between this and the first grade of negligent homicide is, that in this the risk of causing death or other great bodily harm, must be apparent; by which is meant, that it must necessarily be perceived by a common observer, without inquiry or examination, merely by witnessing the act, and reflecting on its consequences.

Art. 523. The words, "lawful act," used in the definition, have the same meaning as is explained in that of the first grade of this offence.

Art. 524. The word, "circumstances," used in the description of this offence, relates to the time, place, and such other concomitants of the act as make it dangerous, although it would not be so at other times, in other places, or attended by other accompaniments.

Art. 525. The word, "manner," relates to the mode in

which the act is done, or in which the instruments, or means that produce it, are used or employed.

Art. 526. The term, "means," is intended to include the instruments with which the act is performed, or the other modes employed to effect it.

Art. 527. The "act," intended by that term, in the last four preceding articles, means the act in the performance of which the homicide takes place.

Art. 528. The "due precaution," mentioned in the description of this offence, is such as a prudent man would deem effectual to prevent the danger.

Art. 529. It is no justification for omitting such necessary precaution as is above described, that time or other circumstances did not permit them to be taken, but that the party did every thing else in his power to avoid the homicide. In such case the act itself, in the doing of which the death happened, ought to be omitted, unless it be one of those acts which are necessary for such defence of person or property as renders homicide justifiable ; in which case, the best precaution that circumstances permitted, is sufficient.

1st Example. Of the crime generally. If one prove a cannon in a public road, and it burst and kill a passenger, it amounts to this offence, whether the passenger had notice of the intended explosion or not ; for no one has a right to stop the passage of a highway, for the purpose of doing an act that ought to be done elsewhere.

But if the operation were performing in a proper place, and one who had notice chose to remain, and is killed, it is no offence, for due caution has been used.

If an act that cannot be done but in a public place, such as pulling down a house, cause the death of a passenger, who perseveres in passing after due notice, it is no offence. If no notice be given, the killing in this case is negligent homicide in the second grade.

2nd Example. Of the "circumstances" which give the character of apparent risk.

The common case of a workman throwing materials

from the roof of a house exemplifies this part of the definition. The criminality of the homicide there depends on the circumstance of the PLACE in which the act is done ; if in the country, or other unfrequented place, without previous inquiry and examination whether any one be in the way, it is ranked in the first grade of this offence ; if in the streets of a populous city, without the precautions required by this code, or by the police of the city, it is a negligent homicide in the second grade ; if in either place, with the caution required under the circumstances of the respective cases, it is no offence.

3rd Example. Of the apparent risk, as applied to the MANNER.

It is lawful for a master to correct his apprentice by ordinary means ; yet if such correction be repeated or continued in a manner apparently cruel or dangerous, and it causes death, although no improper instrument be used, it comes within the definition of this offence.

4th Example. Of risk apparent from the MEANS used.

If death is caused by the employment of deadly weapons, or using greater force than is necessary to repel the attack of an unarmed man upon person or property, the risk of death is apparent, and the party inflicting it is guilty of this offence.

Art. 530. In all the examples of the different kinds of offences designated as negligent homicide, it is understood, as an essential part of such case, that there is no intent to kill, and in all (except the example taken from the law of self-defence) that there was no design to do a bodily harm.

§ 4.

Of negligent homicide in the performance of unlawful acts.

Art. 531. All the definitions, rules, and provisions, with respect to negligent homicide in the first and second grades, except those which regard the legality of the act, in the doing or attempt to do which the homicide is committed, apply to the homicides described in this division of the offence, in all things in which they are not contrary to the following provisions.

Art. 532. Where negligent homicide in the second grade has been committed, in the doing or the attempt to do an act which is an injury, but not an offence, one-fifth shall be added to the punishment. If the act done or attempted, be a misdemeanor, but not an offence against the person, one-fourth shall be added. If it be one of those designated as an offence against the person, but not one of those offences designated as murder, one-half shall be added. If it be a crime punishable with imprisonment at hard labour for any term less than life, the punishment shall be doubled, and the imprisonment shall be at hard labour. And if the act done or attempted to be done, be a crime punishable with imprisonment for life, the homicide shall be punished by imprisonment at hard labour for life.

Art. 533. It is intended, by the preceding article, that the homicide must have been done in the attempt to offer the injury or commit the offences therein specified, that is to say, must have been the consequence of some act done for the purpose of offering or committing such other injury or offence. If the act which caused the death had no connexion with the injury intended to be offered or committed, it does not come within the definition. The same rule of construction applies to the words, " in the doing or in the attempt to do," whenever they are used as giving a character to any act actually done.

§ 5.

Of criminal voluntary homicide.

Art. 534. Voluntary homicide is a CRIME in all cases, where it is neither justifiable nor excusable, according to the rules heretofore laid down. There are two degrees of this species of homicide, each degree forming a distinct class of crime. They are,

1. Manslaughter.
2. Murder.

Art. 535. Manslaughter is voluntary homicide, committed under the immediate influence of sudden passion, arising from an adequate cause.

In considering and applying this definition, the following rules are to be observed.

1. To constitute manslaughter, the homicide must be intentional. Those involuntary homicides, occasioned by want of due care, or occurring in the prosecution of some unlawful act, which were heretofore distinguished by this name, are in this code distinct offences.

2. Manslaughter is homicide committed under the immediate influence of sudden passion; all the terms of this part of the definition are to be strictly observed in its application to any particular act. If the passion be not sudden, that is to say, arising in the same interview in which the act was committed, but entertained before that time; or if thus arising, and the act be not done under the immediate influence of that passion, but after such an interval of time as in the common course of human feelings would give time for reflection, or with the intervention of such circumstances as must naturally produce it : in either of these cases the crime is not manslaughter. That the act be done "under the influence" of such passion, is also a necessary part of the definition. This means, that the passion is the cause of the act; not merely that it is done during the time that the mind is agitated by passion; from which it follows, that passion against one will not qualify the homicide of another with the appellation of manslaughter.

3. The passion intended by the above definition, includes all those called choler, rage, anger, sudden resentment, terror or fear; their great characteristic being a sudden and temporary agitation of the mind, that renders it incapable of cool reflection during the prevalence of this passion.

4. It is not sufficient that the act be committed under the influence of passion, to give to homicide the character of manslaughter : the passion must have an adequate cause. The law admits only such as adequate causes, which it defines as such.

The cause, to be adequate, must be one that in men of ordinary tempers, commonly produces an irritation of mind which renders them incapable of calculating the consequences of their acts. No words whatever are an adequate cause ; no gestures, merely showing derision or contempt.

No assault and battery, so slight as to show that the intent was not to inflict great bodily pain.

An assault and battery made by the deceased, causing great pain or bloodshed, is an adequate cause.

A serious personal conflict, in which great bodily pain was inflicted by means of a weapon or other instrument, used by the person killed, or by means of a great superiority of personal strength or skill, is an adequate cause, even if the person guilty of the homicide were the aggressor in such conflict, or in any manner provoked the contest, provided such aggression or provocation was not made with the intent to bring on a conflict for the purpose of killing.

A discovery of the wife of the accused, in the act of adultery with the person killed, is an adequate cause.

Passion, occasioned by lawful correction of the person accused, is not an adequate cause.

Provocation given by a relation in the ascending line to his descendant, is not an adequate cause ; although it would have been such, if given by a person not standing in the same relation. This does not extend to relations by affinity only.

Injury to property, unaccompanied by violence, is not an adequate cause.

Passion occasioned by the legal performance of duty by an officer of justice, or other person legally authorized to perform any executive duty of justice, is not an adequate cause.

Art. 536. Manslaughter is punished by imprisonment not less than one nor more than five years, at hard labour or in close confinement.

§ 6.

Of murder.

Art. 537. Murder is homicide, inflicted with a premeditated design, unaccompanied by any of the circumstances, which, according to the previous provision of this chapter, do not justify, excuse or bring it within some one of the descriptions of homicide hereinbefore defined.

Art. 538. There are different grades of guilt in the commission of this crime, which are called :

Infanticide,
Assassination,
Murder under trust,
Parricide.

Art. 539. Infanticide is the murder of an infant for the purpose of concealing its birth.

Art. 540. Murder is characterized as assassination, either by the purpose intended to be obtained, by the means used to effect it, or by the condition of the person murdered.

1. *By the purpose.*

When the murder is committed for the purpose of effecting another crime.

When it is committed for the purpose of concealing another crime previously committed.

When it is committed for the purpose of obtaining an inheritance.

When it is committed for HIRE ; and in this case, he who gives and he who receives the reward is guilty of assassination.

2. *By the means used.*

When the murder is done by LYING IN WAIT; by burning the house in which the person murdered is; by POISON.

3. *By the condition of the person murdered.*

When the crime is committed on a woman, a man above the age of seventy, a minor under the age of sixteen, a person asleep, or in a dwelling-house by night or travelling on the high road.

Art. 541. Murder, under trust, is that which is committed by persons under the following relations to the person murdered, that is to say: husband, wife, tutor or curator, ward, collateral relation within the second degree inclusive, master, servant, schoolmaster, host, guest, physician or surgeon; and finally, if the murder be committed by one upon another, who has reposed confidence of safety in him, on an express or implied promise of fidelity or protection. Murder, committed by a guide or conductor on the land, or by the master of a vessel by water, upon a traveller, whom he has undertaken to conduct, are examples of this last description of murder under trust.

Art. 542. Illegitimate children of the same mother, and of the same father by another mother, if acknowledged by the father, are comprehended in the above description of collateral relations.

Art. 543. The word " host " includes as well the gratuitous receiver of the guest, as the one who receives him for hire.

Art. 544. Parricide is murder committed by a relation by consanguinity, in the ascending line upon his descendant, or by a descendant upon his relation by consanguinity, in the ascending line.

Art. 545. Illegitimate children, and such of their

parents as have acknowledged them, are included in the above definition.

Art. 546. Punishment for murder is imprisonment for life.

Each of the aggravated species of murder described in this section has appropriate privations and aggravations of discipline allotted to it in the Code of Reform and Prison Discipline.

Art. 547. An attempt to murder, by administering poison, although it fail in its effects, shall be punished by imprisonment at hard labour, for fifteen years.

SECTION VIII.

Of suicide.

Art. 548. No punishment can be inflicted on him who commits this act : and by the principles on which this system is founded, the law cannot make an innocent survivor suffer for the rashness of another. But any one who shall aid in the act of suicide, or who shall provide the means of executing it, knowing the purpose for which they were intended, or be guilty of any omission with respect to the act or means of suicide, that constitutes homicide by omission, according to any of the preceding provisions of this chapter, shall be imprisoned at hard labour, not less than three nor more than six years.

CHAPTER VI.

Of duels.

Art. 549. If any person shall use any insulting words or gestures of or to, or make an assault upon another with intent, either to provoke any one to give a challenge to FIGHT A DUEL, or as an alternative, to dishonour him, he shall be fined not less than fifty, nor more than three hundred dollars, or imprisoned not less than five, nor more than thirty days, in close custody.

Art. 550. If the defendant, in any prosecution under the last preceding article, shall make any denial, explanation, or acknowledgment, that the court shall think ought to satisfy the honour of the prosecutor, they shall direct the same to be recorded and published, with their judgment declaring the same to be satisfactory; and may, at their discretion, direct the defendant to be dismissed, on the payment of costs.

Art. 551. Whenever judgment shall be pronounced on, for any offence under the said article, it shall contain a clause that it shall be void as to everything but costs, in case the defendant shall make such acknowledgment as shall be satisfactory to the prosecutor.

Art. 552. No conviction on judgment for any offence under the said article, shall be a bar to any prosecution or suit for defamation or assault for the same cause, unless the satisfaction made by the defendant shall be accepted, as is provided in the last preceding article.

Art. 553. In case any offence under the said article should imply a charge affecting the honour or reputation of the person making the complaint, and the investigation on the trial show such charge to be unfounded, the court shall make that declaration in the sentence, and cause the same to be published at the expense of the defendant; and if the party complaining request it, the question, whether the charge be true or false, shall be decided by the jury.

Art. 554. Whoever shall give a challenge to fight a duel, or shall, on receiving such challenge, ACCEPT the same, shall be imprisoned, in close custody, not less than two, nor more than six months, and be suspended from his political rights for four years.

Art. 555. Whoever shall fight a duel, if he in such fight inflicts no wound, shall be imprisoned, in close custody, not less than six, nor more than twelve months, and shall be suspended from his political rights for six years. If he wound his adversary, and such wound do not occasion death, or any permanent bodily disability, the imprisonment shall not be less than twelve, nor more than eighteen months, and the suspension for eight years. If he fight a duel, and shall inflict a wound on his adversary that causes a permanent disability, he shall be imprisoned not less than twelve months, and be suspended from the exercise of his political rights, and his civil rights of the first and third class, for seven years. If in such fight he kill, or inflict a mortal wound on his adversary, he shall be imprisoned not less than two, nor more than four years, and forfeit for ever his political rights, and his civil rights of the first and third class. And if such death or mortal wound be inflicted by treachery, he shall be deemed guilty of murder by assassination, and suffer the punishment in this code directed to be inflicted on those convicted of that crime.

Art. 556. If any one shall advise another to fight a duel, or shall use any reproachful or contemptuous language to or concerning any one for not sending or accepting a challenge, or for not fighting a duel, he shall be fined not less than fifty, nor more than five hundred dollars, or be imprisoned not less than thirty days, nor more than six months.

Art. 557. If any one shall bear a challenge, either written or verbal, to another, knowing the intent with which it was sent, he shall be fined not less than one hundred, nor more than one thousand dollars, be imprisoned, in close custody, not less than two, nor more than six months, and suspended from his political rights for three years.

Art. 558. If a challenge shall be given and accepted in this state, and the parties go out of the state and fight a duel, the punishment for giving or accepting such challenge, shall be the same as if the whole offence were committed within the state.

Art. 559. It is an offence within the meaning of the first article of this chapter, if the insulting words or gestures be used relative to, or the assault be committed upon, either the person whom it is intended to provoke, or any other so nearly connected with or related to him as to show the intent in the said article expressed.

The dishonour, in the same article, means a loss of the esteem of those who think that offences of that nature ought to be avenged by a challenge to fight a duel.

Art. 560. The words "to fight a duel," in this chapter, are used in their common and general acceptation : they mean, to enter into a voluntary combat, one man against another, with deadly weapons.

Art. 561. A challenge is any proposal, either verbal or written, or by message, in whatever language it may be couched, to fight a duel, provided that, from the circumstances attending the proposition, it appeared to be so understood by the party accused, whether he be the party giving or the party accepting it.

Art. 562. The acceptance of a challenge, is an agreement to the proposition to fight a duel, either given by express words or by other terms, either written or oral, from which such agreement may clearly be inferred on by circumstances which show such agreement.

Art. 563. It is treachery, if the death be occasioned by the breach of any rules made for conducting the combat, or by any other advantage, which, although not expressly provided against in those rules, was yet one that could not be supposed to have been intended to be given.

Art 564. It is assassination, if the mortal wound be intentionally inflicted on a party, after he is incapable of further resistance, either from being disarmed, or any other circumstance, with a knowledge of such incapacity by the party inflicting it, whether it be done in pursuance of any previous rule for the combat or not.

Art. 565. It is assassination, and not a duel, if the death or mortal wound be inflicted by a party who has obtained the power of inflicting it without risk to himself, by the effect of a chance previously agreed on. Death inflicted by a party who has obtained a loaded pistol by a chance agreed on, while the one used by his adversary is not loaded, is an example of what is intended by this rule.

Art. 566. In order more effectually to secure the execution of the provisions of this chapter, the attorney-general and district attorneys of this state, and all officers of justice when they are sworn into office, and such of them as are in office at the time of the promulgation of this code, or within fifteen days afterwards, and all grand jurors, when they are sworn, shall sign a declaration in the following form :—" I declare, that I consider the obligation, which my duty requires, of bringing to justice all offenders against the laws, as containing no reservation with respect to duels. And I promise on my honour that I will, within the local bounds to which my official functions extend, by all lawful means prevent, so far as shall be in my power, any duel which I may have reason to suppose is intended, and prosecute all offences which come to my knowledge, against the sixth chapter of the nineteenth title of the second book of the Code of Crimes and Punishments of this state, entitled, ' Of Duels.' "

The word " prosecute," in the said declaration, shall, in the case of grand jurors, be changed for " indict ;" and in the case of officers of justice, it shall be changed for the words " enter complaint against."

Art. 567. And all officers, civil or military, judicial or executive, now in office, shall, within thirty days after the promulgation of this code, if in office at that time, and those appointed or elected afterwards, shall, at the time they take their oath of office, and before they enter on the duties of their office, take before a magistrate, and subscribe a declaration under oath, in the following form :—" I do solemnly swear, that I have not fought a duel, or given or accepted a challenge to fight a duel since the promulgation of the Code of Crimes and Punishments of the state of Louisiana ; and that I shall hereafter consider myself as bound by the ties of honour, as well as the sanction of this oath and of the laws, not to commit any offence against the provisions of the sixth chapter of the nineteenth title of the second book of the said code, entitled ' Of Duels.' " And every person elected or chosen to any office who shall refuse or neglect to take such oath and subscribe such declaration, within the period and at the time above directed, and to send the same to the office of the secretary of state, as is directed in the next article, shall be considered as having resigned or refused to accept the office to which he is elected.

Art. 568. As to all officers appointed or elected, the oath and declaration aforesaid shall be taken and subscribed before the magistrate who administers the oath of office, and shall be deposited, recorded and transmitted as is by law directed concerning oaths of office. And as to all officers in office at the time of the promulgation of this code, the oath shall be taken before any magistrate, and deposited, recorded and transmitted, as is now by law directed with respect to oaths of office.

TITLE XX.

OF OFFENCES AFFECTING INDIVIDUALS IN THEIR PROFESSION OR TRADE.

Art 569. All direct offences of this nature are comprehended in the twelth and eighteenth titles, and the chapter " Of Conspiracies," and those having the same effect indirectly, in other titles of this book.

TITLE XXI.

OF OFFENCES AGAINST CIVIL AND POLITICAL RIGHTS AND CONDITIONS.

CHAPTER I.

Of the substitution, exposure of infants, and of falsifying registers.

Art. 570. If any person to whom an infant, under the age of six years, shall be confided for nursing, education, or other purposes, shall, with intent to deceive the parents, tutors, or curators of such infant, substitute, or attempt to substitute another child in the place of the one so confided, he shall be imprisoned at hard labour not less than three nor more than seven years.

Art. 571. The word "substitute" in this chapter means, to deliver to the person confiding the child, another instead of the one so confided, under the pretence that it is the same.

Art 572. If any one, to whom such a child shall be so confided, or its father or mother, shall expose or desert such child with intent wholly to abandon it, in a place where its life will be endangered, the punishment shall be imprisonment at hard labour not less than five nor more than ten years.

Art. 573. But if such abandonment be made without the knowledge of the father, mother, tutor or curator of the child by the person to whom it shall have been confided, by fraudulently depositing it in an inhabited house, one half of the punishment, mentioned in the last article, shall be inflicted.

Art. 574. If such child shall die in consequence of

such exposure, it is infanticide, murder, or murder under trust, depending on the person who commits the crime. If it receive any other bodily injury, the offence shall be punished in the same manner as the same injury would be, had it been done with intent to kill.

Art. 575. If any one shall, for the purpose of intercepting an inheritance in the whole or in part, fraudulently produce an infant, falsely pretending it to be born of parents whose child would stand in the order of succession to such inheritance before or equally with another person whose condition and civil rights it was intended to intercept, the person so offending, and those who shall aid and assist in the deception, shall be imprisoned in close custody not less than six nor more than twelve months, and shall be suspended from the exercise of their civil rights of the first and third class for five years.

If any one shall, for the purpose of injuring another in his civil or political rights, or in his right to property, destroy, or alter any certificate of birth, or marriage, or burial, he shall be imprisoned not less than seven nor more than fifteen years at hard labour, and shall forfeit his political rights.

If any person, whose duty it is, by law, to make a record of births, marriages, or deaths ; or any curate, priest, minister, or parson, who in any church or religious congregation, is charged with keeping a register of births, marriages, or funerals, celebrated for the members of such church or religious congregation, shall fraudulently make a false entry in such record or register of any such birth, marriage, death, or funeral, with intent to injure any one in his condition, civil or political rights, or his right to property, he shall be imprisoned at hard labour not less than seven nor more than fifteen years.

Art. 576. Other offences affecting political rights will be found in the title of offences against the right of suffrage.

CHAPTER II.

Of bigamy.

Art. 577. A person having a wife or husband living, who shall, without having a reasonable cause to believe such wife or husband to be dead, contract a second marriage, is guilty of bigamy, and shall be imprisoned at hard labour not less than one, nor more than five years.

Art. 578. If the first wife or husband had, at the time of the subsequent marriage, been absent for five years, and during that time the accused had not received any intelligence of his or her being alive, this shall, for the purposes of this chapter, be considered such a reasonable belief of death, as to take away all criminality from the act.

Art. 579. What other cause to believe the death of the former husband or wife shall be deemed a reasonable cause, is matter of fact, to be decided according to the circumstances of the case.

Art. 580. It is not necessary, to constitute this offence, that the first marriage should have been contracted within this state ; but it must, wherever celebrated, have been a valid marriage, according to the laws of the country in which it was contracted.

Art. 581. The subsequent marriage must also be made according to the forms prescribed by law to give validity to marriages in this state.

Art. 582. If a citizen of this state, residing therein, having a husband or wife living, either here or elsewhere, shall go out of this state, and contract a second marriage, with the intent of returning to reside within this state, and shall so return—he or she shall be deemed guilty of the crime of bigamy.

Art. 583. If the first marriage be not null in itself, but only voidable, a second marriage, during the lives of the parties to the first, is bigamy; unless such first marriage had been declared void by a competent authority, or had become so by the operation of law or the act of the party, before the time of contracting the second marriage.

Art. 584. No other divorce but one from the bonds of matrimony is such a dissolution of the first marriage as will exempt the party from the guilt of bigamy or a second marriage, while both parties to the first are living.

Art. 585. A third marriage, during the lifetime of the parties to the second, is bigamy, although the second marriage was contracted during the lifetime of the parties to the first, and in a manner to make it bigamy; and in case of three or more successive marriages, any of the persons, with whom the party accused, contracted either of the former marriages, being alive, at the time of celebrating a subsequent one, he or she may be convicted of bigamy.

TITLE XXII.

OF OFFENCES AFFECTING PERSONS IN THEIR PROFESSION OR TRADE.

THE offences coming under the purview of this title will be found in the titles, "Of offences affecting commerce and manufactures," and in the chapter of "Conspiracies."

TITLE XXIII.

OF OFFENCES AFFECTING PRIVATE PROPERTY.

CHAPTER I.

Of burning and other malicious injury to property.

Art. 586. If any one shall MALICIOUSLY SET FIRE to any DWELLING-HOUSE, with intent to destroy the same ; or shall destroy such house by an explosion of gunpowder or any other explosive matter, he shall be imprisoned, at hard labour, during life. If the house be not a dwelling-house, but contain personal property of the value of one hundred dollars, he shall be imprisoned, in like manner, not less than seven nor more than fourteen years : and if it be empty, or contain personal property of less value than one hundred dollars, the punishment shall be a like imprisonment, not less than five nor more than ten years.

Art. 587. A house, within the meaning of this chapter, is any edifice so built as to come within the denomination of real estate, according to the definition of that term in this code, being closed in on all sides, and having the area, which is enclosed by its sides, covered with a roof. This definition excludes a tent, a booth, or an open shed.

Art. 588. A dwelling-house is one in which some person habitually sleeps or eats his meals, or one that is built and intended for that purpose, although not actually inhabited.

Art. 589. This offence of setting fire to a dwelling-house is also committed by setting fire to any building that communicates, by any combustible matter, with the inhabited building, or that is so near to it as, if the one burns, to cause the other to take fire.

Art. 590. If any one shall, in like manner and with like intent as is above expressed, set fire to any building, not coming within the description of a house, or to any stack of grain or hay, any heap of firewood, or timber, or other collection of combustible produce of the earth, standing or being on the land of another, and of the value of ten dollars or upwards—he shall be imprisoned not less than six nor more than twelve months, or fined not more than five hundred dollars, or both, at the discretion of the court.

Art. 591. The intent must be malicious ; therefore, if the house be the property of the person who does the act, and no other person has any interest therein, he is guilty of no offence. But if there be any other person interested as joint owner, usufructuary, lessee, or in any other manner whatever ; or if another have an incumbrance on the house, or have made insurance thereon—the offence is incurred, although the person committing the act may have some estate in the house. This article applies to all the offences described in this chapter.

Art. 592. If one set fire to his own house, with the intent that the fire shall communicate to that of another, and it does so communicate—he is guilty of this offence.

Art. 593. The offence is not complete merely by the burning of the combustible matter placed for communicating the fire. It must actually have communicated to the house, but it is not necessary for this purpose, that it should be completely destroyed.

Art. 594. If any building destroyed by fire, contrary to the provisions of this section, contain any DOMESTIC ANIMALS, which are destroyed with the building—the punishment shall be increased one-half.

Art. 595. If any one shall, designedly, and with intent to injure, illegally set fire to, or destroy or injure by explosion, any ship or other vessel, boat, flat-boat or raft, which with the cargo, if any there be, is of the value of one hundred dollars or upwards—he shall be imprisoned, at hard labour, not less than three nor more than seven years.

Art. 596. The "intent to injure," mentioned in the articles of this section, means an intent to cause a PECUNIARY loss to some person (other than the offender) having an interest in or upon the property when the act is designedly done. The circumstance that another has an interest in or upon it, is conclusive proof of the intent to injure.

Art. 597. Where death is occasioned by any of the offences described in this section, the offender is guilty of murder ; and of assassination, if he intended the death of the party.

Art. 598. If any bodily injury, less than death, is suffered by the fire or explosion, in the execution of the offence—the punishment shall be doubled in all cases where the punishment is less than imprisonment for life.

Art. 599. If any of the offences described in this section be committed during the NIGHT, the punishment shall be increased one-half.

Art. 600. Whoever shall MALICIOUSLY destroy any personal property exclusively belonging to, and in the possession of another, if of any of the kinds hereinbefore described, by any other means than by fire, or if of any other kind, by any means whatever, being of the value of ten dollars or more; or in like manner injure it to that amount, he shall be imprisoned not less than one month, nor more than one year, or shall be fined not exceeding five hundred dollars, or both, and the imprisonment or part of it may be in close custody. If the offence described in this article be committed by poisoning, killing or disabling any animal of any kind usually employed in husbandry, or raised for sale, the punishment shall be doubled, but shall not be less than imprisonment for thirty days in close custody, or a fine of two hundred and fifty dollars.

Art. 601. If any one shall MALICIOUSLY destroy the fences or enclosure of any real property belonging exclusively to another, and in his separate possession, or shall destroy any trees, shrubs or any CROP of any kind growing thereon, if the fences or other things so destroyed are of the value of ten dollars or upwards, he shall be imprisoned not more than one year, or fined not exceeding five hundred dollars, or both ; and the imprisonment, or any part thereof, may be in close custody.

Art. 602. If any one shall MALICIOUSLY destroy any original written obligations or original acts, giving an interest in, or a right to any real or personal property, of the value of one hundred dollars, belonging to another, or shall in like manner destroy the copy of any such obligation or act, when, by reason of the destruction of the original, or other legal cause, such copy is the only proof of the obligation or act, he shall be imprisoned not less than one month, nor more than one year, or be fined not less than fifty, nor more than one thousand dollars, or both, and the imprisonment or any part of it may be in close custody.

Art. 603. If any one shall maliciously or fraudulently remove or destroy any post, stone, tree, or other thing serving as a land-mark to designate a boundary between two different tracts of land, he shall be imprisoned at hard labour not less than one nor more than three years, and shall forfeit his political rights.

Art. 604. Injuries to property by negligence are not the object of penal law.

CHAPTER II.

Of house-breaking.

Art. 605. Whoever enters a HOUSE secretly, or by force, or threats, or fraud, during the NIGHT, or in like manner enters a HOUSE by day, and conceals himself therein until the NIGHT, with the INTENT in either case of committing a crime, is guilty of the crime of house-breaking, and shall be imprisoned at hard labour not less than ten nor more than fifteen years.

Art. 606. The qualifications of secrecy, force, or fraud, as applied to the entry, in the description of this offence, are intended to exclude every kind of entry but one made by the free consent of the occupant, or of one authorized to give such consent from him, fairly obtained and expressly or impliedly given.

Art. 607. Although a consent be given to an entrance into one part of a house, yet an entrance into any other part, by any of the means and with the intent described in the first article of this section, constitutes the crime of house-breaking.

Art. 608. The term "house," as used in this chapter, comprehends all such as are built for public as well as private use, whether the property of the state, the United States, or any public or private corporation or society.

Art. 609. The entry, in the description of this offence, is not confined to the entrance of the whole body ; the introduction of any part, for the purpose of committing a crime, is sufficient.

Art. 610. If any one shall discharge any fire-arms, or any missile weapon, into a house, with the intent of doing bodily injury to any one in such house, or introduce any instrument for the purpose of drawing out any personal property, it is an entry intended by the description of this offence, although no part of the body of the offender should come within the house.

CHAPTER III.

Of the acquisition or appropriation of property by fraud or force.

Art. 611. Offences of this nature may be committed in the following manner :

1. By the fraudulent appropriation of personal pro-

perty, which had been delivered to the offender for another purpose.

2. By the like appropriation of property which came to the possession of the offender by finding.

3. By the violation of epistolary correspondence.

4. By obtaining personal property under false pretences.

5. By theft or robbery.

6. By receiving property knowing it to be fraudulently obtained.

SECTION I.

Of fraudulent breach of trust.

612. The following are the acts which may severally constitute this offence :

1st. The fraudulent appropriation of personal property by any one to whom it shall have been delivered on deposit, sequestration, pledge, or to be carried or repaired, or on any other contract or trust, by which he was bound to deliver or return the thing received.

2nd. The fraudulent appropriation of certain specific personal property by any one to whom it shall have been delivered on a contract of loan for use, or of letting and hiring, after the time at which, according to the contract, the right of use thereby acquired has ceased, or before that time, by a disposition not authorized by such contract.

Art. 613. These two cases refer to a receiving, with an intent to comply with the contract under which the delivery is made, and a subsequent determination of fraud; if the contract be intended merely as the means of procuring possession, with the intent of making a fraudulent appropriation, it is theft.

Art. 614. The punishment for the offences described in the first article of this section, is imprisonment in close custody, not exceeding six months, if the property be of the value of thirty dollars or under ; and if above that value, the like imprisonment, not exceeding one year.

SECTION II.

Of fraudulent appropriation of property found.

Art. 615. The giving to another the charge or care of property, subject to the immediate orders of the owner, or the use of it in his presence, or for the purposes of his trade, is not a delivery within the meaning of any articles describing this offence. A fraudulent appropriation of property so placed is theft.

Art. 616. If any one shall come, by finding, to the possession of any personal property, of which he shall know, or have reason to believe, any DESIGNATED person to be the owner, and shall fraudulently appropriate the same, or any part thereof, he shall be imprisoned in close custody not less than sixty days nor more than six months, and shall be fined in a sum equal to double the amount of the property so appropriated.

Art. 617. Where property has been casually lost, and the finder has no reason to believe any designated person to be the owner of the property found, if it is of the value of more than twenty dollars, and the finder shall conceal the same, and appropriate it to his own use, he shall be fined in a sum equal to double the amount of the property appropriated.

Art. 618. If the property be found in a place where property of the same description is usually placed, or suffered to be ; or if in an unusual place, in one where the finder knows it to have been designedly put by the owner ; or if the property be domestic animals, and they are found in a place in which they are usually kept, or to which they are suffered to go, or may reasonably be supposed to have strayed, this is not finding within the meaning of the preceding articles; and if the person taking the property fraudulently appropriate it, he is guilty of theft.

Art. 619. If any one shall fraudulently appropriate property, taken or driven on shore from any vessel, wrecked, stranded, or burned, on the sea-coast, or on any of the rivers, lakes or harbours of this state, he shall be imprisoned, at hard labour, not less than one nor more than three years.

Art. 620. The property, described in the last preceding article, shall be presumed to be fraudulently appropriated, within the meaning of that article, in all cases where the property is concealed and the directions contained in the Code of Procedure, on the subject of wrecked property, are not pursued.

SECTION III.

Of the violation of epistolary correspondence.

Art. 621. If any one shall open and read, or cause to be read, any sealed letter, without being authorized so to do either by the writer of such letter or the person to whom it is addressed, or by law, he shall be fined not more than fifty dollars, or imprisoned not less than ten nor more than thirty days.

Art. 622. Whoever shall MALICIOUSLY PUBLISH or CIRCULATE the whole or any part of a letter so opened, knowing the manner in which it was obtained, and without legal authority, shall be fined not less than fifty nor more than two hundred dollars, or imprisoned not less than one nor more than three months.

Art. 623. If property of any assignable value be taken from such letter, it is theft.

Art. 624. If any one shall TAKE any letter, whether sealed or not, or any writing whatever, from the legal possession of another, without his consent, and shall maliciously publish the same, he shall be fined not less than one hundred nor more than five hundred dollars, or imprisoned not less than one nor more than six months.

SECTION IV.

Of obtaining property by false pretences.

Art. 625. If any one, with a fraudulent intent, shall obtain any personal property, or the release of any right, of any ASSIGNABLE value, with the consent of the owner or possessor thereof, by means of any false pretences, without the use of which such consent would not have been given, he is guilty of this offence.

Art. 626. No mere declaration of the value, or cost, or quality, or quantity of the property sold, although such declaration should be false; no promise of a consideration for the delivery of personal property, although such promise be not performed; no mere declaration that the party is able to pay, or perform, or deliver the consideration : is a false pretence under the above definition.

Art. 627. The owner's consent to the delivery of the property is an essential part of the definition of this offence, and a characteristic that distinguishes it from theft. A temporary possession for examination, or any other purpose, while the contract for the transfer is pending, is not such a delivery, by consent, as is required by the description of the offence. And if the fraudulent appropriation be made before such final consent be given, it is theft.

Art. 628. This consent is presumed to have been given whenever the consideration is received, and the property is left, or put in the power of the person to whom by the purport of the contract it appears to be transferred, although such consideration should prove worthless or fraudulent. It is also presumed to have been given whenever credit has been given for the price, however short the time.

Art. 629. Credit is presumed to have been given when, although the sale or other transfer was made on a stipulation of paying cash, the seller shall have taken a draft, or order, or other security for the amount, and voluntarily left the property in the hands of the purchaser.

Art. 630. It is a false pretence for any one to assign or deliver any written contract as his own property, when, to his knowledge, it belongs to another bearing the same name.

Art. 631. It is a false pretence to assume any false description, which would, if true, give greater credit to the party assuming it. By "description" is meant profession, trade, office, or employment.

Art. 632. If any one shall commit this offence by falsely personating another, he shall incur the highest punishment designated for the same.

This modification of the offence is committed —

1. By assuming to be another, whose name or credit shall induce the owner to deliver the property.

2. By assuming to be another person bearing the same name as the person who commits the offence.

Art. 633. The assumption need not be by positive words; it is sufficient if, by any device whatever, the person delivering the property, or releasing the right, is designedly made to believe that he who receives such property, or release, is the person whose name or character he assumes.

Art. 634. It is an offence, under the first article of this section, after a sale of personal property and before delivery, to substitute other property of less value than that sold, with intent to defraud the purchaser of the price paid, or to be received.

Art. 635. It is a false pretence to promise immediate payment for personal property, and, after obtaining possession thereof, to refuse either to restore the property or to pay the price. The offence, described in this article, is committed by a refusal to pay or to deliver the property, on demand, at any time within three days after the purchase, if the property be then in the possession of the purchaser, or within one hour if demand be then made, whether the property be in his possession or not.

Art. 636. It is sufficient to make the party liable under the preceding article, if the demand be made at the place where payment was promised to be made, and the not making the payment there is a sufficient refusal within the meaning of the said article.

Art. 637. It is a false pretence to give in payment, for any personal property sold and delivered as for cash, any check, bill, or order, which the person giving the same affirms will be paid at sight, but which he shall at the time know to be of no value ; unless such check, bill, or order be taken on the credit of the parties thereto, or some of them ; and it shall be presumed to have been so taken whenever it is made payable otherwise than at sight or on demand.

Art. 638. It is a false pretence to sell any merchandize by a sample, taken not from that actually sold, but from other merchandize of a greater value, with intent to defraud.

Art. 639. It is a false pretence to produce a false invoice of merchandize sold, or to produce an invoice of other goods of the same description, affirming it to be the true invoice of the goods sold, for the purpose of deceiving the purchaser as to the cost and value of the property purchased.

Art. 640. It is a false pretence to make, or knowingly to produce, any false letter or other paper, not amounting to forgery, in order to influence another in the purchase or sale, or other disposition of property.

Art. 641. It is obtaining property under a false pretence to procure it by any game, either of skill or chance, or of both, by any other means than those which are given by the regular chances of the game, if it be one of chance ; or by the fair exercise of skill and knowledge of the game, if it be not a game of hazard.

Art. 642. It is a false pretence fraudulently to make any false reports, for the purpose of raising or depressing the price of the public funds, or the stock of any incorporated company; or to circulate them, knowing them to be false.

Art. 643. The enumeration, contained in this chapter, and in other parts of the code, of certain acts which shall constitute the offence described, does not exclude other acts coming within the definition. Nor does the declaration, that certain other acts are not considered as offences, restrict the exception to those particular acts.

Art. 644. If the value of the property, obtained by an offence under this section, shall not amount to more than thirty dollars, the punishment shall be imprisonment, at hard labour, not exceeding three years; and if the value exceed that sum, the imprisonment shall not be less than one nor more than four years.

SECTION V.

Of theft.

Art. 645. Theft is the FRAUDULENTLY TAKING OF CORPORAL PERSONAL PROPERTY, having some ASSIGNABLE value, and belonging to another, from his possession, and without his assent.

Art. 646. The subject on which this offence can operate, is exclusively PERSONAL PROPERTY; but it embraces every species of that property that can be taken, and excludes only incorporeal rights.

Art. 647. The "TAKING," mentioned in the description of this offence, is that which designates it from the other fraudulent appropriations of property heretofore described. The following rules and illustrations show the nature of the taking intended, and the circumstances under which it constitutes the offence :

1. There must be to constitute this offence a taking, and that taking must be from the possession of the owner; therefore, although there has been a fraudulent appro-

priation, yet, if the possession was acquired by the accused in such a way as to bring the case within the description of either of the offences made punishable by the preceding part of this chapter, it is not theft.

2. But every fraudulent taking from the possession of the owner, and subsequent appropriation of personal property, which does not come within the description of some one of the offences described in the former sections of this chapter, is either theft or robbery.

3. If any servant or clerk, or person employed as such by any person, receive on account of his employers, from any other person, or from the employer himself, in trust or charge, to be kept or disposed of under the direction of the employer, any such property as is described in the definition of this offence, the possession of such clerk or servant is, as relates to this offence, the possession of his employer; and if the servant or clerk fraudulently appropriate it, it is theft.

4. Whenever the delivery is extorted by fear, it is a taking, within the definition of this offence, and one of those circumstances which constitutes the offence of robbery.

5. The possession of a factor or agent, entrusted with the sale or other alienation of property, is not such a possession of the owner as will make the factor or agent guilty of this offence, if he appropriate the proceeds.

6. Taking alone, without carrying away, is sufficient within the definition.

7. Taking may be either by a removal, or simply by laying hold upon the article, either directly with the hand or by means of any instrument, in such a way as to evince a design to remove it.

8. The offence is complete by the taking; therefore, a voluntary return of the property will not prevent conviction; but it shall lessen the punishment one-half.

9. No one can be convicted of theft or robbery for any taking of property, in which he has a joint interest with the person from whose possession it was taken.

10. He who has the general property, of personal

property, may commit this offence, by taking the same fraudulently, from one who has a special property in it, with intent to make him answerable for the value.

11. If one of several persons, having a joint interest in personal property, either as partners, husband and wife, or otherwise, deliver it voluntarily to another, who takes it with a fraudulent intent against the other persons interested, it is not theft.

12. Where husband and wife are separated in person and estate, the delivery by the husband of the wife's property, over which she has given him no control, without her assent, to a person who is connusant of the facts, and who takes it with a fraudulent intent, it is theft in both.

13. But where the separation is of property only, no one can be convicted of theft of the wife's property, who shows a voluntary delivery by the husband.

14. The last two preceding rules apply equally to property of the husband, delivered under similar circumstances by the wife.

15. The dispositions of law, in the case of thefts or other offences committed by the wife in company with the husband, are found in the third chapter of the First Book.

16. Neither the ownership nor the legal possession of property is changed by theft alone, without the circumstances required in such case by the Civil Code, in order to produce a change of property; therefore, stolen goods, if fraudulently taken from the thief, are stolen from the original proprietor.

17. The possession of articles of dress or ornament, which are personally used by minor children, who are not of sufficient discretion to know the value of property, is the possession of the parent or guardian; therefore, such property fraudulently taken, although with the consent of the child, is theft.

Art. 648. Although nothing but corporal personal property, as the same is defined in this code, is the subject of this offence, yet if any one shall sever from any BUILDING, fixed on the land of another, any of the materials of which it is formed, or shall take any produce of the soil, growing on such soil, of the value of five dollars or more, for the purpose of fraudulently appropriating the same ; and in pursuance of such intent, shall remove them from the said land, such severance is sufficient to bring the materials, or other produce taken, within the description of personal property, and make the person taking the same, guilty of theft.

Art. 649. Simple theft, if of property not exceeding in value thirty dollars, is punishable by imprisonment, at hard labour, not exceeding three years. If the property be above the value of thirty dollars, the punishment shall not be less than two nor more than four years.

SECTION VI.

Of aggravated theft.

Art. 650. The crime of theft may be aggravated by several circumstances, which are described in the following sections. If theft be not accompanied by any of them, it is simple theft.

SECTION VII.

Of theft by effraction.

Art. 651. If any one shall, in the DAY-TIME, with a fraudulent design, enter a house, or a SHIP or other VESSEL, without breaking or other violence, and shall then and there commit a theft, he shall be imprisoned not less than three nor more than six years, at hard labour.

This article does not relate to domestic servants, or other inhabitants of the house in which the theft is committed.

Art. 652. The last article only relates to property being in the house or ship, not in the personal possession of any one in it. Taking property of this last description may be either simple theft, private stealing from the person, or robbery.

Art. 653. If any one break into a house, or into any ship or other vessel, in the day-time, with intent to commit a theft, whether the theft be committed or not, he shall be imprisoned, at hard labour, not less than four nor more than seven years.

Art. 654. If any one be in the house, or in the ship or other vessel, either at the time the offence mentioned in the last two preceding articles is committed, and resist the offender, or be restrained from resisting by fear, the punishment shall be increased one-fourth.

Art. 655. The breaking intended by the last three preceding articles, means—first, that the entry must be made with actual force —the slightest force brings the offender within their purview—the lifting of a latch of a door that is shut—the raising of a window—the entry at a window, chimney, or other unusual place—the introduction of the hand or any instrument to draw out the property, through any aperture made for the purpose, although the whole body does not enter, is a breaking.

Art. 656. If any theft shall be committed by breaking any closet, box, or other place of the like nature, in which the property stolen was contained, the punishment shall be not less than four nor more than seven years at hard labour.

The breaking meant by this article must be by actual force. Not merely lifting the lid of a box, or opening a door, when either are unfastened, the use of false keys, or of the true one fraudulently obtained, is a breaking.

SECTION VIII.

Of stealing from the person.

Art. 657. If the theft be committed by privately stealing property from the person of another, the offender shall be imprisoned at hard labour, not less than two nor more than six years.

Art. 658. By "privately," is meant either without the knowledge of the party whose property is taken, or so suddenly that he has no time to make resistance before the property is carried away.

Art. 659. If the party perceive the theft, and attempt to resist it, and the theft is completed by violence, it is robbery ; if not completed, after violence or threats, it is an attempt to rob.

Art. 660. If the article be TAKEN, under the definition heretofore given of that word, the crime of private stealing is complete, although, owing to the difficulty of extricating it from the person of the possessor or from his detection of the attempt, it be not actually carried away.

Art. 661. The theft must be from the person ; if the property stolen be in his presence only, it does not amount to this offence.

SECTION IX.

Of robbery.

Art. 662. Robbery is theft, committed by fraudulently taking the property of another from his person or in his presence, with his knowledge and against his will ; whether it be taken by force, or delivered or suffered to be taken through fear of some illegal injury to person, property or reputation, that is threatened by the robber or his accomplice.

Art. 663. The audacity of an open infringement of the laws, and the alarm and danger it creates, are the characteristics of this species of theft. Wherever either of these occurs, in any degree, in the commission of theft, the additional guilt is incurred ; therefore, the law gives no measure for the degree of violence necessary to constitute this crime. Any force that accomplishes the object is sufficient.

Art. 664. No device will be sufficient to give another character to this crime. If the property be fraudulently taken by violence, or thus received when it is surrendered through fear, it is immaterial whether it be done by a direct command, or by a request to give as alms, or under any other pretence.

Art. 665. If, by any of the means which constitute robbery, one is forced to give property for an inadequate price, it is robbery.

Art. 666. If property be stolen by simple theft, and before it is carried away, the owner is forced, by any of the means which constitute robbery, to give up his attempts to recover possession of the property, it is robbery.

Art. 667. Any threat, in order to be an effectual cause for the fear mentioned in the definition of this offence, must be to do some illegal act, productive of injury, either to person, property or character. A threat of withdrawing favour, or doing any other lawful act, is not sufficient.

Art. 668. The threat need not be direct ; it is sufficient, if it be expressed indirectly, or by gestures only, so as to produce the effect.

Art. 669. The punishment for this offence is imprisonment, at hard labour, not less than seven nor more than fifteen years.

SECTION X.

Of receiving property, knowing it to be fraudulently obtained.

Art. 670. Whoever shall receive, either by way of purchase or on any other contract, or for safe keeping or concealment ; or shall conceal, or endeavour to conceal, any property, knowing it to be fraudulently obtained by any of the acts which, by this chapter, are created offences —shall be punished in the same manner with the principal offender.

Art. 671. It is no objection to the conviction of a receiver, under this section, that the principal offender has not been convicted ; but if any one be indicted, and in custody or on bail, for stealing, or otherwise fraudulently obtaining the same property, the person accused as receiver shall not be tried, without his consent, until the prosecution against the principal offender has been disposed of.

Art. 672. The offence, described in this section, is a distinct and substantive offence, not governed by the rules which apply to accessaries.

Art. 673. If any one, knowing that property has been taken by theft, aid the thief in removing it to its final destination or place of concealment—such person is an accomplice in the theft, and not a receiver.

Art. 674. An accomplice in a theft, who is not present at the act, and afterwards receives the property, is punishable as an accomplice.

Art. 675. Nothing in this chapter contained, applies to the taking of property, which the person taking believes to be his own, or that of another who has authorized him to take it.

CHAPTER IV.

Of attempts to defraud by threats.

Art. 676. Whoever, with a FRAUDULENT intent, shall threaten another with an injury to his person, reputation or property, accompanied by a demand of property, or of service, as the means of avoiding the execution of such threat, shall be imprisoned at hard labour, not less than one nor more than five years, provided such offence do not amount to robbery.

Art. 677. The injury intended by the last preceding article, means not only a direct injury, by means of actual violence, but also that which is indirect, such as a threat of bringing an accusation for some offence, either juridically, or by public defamation.

Art. 678. The injury need not be threatened directly against the property, person, or reputation of the person to whom the threat is addressed; if it be against the reputation or person of the wife or husband, ascendant or descendant, of the person whom it is intended to defraud, it is sufficient to constitute the offence.

Art. 679. A threat to vilify the memory of a deceased ancestor, is a sufficient threat to constitute this crime.

Art. 680. This offence is committed, whether the threat be verbal or written; and if written, whether with or without a signature.

Art. 681. It is not necessary that the demand of property, or the threat, should be in direct terms; if such be the plain meaning, it is sufficient.

Art. 682. If any one shall make any such threats by writing, printing, sending or delivering a letter or writing, whether in his own name, in a fictitious name, or anonymously, or shall procure such letter to be written, printed, sent or delivered, without any intent to DEFRAUD, and without any demand of property, as the means of avoiding the execution of the threat, but merely from MALICE, he shall be imprisoned not less than one nor more than six months, and fined not less than fifty nor more than three hundred dollars, and the whole or part of the imprisonment shall be in close custody.

CHAPTER V.

Of conspiracy.

Art. 683. Conspiracy is an agreement between two or more persons to do any unlawful act, or any of those designated acts which become, by the combination, in‧jurious to others.

The several conspiracies that are punishable by law are :

1. A conspiracy to commit an offence.

2. Falsely to accuse and prosecute another of committing an offence.

3. To do certain injuries that are neither crimes nor offences if done by an individual.

Art. 684. The agreement constitutes the offence, and it is a distinct offence from any other that may be committed in carrying it into effect; and to complete the offence, it is not necessary that any act should be proved to have been done in furtherance of the agreement.

Art. 685. But if the accused show that the design was abandoned, before any act was done towards its execution, voluntarily, and not from any obstacle, the punishment shall be lessened one-half.

Art. 686. Where the conspiracy is to commit an offence, the punishment shall be one-half of that denounced by law against the offence which it was the object of the agreement to commit, if it be not carried into effect, and in addition to such punishment, if it is committed.

Art. 687. Where the conspiracy is falsely to accuse and prosecute another of an offence, the punishment shall be one-half of that which would have been inflicted if the offence had been proved.

Art. 688. It is not necessary, for supporting an indictment for a conspiracy to accuse and prosecute, to show that the party has been acquitted on such prosecution ; but if the prosecution, which is alleged to be false, be pending, the defendants in the indictment for conspiracy are entitled to have it tried before they are themselves put upon trial.

Art. 689. The cases not comprehended in the foregoing articles of this chapter, and in which conspiracies become unlawful, are as follows, to wit :

1. Every one has a right, individually, to determine what he will give as a consideration for service or property to be furnished to him : he has the same right to withhold his own service or property, unless the value he shall place upon them be paid. But an agreement, stipulating that the parties to it will not give more than a certain price for any particular species of service or property, or that they will not furnish or render any such property or service for less than a stipulated price, is injurious to that free competition necessary to commerce. And if such agreement be made between two or more persons not being partners, it is a conspiracy, and shall be punished by simple imprisonment, for not more than three months, or by fine not exceeding three hundred dollars, or both.

2. If the agreement be made between employers, not to give above certain wages to workmen, imprisonment shall always form part of the sentence, and the imprisonment cannot be for less than ten days.

3. If the agreement constituting the conspiracy, in any case whatever, purport to inflict any injury on the person, property or reputation of those who will not

enter into such agreement, the punishment shall be doubled.

4. Any malicious combination or agreement to injure any individual, or description of persons, in their reputation, or profession, or trade, or property, by agreeing not to employ them, or by other means that would not otherwise amount to an offence, is a conspiracy, and shall be punished by fine, not exceeding two hundred dollars, or imprisonment, not exceeding sixty days, or both.

5. Any combination or agreement to raise the price of any articles of food, fuel or drink, is a conspiracy, and is punishable by fine, not exceeding five hundred dollars, and imprisonment, not exceeding three months.

6. An agreement of partners, solely between themselves, is not such an agreement as can constitute this offence, unless the partnership be specially entered into for the purpose of making such conspiracy ; in which case, or whenever the benefit (if any) to be derived from the conspiracy is agreed to be participated, the punishment shall be doubled.

7. An agreement to abridge or increase the quantity or time of labour, comes within the description of limiting the price to be given, or determining that which must be received.

GENERAL PROVISION.

Of accessaries.

Art. 690. All accessaries shall be punished by one-fourth of the punishment that would have been suffered by the principal offender ; provided, that it shall, in no case, exceed a fine of three hundred dollars, and imprisonment, in close custody, for one year.

A CODE OF PROCEDURE.

INTRODUCTORY TITLE.

CHAPTER I.

Preamble.

Art. 1. It is not enough to have defined offences and designated the punishments adapted to them : every citizen must not only be taught what actions he is to avoid as offences, but must also be informed by what means he may prevent an injury he apprehends, or bring the offender to justice if the wrong be already suffered.

Judges, other magistrates, and ministers of justice, must have their duties defined, not only for their own guidance, but that, being generally understood, they may receive the high reward of public approbation, or suffer disgrace or punishment, as those duties are performed, neglected, or wilfully abandoned.

These considerations have induced the General Assembly of Louisiana to enact this Code of Procedure, forming a part of their System of Penal Law. It is divided into three books :

The first contains the means of preventing offences, and of putting an end to such as continue : it designates the cases in which the military force may be employed in aid of the civil power, and prescribes the rules by which it shall be governed in that service.

The second directs the mode of proceeding for bringing an offender to punishment, from the complaint to the final judgment.

The third gives the forms to be used in all the judicial proceedings prescribed or authorized by this code.

CHAPTER II.

General provisions.

Art. 2. This code being a part of the general system of Penal Law, all the words used herein are employed in the same sense that is given to them when they are used in any other part of the system.

Art. 3. All the general provisions in the second chapter of the first book of the Code of Crimes and Punishments, and all such general provisions in other parts thereof as apply to the subject of this code, have the same force in this that they have in the Code of Crimes and Punishments.

Art. 4. The objects which the general assembly has endeavoured to effect by this code, are :

1. *The prevention of intended offences.*—This is attained by pointing out on what occasions, and by what means, an individual may call for the interference of the magistrate, or of his fellow citizens, or may use his own physical powers to resist any attempted invasion of his rights or those of others.

2. *The protection of innocence against unjust accusations.*—No laws can in all cases protect against perjury, error, or the combination of circumstances which sometimes gives to innocence the appearance of guilt ; but they can, and ought, to provide every facility that human prudence can suggest and human power can effect, for making truth evident, and detecting error ; they should also, by avoiding all entangling forms, insure an acquittal to every one who is accused, unless his guilt be made apparent.

3. *To take away from the guilty all hope of escape by a resort to formal or technical objections.*—The great object

of penal law is the prevention of offences by the example of punishment, the intent of all codes of procedure is to insure this end ; therefore, every system must be imperfect which permits the form to defeat the substance of the law, and suffers a criminal ever to escape punishment from any defect of form in his prosecution.

4. *To give to criminal proceedings the greatest degree of despatch that is consistent with the prosecution of public justice on the one side, and the defence of private rights on the other.*—Delay inflicts punishment on the innocent, or lessens the force of example, by punishing the guilty after the crime he has committed is forgotten.

5. *To subject the innocent to no expense, and to impose none on the guilty but such as may be measured and apportioned to the offence.*—To add to the evil of an unjust accusation the obligation of paying for it, would be an absurdity and an injustice that no law should sanction ; and the indiscriminate infliction of costs on every conviction, without regard to the circumstances of the offender or the nature of his offence, is scarcely less unjust.

6. *To abolish all forms that produce vexation to the prosecutor, to the accused, or to the witnesses ; and to subject no one who is concerned in a criminal proceeding to any inconvenience, but such as are absolutely necessary for the execution of the law.*—The obligations and restraints imposed by the most perfect laws, are necessarily attended with inconvenience to those who are called on to execute them, or have become subject to their animadversion ; to reduce them to the lowest degree consistent with public safety, is one object of the present code.

7. *To render the whole form of proceeding simple and perfectly intelligible to all.*—The utility of this object is so apparent as to render no illustration necessary.

Art. 5. These objects : security to the innocent, not only from the danger of an unjust conviction, but the apprehension of it ; the prevention of intended offences ; the destruction of all hope of escape from merited punishment by a resort to formal objections ; despatch ;

economy ; the abolition of all vexatious proceedings, and the establishment of simplicity in forms, have been the principal objects in the formation of this code, and they are conspicuously placed here that future legislatures may weigh their importance, examine how far the different provisions of this code are in conformity with them, and in what points they are not adhered to, in order that the proper amendments may be made to give them effect.

BOOK I.

OF THE MEANS OF PREVENTING OFFENCES; OF SUP-
PRESSING THOSE WHICH ARE CONTINUOUS, AND
OF EMPLOYING THE MILITARY IN AID OF THE
CIVIL POWER.

TITLE I.

OF PREVENTING OFFENCES.

Art. 6. Offence may be prevented :
1. By lawful resistance.
2. By the intervention of the officers of justice.

Art. 7. Resistance to the offender in the commission
of the offence may be made in the cases and in the
manner prescribed by law, either by the person about to
be injured or by others, without the intervention of the
officers of justice.

CHAPTER I.

Of resistance by the party offended.

Art. 8. Resistance, proportioned to the degree of aggression, may be used to prevent any of those acts
described in the Code of Crimes and Punishments, as
" Offences against the person."

Art. 9. The same degree of resistance may be opposed

to prevent any illegal attempt by force to take or injure property in the lawful possession of the person holding it.

Art. 10. By the resistance proportioned to the aggression in the above articles is meant, such as is sufficient for the purpose of preventing the offence, and no more.

Art. 11. The Code of Crimes and Punishments in the titles relative to offences affecting person and property, contains rules by which the exercise of this right is elucidated and modified.

CHAPTER II.

Of the rights and duties of third persons in preventing the commission or continuance of offences.

Art. 12. It is the duty of every citizen not only to abstain from offences himself, but to prevent their being committed by another, if he can do so without injury to himself : if he voluntarily incur the risk of such injury it is a merit which entitles him to public esteem, and in certain cases provided by law, to an honorary reward. The cases in which this duty of interfering to prevent offences is permitted, and those in which it is enforced under a penal sanction, are detailed in the following articles of this chapter.

Art. 13. In all cases where an offence is seriously threatened or intended, it is a moral duty in him to whose knowledge such intent may come, to prevent its execution, by notice given either to the party who may be affected, or to a magistrate. It is an offence to have omitted such notice, in all cases where the crime is subsequently committed, and is one of those punishable by imprisonment for life, provided, the intention has been made manifest by express words, or by doing some act preparatory to the commission of the crime ; whoever shall be guilty of this offence shall be fined not exceeding one hundred dollars or imprisoned not exceeding sixty days.

Art. 14. In cases in which the intention has been shown by an act which itself is an offence (such as a conspiracy), and the intent is to commit a crime punishable by imprisonment for life : the person having a knowledge of such conspiracy or other preparatory act, who shall not give notice of it to a magistrate or to the party about to be injured, shall incur the punishment denounced by the last preceding article, whether the intended crime be committed or not.

Art. 15. After an offence has been committed, the mere omission to denounce it is not punishable, if not accompanied by such an act as renders the person an accessary.

Art. 16. Every species of such illegal violence to the person or property as is by the Code of Crimes and Punishments constituted an offence, may be suppressed after it has begun to be exercised, by the resistance not only of the party injured, but by that of others who may come to his aid, but they are bound in exercising this right to proportion the means and degree of resistance to the violence offered, according to the rules that are prescribed to the party injured in the last preceding chapter, and the parts of the code to which it refers.

Art. 17. All those who are legally called on by any magistrate or officer of justice in the execution of his duties, are not only justified in giving their aid in suppressing acts of illegal violence, and arresting offenders, but are bound to do so, under the penalty of a fine not exceeding fifty dollars.

Art. 18. If any one shall voluntarily incur any great danger, or use extraordinary diligence, or show unusual skill in preventing or suppressing an offence, or in arresting an offender, he shall be entitled to an honorary certificate made by the court, having the highest penal jurisdiction in the district of his residence, which certificate shall be entered on the minutes of the court, and published three times in three successive years, and authenticated copies shall be sent to the governor of the state, and to the president of the senate, to serve as recommendations for an appointment to any office in which the qualities he has shown may be useful.

Art. 19. In cases of extraordinary exertion, coming within the intent of the last preceding article, which in the opinion of the judge, and of the governor of the state, shall merit such distinction, a piece of plate of the value of one hundred dollars, with a suitable inscription, to be executed under the direction of the governor, shall be added to the honorary certificate.

Art. 20. Whoever shall give such information to a magistrate as shall lead to the conviction of any one guilty of fighting a duel, or giving or accepting a challenge, or forgery, or any crime punishable by imprisonment for life, shall be entitled to receive, on the certificate of the judge and public prosecutor in the court where the conviction was had, the sum of fifty dollars, from the treasurer of the state, out of the moneys received for fines.

Art. 21. Neither the party immediately injured by any of the crimes referred to in the last article, nor an accomplice in the crime, are entitled to the recompense therein mentioned.

Art. 22. The crime of rape being one of those that can only be prosecuted on the complaint of the party injured, is not included in those for the discovery of which the recompense is offered.

Art. 23. When laws are just, whoever contributes to their execution, renders an acceptable and an honourable service to his country, and he ought no more to be reproached for receiving a recompense for the trouble of denouncing an offender, than for taking a salary for any other public service ; therefore, to repress the effects of a vulgar and injurious prejudice, it is declared to be an offence for any one in writing or in any other way by which defamation may be committed, to use reproachful or insulting words against any person, or endeavour to bring him into contempt, or excite the public indignation against him for having given information against any offender, or for having received the recompense granted by law; and the offender shall be punished by fine not less than twenty nor more than one hundred dollars.

CHAPTER III.

Of the prevention of offences by the intervention of officers of justice.

Art. 24. When any one fears, with JUST REASON, that another intends to commit an offence against his person or property, with violence, he may apply to a magistrate, who shall without delay take the declaration of the applicant, under oath, reduced to writing; and if it appears that he has any reason to fear the commission of such an offence as is above described from any DESIGNATED PERSON, he may cause such person to be arrested and brought before him by warrant, which must substantially state the application.

Art. 25. When any one so arrested is brought before the magistrate, he shall hear any statement or proof the accused has to offer, and if from such statement and evidence it appear that the complainant has mistaken the intention of the accused, and has no cause of fear, the prisoner shall be discharged; if he fail in showing that the application is groundless, the magistrate shall direct him to give bond with sufficient security that he will commit no offence against the person or property of the complainant.

Art. 26. The penalty of such bond shall be determined by the rules laid down in this code, for the government of magistrates in taking bail.

Art. 27. If the bond be not executed according to the

order of the magistrate, the prisoner shall be committed to prison, and shall remain in custody until the bond shall be executed according to the order.

Art. 28. If from the nature of the evidence offered, or from the demeanour of the prisoner, the magistrate has just reason to believe that the prisoner intends an offence against the person or property of any persons who cannot be particularly designated, he may order the bond to be conditioned that he will commit no offence against the person or property of any one.

Art. 29. The bond shall be limited in its operation to the term of twelve months ; but it may be for a shorter time ; and at any time within the last month, the complainant may renew his application, and the order for security may be renewed on the oath of the party, declaring that he still fears the execution of the prisoner's former designs, provided the magistrate, after hearing the circumstances of the case, shall deem such fear well founded.

Art. 30. Any magistrate who is present when any offence, accompanied with violence, is committed, may, without any other proof, order the offender to be arrested, and compel him to give security in the manner above directed, to refrain from the exercise of any illegal force.

Art. 31. Any person who knows or has reason to suspect that an offence, such as is distinguished in this code as one of those against person or property, is intended to be committed, may apply to a magistrate, who shall hear the proof, and if he be convinced of the existence of such intention, shall cause the person accused to be arrested, and compelled to give security in the manner before directed.

Art. 32. Courts may on any conviction add to their sentence that after the execution of the punishment is complete, and before the defendant, if in custody, be discharged, he shall give security in the form and for the time above directed, either that he will not commit any particular offence or any designated species of offences, or generally, that he will commit no offence for the time limited. But this power is only to be exercised where, from the character of the party or his conduct in committing the offence, there is good reason to apprehend a repetition of that offence, or the commission of some other.

Art. 33. If the condition of the bond be forfeited, it shall be put in suit by the public prosecutor, who must specify in his petition in such suit the offence which caused the breach of the condition of the bond, with the same certainty that is required in an indictment, and must prove the same by the same evidence that would be required on a trial for the same offence.

Art. 34. At any time before the breach of the condition of such bond, the surety may discharge himself by surrendering the principal, in the manner herein directed in the case of bail for appearance.

Art. 35. Individuals have also a right to prevent the consequences of a theft by seizing any personal property which has been stolen, or which there is good reason to believe has been stolen, and bringing it with the supposed offender, if he can be taken, before a magistrate for examination, or delivering it to an officer of justice for that purpose ; but this must be done openly, and the whole without delay.

Art. 36. When the nature of the case and the proof offered to the magistrate, of any intended injury to person or property, justifies and requires it in his opinion, he may order a sufficient number of officers of justice to guard the person or property threatened, or may, according to the directions hereinafter contained, require military aid for that purpose.

Art. 37. If any one be brought before a magistrate by virtue of an application under the first article of this chapter, where the complainant has made oath that he fears violence, but it does not appear to the magistrate that from the circumstances such fears are well grounded, he shall, nevertheless, before discharging the prisoner, admonish him of the nature and consequences of the offence which the applicant fears he will commit, and if after such admonition the prisoner shall commit such offence, he shall suffer the maximum of the punishment assigned to the same.

Art. 38. The constitution of the state gives to every citizen the right "freely to speak, write and print on any subject, being responsible for the abuse of that liberty;" therefore, no law can be made to prevent any intended defamation in either of those modes ; but if any one shall make oath that he is informed and believes, and shall convince the magistrate that he has good reason to believe that another is about to PUBLISH, SELL or CIRCULATE, or is continuing to sell, publish or circulate any libel against him, or any such publication as is forbidden by the Code of Crimes and Punishments, in the chapter of offences against morals and decency, the magistrate shall cause the person accused to be summoned to appear before him, and shall admonish him of the nature and consequences of the offence which the applicant fears he will commit ; and if after such admonition the accused shall commit such offence, he shall suffer the maximum of the punishment assigned to the same.

Art. 39. On a conviction for a libel, or for any publication forbidden by the chapter of the Code of Crimes and Punishments concerning offences against morals and decency, the court shall order all the copies of the publication on which the conviction was had, and which remain in the hands of the defendant, to be seized and destroyed ; and if it shall appear that after the commencement of the prosecution was notified to the defendant, he shall have sold or circulated any copies of such publication, he shall suffer the maximum of the punishment assigned to the offence.

Art. 40. The court shall, in like manner, on a prosecution for selling unwholesome provisions or liquors, or adulterated medicines, order them to be seized, and after conviction they shall be destroyed ; and any sale made by the accused during the pendency of the prosecution, shall produce the same effects as to the punishment that is directed in the last preceding article with respect to libels.

Art. 41. Another case in which the court must interfere to prevent offences is, by ordering the removal of all
such obstructions in public and common property, and all
such establishments injurious to public health, as shall be
found by a conviction of the offender to have been made.

CHAPTER IV.

*Of search warrants, as the means of preventing the com-
mission of crimes and the loss of property by theft.*

Art. 42. A search warrant is an order in writing made
by a magistrate, directed to an officer of justice, commanding him to search for certain specified articles,
supposed to be in the possession of one who is charged
with having obtained them illegally, or who keeps them
with the intent of using them as the means of committing
a certain designated crime.

Art. 43. The power of granting this writ is one in the
exercise of which much is necessarily left to the discretion
of the magistrate ; he is, however, bound by the following
rules in granting the warrant, and the ministerial officer
by those which are afterwards laid down for his conduct
in executing it.

Rules for the magistrate in granting a search warrant.

1. Search warrants can only be granted for the following purposes, that is to say :

To discover property taken by theft or under false
pretences, or found and fraudulently appropriated.

To seize forged instruments in writing or counterfeited
coin intended to be passed, or the instruments or materials
prepared for making them.

To seize arms or munitions prepared for the purpose of
insurrection or riot.

To discover articles necessary to be produced on the trial of one accused of a crime under the circumstances hereinafter stated.

2. A search warrant can be granted in no case but on an AFFIDAVIT, made by a credible person.

3. If the application be to search for property taken by theft or under false pretences, the affidavit must state that the property has been lost by one of these offences ; it must describe the property, and state a belief and the reason of such belief, that the property is concealed in a certain place, describing it.

4. If forged papers, false coin, or the instruments or materials for making them, form the object of the application, the affidavit must state a belief and the reason on which it is founded, that those articles or some of them are concealed in a certain place, describing it, with intent to commit a crime.

5. If the application be to search for arms or munitions prepared for insurrection or riot, the affidavit must state a belief and reasonable grounds for such belief, that a conspiracy has been formed, or an unlawful assembly held, for the purpose of preparing the means for executing those offences, and that the arms or munitions were part of such preparation ; and must also describe the place in which it is suspected they are deposited.

6. When any one accused of a crime before a magistrate, to whom it shall appear from the circumstances in evidence before him, that the production of some weapon, implement or other article, will be necessary on the trial of the accusation, if it shall appear by the oath of at least one witness, that there is good reason to believe that such article is concealed in a certain place, this warrant may also issue.

7. The designation of a house by the name of the owner or the occupant, or by the number or situation, is a sufficient description of place under the preceding articles.

8. If the magistrate be satisfied of the truth of the allegations in the affidavit, he shall make his warrant in

the form prescribed for that purpose in this code, but no variation from that form shall affect the validity of the warrant, provided it be not deficient in one of the following requisites:

First. It must be in WRITING, and signed by the magistrate with his name; and the designation of the office he holds, must appear either by the signature or in the form of the warrant.

Second. It must be directed to the sheriff or to some other officer of justice: if to the sheriff, it may be by the designation of his office; if to any other officer of justice, his name as well as his office must be put in the direction.

Third. It must direct him to search for and bring before the magistrate, to be disposed of according to law, the property or articles specified in the affidavit, describing it as set forth in the affidavit.

Fourth. The place to be searched must be specified with reasonable certainty.

Fifth. The officer must be directed to execute the warrant in the day time.

Sixth. The officer must be directed to bring the property described, and the person in whose possession it may be found, before the magistrate for examination, without delay.

9. When the property is brought before the magistrate, if upon the examination and evidence offered him it shall be identified to be the same with that described in the affidavit, and that it was taken or held for the purpose mentioned therein, he shall cause an inventory to be publicly taken thereof, in the presence of the party in whose possession it was found, and of the applicant for the warrant, if they choose to attend; one copy of which shall be given to each of them, one kept by the sheriff, and another filed by the magistrate, with his proceedings, for the purpose of being sent with the articles seized to the court that shall try the offence.

10. If the magistrate discovers either that the property seized is not the same as that described in the affidavit and warrant, or that there is no good reason for

the suspicions set forth in the affidavit, he shall direct the property to be restored, and the possessor, if brought before him, discharged.

11. If the person in whose possession the property was found, shall be brought before the magistrate in obedience to the writ, he shall proceed to his examination in the manner directed for examinations on arrests, and shall either discharge, commit or let him to bail, as is directed in that part of this code.

Rules for the government of officers of justice in the execution of search warrants.

1. If the warrant be directed to a sheriff, it may be executed by him or any of his known deputies previously appointed, but if he make a special deputy for the purpose of the deputation, the name of the person shall be written on the warrant.

2. If the warrant be directed by the magistrate to any other officer of justice, he must see that his name as well as his office is written in the warrant, and in all cases the officer must see that the warrant contain all the requisites above stated, to give it validity; if it do not, he is not bound to execute it.

3. Before executing the warrant, the officer must give notice of its execution to the person who applied for it, that he may be present and identify the property if it be found.

4. The warrant must be executed in the presence of two inhabitants of the parish, who shall sign the return as witnesses.

5. It can only be executed in the DAY TIME.

6. No other place than that designated in the warrant can be searched, but the whole of that may be examined.

7. The officer charged with the warrant, if a HOUSE is designated as the place to be searched, may enter it without demanding permission if he find it open; if the doors be shut, he must declare his office and his business and demand entrance; if the doors be not opened, he

may break them. When entered, he may demand that any other part of the house, or any closet, or other closed space in which he has reason to believe the property is concealed, may be opened for his inspection, and he may break them if it is refused.

8. If required, the officer must show his warrant.

9. He makes himself liable to damages and to the penalties prescribed by the Code of Crimes and Punishments in cases of misbehaviour in office, by any unnecessary force, harshness or ill-usage in the discharge of this duty.

10. An inventory of the property seized must be made before it is removed, and signed by the officer and the two witnesses.

11. No other property but that specified in the warrant must be seized.

12. If the property specified in the warrant be seized, the person in whose possession it was found must be arrested, according to the forms in this code for making arrests, and with the property brought for examination before the magistrate who issued the warrant.

13. A return will be indorsed or annexed to the warrant, stating what was done in obedience to it, and signed by the officer and the two witnesses.

Art. 44. Whoever shall maliciously, and without reasonable cause, procure any search warrant to be issued and executed, shall be fined not less than fifty nor more than three hundred dollars, or imprisoned not less than thirty days nor more than six months, and the imprisonment, or any part of it, may be in close custody.

Art. 45. If any magistrate shall issue a search warrant without a previous affidavit, as required by this chapter, he shall suffer the punishment mentioned in the last preceding article, and be deprived of his office.

Art. 46. Any officer of justice, who, in executing a search warrant, shall exceed his authority to the injury of any one, shall be imprisoned not exceeding sixty days, besides suffering the punishment assigned to any other offence he may have committed by such illegal conduct.

TITLE II.

OF SUPPRESSING PERMANENT OFFENCES.

Art. 47. Permanent offences are such as are renewed by a continued succession of the same acts which first created them. They may affect the public tranquillity, the public health, the public property, or the person, the reputation, or the property of individuals.

CHAPTER I.

Of suppressing permanent offences against the public tranquillity.

Art. 48. The mode in which magistrates and officers of justice are to proceed in the suppression of offences of this nature, is declared in the title that treats of those offences in the Code of Crimes and Punishments, and will be further provided for in the next title of this book.

CHAPTER II.

Of suppressing permanent offences against public health and safety.

Art. 49. Whenever an indictment shall be found against any one for carrying on a business injurious to the health of those in the vicinity, if the indictment shall charge that any persons have actually suffered in their health from the exercise of such business, the court, on the application of those interested, and after hearing the person accused and receiving statements on oath on both sides, may in their discretion enjoin the person accused, in such penalty as they may deem reasonable, not to carry on the said business, or to carry it on in a place or in a manner that will not prove injurious to the health of others until the trial ; and if a conviction shall be had on such indictment, the injunction shall be perpetual in conformity with the provisions of the third chapter of the first title in this book.

Art. 50. In like manner, if an indictment be found against any one for carrying on a manufacture of powder or other dangerous operation, contrary to the provisions of the Code of Crimes and Punishments, a like injunction, and an order for the removal of the dangerous substance to a safe distance, may be made by the court in which the indictment is found.

CHAPTER III.

Of suppressing permanent offences against the public enjoyment of property held for common use of all the citizens.

Art. 51. If any one shall erect any building or make any other permanent obstruction which shall prevent the free use of any public property held for the common use of all the citizens, and which shall have been in such common use for twelve months next preceding the time of erecting such obstruction, the judge of the court of the highest criminal jurisdiction in the district may, on complaint and proof of the facts above stated, cite the party accused of making such obstruction, to appear before him, and in a summary way shall take evidence of the facts, and if the inconvenience to the public from the obstruction be so great, as in his opinion to render it improper to wait the event of a trial for the offence, and the fact of one year's previous possession and use in public is clearly proved, he may order such obstruction to be removed by the sheriff.

Art. 52. No further penalty can be imposed until a conviction take place, on an indictment or information for the offence.

Art. 53. If no indictment or information be filed against the party whose building has been removed, or if on the trial he shall be acquitted by showing title to the property on which it was erected, he is entitled to an indemnity from the person making the complaint, for any damage he may have suffered by the removal.

CHAPTER IV.

Of the suppression of permanent offences against morals and decency.

Art. 54. In cases of publications which come within this description of offences, the suppressive remedy is set forth in the   article of the third chapter and first title of this book ; if the offence be committed by indecent exposure, it is suppressed on complaint and arrest, in the manner directed for other offences, and by taking security for good behaviour.

CHAPTER V.

Of suppressing permanent offences to reputation.

Art. 55. The only cases and the only manner in which the suppression of the offences mentioned in the title of this chapter can be made, are those detailed in the articles of the third chapter and first title of this book.

CHAPTER VI.

Of the suppression of permanent offences affecting the person by assault and battery.

Art. 56. The continuance of assault and battery may be suppressed in the manner heretofore indicated in this and in the Code of Crimes and Punishments, by resistance of the party aggrieved, or of those who come to his aid, and by the arrest of the offender, and forcing him to give security to keep the peace.

CHAPTER VII.

Of suppressing offences against personal liberty.

Art. 57. The suppressive remedy for offences of the nature indicated in the title of this chapter, is by writ of *habeas corpus;* the nature of which remedy, and the mode of applying it, are detailed in the following sections of this chapter.

SECTION I.

Definition and form of this writ.

Art. 58. A writ of *habeas corpus* is an order in writing issued in the name of the state, by a judge or court of competent jurisdiction, directed to any one having a person in his custody, or under his restraint, commanding him to produce such a person at a certain time and place, and to state the reason why he is held in custody, or under restraint.

Art. 59. The writ of *habeas corpus* is to be, as nearly as circumstances will permit, in the following form, *to wit*:—

The state of Louisiana to A. B.   You are commanded to have C. D. in your custody, as is said, or under your restraint, kept, before E. F., judge of (describing the office of the magistrate issuing the writ, or, if issued by a court, inserting the style of such court), on the day of   at   o'clock, in the forenoon or afternoon (as the case may be) of the same day, at (naming the place) or forthwith (as the case may be), and that you then and there state in writing, the cause of detaining the said person, and produce your authority for so doing, and hereof you are not to fail under the heavy penalties denounced by law against those who disobey this writ.   E. F., judge, &c., or G., H., clerk of the court of, &c.

Art. 60. The writ of *habeas corpus* (if issued by a judge) must be signed by him, or (if issued by a court) must be signed by the clerk, and sealed with the seal of such court.

Art. 61. The proceedings under this writ are considered as the most effectual safeguard of personal liberty against public or private attempts to invade it. It is therefore declared, that in all cases where there may be any doubt on the construction of any provision in this chapter, that construction must be given which is most favourable to the person applying for relief under it, and which will give the most extensive operation in all cases to the remedies hereby provided against illegal restraint.

Art. 62. The writ of *habeas corpus* is not to be disobeyed for any defect of form.   It is sufficient, 1st: If the person to whom it is directed, be designated, either by the style of his office (if he have any), or by such other appellation or description as may make it understood by one of common understanding, that he is the person intended, and any one who may be served with this writ, who has, in fact, the custody of the person directed to be produced, or who exercises a restraint over him, cannot avoid obedience thereto, although the writ may be directed to him by a wrong name, a false description, or even although it be directed to another. 2nd: It is sufficient if the person who is directed to be produced, be designated by name, or if the name be unknown or uncertain, if he be described in any other way so as to make it be understood by one of common understanding, who is the person intended. 3rd : The name and office of the judge, or the STYLE of the court issuing the writ, must be either stated in the body of the writ, or by the signature thereof, so as to show sufficiently the authority for issuing the same. If the time of making the return should be omitted, the writ is to be obeyed without delay ; if no place be inserted, it must be obeyed, by making the return at the dwelling of the judge or the usual place of holding the sessions of the court, whichever issued the same.

Art. 63. The insertion of words in the writ, other than those contained in the above given form, or the omission of any which are inserted in such form, shall not vitiate the writ, provided the substantial parts enumerated in the preceding article are preserved.

SECTION II.

Who has authority to issue writs of *habeas corpus*, and in what case and how they are to be applied for.

Art. 64. The district courts and the criminal court, as now established, and all other courts which may hereafter be established, having jurisdiction in civil causes, to the amount of more than three hundred dollars, or of criminal cases where the punishment is more than one year's imprisonment at hard labour ; and the judges of such courts have power to issue writs of *habeas corpus*, directed to any person within their respective districts.

Art. 65. When the judge of any district is absent, interested or incapable, from whatever cause, of acting, and there is no judge of a criminal court in such district, a writ of *habeas corpus* may be issued by a judge of competent authority, in any of the adjoining districts ; provided, the absence, interest or ability of the judge of the district, where the illegal imprisonment is said to exist, be made to appear by the oath of the party applying, or other sufficient evidence.

Art. 66. The writ of *habeas corpus* may be obtained by petition addressed to any court or judge, having authority to grant the same, signed either by the party for whose relief it is intended, or any other person on his behalf. The petition must state in substance :

1. That the party is illegally imprisoned or restrained in his liberty, and by whom, naming both parties, if their names are known, or designating or describing them, if they are not.

2. If the confinement or restraint is by virtue or under colour of any judicial writ, order or process, a copy thereof must be annexed, or it must be averred that such copy has been demanded or refused.

3. If the confinement or restraint be by virtue of judicial process, regular in form, but illegally obtained or executed, it must be set forth in what the illegality consists.

4. If the confinement or restraint is not by virtue of any judicial process, then the petitioner need only state that the party is illegally confined or restrained.

5. The petition must contain a prayer for the writ of *habeas corpus*.

6. It must be sworn to be true, at least according to the belief of the person making the application.

Art. 67. Any court or judge empowered to grant writs of *habeas corpus*, on receiving such petition, shall, without delay, grant the same ; unless it appear from the petition itself, or from documents annexed, that the party can neither be discharged, nor admitted to bail, nor in any other manner relieved.

Art. 68. A writ of *habeas corpus* is granted in court by the signature of the clerk, and affixing the seal of the court to the writ. It is granted by the judge, by his signature only.

Art. 69. Whenever the court or judge, duly authorized, shall know, or have reason to believe, that any one, in the district of such judge or court, is illegally confined or restrained in his liberty, they shall issue a writ of *habeas corpus* for his relief, although no petition be presented, or application made for such writ.

Art. 70. Whenever it shall appear by the oath of a credible witness, or other satisfactory evidence, that any one is held in illegal confinement or custody, and there is good reason to believe that he will be carried out of the state, or suffer some irreparable injury, before he can be relieved in the usual course of law; or whenever a writ of *habeas corpus* has been issued and disobeyed, any court or judge, empowered to issue writs of *habeas corpus*, shall make a warrant, directed to any sheriff or other executive officer of justice, or any other person who may agree to execute the same, commanding him to take and bring the prisoner, so illegally confined, before such judge, to be dealt with according to law.

Art. 71. Where the proof mentioned in the preceding article is sufficient to justify an arrest of the person having the prisoner in custody for any offence against the provisions of the Code of Crimes and Punishments, in favour of personal liberty, the judge may add to the warrant an order of arrest of such person for such offence, who shall be brought before the judge, and shall be examined and committed, bailed or discharged, according to the directions contained in the first title of the second book of this code.

Art. 72. Any officer, or other person to whom the warrant mentioned in the two last preceding articles shall be delivered, shall execute the same by bringing the person held in custody (and the person who detains him, if so commanded by the warrant), before the judge or court issuing the same, who shall inquire into the cause of his imprisonment or restraint, and either discharge, bail, or remand the party into custody, as directed in this chapter in cases of returns of writs of *habeas corpus*.

Art. 73. The person to whom the warrant mentioned in the three last preceding articles may be directed, shall, for the execution thereof, have the same powers, and be bound by the same rules as are designated in the chapter of this code which relates to the execution of warrants of arrest ; but the said warrant may be executed in any parish of the state, into which the party for whose relief it issued, may have been carried, without any indorsement of such writ, as is required in cases of arrest.

Art. 74. No fees or emolument whatever shall be received by any judge, clerk or other officer, for granting a writ of *habeas corpus*, but the expenses of conducting the prisoner before the court or judge, must be tendered to the person having charge of him, at the rate of twenty-five cents for each mile, unless the judge granting the writ be satisfied that the applicant is unable to pay such expenses, and shall, by writing on the back of said writ, direct that they be advanced by the person having the custody of the prisoner, and the judge may, on the return, either direct that such expenses be paid by either party, or by the state, or the parish, as circumstances may render proper.

Art. 75. In all cases where the law does not otherwise specially provide, every one has a right to dispose of his own person UNCONTROLLED by any other individual. When the right is interfered with by detaining the person against his will, within certain limits, either by threats, by the fear of injury, or by bonds, or other physical and material obstacles, the party is said to be CONFINED or IMPRISONED and to be in CUSTODY of the person who continues such detention. A person also has the CUSTODY of another, who does not confine him within certain limits, but by menace or force, directs his movements, and obliges him against his will to go or remain where he directs.

When no such detention within certain limits exists, but an authority is claimed and exercised of general control over the actions of the party against his consent, he is said to be under the RESTRAINT of the person exercising such control.

In all cases whatever, where such imprisonment, confinement, custody or restraint exists, which is not authorized by positive law, or is exercised in a mode or degree not authorized by law, the party aggrieved may have relief by writ of *habeas corpus*.

Art. 76.*

* Art. 76—referring to slaves, claiming to be free, and seeking to be relieved by *habeas corpus*—is omitted, as being no longer required.

SECTION III.

How the writ of habeas corpus is served and returned.

Art. 77. This writ is served by delivering the original to the person to whom it is directed, or to him in whose custody, or under whose restraint the party for whose relief it is intended, is detained. If he refuse to receive it, he must be informed verbally of the purport of the writ. If he conceal himself, or refuse admittance to the person charged with the service, the writ must be fixed in some conspicuous place on the outside, either of his dwelling-house, or of the place where he is confined.

Art. 78. Any free white male person, capable of giving testimony, may serve the writ.

Art. 79. Its service is proved by declaration on oath and in writing of the person making the service.

Art. 80. It is the duty of the person upon whom a writ of *habeas corpus* is served, whether such writ be directed to him or not, to obey and return the same without delay.

Art. 81. This is done by producing, as directed, the person intended to be released, if in his custody, or under his power or control, and by making a return in writing on the back of the writ, or annexed to it, which must state plainly and unequivocally :

1. Whether he have or have not the party in his power or custody, or under his restraint.

2. By virtue of what authority, or for what cause he took or detains him.

3. If he had the party in his power or custody, or under his restraint at any time within three days prior to the date of the writ, but has transferred such custody or restraint to another ; then stating particularly, to whom, at what time, for what cause, and by what authority such transfer took place.

4. If he have the party in his custody, or under his

restraint, by virtue of any writ or warrant, or other written authority, the same must be annexed to the return.

Art. 82. The return must be signed by the person making the same, and attested on oath.

Art. 83. Whenever a writ of *habeas corpus* shall be taken out for any one in custody, by virtue of an order or execution issued for carrying into effect the final judgment, sentence or decree of any COMPETENT tribunal, either of civil or criminal jurisdiction, the officer having legal custody of such person, need not produce him, unless specially directed to do so, notwithstanding such execution or order, in the cases hereafter provided for ; but it shall be sufficient to make a return in writing, annexing the order or execution, by virtue of which the party is detained. Provided always : that for any special cause for which relief may legally be granted, either set forth in the affidavit, on which the writ of *habeas corpus* is issued, or appearing on the return, the judge may order the prisoner to be brought up, notwithstanding such final judgment, sentence or decree, and may proceed to give the relief to which the party is entitled.

Art. 84. The return to a writ of *habeas corpus* must be made within twelve hours after the service, or sooner, if required by the writ, if the party to be relieved by it is within twelve miles of the place of return. If he be at a greater distance, then he must make the return, allowing one day for every twenty miles' distance, which the party must travel, in order to make the return, and in proportion for a greater or less distance.

SECTION IV.

The mode of enforcing a return.

Art. 85. When it appears to the court or judge, issuing the writ, that it has been duly served, if the person intended to be relieved is not produced at the time, which is required by the provisions of this chapter, the judge, who issued the writ, or if issued by a court, the said court, or any judge thereof, shall make a warrant, directed to any executive officer of justice, or other person willing to execute the same, commanding him to take the person, who has disobeyed the writ, into custody, and to bring him before the judge or court, which issued the warrant, to be dealt with according to law; and if, on being brought before the court or judge, he shall refuse to return the writ, or does not produce the person he was ordered to bring up, in the cases wherein he is by the provisions of this chapter obliged to produce him, he shall be committed to prison, and remain there until the effect of the writ shall be produced, and until he shall pay all the costs of the procedure, and shall moreover be liable to the penalties imposed by law, for disobedience to the said writ, and for any other offence against personal liberty, of which he may have been guilty, in the imprisonment or detention complained of.

Art. 86. In the case provided for by the last preceding article, the person intended to be relieved by the writ of *habeas corpus*, must be brought up in the manner directed by the second section of this chapter.

Art. 87. Whenever, from sickness or infirmity of the person directed to be produced, he cannot, without danger to his life, be brought before the judge, the party in whose custody he is, may state that fact in the return of the writ; and if it be made to appear, by the certificate of a physician regularly admitted to practice, and the testimony of two other witnesses, and the signature of the party intended to be relieved, if he can write; then, if the judge be satisfied of the truth of the allegation, and if the return be otherwise sufficient, it shall be good without the production of the person, and the judge may either go to the place where the prisoner is confined, if he think justice requires it, or he may proceed, when he is satisfied with the truth of the allegation, as in other cases, to decide on the return.

Art. 88. The death of the prisoner, or any other

INEVITABLE ACCIDENT, or SUPERIOR FORCE, will be a good return to excuse the production of the prisoner ; provided proof of such fact be given to the perfect satisfaction of the court or judge issuing the writ ; but this, as well as any other matter alleged in any return, may be contested in the manner hereinafter mentioned.

Art. 89. When any one shall die, while under imprisonment, it shall be the duty of the person in whose custody he was at the time of his death, without any delay, to give notice thereof to the coroner of the parish, or in case of his absence or inability to attend, to a justice of the peace, who shall summon a jury of householders in the said parish, to consist of not less than nine, nor more than eighteen, who shall view the body, and being first duly sworn, shall inquire into the manner in which the person came by his death ; and the said jury shall, in all cases, cause the body to be inspected by a surgeon or a physician duly admitted, and examine him as well as all other persons they may call as witnesses, and if they do not appear, compel their attendance by warrant. And the said jury, or a majority of them, shall make and sign an inquest or certificate, stating that they have examined witnesses, and are satisfied that the body produced to them, is that of such a person (naming him), and setting forth the manner in which he came by his death, unless it shall appear to the said inquest, that the death of such prisoner was caused by a crime; in which case the coroner or justice shall send the inquest to the court having cognizance of the crime, and shall immediately issue a warrant for the arrest and commitment of the party, who shall appear by such inquest to be guilty. And wherever the death of a prisoner is returned as a reason for not producing him in the return of *habeas corpus*, the inquest proving such death must be annexed to the return.

SECTION V.

Of the proceedings on the return.

Art. 90. The judge or court before whom a person is brought on a *habeas corpus*, shall examine the return and the papers, if any, referred to in it, and if no legal cause be shown for the imprisonment or restraint ; or if it appear, although legally committed, he has not been prosecuted, tried or sentenced, within the periods for those purposes respectively limited by law, or that for any other cause the imprisonment or restraint cannot legally be continued, he shall discharge him from the custody or restraint under which he is held.

Art. 91. If it appear that the party has been legally committed for an offence, BAILABLE OF RIGHT, or if he appear, by the testimony offered with the return, to be guilty of such an offence, although the commitment be irregular, or there be no commitment, he shall bail the prisoner, if good bail be offered.

Art. 92. In cases which are not BAILABLE OF RIGHT, the judge has a discretion, the exercise of which involves a high responsibility. It must of necessity be left to his sagacity and prudence to distinguish between those presumptions which leave a strong probability of guilt and those which are too slight to justify imprisonment, previous to the trial. In the latter case only of presumptions, which are not strong, he may admit to bail. This discretion, however, cannot be exercised at all : 1st, Where the crime has been freely confessed before a magistrate. 2nd, Where it is positively and directly charged by the oath of a credible witness present at the act. 3rd, Where an indictment has been found, charging the prisoner with an offence not BAILABLE OF RIGHT.

Art. 93. If the party be not entitled to his discharge, and cannot be bailed, the judge must remand him to the custody, or place him under the restraint from which he was taken, if such custody or restraint be legal, or otherwise place him in the custody or power of such person, as by the law of the state is entitled thereto.

Art. 94. If the judge cannot immediately determine the case, he may, until judgment be given on the return, either place him in the custody of the sheriff of the parish where the return is made, or place him under such care, and in such custody, as his age or other circumstances may require.

Art. 95. If it be shown by the return that the person is detained by virtue of an informal or void commitment, yet if, from the documents on which it was made, or from other proof, it appear that there is good cause for commitment, the prisoner shall not be discharged—but the judge or court before whom he is brought, shall either commit him for trial, or admit him to bail, in cases where, by law, he may be bailed.

Art. 96. In order to enable the judge, before whom a return to a writ of *habeas corpus* is made, to perform the duty required by the last preceding section, the officer having the custody of any person committed for any offence, for whose relief such writ is granted, must show the same to the magistrate who made the commitment, or to the clerk of the court (if the papers relative to the commitment have been delivered to him), and it shall thereupon be the duty of such magistrate or clerk, to attend at the hour and place of the return, and exhibit to the judge or court, to which the same is made, all the proofs and documents relative to the said commitment; and if such magistrate or clerk neglect to attend, the judge or court is authorized, on proof of his having had the notice required by this article, to enforce his attendance by warrant of arrest, and the party, when arrested, shall be kept in custody until he perform the duty required by this article.

Art. 97. When it appears by the return that the person soliciting his discharge is in custody, on any civil process, or that any other person has an interest in continuing his imprisonment or restraint, no order shall be given for his discharge, until it appear that the plaintiff, in such civil suit, or the person so interested, or their attorneys or agents, if either are within twenty miles, have had reasonable notice of the issuing of such writ of *habeas corpus.*

Art. 98. The party brought before the judge on the return of the *habeas corpus,* may deny any of the material facts set forth in the return, or allege any fact, to show either that the imprisonment or detention is unlawful, or that he is entitled to his discharge, which allegations or denials must be on oath ; and thereupon the judge shall proceed in a summary way, to hear testimony, and the arguments, as well of the party interested civilly, if any there be, as of the prisoner, and the person who holds him in custody, and shall dispose of the prisoner as the case may require.

Art. 99. If it appear on the return, that the prisoner is in custody by virtue of process from any court legally constituted, he can be discharged only in one of the following cases :

1. Where the court has exceeded the limits of its jurisdiction, either as to matter, place, sum, or person.

2. Where, though the original imprisonment was lawful, yet by some act, omission or event, which has taken place afterwards, the party has become entitled to his liberty.

3. Where the process is defective in some substantial form required by law.

4. Where the process, though in proper form, has been issued in a case, or under circumstances where the law does not allow process or orders for imprisonment, or arrest to issue.

5. Where, although in proper form, the process has been issued or executed by a person either unauthorized, or improperly authorized to issue or execute the same, or where the person having the custody of the prisoner under such process, is not the person empowered by law to detain him.

6. Where the process appears to have been obtained by false pretences or bribery.

7. Where there is no general law, nor any judgment, order or decree of a court, to authorize the process, if in a civil suit, nor any conviction, if in a criminal proceeding.

But no judge or court, on the return of a *habeas corpus*, shall in any matter inquire into the legality or justice of a judgment or decree of a court legally constituted, and in all cases where it appears that there is sufficient legal cause for the commitment of the prisoner for an offence, although it may have been informally made, or without due authority, or the process may have been executed by a person not duly authorized, the judge shall make a new commitment, in proper form, and directed to the proper officer, or admit the party to bail, if the case be bailable.

Art. 100. The order of discharge made by a court or judge, on the return of a *habeas corpus*, has no other effect than that of restoring the party to liberty, and securing him from any future imprisonment or restraint for the same : it is not conclusive, as to any other civil right.

Art. 101. No person who has been discharged by order of a court or judge, on a *habeas corpus*, shall be again imprisoned, restrained, or kept in custody for the same cause, unless he is afterwards indicted for the same offence. But it shall not be deemed to be the same cause :

1. If, after a discharge for defect of proof, or for any material defect in the commitment, in a criminal case, the prisoner should be again arrested on sufficient proof, and committed by legal process for the same offence.

2. If, in a civil suit, the party has been discharged for any illegality in the judgment or process, and is afterwards imprisoned by legal process, for the same cause of action.

3. Generally, whenever the discharge has been ordered on account of the non-observance of any of the forms required by law, the party may be a second time impri-

soned, if the cause be legal, and the forms required by law observed.

Art. 102. When a judge, authorized to grant writs of *habeas corpus*, shall be satisfied that any person in legal custody, on a charge for any offence, is afflicted with a disease, which will render a removal necessary for the preservation of his life, such judge may order his removal, on his giving bail, with two securities, in such sum as shall be ordered by the judge, that he will surrender himself to the same custody, whenever he shall be thereunto required; or the judge may, in such case, where the prisoner is manifestly unable to procure bail, put him in the custody of an executive officer of justice, whose duty it shall be to watch over the said prisoner in the place to which he may be conveyed, to prevent his escape. Provided, that the fact of such disease, and the necessity of removal, shall appear by the oaths of two physicians or surgeons duly admitted to practice, and that the physician who shall attend on such prisoner after his removal, shall also take an oath that he will give notice to a magistrate as soon as in his opinion the said prisoner may safely be returned to his imprisonment, which magistrate shall, on receiving such notice, issue a warrant for his removal to the place in which he was formerly confined.

SECTION VI.

General provisions.

Art. 103. No person shall be discharged under the provisions of this chapter who is in custody on a commitment for any offence exclusively cognizable by the courts of the United States, or by order, execution, or process, issuing out of such courts, in cases where they have jurisdiction, or who is held by virtue of any legal engagement, or enlistment in the army, or who, being subject to the rules and articles of war, is confined by any one legally acting under the authority thereof, or who is held as prisoner of war, under the authority of the United States.

Art. 104. There is no other writ of *habeas corpus* known in the law of this state, but that described and provided for in this chapter. Courts having occasion to direct the production of prisoners before them, either to prosecute, to give testimony, or for any other purpose than that of examining into the cause of their imprisonment, may command the production of such prisoners by an order of court, entered on their minutes, and certified to the officer having charge of such prisoner.

SECTION VII.

Penalties for the breaches of the duties enjoined by this chapter.

Art. 105. Any judge empowered by this chapter, to issue writs of *habeas corpus,* who shall refuse to issue such writ, when legally applied to, in a case where such writ may lawfully issue, or who shall unreasonably delay the issuing of such writ, or who, in cases where such writ is allowed to issue without any proof, shall WILFULLY omit to issue, or wilfully and unreasonably delay the issuing such writ, shall for every offence be fined in the sum of two thousand dollars.

Art. 106. Any judge so authorized, who shall refuse, or wilfully omit to perform, any other of the duties imposed on him by this chapter, or shall unreasonably delay the performance thereof, by which refusal, omission or negligence, any illegal imprisonment is caused or prolonged, shall be fined in the sum of one thousand dollars.

Art. 107. Any executive officer of justice to whom a writ of *habeas corpus,* or any other warrant, writ or order, authorized by this chapter, shall be directed, delivered or tendered, who shall refuse, or neglect to serve or execute the same, as by this chapter is directed, or who shall unreasonably delay the service or execution thereof, shall be fined in the sum of one thousand dollars.

Art. 108. Any one having the person in his custody,

or under his restraint, power or control, for whose relief a writ of *habeas corpus* is issued, who, with the intent to avoid the effect of such writ, shall transfer such person to the custody, or place him under the power or control of another, or shall conceal him, or change the place of his confinement, with intent to avoid the operation of such writ, or with intent to remove him out of the state, shall be fined in the sum of two thousand dollars, and may be imprisoned at hard labour, not less than one nor more than five years.

Art. 109. In a prosecution for any penalty incurred, under the last preceding article, it shall not be necessary to show that the writ of *habeas corpus* had issued at the time of the removal, transfer or concealment therein mentioned, if it be proved that the acts therein forbidden, were done with the intent to avoid the operation of such writ.

Art. 110. Any one having the person for whose relief a writ of *habeas corpus* is issued, in his custody, or under his power or control, who (without being guilty of any of the acts made punishable by the last preceding article) shall, after being legally served with such writ, neglect or refuse to produce such person, in cases where, by the provisions of this chapter, he is bound to produce him, shall be fined in the sum of one thousand dollars.

Art. 111. Any person to whom a writ of *habeas corpus* is directed, and to whom it is duly served, who shall neglect or refuse to make a return thereto, in the manner directed by the third section of this chapter, shall be fined in the sum of five hundred dollars, even if he have not the party whom it is intended to relieve in his custody, or under his power or control.

Art. 112. Any sheriff or his deputy, any jailor or coroner, having custody of any prisoner, committed on any civil or criminal process of any court or magistrate, who shall neglect to give such prisoner a copy of the process, order or commitment, by virtue of which he is imprisoned, within three hours after demand, shall be fined in the sum of five hundred dollars.

Art. 113. Any magistrate who, on receiving notice of the issuing of a *habeas corpus* for any person committed by him for any offence, shall neglect to attend at the return of the *habeas corpus*, in the manner directed in this chapter, shall be fined in the sum of three hundred dollars ; unless, before receiving such notice, he shall have returned the papers relative to such commitment, to the clerk of the court having cognizance of the cause.

Art. 114. Any person who, knowing that another has been discharged by order of a competent judge, on a *habeas corpus*, shall, contrary to the provisions of this chapter, arrest or detain him again for the same cause, which was shown on the return of such writ, shall be fined in the sum of five hundred dollars for the first, and one thousand five hundred dollars for a second offence.

Art. 115. Any able-bodied male inhabitant of this state, above the age of eighteen and under fifty years of age, who shall, when legally called on for that purpose, refuse to aid a magistrate, executive officer of justice, or other person, legally authorized to serve or execute any writ, commitment or order, issued by virtue of this chapter, in the service or execution of such writ, warrant or order, shall be fined in the sum of fifty dollars.

Art. 116. The recovery of the said fines shall be no bar to a civil suit for damages, or to a criminal prosecution, for such of the said acts or omissions as may, in the third book of this code, be declared to be an offence.

CHAPTER VIII.

Of suppressing permanent offences against property, and of the disposition of personal property, seized and supposed to be stolen.

Art. 117. Permanent offences against personal property, by a criminal taking, may be suppressed either by civil suit for its restoration or by the means hereinbefore directed of a search warrant, or by resistance to the unlawful taking.

Art. 118. In all cases of a conviction for a criminal taking or detention of personal property, which is taken with the offender or in his possession, or where without such conviction the property is found on a search warrant, or is detained in the hands of an officer of justice on suspicion of being stolen; on satisfactory proof of ownership, it shall be restored to the owner.

Art. 119. No property coming to the possession of a magistrate, court or officer of justice, by any of the means described in the last preceding article, shall be restored to any one claiming as owner until after notice published for fifteen days, describing the property and designating the person from whom it was taken, or the place where it was found, and requiring all persons having any claims, to make them known.

Art. 120. If no more than one claimant appear, the property shall, without prejudice to any other civil claim, be delivered to him on his making oath to the ownership. If more than one claimant appear, the property shall remain sequestered in the hands of the sheriff, until by a civil suit the rights of the parties be determined.

Art. 121. If no claimant appear, the property shall be sold at auction, and the proceeds paid to the treasurer of the state, and if no claim be made on him by any person claiming as owner within one year, it shall be carried to account of the Recompense Fund, hereinafter designated.

Art. 122. If an indictment or information be presented against any one for a violent dispossession of real property, contrary to the provisions of the Code of Crimes and Punishments, it shall be tried in preference to any other, except those for offences punishable with imprisonment for life, and an information may be filed when the court is not in session by permission of the judge, who shall thereupon hold a special court for the trial of such offence.

Art. 123. If the defendant be convicted, the person aggrieved shall be restored to, and maintained by the court in, possession of the property against the person convicted, until the right shall be determined by a civil suit, if any be brought.

TITLE III.

OF THE MANNER OF CALLING FOR AND EMPLOYING THE MILITARY FORCE OF THE STATE IN AID OF THE CIVIL POWER.

Art. 124. Neither the militia nor any other military force shall be employed in the aid of the civil power, or brought to act in a military capacity against any persons in the state, unless it be called for in the manner directed by this title ; and when so called for shall be subject to the regulations hereinafter prescribed.

CHAPTER I.

Of the manner and cases in which the military force may be required.

Art. 125. When any three magistrates, of whom a judge must always be one, shall be convinced by the affidavits of two inhabitants of the state, that a RIOT or INSURRECTION has taken place in the parish in which the persons making the affidavit reside, and that the persons engaged therein cannot be arrested or dispersed by the ordinary force of civil authority, they shall make a written application to the governor, requesting military aid.

Art. 126. If the governor be at such a distance from the place at which the riot or insurrection exists, as is too great to enable him to give the necessary orders in time for its suppression, a copy of the application shall be also sent to the nearest field officer of ordinary militia or of any independent corps, containing the same request.

Art. 127. The application must be signed by the magistrates, must state the substance of the testimony offered to them, and the place and probable object of the riot or insurrection, and it must designate the number of men required for the purpose of suppressing it.

Art. 128. Immediately after receiving such application, the governor, or officer to whom it is directed, shall order the number of men specified therein, to march with arms and ammunition under the command of the requisite officer, and place themselves under the direction of the magistrates signing the application.

Art. 129. The governor, or the officer to whom the application is made, may, notwithstanding the designation of the number of men in the application, order as many more as he may deem necessary, to be embodied and hold themselves in readiness, if those sent for the purpose should prove insufficient to overcome the resistance that may be offered ; and if the resistance should be continued, the men so kept in readiness may be employed without further requisition from the magistrate.

CHAPTER II.

Of the manner in which the military force is to be employed.

Art. 130. The officer commanding the troops detailed in compliance with the application of the magistrates, shall immediately repair to the place designated, and post the troops in such a manner as to intervene between the persons or the property that it may be the intention of the rioters or insurgents to attack. He shall then act entirely on the defensive, not suffering the men to fire, and permitting them to use their edged or pointed weapons only to repel actual violence, except in one of the following cases :

1. If an attack be made on any one of the militia by which his life is in danger, or if an attempt be made to disarm him, which he cannot otherwise avoid, he may defend himself by discharging his fire-arms.

2. If a general attack be made by the insurgents or rioters upon the militia with fire-arms, or by missile or other weapons, by which the lives of the men are indiscriminately put in danger, the officer may order the men to fire, but not until an endeavour has been made to disperse the rioters by means less dangerous to persons who may not be engaged in the offence.

3. If the troops cannot be so placed as to intervene between the rioters and the persons and property which they apparently intend to attack, and the illegal purpose of the riot is persevered in, by means evidently dangerous to the lives of others, although no attack be made on the troops themselves, the magistrates, or any two of them, may direct the officer to disperse the rioters, which he is authorized to do, by ordering the men first to use the bayonet or sword, and if they prove ineffectual to disperse the assembly, but not otherwise, then to discharge their fire-arms against them.

4. The troops shall not be brought up to the place until the white flag has been displayed by a magistrate, and warning given to disperse, in the manner directed by the   article of the Code of Crimes and Punishments, and unless in defence against an attack dangerous to life, no order shall be given or obeyed to make any discharge of fire-arms, or other use of any other arms than for defence, until half an hour shall have elapsed after the displaying of the white flag and the giving the warning to disperse.

5. Every endeavour must be used both by the magistrates and officer commanding the troops that can be made consistently with the preservation of life, to induce or force the rioters or insurgents to disperse, before any attack is made upon them by which their lives may be endangered.

BOOK II.

TITLE I.

OF ARREST AND BAIL.

CHAPTER I.

Definitions and general principles, relative to the subject of this title.

Art. 131. A complaint is the allegation made to a proper officer, that some person, whether known or unknown, has been guilty of a. designated offence.

Art. 132. No complaint can have a legal effect, unless it be supported by such evidence as shall show that an act which constitutes an offence has been committed, and renders it certain or probable that it was committed by some person named or described in the complaint. It is then called an ACCUSATION.

Art. 133. The evidence mentioned in the last preceding article may be taken without the knowledge of the party accused, or the effect of the law might be evaded by his escape. But he cannot be condemned on such evidence; he must have an opportunity of explaining or contradicting it before the judges who are finally to decide on his innocence or guilt. The investigation is called the TRIAL. It necessarily requires some delay, but public justice requires that during this interval, the person of the accused should be secured, in order that he may undergo the penalty of the law, if he be found guilty. This is effected by an ARREST.

Art. 134. As it would be oppressive in most cases to deprive the accused of his liberty before trial and conviction, if he can give a sufficient pledge for his appearance at the trial, the law restores him to his liberty on his giving such a pledge. This pledge is called BAIL.

Art. 135. There are cases in which the accused is bailable of right, others in which it is discretionary with the judge to admit to bail, and some in which no bail can be taken. The rules relative to these several distinctions are laid down in a subsequent chapter of this title, and in the chapter of the preceding book relative to writs of *habeas corpus.*

CHAPTER II.

Of the mode of making a complaint and accusation, and of ordering an arrest.

SECTION I.

Of complaints and accusations, and who may receive them.

Art. 136. Any judge of any court, any mayor or justice of the peace, of the state, is authorized to receive complaints and accusations for offences ; to issue warrants, order arrests, make commitments, and take bail in the manner directed by this code. They are designated under the general term MAGISTRATE.

Art. 137. Any person, even those incapable of giving testimony, may make a complaint to a magistrate.

Art. 138. When a complaint shall be made to a magistrate, he shall reduce the declaration of the complainant to writing, and if he be a person capable of giving testimony, shall administer an oath, that the said declaration contains the truth, and shall cause it to be signed in his presence, and shall then proceed to take such other testimony as shall be offered him to prove the offence, or designate the offender, causing each declaration to be SIGNED by the declarant, and attested on oath.

Art. 139. If it appear probable to the magistrate that any other persons have knowledge of any material fact or circumstance relative to the complaint, it is his duty to summon and examine them on oath, touching the matter of the complaint.

SECTION II.

Of warrants of arrest, and citation.

Art. 140. When a magistrate, from the complaint or accusation, or other evidence taken before him, is convinced that an offence has been committed, and has reason to believe that any person who can be sufficiently designated by name or description, has committed such offence, it shall be his duty to issue a WARRANT OF ARREST, or CITATION, according to the discretion hereinafter vested in him.

Art. 141. When an offence is committed in the presence of a magistrate, he may issue a warrant of arrest, although no complaint or accusation be brought before him ; but in such case the warrant must be *returnable* before some other magistrate, and the magistrate signing the same, must reduce his own testimony to writing, and prior to any commitment or holding to bail, attest the same before such other magistrate on oath.

Art. 142. A warrant of arrest is an order in writing, directing a person, accused or suspected of having committed an offence, to be brought before a magistrate or court of examination.

Art 143. This warrant may be issued by the governor

of the state, by any court having any criminal jurisdiction, or any magistrate.

Art. 144. It must be directed to the person who is to execute it, either by name, or by his official designation. In the latter case it may be directed specially to a particular officer, or generally to all officers of the same description : when so generally directed, any officer of that description, to whom it is delivered, must execute it.

It must describe the party suspected or accused, by name, or by such other designation, as may sufficiently distinguish him, and it must contain an order to arrest and bring him before some court or magistrate for examination. The offence of which the person to be arrested is accused or suspected, must be set forth either by its legal appellation, or it must be substantially described.

It must be signed by the magistrate, or by the clerk of the court which issues it.

Art. 145. Warrants of arrest may be directed to a sheriff or his deputy, or to a constable. These are called officers of justice, and they are bound to execute any legal warrant directed to them. Warrants may also be directed to individuals, who are not such officers, but they are under no obligation to execute such warrant unless they have undertaken so to do; in which case they are bound by the same rules, and are subject to the same penalties for neglect or misconduct, as officers are.

SECTION III.

In what cases an arrest may be made without warrant.

Art. 146. Where a CRIME or a BREACH OF THE PEACE has been committed, and the offender shall endeavour to make his escape, if there is a good reason to believe that he will effect it before a warrant can be obtained, he may be arrested by virtue of a verbal order of any magistrate, or without such order, if no magistrate be present.

Art. 147. Any one in the act of committing a crime, may be arrested by any person present, without a warrant.

Art. 148. Whenever a CRIME is committed, and the offenders are unknown, and any person shall be found near the place where the crime was committed, either endeavouring to conceal himself, or endeavouring to escape, or under such other circumstances as justify a REASONABLE SUSPICION of his being the offender, such person may be arrested without warrant.

Art. 149. In cities and towns, even in cases where it is not certain that an offence has been committed, it is the duty of officers of justice and persons employed in such cities and towns as watchmen, without warrant to arrest and detain for examination, such persons as may be found at night, under such circumstances as justify a reasonable suspicion that they have committed or intended to commit an offence.

SECTION IV.

Of citations.

Art. 150. In cases of misdemeanor, when no danger appears of the defendant's absconding, the magistrate, instead of a warrant of arrest, may issue a citation in the form provided for by this code.

Art. 151. The citation may be served, either by leaving a copy with some person above the age of puberty who shall be found at the dwelling house of the defendant, or by delivering such copy personally to him.

Art. 152. If the defendant do not appear at the time and place of the return of the citation, when it has been duly served, the magistrate shall issue a warrant of arrest.

CHAPTER III.

Of the duty and powers of officers of justice and others in making arrests.

Art. 153. At or before the time of making an arrest, the person who makes it must declare that he is an officer of justice, if such be the case. If he have a warrant, he must show it if required ; or if he make the arrest without warrant in any of the cases in which it is authorized by law, he must give the party arrested clearly to understand, for what cause he undertakes to make the arrest, and must require him to submit and accompany him to the magistrate.

Art. 154. The arrest is complete as soon as such notice is given as is required by the last preceding article ; provided, the party intended to be arrested, from his situation and other circumstances, may reasonably be supposed to have heard the said notice, and to have known that it was addressed to him.

Art. 155. In all cases where the person arrested refuses to submit to the arrest, or to proceed to the magistrate for examination, or attempts to escape, such degree of force may be used as is necessary to compel his appearance. But when he submits to the arrest, and neither attempts to escape nor make resistance, PERSONAL VIOLENCE shall not be used, nor shall BLOWS, STRIPES or WOUNDS be inflicted in any case, as a means of enforcing submission to the arrest, except so far as is hereinafter specially provided.

Art. 156. He who makes an arrest, may take from the party arrested all OFFENSIVE WEAPONS which he may have about his person, and must deliver them to the magistrate who takes the examination, to be disposed of according to law.

Art. 157. No person who shall kill or wound another, intentionally or unintentionally, by the use of such means as would probably produce death, shall be justified or excused for such killing or wounding, although he prove that the party killed or wounded endeavoured to escape from an arrest; but if the party arrested or attempted to be arrested, shall, after receiving the notice provided for in the first article of this chapter, make resistance with DEADLY WEAPONS, the person making the arrest may also use such weapons, where they are necessary for his defence and to repel any forcible opposition to the execution of the arrest; and in such case, if wounds or death ensue, the party making the arrest shall be justified. This article does not extend to prisoners breaking out, or endeavouring to break out of prison when lawfully arrested; in such case, the person having custody of the prisoner, and others employed by him, may lawfully use offensive weapons to prevent the breach of the prison.

Art. 158. If, after a lawful arrest has been made, any one shall, by force, rescue or attempt the rescue of the prisoner, or before the arrest has been made, shall by force attempt to prevent it from being made, the person having the prisoner in custody, or authorized to make the arrest, and others who may be lawfully aiding him, may resist such force, and in doing so may use deadly weapons, whenever it may be necessary to prevent this rescue, or overcome resistance to the arrest.

The provisions of this article extend to all cases where a person is in lawful custody.

Art. 159. In all cases of arrest for examination, the person making the same must, without unnecessary delay, conduct the party arrested before the court or magistrate by whom the warrant was issued, or, if the arrest was made without warrant, before the nearest magistrate in the parish.

Art. 160. Until the person arrested can be brought before the court or magistrate, and during the examination he remains in the custody of the person making the arrest, or of some officer of justice appointed by the magistrate or court.

Art. 161. Watchmen in cities or towns, and officers of justice having charge of prisoners anywhere, are authorized to receive persons arrested for examination, when necessary, for their safe custody during the night or at other times when they cannot be brought before the court or magistrate for examination, and to deliver them again to the party who made the arrest; but in all such cases, the person having charge of the prison, shall take a copy of the warrant if the arrest is made by warrant, or of a declaration of the cause of the arrest in writing, signed by the party making the arrest, if it be one made without warrant.

Art. 162. If the magistrate who shall issue any warrant of arrest, shall be absent at the time when it is returned, or unable from whatever cause, to examine the prisoner, the person, in whose custody he is, must conduct him before some other magistrate in the same parish, and in such case the complaint and affidavit on which the warrant was granted must be sent to the magistrate before whom the prisoner was taken, or if they cannot be procured, the complainant and witnesses must be summoned to give their testimony anew.

Art. 163. Warrants of arrest may be executed in any parish of the state, provided the person authorized to execute such warrant shall procure the allowance of some magistrate in such parish, which he is required to give on being satisfied that the warrant is not forged, and that the person presenting it, is the person to whom it is directed.

This allowance shall be made by writing on the warrant the word "allowed," with the name of the parish and the date of the allowance signed with the name of the magistrate who makes it. In whatever parish the arrest be made, the prisoner shall be brought to the parish in which the warrant for his examination was issued.

Art. 164. Arrests may be made on any day and at any hour of the day or night, and at any place within the state, under the several modifications provided in this section.

Art. 165. If the person accused shall fly into any HOUSE, or other BUILDING, in order to avoid arrest, any one having authority in the manner directed in this chapter to arrest him, may follow him into the said house, and when entered, he may, for the purpose of making the arrest, break any inner door of any apartment, in such house where the accused may be, if entrance be refused.

Art. 166. If the door be not opened when required, it is a refusal of entrance.

Art. 167. No one is authorized to break the outer door of a house in order to make an arrest, but an officer or other person having a warrant of arrest, and those who are lawfully assisting him, except as is provided in the next article.

Art. 168. In cases where, by any of the preceding articles, arrests are authorized to be made without warrant, the person so authorized, may justify breaking the outer door of any house, or in any other manner forcing an entrance therein, without warrant, in cases of such crimes only as are punishable by an imprisonment for life.

Art. 169. No outer door of any house can in any case be broken, or an entrance forced therein, in order to make an arrest, without the following formalities :

Entrance must be demanded in a loud voice.

Notice must be given in the same manner that the party is the bearer of a warrant of arrest.

Or if it is a case in which the arrest is lawful without warrant, that information must be substantially given in an audible voice.

If the arrest is attempted to be made *at night*, two householders of the parish, required for the purpose, must be present, who must announce their names to those within.

Art. 170. All inhabitants of the state, when called on by a magistrate or officer of justice, are bound to assist in making arrests and securing the persons arrested, and are justified in doing all acts in rendering such aid, which the officer himself might do.

Art. 171. If any person who has been lawfully arrested shall escape or be rescued from custody, either before or after commitment, the person from whose custody he escaped, may lawfully pursue and arrest him by virtue of the original warrant or commitment in any part of the state, and convey him back to his former custody.

CHAPTER IV.

Of the duty of magistrates in taking examinations and making commitments.

Art. 172. When the person accused is brought before a magistrate for examination, he shall be informed of the accusation against him ; the examinations of the witnesses, which have been taken, shall be read to him ; and, if he request it, the witnesses (if they are yet alive and within the state) shall be summoned to attend, and they, as well as any additional witnesses who are produced, may be cross-examined by the accused or his counsel.

Art. 173. The magistrate shall then proceed to the examination of the person accused in the following manner :

1st. He must be informed that, although he is at liberty to answer in what manner he may think proper to the questions that shall be put to him, or not to answer them at all, yet a departure from the truth, or a refusal to answer without assigning a sufficient reason, must operate as a circumstance against him, as well on the question of commitment as of his guilt or innocence on the trial.

2nd. The magistrate shall next put the following interrogatories to the person accused :

What is your name and age ?

Where were you born ?

Where do you reside, and how long have you resided there ?

What is your business or profession ?

Where were you at the time the act (or omission) of which you are accused is stated by the witnesses to have taken place ?

Do you know the persons who have been sworn as witnesses on the part of the accusation, or any, and which of them, and how long have you known them ?

Give any explanation you may think proper, of the circumstances appearing in the testimony against you, and state any facts that you think will tend to your exculpation.

3rd. If any writing, or any article of property, be produced in evidence, it must be shown to him, and he must be asked whether he recognizes it.

4th. The answers of the accused to the several interrogatories shall be reduced to writing by the magistrate, or some one by his order. They shall be shown or read to the accused, who may correct and add to them ; and when made conformable to what he declares is the truth, may be SIGNED by him ; but if he refuses to SIGN, his reason shall be stated in writing, as he gives it, by the magistrate himself ; and the examination shall be signed and certified by the magistrate, whether the accused sign it or not.   This examination is not to be on oath.

Art. 174. After the examination of the accused is finished, his witnesses, if he have any, shall be sworn and examined, and their examinations reduced to writing and signed by them respectively, after they have been read, corrected (if necessary) by them, and approved.

Art. 175. The witnesses shall not be present at the examination of the person accused ; and while one of them is examined, the others shall be kept apart.

Art. 176. All the examinations, depositions, and other proof, shall be kept by the magistrate, to be disposed of as is hereinafter directed.

Art. 177. If the accused or the public prosecutor

request that a further examination take place, the magistrate may, at his discretion, postpone the examination to a future day ; and either continue the prisoner verbally in the custody of the officer by whom he was brought before him, or give a written commitment to the keeper of the prison of the parish ; in which commitment it will be necessary only to state, that the party is committed for further examination on a complaint of (stating the offence).

Art. 178. After being once committed for further examination, the prisoner may be verbally ordered to be brought up and REMANDED from time to time, as long as the examination continues.

Art. 179. The effect which the examinations and depositions, taken before the magistrate, is to have on the trial, is set forth in the Code of Evidence.

Art. 180. It is the duty of the magistrate, before whom a prisoner is brought for examination, to address him without passion. He must neither use menace, nor hold out hopes of impunity or reward, in order to influence him.

Art. 181. In cases of difficulty, other magistrates of the same parish may assist at the examination and offer the sitting magistrate their advice, but he must decide, except on questions of bail, as is hereinafter provided.

Art. 182. The prisoner may have the assistance of such counsel as he may employ, but the magistrate has no authority to assign counsel.

Art. 183. Whenever the accusation is for a crime, the magistrate shall, and on all other occasions may, give notice to the public prosecutor to attend the examination ; and it shall be his duty, on such occasions, to attend and examine the witnesses, and argue all questions of law and fact that may arise in the course of the investigation.

Art. 184. The magistrate has the same powers for preserving order, during the examinations, that are vested in courts by the chapter of the Code of Crimes and Punishments relative to offences against the judiciary power committed in a court of justice; and the magistrate may, on his own view, immediately make a commitment for trial for any of the said offences.

Art. 185. The magistrate shall, on the application of the accused or the public prosecutor, issue summonses to the witnesses that may be required by either, which shall be served by any officer of justice; and if they refuse to attend, they may be brought up by warrant; and any witness refusing to answer a legal question, may be committed to prison until he shall agree to answer.

Art. 186. After hearing the proof, and considering the allegation, if any be made by the accused, the magistrate must determine, whether he be legally charged with the offence of which he is accused, or any other offence, or there be sufficient reason to believe him guilty thereof. In either case, that is to say, if the charge be positively proved by a credible witness, although there be exculpatory proof, or although there be no such direct proof, but the circumstances detailed induce a belief that he is guilty, he must be bailed or committed.

Art. 187. A commitment is an order directed to the sheriff of the parish, commanding him to keep the prisoner in safe custody, to answer a charge for the offence of which he is accused (specifying the same particularly), until he shall be released by law. This commitment must, in substance, contain a direction to the sheriff or his deputy, or the keeper of the jail, either by the style of his office, or by name, or both.

An allegation that the person (naming or describing him) is charged on oath with an offence (specifying it either by the legal appellation of the offence, or substantially stating the act which has been charged).

An order to receive the prisoner and detain him until he shall be discharged by law.

It must be signed by the magistrate issuing it, or if issued by a court, the commitment must be under its seal and signed by the clerk.

Art. 188. No person shall be discharged for any defect of form in the commitment, if it can be sufficiently understood from the language thereof, in its usual signification, that the officer detaining him is the person to whose custody persons accused of offences may be legally committed; that the prisoner is legally charged with some offence; and that the commitment be signed by a magistrate authorized to make commitments.

Art. 189. The commitment shall be delivered to an officer of justice, whose duty it shall be to take charge of the prisoner, without other warrant, and convey him without delay to the officer who is directed to receive him.

Art. 190. But if the offence be BAILABLE OF RIGHT, or if not bailable of right, and the proof is not evident nor the presumption great, the magistrate cannot commit the prisoner, if he offers good bail. His duty, in taking bail, is set forth in the next chapter.

Art. 191. If it appear from the testimony, that the prisoner is guilty of any other offence than the one of which he was originally accused, he shall be committed or bailed for such offence.

CHAPTER V.

Of the duty of the magistrate in taking bail.

Art. 192. The constitution declares, that "all persons shall be bailable, except for capital offences, whenever the proof is evident or presumption great." At the time of adopting the constitution the capital offences were murder, rape, exciting insurrection among slaves, and stabbing or shooting or poisoning with intent to murder; therefore, all other offences are and must be bailable. Persons accused of the offences above enumerated, are also to be bailed when the proof is not evident nor the presumption strong.

Art. 193. A single justice of the peace may admit to bail in all cases of misdemeanor, and in cases of crime where the punishment is imprisonment at hard labour for a term not exceeding six years. In cases where the punishment exceeds that term, but is less than fifteen years, the assent of two justices is necessary for determining the amount of bail and approving the security. In all other cases the bail must be taken before a judge.

When homicide is directly proven or admitted on an examination before a justice, the prisoner cannot be admitted to bail by the justice alone without the assent of a judge, notwithstanding any allegation or proof of justification, excuse or alleviation. He must, in such case, be committed ; and, if the circumstances require it, afterwards bailed, or relieved on *habeas corpus*.

Art. 194. Bail is given by the prisoner and his surety signing a RECOGNIZANCE, conditioned for the appearance of the prisoner at the next session of a court of competent jurisdiction, to be named in the condition, and to abide the judgment of such court.

Art. 195. When bail is given, the prisoner must be discharged, without exacting from him the payment of any fees.

Art. 196. In all cases where a crime is charged, and from the nature of the offence any proof or presumption of guilt may reasonably be supposed to be drawn from any article in the possession of the prisoner, the magistrate may direct him to be searched in his presence, and shall preserve all things found on him which may be useful to be produced on the trial, and afterwards disposed of according to law.

Art. 197. Where the offence charged is the illegal infliction of a wound, or any other injury, which may terminate in the death of the person injured, and the offence be proved or confessed, the magistrate cannot discharge, if it appear from the examination of surgeons that there is a probability that death will ensue in consequence of such injury. In this case the party must be committed for further examination, until the consequences of the injury can be ascertained.

Art. 198. No justice of the peace can let any prisoner to bail after he has been committed for trial ; the power of these magistrates, on this subject, is confined to cases where the persons are brought before them for examination.

Art. 199. The amount of bail cannot be apportioned by law to the circumstances of every case. It forms one of the most important and delicate exercises of judicial duty. It should be so performed as neither to suffer the wealthy offenders to escape by the payment of a pecuniary penalty, nor to render the privilege useless to the poor. In order to make it a sure pledge for the appearance of the party, it must be determined by considering :

1. The nature of the punishment to be inflicted on conviction.

2. The pecuniary circumstances of the party accused.

If the offence be punishable by hard labour, imprisonment or privation of civil rights, the desire to avoid punishment being greater, it should be counteracted by an increase of penalty.

The wealth of the party must also be considered. The poor might be oppressed by requiring an amount of security which would be no pledge whatever for the appearance of the rich. For these reasons, the law leaves to the discretion of the judge to determine the amount of bail, guided by the above principles, and within the limits contained in the following articles.

Art. 200. Where the punishment of the offence is a pecuniary penalty only, the bail must be greater than the highest fine that can be imposed.

Art. 201. When simple imprisonment forms a part of the punishment, one dollar at least must be added to the amount of bail for every day that the party may be sentenced, if not exceeding one year; if the imprisonment may exceed one year, then any further addition must be left to the discretion of the magistrate.

Art. 202. If hard labour form part of the punishment on conviction, then two dollars at least is to be added to the amount of bail for every day to which the party may be sentenced, not exceeding one year ; if the punishment may exceed one year, then any further increase must be left to the discretion of the magistrate.

Art. 203. If a suspension or forfeiture of political or civil rights, without imprisonment at hard labour, form a part of the punishment, then the sum of five hundred dollars at least must be added to the amount of the bail.

Art. 204. The five last preceding articles shall also govern the judges who may bail prisoners on writs of *habeas corpus*.

Art. 205. No person shall be received as surety for the appearance of the party accused who is not a HOUSE-HOLDER who has resided at least one year in the state, and who does not own or possess property either real or personal to double the amount of the sum for which he is bound, to prove by his oath, in all cases where the magistrate has any doubt of his sufficiency.

Art. 206. A woman cannot be received as bail.

Art. 207. In all cases of crime, two sureties are required.

Art. 208. A single surety will be sufficient, if he possess and own unincumbered real property to double the amount of the sum for which he is bound.

Art. 209. When the person admitted to bail is a minor or a married woman, the engagement shall, notwithstanding, be valid.

Art. 210. If, owing to mistake or misrepresentation, insufficient bail has been taken, or if the sureties become afterwards insufficient, the accused may be ordered to find sufficient sureties by any magistrate, and on his refusal may commit him for trial.

Art. 211. In all cases where a magistrate shall either commit for trial or bail the accused, he must cause each of the witnesses who has been examined, and has testified to any material fact or circumstance in the case, to enter into a recognizance, without surety, in a sum fixed by the magistrate, conditioned for his appearance at the next sitting of the court, at which the accused is bound or committed to appear ; and if a witness shall refuse to sign such recognizance when required, he may be committed to prison by the order of the magistrate, and shall be confined until he shall be brought before the court to testify, or until he shall sign the recognizance.

Art. 212. Those who may have become bail for any one, may at any time discharge themselves by surrendering him to the custody of the sheriff of the parish in which the court at which he was bound to appear shall sit.

Art. 213. The magistrate who took the recognizance of bail, is bound, on request, to deliver a copy thereof to the bail, if he have not yet transmitted the same in the manner hereinafter directed, or if he have so transmitted it, then the clerk of the court having custody thereof, must, on like request, deliver such copy, which shall be a sufficient warrant for the bail to arrest the person for whom they have become bound. In making which arrest the bail are authorized to do the same acts and are bound by the same rules as are hereinbefore prescribed to persons having warrants of arrest for examination on accusations for the same offences.

Art. 214. The sheriff to whom a surrender is legally made, as authorized by the preceding articles, is bound to receive the person so surrendered, and the bail must deliver to him with the prisoner the certified copy of the recognizance of the bail, as his authority for detaining such prisoner, and he shall, on the request of such bail, give them a transcript of the recognizance with an acknowledgment that he has received the person mentioned therein, in discharge of his bail. Which transcript and acknowledgment being proved by the oath of two witnesses to have been executed by such sheriff shall be a sufficient warrant for the officer or magistrate having custody of the recognizance to cancel the same.

Art. 215. The magistrate who shall make any commitment, or let any person to bail, shall, without any unnecessary delay, at the furthest within three days, transmit to the clerk of the court, which has legal cognizance of the offence charged, all the complaints, accusations, depositions, recognizances of bail, bonds for the appearance of witnesses, and all other documents in his possession relative to the accusation.

Art. 216. If there be proof made before a magistrate of the commission of any offence, and the party accused shall not be found on the warrant of arrest for examination, it shall notwithstanding be the duty of the magistrate to transmit to the court having cognizance of the offence, all the depositions and other documents he has taken in the manner directed by the last section, in order that the same may be laid before the grand jury in the manner hereinafter directed. But the said depositions and other documents need not in this case be transmitted to the court until the first day on which it shall sit, after the said depositions shall have been taken.

Art. 217. Further rules respecting bail are given in the chapter regulating the practice on writs of *habeas corpus*.

TITLE II.

OF THE PROCEEDINGS SUBSEQUENT TO THE COMMITMENT OR BAIL.

CHAPTER I.

Of appearance, and the manner of enforcing it against parties and witnesses.

Art. 218. The names of all persons who have given bail or have become bound by recognizance to appear in any court of criminal jurisdiction, shall be called in open court on the day they are respectively bound to appear, and if they fail to appear before the adjournment of the court, and no sufficient cause is shown according to the provisions of the next article, their defaults shall be entered, and such entry shall be evidence of the breach of their appearance, bonds or recognizances.

Art. 219. If it be satisfactorily shown on the part of the sureties or of the accused, that he is prevented from appearing by inevitable necessity, the court must direct an entry to be made on the back of the appearance bond, that time is given for the accused to appear until such day as the court, under a consideration of the circumstances of the case, shall appoint.

Art. 220. Courts may also, on the motion of the public prosecutor, order the sheriff to arrest and bring before them any person who has been bound by recognizance or summoned to appear and give testimony, and who has not attended at the time appointed ; and when so arrested the said witnesses may be also fined in any sum not exceeding fifty dollars for their neglect, and must remain in custody until they give their testimony and are discharged from further attendance, or until they give such security as shall satisfy the court (either by their own recognizance or with sureties) for their appearance to testify. Provided, that if a witness shall show that he was prevented from appearing by inevitable necessity, the court must remit the fine, and take the witness's own recognizance for his appearance.

Art. 221. Witnesses bound to appear, and persons let out on bail, must not only attend on the day appointed in their respective obligations, but at such other times as the court shall direct, and the obligation continues, until they are discharged by the court.

Art. 222. If the public prosecutor discover that it will be necessary to have any person examined before the grand jury, who has not been bound by recognizance to appear, he may apply to a magistrate, who shall summon such witness and cause him to enter into recognizance for his appearance, to testify in the manner prescribed in the first chapter of this book, or he may obtain a summons from the clerk of the court under his signature and the seal of the court, commanding such witness to appear at a day therein to be appointed, to give testimony in such cases as shall be required of him, and courts and magistrates may, whenever they think proper, cause witnesses to enter into recognizance for their appearance to testify.

CHAPTER II.

Of the duty of public prosecutors, sheriffs and clerks, preparatory to the meeting of the grand jury.

Art. 223. On the first day of each term of any court, at which a grand jury is summoned, the sheriff of the parish in which the court shall sit, shall make out and deliver to the judge of such court, two copies of a calendar, on which shall be entered the names of all the persons in his custody committed for trial for any offence, stating when they were committed, by whom, and for what offence, and entering on the said calendar the names of all such persons as having been committed for any offence were bailed, since the last term of the court, and by what judge. And the clerk of the said court shall also make out (and deliver to the judge) two copies of a calendar, on which he shall enter the names of all the persons who appear by the returns of the magistrates to have been either committed, or bailed, or who have been accused without having been arrested, for any offence, together with the dates of the accusation, the name of the magistrate who committed or bailed, and distinguishing whether each person was committed or bailed, or could not be found ; and the judge shall deliver to the grand jury, as soon as they are sworn, one copy of each of the said calendars, together with all the examinations, depositions, and other documents returned by the magistrate, and shall also send to them all such other returns as shall be afterwards made by any magistrate during the session of the grand jury. Provided that the said calendar, before it is sent to the grand jury, shall be submitted to the public prosecutor, who shall mark thereon such cases of misdemeanor as he shall choose to prosecute by information, and the papers and documents relative to such cases shall not be sent to the grand jury, and it shall be the duty of the public prosecutor to file informations in all such cases before the end of the term.

CHAPTER III.

Of the grand jury, its organization and its duties.

Art. 224. The grand jury is a body of men, taken at stated periods, from the mass of citizens, to perform a most important function in the administration of justice. It is their duty to protect the innocent from accusation, but to discover and bring the guilty to trial. They have no political nor any other civil powers, and must confine their deliberations to inquiries whether there have been infractions of the penal laws of the state, and who have been the offenders : no other presentments or expressions of their opinions can be received in a court of justice, except in cases where special duties may be imposed upon them by law.

Art. 225. The grand jury consists of twenty-three members, who are selected in the manner prescribed by special laws for that purpose : the consent of a majority of the whole number is necessary to make an indictment ; but a majority of those present may decide on any other question arising in the course of their deliberations. No grand jury can proceed to any business, unless thirteen members at least are present.

Art. 226. The grand jurors, before they enter on the

exercise of their duties, shall each take the oath prescribed for that purpose by this Code.

Art. 227. A judge of the court in which the grand jury shall be convened, shall, immediately after they are sworn, give them such information as he may deem proper as to the nature of their duties, and draw their attention to such offences as are on the calendar, or as he has reason to believe will be brought before them ; confining his observations to the subjects connected with their duties as jurors, and carefully avoiding all topics of political or party nature : he shall read to them such parts of the Penal Code as relate to the several offences on their calendar, together with the whole of this chapter.

Art. 228. When the grand jury has received the address of the court, they shall retire to the chamber appointed for their deliberations. Two constables or deputies of the sheriff shall be appointed to be constantly in attendance on them, the one as door-keeper, the other as messenger to carry the orders and citations which they may issue.

Art. 229. The first act of the jury, after having retired, shall be to organize themselves, by electing two of their members, the one to preside at their sittings, to be called the foreman of the grand jury, the other to be their clerk ; this choice shall be made by ballot, and the members having the greatest number of votes for these places shall respectively be elected. If two persons shall have an equal number of votes for the same place, this fact shall be reported to the court, and the judge shall determine which shall be elected. As soon as an election shall be made, a message shall be sent by one of the members of the grand jury to the court, stating which members have been respectively chosen.

Art. 230. The deliberations of the grand jury shall be secret : no one shall be admitted while they are sitting but the public prosecutor, and such persons as may be sent for or appear as witnesses, or may come to make complaint or give information relative to the infraction of any penal law. Every one announcing himself as complainant or informant against such infraction, must be admitted and heard at such time as the grand jury will permit.

Art. 231. The public prosecutor shall have access to the grand jury whenever he may have any information or advice on any point of law to give, or any complaint or evidence to lay before them, or whenever his attendance is required by the grand jury or any member thereof who may desire his advice; but he must not be present at their deliberations or decisions.

Art. 232. The grand jury are to decide on all the cases on the two calendars whether there is matter for accusation; this is not left to the discretion of the public prosecutor: therefore, it shall be the duty of the public prosecutor to prepare bills of indictment in all cases of crimes appearing on the calendars, and in all such cases of misdemeanor as he shall not choose to prosecute by information and to send them to the grand jury, beginning with the cases of those who are in actual custody, and among those, sending in first the cases of crimes highest in degree. He can only depart from this order when material witnesses summoned or under recognizance to appear, have not appeared, and he has reason to expect their attendance. For the purpose of preparing these indictments, copies of the examinations, depositions and other papers returned by the magistrates, shall be sent to him by the clerk within three days after they are filed, and except in cases in which the returns are made within three days of the meeting of the grand jury, it is the duty of the public prosecutor to prepare all such bills of indictment by the first day of the term.

Art. 233. If any of the grand jury know or have reason to believe that an offence has been committed within the jurisdiction of the court in which they are sworn, he is bound by his oath to declare the same to his fellow jurors, excepting such offences as can be presented on the complaint of the party injured only, and the jury shall thereupon take up the consideration thereof in their order.

Art. 234. Any individual having a knowledge of the

commission of any offence, may apply to the grand jury, who are bound to hear his complaint and take his own declaration or oath, and that of such other witnesses as he may point out to them.

Art. 235. The grand jury may issue a summons ordering the attendance of any witness, and if he fail to attend, may issue an order directing the sheriff to arrest and bring him before them, and if he shall refuse to be sworn or to testify, they may by a like order commit him to prison, and he shall not be released until the grand jury are finally discharged, unless he consent to be sworn and give testimony as ordered, and he shall moreover be liable to such punishment as in such case is provided by the Code of Crimes and Punishments.

Art. 236. Every summons, order of arrest or other order of the grand jury, shall issue in the name of the grand jury (specifying the parish or district for which they are sworn), and shall be signed by the foreman and attested by the clerk.

Art. 237. When the foreman or clerk is disabled from sickness, or for other cause has been discharged or excused from attendance by the court, another member of the jury may be chosen in his place during such disability.

Art. 238. When an indictment is found or the jury decide in the manner hereinafter provided, that there is matter of accusation for any offence against a person who is neither in custody nor on bail, or if on bail, is bailed for an offence less in degree than that found, it shall be the duty of the public prosecutor to apply for, and of the judge to grant, a warrant of arrest for the offence stated in the indictment or presentment, commanding the sheriff to arrest and keep in safe custody the person therein named, who is charged with the commission of an offence (naming it) by the grand jury.

Art. 239. The warrant shall be in the form hereinafter prescribed, and shall be executed in the manner directed with respect to ordinary warrants for arrest, except that no examination can take place before the magistrate on any other point than that of the identity of the person ; if no objection of this nature be made, or if made, be not supported by proof, the magistrate must either commit or bail the prisoner, according to the rules established for that purpose on ordinary arrests.

Art. 240. In their deliberations, the grand jury are to proceed in the following order : the calendars are to be read and they shall take up for consideration, first : the causes of those who are in custody, beginning with the greatest in degree. The indictment sent in by the public prosecutor shall be then read, together with the examinations and other documents returned by the magistrates. The witnesses shall then be examined, and if any member requires the advice of the public prosecutor, he may be called, heard, and after he has retired, the foreman shall again read the indictment and put the following questions to the jury :

1. Whether they find that the offence stated in the indictment has been committed ?

2. Whether it was committed by the person accused in the indictment ?

Each of these questions shall be debated and decided separately, and on each the jury may, with the assent of twelve members, make any amendments or alterations in the indictment, either in the description and circumstances of the offence, according to their view of the testimony and law, or in the name or description of the offender, if another person than the accused in the indictment appears to have committed the offence.

If both the questions above stated are decided in the affirmative by twelve jurors, the indictment shall then be signed by the foreman and clerk, respectively by each, adding to his name the quality in which he signs. When thus signed, the indictment is said to be found.

Art. 241. In cases where the public presecutor has not sent an indictment, the grand jury, after hearing the testimony, shall in like manner decide, 1 : Whether an offence has been committed, and what that offence is ; and, 2 : Who is the offender. And if it result, from the decision of these questions, that twelve jurors are of opinion, that any designated person has been guilty of an offence, the clerk shall certify that there is matter for accusation against the person (naming him) for such an offence (designating it), and shall deliver such certificate with a minute of the evidence to the public prosecutor ; who shall immediately send an indictment to the grand jury, conformable to the fact and law, which indictment, before it can have any force, must be found in the manner above directed.

Art. 242. If the grand jury decide that they have not sufficient evidence, either that the offence was committed, or that it was committed by the person accused (whether this decision be made on an indictment or under the last preceding clause, where no indictment has been presumed), a certificate shall be sent to the court, stating that the grand jury find no cause of accusation against such person (naming him) for the offence of which he is charged (specifying it), which certificate shall be signed by the foreman and attested by the clerk. Whereupon such person, if in custody, shall be discharged, or if bailed, the bail bond shall be cancelled ; but such finding and discharge shall not prevent another accusation for the same cause, if other testimony be produced ; nor shall the party be discharged either from custody or from his bail, if he be detained or bailed for any other cause than that which has been examined by the grand jury : Provided also, that no discharge shall be ordered on any such certificate until the public prosecutor have had notice thereof, and if he shall declare to the court that he has other evidence against the accused, which in his opinion will justify a commitment, the discharge shall be delayed twelve hours to enable him to produce such testimony.

Art. 243. No record shall be kept of the manner in which any member of the grand jury has voted on any question before them ; nor can any member be obliged or allowed to declare, even in a court of justice, in what manner he or any other member of the grand jury voted on any such question, or what opinions they expressed. But they may be called on in any court of justice (in cases where evidence of that nature is otherwise legal) to show that the testimony of a witness examined before the grand jury was different from or consistent with that given before such court.

Art. 244. Every indictment found by the grand jury shall be delivered by the clerk into the hands of the presiding judge in open court, and if the person indicted be in custody or bailed for the offence of which he is indicted, the judge shall deliver the indictment to the clerk to be filed. But if the person indicted be not in custody, or not bailed for the offence of which he was indicted, then the judge shall retain such indictment until the party be arrested, or until the last day of the term, if he be not arrested before, and shall then deliver it to the clerk to be filed.

Art. 245. The grand jury cannot be discharged during the term, until they have decided on all the causes on the calendar, and on all complaints before them, nor then without the order of the court; until discharged, they must meet every day while they have any business before them; but they may determine their own hours of meeting and adjournment. When they have no business immediately before them, but are waiting for witnesses, or on any other account, they may adjourn with leave of the court, for any term not exceeding three days.

When the term of the court to which the grand jury is summoned, expires, either by its limitation or the adjournment of the court, the functions of the grand jury cease.

Art. 246. The grand jury has a right to ask the instruction and opinion of the court on any point of law on which one-third of the grand jurors present may be dissatisfied with the opinion of the public prosecutor. In order to obtain such instruction the grand jury shall come into court, and if the matter on which they desire to consult the court requires secrecy, the foreman shall so state to the judge, and thereupon the judge shall cause all persons to leave the court until he shall have heard the questions of the grand jury and given his opinion and instruction thereon. After hearing which, the said jury shall retire to their own chamber to deliberate, but are not bound to decide in conformity with such opinion or instruction.

Art. 247. Fines not exceeding for any one infraction thirty dollars, may be imposed by the court on such grand jurors as fail in their attendance at any time during the term. The grand jury may themselves, in addition thereto, impose fines not exceeding ten dollars, to insure punctuality in attending at the hour to which they may have adjourned. Such fines to be collected in the same manner with other fines by the sheriff, on the warrant of the foreman, and appropriated to such charitable institution as the grand jury shall direct.

Art. 248. Grand jurors cannot, during the time of their attendance as such, be arrested for any misdemeanor, nor on any civil suit, except for a breach of the peace committed during the time they are thus privileged; nor for five days previous to the day for which they are summoned, nor two days after their discharge : and any one who shall arrest or cause to be arrested, any person summoned as grand juror, knowing him to be such, contrary to the provisions of this act, shall be fined not less than thirty nor more than one hundred dollars; and the grand juror so arrested shall be discharged from such arrest, and may recover such damages as he may be entitled to by a civil suit.

Art. 249. The functions of a grand juror require to be exercised with the most perfect freedom of opinion, of debate and action; therefore it is his duty to keep secret whatever he himself or any other juror may have said, or in what manner he or they may have voted, on any particular question or matter legally before them ; and any person offending against the provisions of this article is guilty of a misdemeanor, and shall be fined not less than thirty dollars nor more than one hundred dollars.

Art. 250. No grand juror shall, directly or indirectly, give information to any one that an accusation or complaint is pending before the grand jury, if the person accused has not been arrested on such accusation or complaint; and any one offending against this provision is guilty of a misdemeanor, and shall be fined not less than fifty nor more than two hundred dollars, unless such information was given with intent that the person accused should escape or avoid an arrest, in which case, the juror giving such information shall also be deemed to be an accessary to the offender, whose escape he intended to promote.

Art. 251. No grand juror shall be prosecuted or sued for any thing he may say or any vote he may give, in the grand jury, relative to any matter legally pending before the jury; provided, that nothing herein contained shall prevent the prosecution and punishment of any grand juror who shall be guilty of perjury in making any accusation or giving any evidence to his fellow-jurors; and in the case contemplated by this proviso, the jurors are not bound by their oath nor by any of the preceding articles, to keep such perjury secret.

CHAPTER IV.

Of indictments and informations.

Art. 252. No OFFENCE can be prosecuted except by indictment or information. This rule is modified in cases of certain fines and of contempt, in the manner specially provided for.

Art. 253. An indictment is an act in writing made by a grand jury legally convoked and sworn, declaring that a person therein named or described, has done some act or has been guilty of some omission which is by law declared to be an offence.

The indictment shall be in the following form :

" To the district court of the district (or the criminal court, giving the style of the court as the case may be).

"The grand jurors for the (name the parish and district) on their oath present, that A. B. on the day of   in the year   in the parish of did (here insert the act constituting the offence) contrary to the laws of this state and the peace and dignity of the same.

C. D. Foreman.

E. F. Clerk."

Art. 254. No indictment shall be deemed deficient in form for any variance from that contained in the preceding article, provided it can be understood :

1. That the same was presented to some court having jurisdiction of the offence stated in the indictment, although the title of the said court may not be accurately set forth.

2. That it may be also understood from the said indictment that it was found by a grand jury, convened for the parish or district in which such court sat.

3. That the person accused is named, or if his name cannot be discovered, that he be described as "a person refusing to discover his name," which shall be sufficient description ; but if on his arraignment the accused, so described, shall assume some name, the name so assumed shall be inserted in the indictment and taken as the true name. No addition is necessary to the name, but if a false one be given, it can only be corrected in the manner stated under the head of arraignment.

4. That the offence is alleged to have been committed at some place which is within the jurisdiction of the court, except in cases where the act, though done without the local jurisdiction of the court, is made cognizable therein by law.

5. That the offence is alleged to have been committed at some time which is prior to the time of finding the indictment, and where there is a limitation of time for commencing the prosecution, within such limitation.

6. That the act or omission charged, be so clearly and distinctly set forth, as to enable a man of common understanding to know what is intended.

7. That the indictment be signed by the foreman and the clerk of the grand jury, and that the day on which it was presented to the court be noted thereon.

8. That the name be set forth of the party injured, if a private offence, but if the names are unknown to the grand jury, it may be so stated.

9. That it concludes with the words "contrary to the laws of this state, and the peace and dignity of the same," which are required by the constitution.

Art. 255. The words used in an indictment, shall be taken and construed in their usual acceptation in common language, except such words and phrases as are particularly defined, which are to be taken in the sense herein given to them.

Art. 256. It is not necessary to state in the indictment any particular place in the parish for the commission of the offence, or to aver that it was done within the jurisdiction of the court, but it will be sufficient to state that it was done within the parish, naming it, if such parish be actually within the jurisdiction of the court.

Art. 257. Where the offence shall have been begun in one parish or district, and become complete in another parish or district, the offender may be tried in either of the districts or parishes, and the offence may be stated to have been done in either of the said parishes or districts, and proof that the offence was either begun or completed in the parish or district where it is charged to have been done, shall be sufficient to support the indictment.

Art. 258. Accomplices and accessaries to offences begun in one parish or district, and which become complete in another, may in like manner be prosecuted in either of the said parishes or districts, and the offender may also, as in case of principals, be stated in the indictment to have been done in either, and proof thereof shall in like manner support the indictment.

Art. 259. Where any act done out of the state is made an offence by the Penal Code, the offender may be tried in the parish or district in which he is apprehended.

Art. 260. If any one out of the state or in one parish or district of the state, shall procure another person to commit an offence within another parish of the state, he may be indicted and tried in the place where the offence was committed, and that whether the person doing the act were an innocent or guilty agent.

Art 261. It is not necessary to state the place in which an indictment is found in the margin of the indictment.

Art. 262. Every thing necessary to be stated must be truly stated in the indictment : there are no legal fictions.

Art. 263. Every indictment must describe the offence with such certainty, as to enable the accused to plead the judgment that may be given on it, in bar of any prosecution for the same offence.

Art. 264. The precise time at which the offence was committed need not be stated in the indictment, provided it be laid to have been done before the time of presenting the indictment ; but where the time is material to the description of the offence, it must be alleged with the same certainty that is described in the definition of the offence.

Art. 265. Rules and forms are given in a subsequent chapter for drawing indictments and informations, in each particular offence ; where those forms or rules vary from those contained in this chapter, the particular rules or forms are to prevail in that offence for which they are intended.

Art. 266. When any circumstance is expressly made an aggravation of the offence, such circumstance must be set forth in the indictment.

Art. 267. Where a repetition of the offence is intended to be relied on as an aggravation of the punishment, the indictment must set forth the preceding conviction, with the exceptions hereinafter mentioned.

Art. 268. Where the intent is a material part in the description of the offence, it must be stated in the indictment.

Art. 269. Every indictment for forgery, or for making, altering, passing, or having in possession any instrument in writing, contrary to any of the provisions of the chapter of the Code of Crimes and Punishments relative to " Offences affecting the credit of written instruments," or for any other offences founded on written instruments, shall, with the exception contained in the next article, contain an exact copy of such instrument, expressing in words whatever is so expressed in the instrument, and in figures, what in the instrument is expressed in figures, but no ornamental engraving or writing contained in the instrument, need be imitated in the copy.

Art. 270. The only case in which an indictment for either of the offences mentioned in the last article, shall be good without containing a copy of the instrument, is, where the instrument has been destroyed by the act or procurement of the accused, in which case that fact may be charged in the indictment, and must on the trial be proved ; and instead of the copy, the instrument must be described in the indictment with so much certainty as to make it appear that it was one of those which are made punishable by the system of Penal Law.

Art. 271. To every indictment for any of the offences above enumerated, except in the case mentioned in the last article, and in the case of forgery or other offence relating to a public record, the foreman of the grand jury shall annex the instrument on which the indictment is found, and shall mark the same, by writing on some part thereof, the initials of his name, and the said instrument shall remain annexed to the said indictment, unless it shall be withdrawn by leave of the court.

Art. 272. In the case above of an offence relating to a public record, the book in which it is kept shall be produced and marked by the foreman of the grand jury ; and shall again be brought into court, and verified to be the same, without alteration, as it was produced to the grand jury; and shall be exhibited to the defendant, previous to his arraignment, when he is called on for his exceptions to the indictment, in the manner prescribed in the next chapter.

Art. 273. In case of any defamation by writing or painting, painted or inscribed on a building, or on an article, too bulky to be produced in court, a copy or description may be inserted in the ACT OF ACCUSATION, and proof of the fact be given on the trial, without producing the painting or writing, or showing it to the accused.

Art. 274. In cases of libel, the indictment or information need not contain the whole of the work, but only so much as is charged to be libellous, but the whole must be annexed to the act of accusation.

Art. 275. In an indictment for any of the offences created by the said chapter of offences affecting the credit of written instruments, it shall not be necessary to charge that the instrument on which the indictment is brought would, if true, have had any of the effects enumerated in the article containing the definition of the offence, or specifying what the effect would be, or to name any particular person, whom it was the intent of the accused to defraud; or to state otherwise than by the copy thereof, what the said instrument purported to be, or in any act of accusation whatever, to charge that the offence was committed against the form of any particular statute.

CHAPTER V.

Of the proceedings between the indictment and the trial.

Art. 276. It shall be the duty of the clerk of the court, in which any indictment or information for any offence is filed, within three days after the same shall have been filed, to make a copy thereof, and to deliver the same to the sheriff, to be served on the accused, or on his bail;

and no one shall be, without his assent, arraigned or called on to answer any indictment or information, until three whole days have elapsed after the copy shall have been served as aforesaid, exclusive of the days of service and arraignments.

Art. 277. Two days, at the least, after having received the copy of the indictment, and one day at the least before his arraignment, the accused shall be brought into court, and the instrument (if there be any) annexed to the indictment shall be exhibited to him ; and he and his counsel shall, in the presence of an officer of the court, have reasonable time allowed them to compare the said instrument with the copy set forth in the indictment, and to consider of any exception they may think proper to make to the indictment.

Art. 278. After the exhibition of the instrument, as is above provided for, and after the expiration of the time allowed for the examination thereof, in cases where there is any instrument annexed, and in cases where there is no instrument annexed, then at such time as the court shall direct, at least two days after the service of the indictment, and at least one day before the arraignment, the accused shall be brought into court, and he must be told by the clerk that if he has any exception to make to the indictment, for any want of substance or form, or for any variance between the said indictment and the instrument thereunto annexed, or for that he, the accused, is not indicted by his true name, that he must then make such exception, or that no such exception will hereafter be heard.

Art. 279. If the accused shall make no such exception, an entry shall be made on the back of the indictment to that effect, and the accused shall be remanded to prison if in custody, or to his bail, if he be out on bail, until the time of his arraignment ; and no motion for quashing the indictment, or for an arrest of the judgment, shall be made on account of any of the exceptions mentioned in the last article, except as is hereafter provided in this chapter.

Art. 280. If the accused shall allege for exception, that he is not indicted by his true name, he must state what such true name is ; and the prosecuting officer may then immediately amend the indictment by inserting such name, which the accused shall not be permitted at any time afterwards to disavow.

Art. 281. If the accused shall make any exception to any want of form in the indictment, or to any variance between the instrument of writing and the copy in the indictment, the public prosecutor may, if he think the said exceptions well taken, immediately amend such defect of form or variance.

It shall be optional with the accused to make the exceptions mentioned in the preceding articles, verbally or in writing ; if verbally made, the judge shall take a note of them in writing, which shall be read to the accused.

Art. 282. In case any amendments shall be made either in virtue of the two preceding sections, or by permission of the court, as is hereinafterwards provided for, the court may allow such further time for the arraignment and trial, as they may deem necessary to enable the accused to prepare for his defence.

Art. 283. Whether the accused except to any irregularity in the form of the indictment, or to any variance between the indictment and the copy of the instrument annexed to it, or not, the public prosecutor shall be permitted to amend the same, at any time before the arraignment. If the public prosecutor shall not choose to amend the indictment according to any exception made by the accused, or if the court shall be of opinion that such exception relates to matter of substance, and is not amendable under the provisions of this chapter, a day shall be assigned for the argument of such exceptions, previous to the arraignment ; and if the court shall allow such exception, and consider them as matter of substance, the accused may be again indicted for the same offence, and shall not be, on that account, discharged ; but if the court shall allow the exceptions, after argument, but consider them matter of form only, the public prosecutor may immediately amend them.

Art. 284. If the grand jury which found the indictment was illegally constituted, or not drawn or selected in the manner directed by law, or not sworn; the accused may except thereto, in the manner directed by the article; but if such exception be allowed, it shall be considered as a matter of substance, and no amendment shall be allowed.

Art. 285. If the exception be that it does not appear by the indictment, for what district the grand jurors were summoned, or in what court, or whether they were sworn or not, or whether they were drawn and impanneled in the manner directed by law; it shall be considered as matter of form and amendable, unless the exception state, that in point of fact the grand jury were not summoned from the proper district, or were not sworn, or that they were impanneled in another court, or that the forms prescribed by law were not pursued in the drawing or impanneling their names, in which case, if either of the said last mentioned exceptions of fact are allowed, it shall be considered matter of substance, and shall not be amendable.

Art. 286. If the exception be that the copy of the instrument in writing on which the prosecution is founded, is not contained in the indictment, or that the original is not annexed in cases where, by law, such copy ought to have been inserted, and such original annexed; or that the time and place is not set forth at which the offence is said to have been committed; or that the action or omission alleged, is not one that is by law created an offence; or that where the intent is made a material part of the offence, such intent is not charged; either of these exceptions shall be considered as matter of substance, and shall not be amendable.

Art. 287. All exceptions, other than those enumerated in the three last preceding articles, and therein designated as exceptions to matter of substance, shall be considered as exceptions to matter of form; and shall be amendable in the manner hereinbefore provided for.

Art. 288. After a conviction, no judgment shall be arrested for any allegation of a defect, either in substance or form, other than this; that the act of accusation contains no charge of any thing amounting to an offence, and if such objection be allowed, another indictment or information may immediately be filed, and the defendant shall not be discharged, if the proof adduced on the trial be sufficient to have warranted his arrest.

Art. 289. At the time when the accused is called to make his exception to the indictment, he shall be asked by the court whether he has counsel; and if he shall allege that he is unable to procure counsel, the court shall assign some licensed attorney to conduct his defence under his direction. But the accused may in all cases have the advice and assistance of any one whom he may have engaged, whether licensed or not, to aid him in his defence. But such employment shall not deprive the prosecutor of the right of examining such person as a witness, to state any facts which came to his knowledge, either prior to the prosecution, or which were not confided to him by the accused, after such prosecution was commenced.

Art. 290. If the defendant make no exceptions to the act of accusation, or if, having made any, they are over-ruled, he must next be arraigned : this is done by the clerk, who must read to him the act of accusation in an audible voice, and the judge must interrogate him by asking, " Are you guilty of the charge you have just heard read, or not guilty ?"

Art. 291. This form must not be dispensed with, either on a suggestion that the defendant knows the contents of the act of accusation, or out of delicacy to any defendant.

Art. 292. To this interrogatory of the arraignment, unless he plead the special plea mentioned in the next article, the defendant can only answer in the negative or the affirmative : a refusal to answer, or an evasive or explanatory answer, shall be taken and recorded as an answer of not guilty.

Art. 293. If the defendant have before had judgment

of acquittal, or been convicted of the same offence, he must state that matter specially in writing, and to this plea the public prosecutor may either demur if it be deficient in substance, or reply either that there is no record of any such conviction or acquittal as is pleaded, and on the trial the defendant must produce the record and prove that he is the same person mentioned therein.

Art. 294. If the defendant answer in the affirmative, it shall not be recorded until the court shall have explained its consequence, and desired him to reflect, and if he wishes it, to consult with his counsel : if after this he persevere, the confession shall be recorded ; provided there is no reason to suppose the confession proceeds from insanity, for which purpose, in all cases of CRIME when the party making the confession is in custody, the officer in whose charge he was, shall be interrogated.

Art. 295. When the plea of not guilty is recorded, the public prosecutor shall, under the direction of the court, designate to the defendant a day for the trial, which shall not, without the consent of the defendant, be less than the third day after that on which the notice is given, and this time may be prolonged at the instance of the defendant or of the public prosecutor, under the limitations hereinafter contained.

Art. 296. On application to the clerk, process for summoning the witnesses, as well on the part of the defendant as the public prosecutor, shall be made out, directed to the sheriff of any parish where the witness may be found, who shall be bound to execute the same.

CHAPTER VI.

Of the mode of drawing and summoning the jury.

Art. 297. All offences whatever must be tried by jury.

Art. 298. All free white persons of full age and not

exceeding sixty years of age, who have resided one year in the parish in which they are called to serve, and have paid taxes or been rated on the tax list either for parish, city or state tax, or who have resided six months in the parish and own real property therein, whether they have paid taxes or not, are qualified jurors.

Art. 299. The names of all grand jurors and petit jurors must be drawn by lot before they are put on the panel.

Art. 300. For this purpose, in each of the parishes of this state in which a court, having criminal jurisdiction, shall sit, the parish judge, the sheriff, and two justices of the peace to be designated by the judge, or a majority of them, shall within thirty days after the promulgation of this code, form and sign a list containing the names of the persons having the qualifications above enumerated, who are in their opinion the best qualified, from their education and character, to serve on juries. Such list shall contain a number of names equal at least to two-thirds of the number of voters at the last general election in such parish.

Art. 301. In forming such list, the persons aforesaid shall consult the assessment roll of taxes, and the list of votes taken at the general election next preceding the time of making the list.

Art. 302. No name on the tax list or list of voters shall be excluded from the list to be formed but by the unanimous consent of all the persons hereby appointed to form it.

Art. 303. Any inhabitant of the parish, having the qualifications required, whose name has been omitted on such list for one year, may, if he desire it, have it inserted in the next year's list, by applying either to the sheriff or the parish judge.

Art. 304. When the list is so signed, the same shall be delivered to the parish judge to be filed, and the sheriff shall immediately, in the presence of the judge, of at least one justice, and of as many other citizens as choose to attend, proceed to write each name contained on such list on a separate ballot, all as nearly as may be of the same size and appearance.

Art. 305. The sheriff shall also provide two boxes, each having an opening in the top, that may be closed and locked with two different locks, and shall deposit the said ballots in one of the boxes and lock the openings of both, delivering one of the keys of each to the judge, and keeping the other himself, and shall keep both boxes in his own custody.

Art. 306. At some day, to be designated by the parish judge, between thirty and fifteen days before every session of any court of criminal jurisdiction in the parish, the said judge shall cause notice to be given to the sheriff and to two justices of the peace, to meet at such place as he shall direct ; and the judge shall, in their presence or that of a majority of them, as often as a grand jury shall be required for such court, draw at hazard from the box containing the ballots the names of fifty persons, out of which the sheriff shall elect ten and the judge seven, and the justices of the peace each three names, which shall be inserted on a list to form the panel for the grand jury, but if only one justice attend, he shall select six names, and the ballots containing the names so selected shall be put in the second box, and the residue of the ballots returned to that from which they were taken.

Art. 307. Forty ballots shall in like manner be taken from the first box, and the names contained on them shall be written on a list to form the panel of petit jurors, for the trial of causes in such court at its next session ; and the ballots shall be put in the second box, and both boxes shall then be locked, the keys delivered as before, and the boxes kept in the custody of the sheriff.

Art. 308. The two lists, or the one (in case no grand jury is drawn), shall then be certified by the judge, the sheriff, and at least one justice, to contain the names of those who were drawn and selected to serve as grand jurors, or drawn to serve as petit jurors, and shall be delivered by the sheriff to the clerk of the court, who shall file and record the same.

Art. 309. Any court may by rule direct grand or petit jurors to be summoned at other periods, where the business of the court renders the attendance of one set for a whole session too oppressive.

Art. 310. Every year, within thirty days of the time the first list was made out, a new list shall be in like manner made, and the ballots containing the names shall be put into the box after destroying those of the first year.

Art. 311. So many of the names contained on the list of one year, may be put on that of the succeeding year, as the persons entrusted with the duty may deem proper.

Art. 312. As often as the first box shall be exhausted, the ballots contained in the second shall be transferred to the first.

Art. 313. On receiving such lists, it shall be the duty of the clerk to make out a writ in the form hereinafter in this code contained, with a schedule annexed, containing a true copy of the list of grand jurors, commanding the sheriff to summon the persons named in such list to attend as grand jurors at the next session of the court.

Art. 314. The clerk shall in like manner make out a writ for summoning the petit jury.

Art. 315. The sheriff shall execute such writs in the manner they command, by leaving a printed notice, containing the day and place of attendance, with each juror, or at his place of abode, at least six days before the return of the writ.

Art. 316. Jurors who do not appear when regularly summoned, or who depart without leave of the court, or who violate any legal rule for preserving order in the course of judicial proceedings, may be fined, for each offence, not exceeding ten dollars, and the court may command process to issue immediately for collecting it.

CHAPTER VII.

Of proceedings in court previous to the trial.

SECTION I.

Of postponing a trial.

Art. 317. At any time before the trial, the public prosecutor or the defendant may apply to put it off to a future day, which shall be granted whenever such circumstances shall appear to the court by affidavit, as show justice requires it. But the defendant, if in custody, may be discharged, if he is not brought to trial in the second term after his arrest; and if on bail, during the fourth term after such arrest : provided the delay have not taken place on his application, and that he have been guilty of no contrivance to deprive the prosecutor of his testimony.

Art. 318. The trial must also be postponed if it appear that a copy of the panel of jurors has not been delivered according to the provisions hereinafter contained.

Art. 319. On the day of the trial, the defendant shall be called, if he be on bail, or brought into court, if in custody : the names of the jurors shall then be called, and if not challenged, or if the challenge be overruled, shall be sworn.

Art. 320. If the trial be for a misdemeanor, it may proceed if the defendant appear by his counsel ; if it be for a crime, the defendant must be personally present ; and if on bail, must then be surrendered into the custody of the sheriff, and remain in custody until discharged by due course of law. But the court may at their discretion, when sex, age, or state of health require it, permit the defendant to remain in the custody of his bail during the recess of the court, if the cause cannot be finished in one sitting, or while the jury are out, if any great delay should take place in rendering the verdict.

SECTION II.

Of challenge.

Art. 321. A challenge is an objection made to the jurors who are returned to try the cause, and is of two kinds.

1. To the panel.
2. To any individual juror.

Art. 322. The panel is the list of jurors, either for the grand or trial jury, made by the officers authorized for that purpose, when the names are drawn according to law.

Art. 323. A copy of the panel of the trial jury must be delivered by the sheriff to every defendant, if in custody, or to his bail, if he be delivered to bail, at least three whole days before the day of trial, for the purpose of enabling him to make his challenge.

Art. 324. A challenge to the panel is an objection made to all trial jurors who are summoned ; it can only be grounded on some material departure from the forms prescribed by law for drawing and impanneling juries. But it is not a good cause of challenge to the panel, that one or more persons not having the legal qualifications, have been put on the jury list.

Art. 325. A challenge to the panel must be made in writing, stating the cause of challenge, before any juror is sworn, and the officers, whether judicial or ministerial, as well as any other persons, may be examined, to prove or disprove the irregularity alleged, if the public prosecutor deny the fact. If he admit the fact, but deny the irregularity complained of is material, he may demur to the challenge.

Art. 326. Challenges to individual jurors are of two kinds; peremptory and for cause.

Art. 327. A peremptory challenge is an objection made to a juror for which no reason need be given; it is enough for the defendant to signify his desire that any particular juror who is about to be sworn, shall not serve on the jury, and he shall be set aside; but this right can be exercised only with respect to nine jurors.

Art. 328. Where there are several defendants, each one is entitled to his challenge, both peremptory and for cause; but if they do not agree to let one challenge for the whole, they must be separately tried.

Art. 329. A challenge for cause is an objection made to a particular juror on the allegation of some circumstance that renders him either incapable to serve as a juror in any case, or unfit to serve as such in the one about to be tried. Of the first kind are:

1. Conviction of any offence which by the Code of Crimes and Punishments incurs a forfeiture of the right of serving as a juror.

2. A want of qualifications designated by law as necessary for a juryman.

3. Insanity, or such defect in the organs of hearing, seeing or speaking, or other bodily or mental defect or disease as renders him incapable of performing the duties of a juror.

All these are called principal causes of challenge. When a particular exemption from service on juries is granted by law, it is not a cause of challenge to such person, but a right of which he may avail himself or not.

Art. 330. The causes of challenge of the second kind are either in chief, by the allegation of a fact, which, if proved, is a disqualification by law, or to the favour, by the allegation of some circumstance which is supposed to evince the want of that perfect impartiality necessary in a juror. The causes of challenge in chief are:

1. Relationship within the ninth degree to the person alleged to be injured or attempted to be injured by the

offence charged, or to the person on whose complaint the prosecution was instituted, or to the defendant.

2. Standing in the relation of husband, master or servant, landlord or tenant, tutor or curator, sponsor for the child of one of the said parties, being in his employment on wages, or plaintiff or defendant against him in any civil suit, or having complained against him, or being accused by him in any criminal prosecution.

3. Having served on the grand jury which found the indictment against the defendant on which he is about to be tried.

4. Having served on a petit jury which has convicted or acquitted another person charged with having committed the same offence now about to be tried.

5. Having been one of a jury which was sworn in the same cause against the same defendant, and which jury either gave a verdict which was set aside, or was discharged after hearing evidence for any other cause, except in the case hereinafter provided.

6. Having served as a juror in a civil suit brought against the defendant for the same act.

7. Having formed such an opinion of the guilt or innocence of the defendant, as in the opinion of the juror himself, renders him not an impartial judge.

Art. 331. If either of the facts stated as causes of challenge in the two last preceding articles, be alleged and proved to the satisfaction of the court, the juror challenged for such cause shall not be sworn.

Art. 332. The juror challenged may be sworn, and other evidence may be produced, to show the truth of the cause of challenge, and in the case of the seventh cause above enumerated for challenges in chief, if the juror have formed an opinion, but does not think it disqualifies him, this may be made a case of challenge to the juror in the manner provided by the next article. But no juror shall be obliged to answer, whether he has been convicted or not of a certain crime that would disqualify him.

Art. 333. A juror must come to the performance of his

high duty with a mind perfectly unbiassed ; therefore, if no challenge in chief be made, or, being made, is not proved, the defendant, if he can prove any other circumstance that shows either prejudice against him, or favour to his accuser, may make it a cause of challenge to the favour.

Art. 334. This challenge, like those in chief, is made verbally, and if it be to the first juror who appears, it must be tried by three persons called triers, to be named by the court ; if one juror has been sworn, he, together with two persons named, are the triers ; if two are sworn, the court must name another trier, and when three jurors are sworn, they are the triers of all subsequent challenges to the jurors.

Art. 335. The triers shall be sworn to decide whether the juror challenged is perfectly unbiassed, and free from all prejudice against the defendant, and as a majority of the said triers decide, the juror shall be sworn or the challenge allowed.

Art. 336. A juror against whom a challenge in chief or the favour has been overruled, may be challenged peremptorily.

Art. 337. The public prosecutor may make challenges to the panel or for cause to individual jurors, for the same causes in which they are allowed to the defendant. He has also a right of peremptory challenge to three jurors.

Art. 338. All challenges to individual jurors must be made when they are called to be sworn, but before they are sworn.

CHAPTER VIII.

Of the trial.

Art. 339. The names of all the jurors on the petit jury panel, shall be called, and those who do not appear shall be fined not exceeding ten dollars, which fine on the subsequent appearance of the juror and on his offering a sufficient excuse, to be approved at the discretion of the court, may be remitted.

Art. 340. Either the public prosecutor or the defendant may require, before proceeding to trial, that an attachment issue against the jurors who have made default, on which they shall be arrested and brought forthwith into court.

Art. 341. After waiting such time as the court shall deem reasonable for the return of the attachment, the clerk shall, in open court, put the names of all the jurors on the panel, each written on a separate ballot, folded as near as may be of the same size and shape, into a ballot box, from which they shall be drawn successively, and, if not challenged, sworn in the order in which they are drawn, until the number of twelve shall be complete.

Art. 342. The court has power to excuse any juror from attendance, for reasonable cause, and whenever any number exceeding five have been so excused, or when a sufficient number cannot be brought up on attachment for the trial of a cause, the court may direct the names of a sufficient number of jurors to be drawn from the box, and order them to be summoned to attend immediately, and their names shall be put into the court box and drawn for the trials as is before directed.

Art. 343. Any less number than twelve that may be agreed on between the public prosecutor and the defendant, may try a misdemeanor, but a crime shall not be tried by less than a full jury, drawn by lot in the manner above directed.

Art. 344. The trial shall proceed in the following order:

1. The clerk shall read the indictment or information to the jury, and inform them what answer has been recorded.

2. The public prosecutor shall open the case by reading from the code the description of the offence, and stating, summarily, by what evidence he expects to prove the guilt of the defendant.

3. The public prosecutor shall offer the evidence in support of the prosecution.

4. The defendant, or his counsel, shall open his defence, state in what facts or law he intends to rely, and whether he thinks the evidence for the prosecution insufficient or inapplicable.

5. The defendant shall produce his testimony.

6. The public prosecutor may then introduce testimony to rebut any that has been introduced by the defendant, or, if he do not, he may offer his concluding argument.

7. The defendant closes the argument : previous to which he may introduce testimony to repel that last offered by the prosecutor.

Art. 346. The public prosecutor may at any time during the term request the court to give a direction to find a verdict for the defendant, if he finds that the prosecution cannot be supported, and if the court give such direction, the jury are bound to acquit the defendant, and if they refuse, a new trial shall be immediately granted, or, at the option of the defendant, entry made that the public prosecutor will no longer prosecute for the offence.

Art. 347. The court cannot, for any defect or supposed deficiency of testimony, prevent the jury from giving a verdict.

Art. 348. If a juror on any trial for a crime should be taken with some malady that prevents his performing his duty, the court may order him to be discharged ; and in that case a new jury must be sworn, and the trial must begin again : the same jurors may, if drawn, serve on the new jury, but may be challenged although they were not before.

Art. 349. In misdemeanor, a new juror may be added, or the trial may proceed with those who remain, by the consent of the prosecutor and the defendant.

Art. 350. The court has a discretionary power of adjourning the trial from day to day, if, from the length of the proceedings, it cannot be conveniently finished in one or more sittings, or if any unforeseen circumstance should make it necessary for the attainment of justice to do so.

Art. 351. In the case provided for by the last preceding article, the jury must, unless by consent, be kept together during the recess of the court, at the public expense, under the charge of an officer, who shall be sworn not to permit any one to speak with them touching any matter relative to that trial. This consent cannot be given in cases of crimes punishable with imprisonment for life.

Art. 352. The court may also discharge the jury : 1st. Whenever it appears to them, by the examination of a physician, that a witness on either side, who has not been examined or discharged, and who is proved to be a material one, has been taken sick since the commencement of the trial, and cannot be examined in court without danger to his life, and there is no probability of his speedy recovery. 2nd. Where the defendant himself is so taken sick. 3rd. Where a material witness on the part of the prosecution has been concealed, or induced to abscond or conceal himself by the defendant, or any one employed by him ; or where such witness for the defendant is concealed, or has been induced to conceal himself or abscond, by the public prosecutor, the complainant, or the person supposed to be injured by the offence, or by any one employed by either of them.

Art. 353. The judge shall decide all questions of law arising in the course of the trial, and shall keep notes of all the testimony offered on either side.

Art. 354. When the pleadings are finished, the judge shall give his charge to the jury, in which he shall state to them all such matters of law as he shall think necessary for their information in giving their verdict. But he shall not recapitulate the testimony unless requested so to do by one or more of the jurors, if there should be any difference of opinion between them as to any particular part of the testimony, and then he shall confine his information to the part on which information is required : it being the intent of this article that the jury shall decide all questions of fact, in which is included the credit due to the witnesses who have been sworn, unbiassed by the opinion of the court.

Art. 355. After hearing the charge, the jury may either decide in court, or retire for consultation. If they cannot immediately agree, an officer must be sworn, in the manner set forth in the subsequent chapter, to take charge of them; and they must then retire to a chamber prepared for them.

Art. 356. Before leaving the court, the jury must appoint one of their number to be foreman: whose duty it is to preside in their debates, to deliver the verdict, or ask any information from the court that may be required by the jury. If a majority do not agree in the appointment of a foreman, he shall be named by the court.

Art. 357. Whenever, in the opinion of the court, it may be deemed proper and convenient that the jury should have a view of the place in which the offence is said to have been committed, or of any other place in which any other transaction material to the inquiry on the trial took place, an order shall be made to that effect, and the jury shall be conducted in a body under the care of the sheriff, to the place, which shall be shown to them by a person appointed by the court, and it shall be the duty of the sheriff to suffer no other person to speak to the jury, and they shall, when the view is finished, be immediately conducted into court.

CHAPTER IX.

Of the conduct of the jury after receiving the charge.

Art. 358. When the jury have retired, they must proceed to deliberate on their verdict. If there be any disagreement between them as to any part of the testimony, or if any juror wish to be informed of any point of law arising in the cause, the officer having charge of them shall bring them into court, where the information shall be given in the presence of, or after notice to, the defendant or his counsel, and to the public prosecutor.

Art. 359. After having received the information required, the jury may again return, and shall not be discharged until they are all agreed on their verdict, unless it shall appear to the court that there is no probability that they will agree, and that the health of one or more of the jurors will be endangered by the confinement.

Art. 360. The jury to be kept during the time of their retirement without any other sustenance than bread and water, except during the adjournments from day to day, mentioned in the last chapter ; and they are to speak to no one, except in case of such adjournment, but the officer who attends them, and with him they are to have no other communication than necessity requires.

Art. 361. If one of the jurors, after they have retired, should be taken so sick as to prevent the continuance of his duty, the jury must be discharged, unless, in cases of misdemeanor, it is agreed between the public prosecutor and the defendant, that the remaining jurors shall decide the cause. This agreement cannot be made in case of crime.

Art. 362. In all cases where power is given to the court to discharge a jury, it operates no discharge of the defendant, but a new jury must be sworn to try the cause.

Art. 363. The court may adjourn while the jury are deliberating on their verdict, and if the jury should agree before the next meeting of the court, if the cause in which they are impanneled be a misdemeanor, they may write and sign their verdict, which must be left with the foreman, sealed, and the jurors are then at liberty to disperse, but must be all present in court at its opening ; when the foreman must deliver it to the court, which shall be openly read, and, if agreed to by all the jurors, shall be recorded.

Art. 364. A sealed verdict cannot be given in cases of crime even by consent.

Art. 365. The jury shall take with them all papers that have been received as evidence in the cause, or copies of such parts of public records, books or other documents as cannot without inconvenience be taken from the persons having charge of them. They may also take with them notes of the testimony which one or more of them have taken, but none made by any other person.

Art. 366. If a juror have any personal knowledge respecting any fact in controversy in the cause, it is his duty to make the declaration in open court during the trial. If, during the retirement, any juror declare any fact that could be evidence in the cause, to his fellows, as of his own knowledge, it is the duty of the other members to return with him into court ; and, in both cases, the juror making the statement must be sworn as a witness, and examined in the presence of the parties.

Art. 367. A mere declaration of the credit or want of credit any juror gives to a witness, does not come within the last preceding article.

Art. 368. The court may punish by fine not exceeding twenty dollars, any such breach of the duties prescribed to grand or petit jurors as are imposed upon them by law, other than such as are specially created offences, which must be prosecuted by information.

Art. 369. No juror shall be punished for any opinion or vote he may have given in deliberating on or in giving his verdict.

CHAPTER X.

Of the verdict.

Art. 370. When the jury have agreed in their verdict, they shall be conducted by the officer having charge of them into court ; when their names shall be called, and if all do not appear, the rest shall be discharged without giving a verdict.

Art. 371. If the whole jury appear, the defendant shall

be called if he be out on bail, or brought into court if he be in custody.

Art. 372. In case of misdemeanor, the defendant may answer, when called, by his attorney or counsel, both at the trial and when the verdict is brought in, and the bail is answerable in the amount of the recognizance if the defendant do not surrender himself to receive judgment. When imprisonment forms a part of the judgment, it may at any time afterwards be inflicted if the defendant be found, notwithstanding the payment of the penalty of the recognizance.

Art. 373. When the jury have returned into court, they shall be asked whether they have agreed on their verdict, and if the foreman answer in the affirmative, they shall, on being required, give the same verbally, or, if it be written, the foreman shall read the same.

Art. 374. The form must be either " guilty " or " not guilty," which is a general verdict, and imports an acquittal or conviction on all the facts charged ; or, in cases where the jurors are in doubt whether the facts that have been proved amount to any offence on which they can decide under the charge in the act of accusation, they may find a special verdict.

Art, 375. A special verdict is a statement of the facts which have been proved to the satisfaction of the jury, with a conclusion that, being uncertain whether such facts are sufficient to establish in law the guilt of the defendant, they submit that point to the decision of the court.

Art. 376. A special verdict shall be argued at such time and in such manner as shall be directed by the rules of court, but the counsel for the defendant shall conclude the argument.

Art. 377. If, after argument, the court shall be of opinion that the facts found prove the defendant is guilty of the offence charged in the act of accusation, or of any other of which he could be convicted under that act of accusation, according to the rules hereinafter established, they shall proceed to pronounce judgment accordingly.

Art. 378. If the facts found show that the act does not amount to any such offence as the defendant could have been convicted on, under that act of accusation, they shall pronounce a judgment of acquittal.

Art. 379. In either of the cases mentioned in the two last preceding articles, the judgment shall be a bar to any future prosecution for the same offence.

Art. 380. If the jury do not pronounce affirmatively or negatively on facts necessary to establish the guilt or the innocence of the defendant, the court shall direct a new trial.

Art. 381. On an act of accusation for any offence coming within the general description of homicide, the jury may find the defendant guilty of homicide in any degree lower than that charged in the indictment; the degrees are measured by the order in which the offences are described in the code, those first described being lowest in degree.

Art. 382. On acts of accusation for battery, aggravated by any of the circumstances which enhance the guilt of the offender, the jury may find him guilty only of simple assault and battery; if several circumstances of aggravation are charged in the act of accusation, they may find him guilty of one or more; but no one can be found guilty of an act of aggravation not charged.

Art. 383. If the charge made by the act of accusation be of theft, aggravated by any of the circumstances which would enhance the guilt of the offence, whether such circumstances as give it another denomination (such as robbery or stealing from the person) or not, the defendant may be found guilty of simple theft, or of theft aggravated by any one or more of the circumstances charged.

Art. 384. If the charge be simple theft, a verdict may be given for any fraudulent appropriation of property that by law is created an offence.

Art. 385. In the cases coming within the purview of the three last preceding articles, the acquittal or conviction is a bar to any other prosecution for the same act, although the subsequent accusation should add a charge of other intent or circumstance.

Art. 386. If a former conviction be charged, either in the act of accusation or by notice, it may negative that fact, or affirm it specially, or by a general verdict.

Art. 387. In every other case not herein specially provided for, the defendant may be found guilty of any offence, the commission of which is necessarily included in that of which he is accused in the act of accusation.

Art. 388. If the defence in any accusation of crime be insanity in the defendant, and the jury acquit him on that ground, they must add that finding to their verdict ; and thereupon the court is authorized to make such order for the confinement of the defendant in a hospital or otherwise, or for the delivery of him to his relations, as humanity and public safety may require.

Art. 389. If, on the trial for any offence, it should appear by the testimony that an offence of a higher nature has been committed than the one charged as arising from the same circumstances, the court must direct the jury to be discharged, and a new indictment sent to the grand jury for the higher offence.

Art. 390. They may also direct the jury to be discharged where there is any such defect in the indictment or other proceedings, as will prevent a trial on the merits, and may, in such case, order the defendant to be committed for any offence that the testimony had shown he had committed.

Art. 391. If a verdict of acquittal shall be given on any act of accusation, so defective that no judgment could have been given against the defendant if he had been convicted, he shall not be discharged, but may again be indicted and brought to trial for the same offence.

Art. 392. When the jury shall find the defendant not guilty on an accusation, for any offence founded on a written instrument, under the chapter of the Penal Code entitled " Of offences affecting the credit of written contracts," the court shall inquire, and the jury must declare whether they find such instrument to be false or forged, or made contrary to any of the provisions of that chapter, and if they find that the instrument is not false or forged, nor made contrary to any of those provisions, the instrument shall be delivered to the person from whose possession it was taken.

Art. 393. If on such accusation the defendant is convicted, or if the jury, under the direction of the last preceding article, have found that the instrument was false, forged, or made in contravention of any provision in the chapter above referred to, the instrument shall remain attached to the indictment, until the court shall make other order, which they may do in case any civil suit be recommended which may render the production thereof necessary to any party in such suit; but on such terms and on such security, as the court may deem proper to prevent fraud.

Art. 394. When there is a verdict of acquittal, the court cannot require the jury to reconsider it; but when there is a verdict of conviction, in which it appears to the court that the jury have mistaken the law, they may explain the reason why they think so, and direct the jury to go out and reconsider the verdict; but if after such reconsideration they return with the same verdict, it must be entered.

Art. 395. In like manner, if the jury bring in a verdict that is neither an acquittal, nor a conviction, nor a special verdict, the court may direct the jury to reconsider the verdict, and it shall not be recorded until it is brought in in some form from which it can be clearly understood what is the intent of the jury, whether to acquit, to convict, or state facts and leave the judgment to the court.

Art. 396. If the jury persevere in finding an informal verdict, from which, however, it can be clearly understood that their intent is to acquit, it shall be entered in the terms in which they found it, and the court shall give judgment of acquittal; but no judgment shall be given against a defendant unless the jury expressly find him guilty, or judgment be given against him on a special verdict.

Art. 397. If the court or either of the parties think that all the jurors have not agreed to the verdict that may have been given by the foreman, they shall severally be asked whether they agree, and if any one answers in the negative, the whole jury shall be sent out for further deliberation.

Art. 398. When the verdict is given, and is such as the court must receive, the clerk records it on the minutes of the court, which he must do immediately, without attending to any other business ; and when it is recorded in full, he must read it to the jury, and demand whether they all agree : if any juror disagree, the record must be cancelled, and the jury again sent out ; if no objection be made, the jury must be discharged.

CHAPTER XI.

Of the proceedings after verdict to judgment.

Art. 399. If the defendant be acquitted, and is not detained for any other legal cause, he is entitled to his discharge as soon as the verdict is recorded, except in the cases hereinbefore provided, where the court may order a detention and a new act of accusation ; unless the public prosecutor shall declare that he intends to move for a new trial for some of the legal causes hereinafter set forth, or shall request that he may be detained on an allegation that he has other charges to exhibit against him : but such motion must be made, or such charges must be exhibited in a legal form, within twelve hours after the acquittal, or the defendant must be discharged, if in custody, and his bail is exonerated if he be delivered to bail.

Art. 400. No prisoner acquitted by a verdict or discharged for want of prosecution, shall be detained for any costs or fees of office, or any debts incurred for his subsistence while in custody.

Art. 401. If the defendant be convicted, he must be remanded, if in custody, to the prison, until judgment shall be pronounced.

CHAPTER XII.

Of new trials and motions in arrest of judgment.

SECTION I.

Of new trials.

Art. 402. A new trial is a rehearing of the cause before another jury, after a verdict has been given on the same act of accusation.

Art. 403. The allowance of a motion for a new trial places the parties precisely in the state in which they were immediately before the first trial. All the testimony must be heard again ; and the first verdict cannot be made use of either as evidence or in argument.

Art. 404. Courts have power to grant new trials in the cases enumerated in this section.

Art. 405. After acquittal, either by general verdict or when a special verdict is found, new trials may be granted on the motion of the public prosecutor in the following cases, and no other :

1. When the defendant, or any one for his benefit, has bribed a juror, or suborned or bribed a witness, or has given any forged paper in evidence, on the first trial, which might, in the opinion of the court, have changed the verdict.

2. When the defendant, or any one for his benefit, has either by force, threats or persuasion, prevented any material witness from appearing against him on the first

trial ; or has destroyed or secreted any written document, material to the prosecution, and which might otherwise have been produced.

3. When evidence in favour of the accused shall have been given to the jury out of court, without the order of the court, and the consent of the public prosecutor.

4. When by the procurement of the defendant, or of any one for his benefit, the jury which tried the cause was illegally impanneled, but no illegality in the panel unless caused by such procurement, shall be a good cause for a new trial after acquittal.

Art. 406. No irregularity committed by the jury shall be a good cause for setting aside a verdict of acquittal.

Art. 407. New trials, after a verdict of conviction, may be granted on the application of the defendant, in the following cases and no other :

1. When the defendant, being in custody, was not brought into court at the trial or at the time the verdict was delivered.

2. When he has been tried without being called on to make his exceptions to the act of accusation and other proceedings in the manner directed in the fifth chapter of this title.

3. When any one has bribed a juror to give a verdict against the defendant ; or has forged an instrument in writing which has been produced in evidence against him ; or when any of his material witnesses have by force, threats or persuasion, been prevented from attending on the trial ; or when a written instrument, material to his defence, has been intentionally destroyed or secreted for the purpose of procuring his conviction—provided in this last case, that the instrument was legal testimony, and that the defendant had reason to expect its production on the trial.

4. When material evidence has been discovered since the trial which may be procured on a new trial, which could not by due diligence have been discovered before ; and which, in the opinion of the court, might have changed the verdict had it been produced.

5. When the jury has received any other evidence, out of court, than that resulting from a view as hereinbefore directed, without leave of the court and the consent of the defendant : when they have decided their verdict by chance ; or have separated after they had retired to consult on their verdict, and before they have given it in, except in cases of sealed verdicts, as is hereinbefore provided.

6. When the verdict is, in the opinion of the court, contrary to law or evidence ; but no more than two new trials shall be given for this cause alone.

7. When the defendant has been tried without the assistance of counsel, when he has prayed that counsel should be assigned him.

8. When the court has misdirected the jury on any point of law, or given them any direction how to find any point of fact, to the prejudice of the defendant.

Art. 408. No new trial shall be granted on the allegation of the perjury of a witness, or the production of forged papers, unless the fact of perjury or forgery appear by the oath of two credible witnesses, or of one witness and strong circumstantial proof ; and unless it shall appear, that the party making the application was surprised by the production of such false evidence, and could not, by reasonable diligence, have been apprised of the intention to produce it ; or that the evidence to prove the forgery or perjury came to his knowledge after the trial, and could not, by reasonable diligence, have been discovered before.

Art. 409. In all cases of applications for a new trial, such of the facts on which it is founded, as may reasonably be supposed to be within the knowledge of the party making it, must be declared by his affidavit, supported by such other testimony, where the case admits of it, as may be satisfactory to the court.

Art. 410. Applications for a new trial, on the part of the defendant, must be made within three days after the entry of the verdict on the part of the prosecution ; it must be made in the manner and within the time specified by the first article of the eleventh chapter of this title. All applications for new trials must be in writing.

SECTION II.

Of motions in arrest of judgment.

Art. 411. A motion in arrest of judgment is a request made to the court, after conviction, praying that no judgment be rendered on the verdict. It must be founded on a defect apparent on the act of accusation.

Art. 412. No judgment can be arrested for a defect of form.

Art. 413. The only matter of substance for which a judgment can be arrested is this, that the act of accusation contains no charge of any fact, or of any fact coupled with an intent, that is by law declared to be an offence. The court may, on its own view of this defect, arrest the judgment without motion.

Art. 414. The effect of allowing a motion in arrest of judgment is to place the defendant in the same state, with respect to the prosecution, in which he was before the indictment was found, or the information was filed. If from the testimony, on the trial, there is sufficient reason to believe him guilty of the offence for which he was first arrested, a new indictment shall be sent to the grand jury; or a new information shall be filed, as the case may require; and the defendant shall remain in custody, or be delivered to bail. If the evidence show him guilty of another offence, he shall be committed or bailed on such charge : and in neither case shall the verdict bar a new prosecution. If no evidence appear sufficient to charge him with any offence, he shall be discharged, and the arrest of judgment shall operate as an acquittal of the charge on which he was arrested.

Art. 415. Motions in arrest of judgment must be made within three days after the entry of the verdict.

CHAPTER XIII.

Of the judgment and its incidents.

SECTION I.

Of the judgment.

Art. 416. If, within three days after a verdict has been entered, no motion in arrest of judgment, or for a new trial, has been made, or, having been made, has been overruled, the court shall proceed to render judgment.

Art. 417. For this purpose the defendant shall be brought into court, if in custody; or surrendered, if delivered on bail.

Art. 418. In cases of misdemeanor, where the defendant has been bailed, and has appeared by attorney, or in person, at the trial, and when the verdict was delivered, but does not appear to receive judgment, sentence may be pronounced in his absence. If the sentence be fine only, it shall be recovered from the bail, but only to the amount of the recognizance, and after DISCUSSION of the property of the defendant.

Art. 419. If, under the circumstances set forth in the last preceding article, the judgment be fine and imprisonment, or imprisonment alone, and the defendant does not surrender himself before the return of the process of execution, the bail is liable to the amount of the recognizance, and the sentence of imprisonment may afterwards be executed whenever the defendant is found.

Art. 420. The defendant being at the bar, the verdict shall be read to him, and he shall be asked whether he have any legal cause to show why judgment should not be pronounced against him.

Art. 421. It will be good cause to show, in answer to this address :

1. That the defendant has received a pardon from the constitutional authority. On the production of which, legally authenticated, the defendant shall be discharged, if the pardon be unconditional, and if there be no other legal cause for his detention but that on which the pardon operates ; but if the pardon be conditional, and the fulfilment of any of its conditions requires his further detention, he shall be recommitted.

2. It may be alleged on behalf of the defendant, that he is INSANE ; and, if the application be supported by such proofs as satisfy the court of the fact, judgment shall not be pronounced, unless a jury, to be impanneled for that purpose, in the manner hereinafter directed, shall decide that he is not insane.

3. The defendant may state, that he has good cause to offer either in arrest of judgment or for a new trial, and that by some unavoidable accident, or cause, over which he had no control, he was prevented from submitting the motion in the time prescribed ; and if such accident, or cause, be shown to the satisfaction of the court, the judgment shall be deferred ; and they shall proceed, as in other cases, to decide on the motion in arrest of judgment, or for a new trial.

4. He may allege that he is not the person against whom the verdict was pronounced, and pray that his identity may be inquired of by a jury ; and if he shall make affidavit of the truth of such allegation, a jury shall be impanneled to try and determine on the identity of the person, at such time as the court shall direct.

Art. 422. If a defendant, sentenced to imprisonment, shall escape before he has been committed, the sentence cannot be executed on any person who shall be apprehended under an allegation, or suspicion, of his being the delinquent, until he has been brought before the court, and asked if he have any cause to show why the sentence should not be executed : when, if an allegation of non-identity be made, and supported by affidavit, the same proceedings shall take place as are provided for by the last article; and until such decision, he shall be kept in custody.

Art. 423. In cases where the court has a discretionary power as to the measure or selection of the punishment, if either the public prosecutor or the defendant shall allege that he has matter to offer which ought to produce an increase or diminution of the punishment, which did not appear on the trial, the court may hear the same, or in their discretion give time to produce it : provided it apply to some one of the points set forth in the next following section. But no evidence shall be taken of any circumstance in aggravation which was, or ought to have been, alleged in the act of accusation ; or in alleviation, which might have been produced on the trial to show the defendant not to be guilty.

Art. 424. If no application, in either of the modes above provided for, shall be made for arresting or suspending the judgment, or if, being made, they should be overruled, the court shall proceed to enter their judgment on the minutes of the court, and to declare it to the defendant, which is called passing the sentence.

Art. 425. In all cases of crime and of misdemeanor, prosecuted separately, the sentence of each prisoner shall be pronounced severally, but in the presence and hearing of all who may have been convicted during the same term of the court.

Art. 426. The judge who pronounces sentence must perform this duty in a manner that he may deem the best calculated to give effect to the example upon the hearers ; the strictest silence must be observed by those who are present ; and it should be accompanied with such reflections as may impress on the mind the importance of obedience to the laws, and the dangers and infamy of infringing them.

Art. 427. When sentence is pronounced for murder, the seat and table of the court shall be hung in black, and the prisoner shall, immediately after the sentence is pronounced, be enveloped in a black mantle that shall cover his whole body, with a cowl or veil drawn over his head ; and shall be thus conveyed in a cart, hung with black, to the place of his confinement.

Art. 428. If the judgment be the imposition of a fine, the clerk shall, without delay, issue execution for its recovery in the manner directed by law.

Art. 429. If the sentence direct the forfeiture of, or suspension from, the exercise of any office, or of any political or civil right, one copy of the judgment shall be sent to the governor, who shall cause it to be filed and recorded in the office of the secretary of state, and published for one week in the gazette printed by the state printer.

Art. 430. If the sentence be for imprisonment, the sheriff shall deliver a copy of the judgment, together with the body of the defendant, to the keeper of the prison in which the sentence is to be executed.

SECTION II.

Of the exercise of the discretionary power given to the court in the selection and apportionment of punishments.

Art. 431. Laws apparently equal in their provisions become unequal and unjust if indiscriminately applied, without modification, to all who become subject to their operation. A difference of physical force or moral feelings, in several culprits, may render the same punishment light to one which would be intolerable to another. Certain circumstances, moreover, attending the commission of the same kind of offence, may render it more or less immoral, injurious or difficult to be repressed. No legislation can be sufficiently minute to provide for all these gradations. The deficiency can only be supplied by vesting in the judge, who applies the law, a discretionary power, within certain limits, to select the kind of punishment adapted to the case, and to increase or diminish its degree. The exercise of this discretion forms one of the most important and difficult functions of the judiciary power: in practice, it must of necessity be irregular ; but, in order to render it as uniform as the nature of the case will admit, the following rules are established, and these principles are enounced in order more effectually to impress on the mind of the judge that the discretion, vested in him by law, is not an arbitrary power, to be exercised according to his caprice, or his feelings, or to gratify his passions ; but that it is required to be an act of sound judgment, guided by views of utility, justice, and good morals ;—and that in using the power vested in him, of selecting, of increasing, and of diminishing the punishment, he must act as he supposes the legislature would have done, had it been possible for them to provide for the particular case under his consideration.

Art. 432. The scale of punishment, in this system of penal law, is so graduated, that the medium between the highest and lowest punishments, where a discretion is given, is intended to be applied to offences marked by no circumstances of extenuation or aggravation.

Art. 433. The following are to be considered as circumstances of aggravation. The effect they are to have in the increase of punishment cannot be prescribed, but is left to the discretion of the judge, within the limits given by law, in each case :

1. If the person committing the offence was, by the duties of his office, or by his CONDITION, obliged to prevent the particular offence committed, or to bring offenders committing it to justice.

2. If he held any other public office, although not one requiring the suppression of the particular offence.

3. Although holding no office, if his education, fortune, profession, or reputation, placed him in a situation in which his example would probably influence the conduct of others.

4. When the offence was committed with premeditation.

5. Or in consequence of a plan formed with others.

6. When the defendant endeavoured to induce others to join in committing the offence.

7. When the CONDITION of the offender created a trust which was broken by the offence, or when it afforded him easier means of committing the offence.

8. When, in the commission of the offence, any other injury was offered than that necessarily suffered by the offence itself; such as wanton cruelty, or humiliating language, in cases of personal injury.

9. When it was attended with the breach of any other moral duty than that necessarily broken in committing the offence; such as personal injury accompanied by in-gratitude.

10. When the injury was offered to one whose age, sex, office, conduct, or CONDITION, entitled him to respect from the offender.

11. When the injury was offered to one whose age, sex, or infirmity rendered incapable of resistance.

12. When the general character of the defendant is marked by those passions or vices, which generally lead to the commission of the offence of which he has been convicted.

13. Whenever the injury has been offered without any provocation on the part of the person suffering by it, and no other circumstances of aggravation or extenuation appear, the medium punishment is that which ought to be inflicted. The existence of such provocation is herein-after made a motive of extenuation; but when the act was done from mere malignity of disposition, and not under the influence of any of those passions which gene-rally actuate mankind, it is an aggravation of the offence.

Art. 434. There are also circumstances which ought to enhance the punishment, although they form no aggra-vation of the offence; these are:

1. The frequency of the offence. In most cases where the law is well administered, this can only take place when the gratification derived from the offence is more than equivalent to the evil produced by the punishment.

When the observation of the magistrate induces him to believe that this is the cause of the increase of the crime, it should be a motive with him to exercise the discretion given him to augment the punishment.

2. The wealth of the offender. Where this is great, in all cases of fine, the penalty must be increased in proportion. In all cases where the punishment is an alternative of fine or imprisonment, or cumulation of both, and the wealth of the offender is so great as to render the payment of the highest fine that can be imposed a matter of little importance to him, imprisonment ought to be inflicted, unless some of the other circumstances, which are herein directed to be considered, should render it improper.

Art. 435. The following circumstances are to be considered in alleviation of the punishment :

1. The minority of the offender : if so young as to justify a supposition that he was ignorant of the law, or that he acted under the influence of another, although he may have attained the age fixed by law for rendering him responsible, and although he have not committed the offence by such command, persuasion, or aid, as by the " Penal Code " entitle him to a certain diminution of punishment.

2. If the offender was so old as to render it probable that the faculties of his mind were weakened.

3. The CONDITION of the offender. This in the several relations of wife, child, apprentice, and ward, is specifically provided for under certain circumstances, in the Penal Code. Those CONDITIONS under other circumstances than those there detailed ; and all other CONDITIONS, which suppose the party to have been influenced in committing the offence by another, standing in a correlative superior situation to him, afford inducements for diminishing the degree of punishment.

4. The order of a superior military officer is no justification for committing a crime, but under circumstances of misapprehension of the duty of obedience, may be shown in extenuation of the offence.

5. When the offence was committed under a combination of circumstances, and under the influence of motives which may not probably recur either with respect to the offender or to any other.

6. The measure of increased punishment for a repetition of offences of the SAME NATURE, is prescribed by the Penal Code; therefore, the medium punishment is that which is intended for the first offence when it is not attended by any circumstance of aggravation or extenuation: but if the party, convicted for the first offence, have previously sustained a good character, and that offence be the only one of ANY NATURE that he has committed, such good character and exemption from other offences, is a motive for lessening the punishment.

7. When the offence has been caused by great provocation, or other cause sufficient to excite in men of ordinary tempers such passions as require unusual strength of mind to restrain.

8. The state of health of the delinquent and the sex (if a female) must be considered in the nature and duration of imprisonment, where that is a part of the sentence.

Art. 436. In selecting the particular kind of punishment, where there is a discretion, attention should be paid to the sex, the constitution, the fortune, the education, and habits of life of the offender. It is apparent that hard labour is not the same punishment, when applied in the same degree, to one used all his life to bodily exertion, and to another bred up to literary pursuits; to a robust man and to a delicate woman. That incapacity to be elected to public office will be a greater penalty to one used to public life, than to him whose pursuits and education have fitted only for attention to his own affairs; and that the possessor of a large fortune will consider a moderate fine as no punishment.

Art. 437. This section is from its nature recommendatory; and obligatory only on the conscience of the judge; it is intended to direct, not to confine, the exercise of his discretion. The only obligation it creates is the moral one of exercising his power on this subject so as to apportion his punishment, not only to the offence, but to the motives and other circumstances of the offender; so as to equalize, as far as possible, the effects of the punishment, and cause it, by a proper selection, to counteract the passions which produced it.

Art. 438. All matters in aggravation, which form no part of the charge in the act of accusation, and matters of extenuation which do not amount to a legal defence, and which have not necessarily or incidentally appeared to the court on the trial, may be produced, either by the examination of witnesses in open court, or by their affidavits, as the court may deem most conducive to justice in each particular case ; but the opposite party must, in all cases, have an opportunity of cross-examining the witnesses, if he require it, and of producing counter-proof.

CHAPTER XIV.

Of forms to be used in judicial proceedings in court.

SECTION I.

Of oaths and affirmations.

Art. 439. An affirmation is a solemn declaration made before a person authorized to receive it, attesting the truth of a statement already made, or about to be made, by the affirmant, or the truth or sincerity of a promise made by him.

Art. 440. An oath is a similar declaration, accompanied by a religious invocation of the Supreme Being to bear witness to the truth of the declaration or the sincerity of the promise, and agreeing to renounce the blessing of God and the respect of man if the engagement should be broken.

Art. 441. In order the better to enforce the obligation of an oath upon those who might disregard its religious and penal sanctions, an honorary engagement is expressly added in the form established by this Code.

Art. 442. An oath or affirmation can be legally administered, only by a court, a magistrate, or some one specially commissioned to perform that function.

Art. 443. If the person to whom the oath is to be administered profess the Christian religion, the oath shall be taken in the following form. The deponent shall lay his hand on the scripture of the New Testament, and shall, with an audible voice, repeat the following formula : " I swear, in the presence of Almighty God, and by His holy word ; and on the faith of a person of probity and honour declare that [here he shall repeat the purport of the oath]—and may God so bless and man so honour me as this oath is truly and sincerely made."

Art. 444. If the person to whom the oath is to be administered be one of the Jewish religion, he shall take it with his head covered, with one hand on the gospels of the Old Testament, and shall repeat the formula denoted by the last preceding article.

Art. 445. If the deponent profess any religion, according to the tenets of which any other ceremony is necessary to give the sanction of religion to the oath, such ceremony shall be observed.

Art. 446. The sanction of religion is added only to strengthen the legal force of the engagement ; any error, therefore, in that part of the form, either as respects the Christian or any other religion, will not affect the civil obligation or the penal consequences of its breach, nor can any ecclesiastical power dissolve or lessen its force.

Art. 447. If the person professing the Christian religion, to whom an oath is tendered, shall declare that he has religious scruples against swearing with his hand on the scriptures, that part of the ceremony shall be omitted ; but he shall raise his right hand, repeat the same formula that is above directed for those professing that religion, omitting only the words, " and by His holy word."

Art. 448. Instead of an oath, in all cases where it is required or permitted by law, an affirmation shall be made by those who are members of any religious sect, according to the tenets of which it is considered irreligious to take an oath, and such affirmation is declared, in all respects, to be equivalent to an oath; and its breach, or falsity, incurs the same penalties with the breach or falsity of an oath.

Art. 449. The declaration of the affirmant that he belongs to such sect as is mentioned in the last preceding article, shall be sufficient proof of the fact; but, although it should be false, the affirmation shall be as valid, and its breach or falsity shall produce the same consequences as if his declaration had been true.

Art. 450. The affirmant shall pronounce, in an audible voice, the following formula: "I do solemnly, sincerely, and truly declare and affirm, that [the purport of the affirmation must be here enounced.]"

Art. 451. No oath need be administered to an executive officer of justice (after he has taken his oath of office), that he has done or will do any act that is required of him by the duties of his office; a declaration to that effect, signed by the officer in cases where his signature is required, is sufficient; and the breach or falsity of such declaration incurs all the penalties that would have ensued on the breach or falsity of an oath.

Art. 452. Nothing in the last article contained shall prevent the swearing and examination of an officer of justice as to the manner in which an official act was performed, when those circumstances become a matter of controversy; the intent of the said article being to avoid the multiplicity of oaths which occurs by the swearing of executive officers to the truth of their returns, in order to fine witnesses or jurors for non-attendance, making affidavits to the service of notices, swearing them to go out with a juror, or with the jury when they retire to deliberate, and other official acts of the like nature ordered by the court.

Art. 453. All returns of the manner in which any

written order has been executed, or any written notice has been delivered, must be in writing, endorsed on or annexed to the order or notice, or on copies thereof, and signed by the officer who has executed it.

Art. 454. When the duty which has been performed, is not the service of any written order or notice, it shall be proved by verbal declaration of the officer, in open court, and noted on the minutes.

Art. 455. The formula of the verbal declaration of any official act that has been performed, and referred to in the preceding article, is as follows : " I do declare, under the sanction of my oath of office, that I did, &c. [enounce the particulars of the service performed.]"

Art. 456. When the duty is an official one, but to be performed by an officer especially designated by the court for the purpose, the obligation to perform it is incurred by the clerk stating, in the form prescribed, the duty that is to be performed, and the assent of the officer verbally given to perform it.

Art. 457. The formula for the statement to be made by the clerk, under the last preceding article, is as follows, addressing himself to the officer, he shall say : " You are required, under the sanction of your oath of office, to [keep this jury, &c., or any other official act.] Will you perform this duty ? " To which the officer shall answer, " I will."

Art. 458. The oaths, affirmations, and declarations, to be administered in the course of judicial proceeding, in a court of criminal jurisdiction, are the following, each of them to be begun and concluded by the formula hereinbefore prescribed for each of these engagements :

1. That of a grand juror. " I swear, &c., as one of the grand jurors for this district, I will diligently inquire, and true presentment make, of all such offences as this court has cognizance of : that I will present no one from hatred or malice, nor leave any one unpresented from favour, affection, reward, or the hope of reward. But that I will, to the best of my ability, perform all the

duties enjoined upon me as a grand juror, and may God so bless, &c."

2. The oath of a petit juror. " I will, without passion, prejudice, or favour, hear the proofs and arguments offered in this cause, and determine on the truth of the accusation submitted to my decision ; and give a true verdict according to law and the evidence, and, &c."

3. The oath of a witness. "The evidence I am about to give, shall be the truth, the whole truth, and nothing but the truth, under the direction of the court as to the legality of the testimony."

4. The oath of a deponent to an affidavit. " What is stated in this affidavit, as of my own knowledge, is true, [if any other matter be stated, add] and all the other matters stated as true, I believe to be true."

5. Declaration of an officer of the service of a verbal order or notice. " That I did, on the   day of now last past, give notice to A. B. that his attendance was immediately required in this court as a juror or witness."

6. Statement and direction to an executive officer to perform the duty of going out with a juror or jurors during a trial. " You are required, &c., to go out with such of the jurors as have leave of the court. You shall not suffer any one to speak to them, nor shall you yourself speak to them, unless it be to require their return to the court, and you shall return with them without any unnecessary delay."

7. The like direction to keep the jury during their retirement. " You are required, &c., to keep this jury in some convenient place, without food and drink, save bread and water, unless with leave of the court. You shall suffer no one to speak to any of them, neither shall you speak to them yourself, without such leave ; unless it be to ask them whether they be agreed on their verdict ; and you shall return with them into court when they are so agreed ; [in cases where a secret verdict is permitted, the following clause shall be added,] or you shall suffer them to disperse after having made a secret verdict, if they shall obtain leave of the court for that purpose."

Art. 459. All affidavits must be certified to have been sworn or affirmed by the clerk of the court, if taken in court, with the style of the court ; or by the magistrate or commissioner, with the addition of their offices ; and must be signed by the deponent in his handwriting if he can write, or with his mark if he cannot.

Art. 460. An oath, taken in court, shall be administered by the judge or the clerk, by either enouncing the formula of the oath to the person who takes it, and causing him to repeat it after him, or giving it to him in writing that he may read it aloud.

Art. 461. Strict silence shall be observed by all but those occupied in administering and repeating the oath ; and the court shall, during that time, transact no other business.

Art. 462. If any one who is legally called on to take an oath, or affirmation, or to be examined as a witness in any court of civil or criminal jurisdiction, shall refuse so to do, he may be committed to prison, in close custody, until he shall consent, besides incurring such other penalties as are provided by law ; provided, that such imprisonment shall not continue longer than the end of the term in which he was committed, unless the commitment be within three days of the end of the term ; in which case the imprisonment may continue for three days after.

SECTION II.

Of the opening and adjournment of courts, and of the form in which the minutes are to be kept.

Art 463. No COURT, according to the definition of the term, can do any legal act before it is opened by a public proclamation, which may give notice that the persons authorized to constitute the court have met, under the circumstances necessary to give existence to that body ; which opening must be entered on the minutes, stating the day, hour and place, at which it took place.

Art. 464. Adjournments must, in like manner, be made by proclamation, entered on the minutes ; and if, from the continuance of a trial or other cause, the court shall continue its sessions until after twelve at night, the entry shall be made in this, as in all other cases, according to the truth.

Art. 465. The minutes of a court are a record of all the proceedings of such court ; and, in order to secure their correctness, a book shall be kept by the clerk, in which he shall enter a note of each proceeding at the time it takes place. This book shall be open for the inspection of all persons interested, until the opening of the court on the next day ; and immediately after the opening, the minutes of the preceding session shall be openly read by the clerk, and all errors therein shall be corrected by order of the court, and the minutes shall then be fairly copied into the record-book of minutes.

Art. 466. The names of the defendants in each trial, of the witnesses, and of the jurors who are sworn, and of the counsel who appear, shall be entered on the minutes, distinguishing the witnesses called for the prosecution from those called by the defendant.

Art. 467. When any instrument in writing is produced in evidence, a short note or description of it, containing the general tenor, the parties, and the date, shall be entered on the minutes, and some mark made on it by the clerk to identify it.

Art. 468. All the orders, and judgments, and every other act of the COURT whatever, shall be recorded on the minutes.

Art. 469. A note of every application made to the court during its session, and by whom made, and for whom, must be entered on the minutes, together with the decision of the court thereon, whether granting or refusing the application.

SECTION III.

On the order of proceeding on the first day of the term.

Art. 470. The judge having taken his seat, shall order the court to be opened. The clerk shall then say, "Crier, make proclamation." The crier then, with a loud voice, proclaims, "Silence! while I proclaim the orders of the court. This court [repeating the STYLE of the court] is now open : of this all persons are required to take notice, and to demean themselves with the reverence due to the laws, and the respect they require to be paid to the important functions of those who administer them."

Art. 471. The clerk shall then, after entering the opening of the court on the minutes, order the crier to call the officers of justice, whose duty it shall be, according to law, to attend; which he shall do by repeating the formula, "Silence! while I proclaim the orders of the court,"— which formula shall introduce all proclamations hereby directed to be made. He shall then say, "All officers of justice, whose duty it is to attend this court, answer to your names, or you will incur the penalties of law." He shall then call each name three times, and the clerk shall enter on the minutes the appearance or default of each.

Art. 472. On the appearance of the officers, the sheriff shall assign to each his separate duty.

Art. 473. The clerk shall then order proclamation to be made for calling the grand jury, which shall be done in the following form : " You good men, who have been selected to perform the important duties of grand jurors, answer to your names, and take your seats as you are called." If a sufficient number of the jury appear, they shall be sworn.

Art. 474. When the grand jury are sworn, the court shall proceed to give them their charge, and to have that part of this code read to them which concerns their duties, and to deliver them the copy of the calendar as is hereinbefore directed. Previous to which the clerk shall direct proclamation of silence to be made when the charge is being given to the grand jury.

Art. 475. When the grand jury has retired, the clerk shall order proclamation to be made for the calling of the petit jury, in the following form : " You good men, whose duty it is to decide, as jurors, between the state of Louisiana and those who are accused of offences against the laws, answer to your names as they are called." The names on the panel shall then be called, and the clerk shall take note of the defaulters.

Art. 476. When any grand juror shall appear, after the others are sworn, the oath shall be administered to him, and he shall, with a certificate of its being taken, be sent to the grand jury.

Art. 477. Proclamation shall then be made, requiring all magistrates who have taken any recognizances or examinations, which have not been delivered to the clerk, forthwith to bring them into court.

Art. 478. Persons bound by recognizance shall then, by proclamation, be called as follows : " All you who are bound by recognizance to appear at this court to answer complaints against you, come forth when your names are called, or your recognizance will be forfeited." The defaulters shall then be noted, and proclamation shall be made, with respect to such defaulters, in the following form : A. B. and C. D., [repeating the names of the bail] produce E. F., [the person delivered to bail] for whose appearance you are answerable, or you will forfeit your recognizance."

SECTION IV.

Of the forms to be used after an indictment or information has been filed.

Art. 479. When an act of accusation has been filed, founded on any written instrument, the original of which is annexed according to the former provisions of this code, the defendant, at the time for that purpose prescribed, shall be brought into court, and the court shall inquire whether he has employed counsel for his defence; if he has not, counsel shall be assigned him. The clerk shall then address him to this effect : "A. B., an indictment [or information] has been filed against you, of which you have been served with a copy; here is the original of the instrument annexed to that act. You are at liberty, under the inspection of an officer of the court, to examine the said instrument, and to compare it with the original, to see that the copy is correct."

Art. 480. After the defendant shall have had an opportunity of examining the instrument when one is annexed, and in all cases when no instrument is annexed, the clerk shall, at the time for that purpose hereinbefore prescribed, address the defendant to this effect : " A. B., if you have any exception to make to the indictment [or information] of which you have received a copy, either for any defect of substance or form, [or " because there is a variance between the copy of the instrument in the indictment and the original which you have seen," in cases where there is an instrument,] or because the name by which you are called in the act of accusation is not your true name, this is the time to make such exception; hereafter it will be too late."

Art. 481. If no exception be made, the clerk shall write on the back of the indictment : " This   day of   the defendant in this indictment was personally called on to make exceptions, if any he had thereto, and warned that they would not hereafter be received, but made none."

Art. 482. The arraignment shall be made in the form before prescribed.

Art. 483. On the day appointed for the trial, the witnesses, as well on the part of the prosecution as of the defendant, shall be called; and if any do not attend, process may be applied for, to compel their attendance; or if an application to postpone the trial be intended, it must be made before a juror is sworn.

Art. 484. If the trial is ordered on, the clerk shall address the defendant to this effect: " A. B., the jurors who are now to be called are those who are to decide on your innocence or guilt. If you do not desire to be tried by any particular jurors, you may set aside nine of them, without assigning any cause ; and if you have good cause to set aside any others, you may do so by declaring it : what is good cause, your counsel will explain to you. If you have any objection to make to the manner in which the jury has been drawn, you must now do so, or you will hereafter be precluded. Your objections to individual jurors must be made when they come to be sworn, but before they are sworn."

Art. 485. The clerk shall then proceed to draw the names of jurors, and as each shall come to be sworn, the clerk shall, in case of CRIME, say, " Defendant, look on the jury ! Juror, look on the defendant ! "—And if no challenge is made, shall proceed to administer the oath.

Art. 486. When a full jury shall be sworn, the clerk shall address them thus : " Gentlemen of this jury, an indictment [or information, as the case may be,] has been filed against A. B., [the defendant] in the following words. To this accusation he has pleaded not guilty. You are the persons upon whom the task is imposed of deciding whether he be guilty or not guilty. This you are to determine according to the evidence which will be offered to you."

Art. 487. Courts of criminal jurisdiction may make such rules for the order of proceeding therein ; but copies of all such rules must be sent to the governor, the senate, and the house of assembly, on the first day of the session after they shall have been made, or if the legislature be in session when such rules are entered, within five days afterwards ; provided, that no such rule shall be contrary to any provision in this system of penal law.

CHAPTER XV.

Of the officers of courts of criminal jurisdiction.

Art. 488. There shall be in every court of criminal jurisdiction the following officers : a clerk, an interpreter, a reporter, a crier, and a sheriff with his deputies.

SECTION I.

Of the clerk.

Art. 489. The duties of the clerk are, to keep correct minutes under the direction of the judge ; to preserve all the papers and records of the court ; to administer oaths in court ; to direct the crier to call the persons whose attendance may be required ; to file all papers directed to be filed, by endorsing on them some description by which they may be known, together with the date of their being filed ; to receive and record all indictments and informations, and to arraign the defendants ; to demand, receive, and record their answers ; to give authenticated copies of the minutes and records ; and to do all such other things as he may be required by law to perform.

Art. 490. The clerk may appoint a deputy, whose official acts shall be valid ; provided the deputation be in writing and recorded on the minutes of the court. When neither the clerk nor his deputy appears, the judge may appoint some person to officiate, whose appointment shall be entered on the minutes of the court, and whose official acts shall be valid.

Art. 491. The clerk is civilly liable for all the acts of his deputy, and criminally for all such as he shall have authorized, or knowingly permitted, in the manner described in the criminal code.

Art. 492. The clerk shall keep an office, in which all records and papers of the court shall be kept, and methodically arranged in such manner as the judge shall order; and the court shall, by rule, direct at what hours such office shall be kept open; and during such hours the clerk is bound to show any paper filed in such office, to any person who may require to see the same; but no acts of accusation, or evidence in support of the same, shall be shown, or copies thereof given, to any but the court, the party accused, the grand jury, or the public prosecutor, before the trial of the cause.

SECTION II.

Of the interpreter.

Art. 493. An interpreter shall be appointed for each court of criminal jurisdiction, who shall be well acquainted with the English, French, and Spanish languages, and who shall be sworn faithfully to perform the duties of his office.

Art. 494. It shall be the duty of the interpreter to translate such papers as are produced, and to interpret such declarations and proceedings as are made in court, so that they may be understood by the court, the jury, the parties, and others present who ought to know the contents, if any of them are ignorant of the language in which such papers are written, such declarations given, or such proceedings had.

Art. 495. Whenever the defendant cannot understand English, a translation of the act of accusation and of all papers annexed to the same, into some language which he understands, shall be given to him, with the copy hereinbefore directed to be served on him; and if he require it, his arraignment shall be postponed until such copy be given.

Art. 496. Whenever any translation or interpretation is required into, or from, a language with which the interpreter is unacquainted, or in the absence or sickness of that officer, or of a vacancy in the office, the court may appoint a proper person to do the particular service required, first administering an oath for the faithful performance of the duty.

SECTION III.

Of the reporter.

Art. 497. A reporter shall be appointed by the governor for each court having criminal jurisdiction, who shall receive such emolument as the legislature shall, by special law, direct: he shall be sworn faithfully to perform the duties of his office. The reporter shall not practise as counsellor or attorney in any criminal cause in that or any other court.

Art. 498. The duty of the reporter shall be to attend at all the sittings of the court; to take notes of all the acts of accusation, testimony, arguments, verdicts, judgments, and other proceedings, in each criminal cause that shall be brought before such court; to perform which duty a convenient seat shall be assigned to him; and from these notes he shall make a faithful report.

Art. 499. Within one month after every term of such court, or oftener at his discretion, he shall publish such reports in some gazette printed in the city of New Orleans.

Art. 500. The governor is authorized to contract with the proprietors of a gazette for the publication of such reports; and as an equivalent for the expense—all judicial orders, directed to be published by any court—all advertisements for sheriff's sales, either on execution or for taxes—all advertisements directed to be made by syndics—shall be published in such gazette, at the usual rates now allowed by the court.

Art. 501. The proceedings in the causes designated or

presented in the chapter next following, are excepted from the operation of the three last preceding articles, and from any other provision in the system of penal law, contrary to the directions of the said chapter.

Art. 502. It shall also be the duty of the reporter to make and deliver to the governor, and the attorney general, once in every three months, a return of names of all the persons bailed or committed to prison by any court or magistrate in the district, designating, in separate columns, the offence charged ; whether bailed or committed, and whether the accusation has been followed up by an indictment or information, and whether the indictment or information be for the same offence as originally charged by the commitment ; whether the party has been discharged, and by what authority, and for what cause ; and whether tried and acquitted, or convicted, and if convicted, of what offence ; and how sentenced, and whether sentence has been executed, and how : designating also, the sex, age, place of nativity, and profession or trade, of the defendant ; whether he could write or read, together with the dates of the commitment and other proceedings, according to forms to be furnished by the governor, who may require by them such additional information as may show the prevalence or suppression of different offences, and the general operation of the penal laws.

Art. 503. Once in every year the governor shall cause an abstract to be made of all the returns, omitting the names in cases of misdemeanor, and cause the same to be published ; to which abstract shall be added (from the return directed by the Code of Reform and Prison Discipline to be made by the keeper) opposite to the name of each convict, who has been committed to the state prison, whether he is still in custody, or discharged, and how ; and if in custody, whether at labour, or in solitude ; and if at labour, how employed.

SECTION IV.

Of the sheriff and other officers of justice.

Art. 504. It is the duty of the sheriff of the district in which any court of criminal jurisdiction shall sit, to attend its sessions by himself or his deputy; and he, or such deputy who acts for him, shall have at least two other deputies constantly in attendance, to execute the orders of the court.

Art. 505. The sheriff shall also present to the court, at the opening of its session, a list containing the names of all the constables; and the court shall also designate the number of them required for daily attendance, who shall serve in rotation.

Art. 506. The constables, during the session of the court, shall be under the direction of the sheriff.

Art. 507. The judge may, in or out of court, whenever he shall deem it expedient for the preservation of the peace or the execution of the orders of the court, appoint any number of special constables he may think proper, who shall continue in office during the time, or for the occasion, for which they are named.

Art. 508. The sheriff's officers and constables may, when the sheriff or the court deem it necessary, be armed with staves; but no man, armed in any other manner, shall be allowed to enter the hall in which the court is sitting. An armed guard may, with the approbation of the judge, be employed by the sheriff, to guard a prisoner to and from the court whenever there is danger of a rescue, but they cannot enter with their arms. Nothing in this article shall prevent officers in the army or navy from entering the court with their usual side-arms.

Art. 509. The crier is an officer of justice appointed by the court; his duty is to make proclamations for opening and adjourning the court; to call and swear the jurors and witnesses; to preserve silence and order in court, and to remove those who disturb its proceedings: the whole under the orders of the court.

CHAPTER XV.

*Of cases in which the publicity of legal proceedings may be
limited.*

Art. 510. In all prosecutions for the following offences,
that is to say : for assault, accompanied by any of the
circumstances set forth in the fourth article of the fourth
section of the first chapter, nineteenth title, and second
book of the Code of Crimes and Punishments ; for
assault with intent to ravish ; for rape, adultery, offences
against decency, and defamation implying a charge of
either of the offences above enumerated; during the examination of witnesses, previous to the commitment for those
offences, no person shall be present but the magistrate before
whom the complaint shall be made, and such other magistrates as he may request to aid him in the examination, the
public prosecutor, the accused and his counsel, the person
complaining, the sheriff, and other officers of justice
attending on the magistrate, the witnesses, and such
persons, not exceeding ten for each party, as the complainant and the accused may desire to have admitted.

Art. 511. On the trial, the persons admitted into court
shall be restricted to those mentioned in the preceding
article, with the officers of court, and the jurors sworn to
try the cause.

Art. 512. In making the report of any such trial, the
reporter shall not give the details of the evidence, or
publish the names of the witnesses.

Art. 513. Any person who shall publish any account
of such trial, containing any indecent or wanton details,
shall be fined not exceeding two hundred dollars, and
imprisoned not exceeding sixty days, if the account be
substantially true ; but if it be false, the punishment shall

be doubled, and the prosecution and trial for such offence shall be conducted according to the rules laid down in this chapter.

CHAPTER XVI.

Of costs.

Art. 514. Until the system by which magistrates and officers of courts of justice are remunerated for their services by fees, shall be abolished, the state shall pay costs in all cases where the accused is discharged on an acquittal, or for want of prosecution.

Art. 515. The payment of costs is not to be awarded in all cases on conviction. The defendant may, in some cases, be exonerated from them altogether, or he may be directed to pay a certain sum towards the payment of costs. This is at the discretion of the court, and must be exercised so as to proportion the amount of costs to the punishment inflicted.

Art. 516. Costs can only be recovered by execution, in the manner directed for the recovery of a fine ; and no one shall be detained in prison to enforce the payment of costs, until after the DISCUSSION of his property, and then only in the manner directed in the case of fines.

CHAPTER XVII.

Of prescription as applied to offences.

Art. 517. There is no prescription against prosecutions for any offences other than those especially provided for in this chapter.

Art. 518. Prosecutions for all misdemeanors, except

public offences, are prescribed by the lapse of three years after the commission of the offence.

Art. 519. Whenever the indictment is for a crime, and the party is found guilty of a misdemeanor, according to the rules hereinbefore established in the chapter of Verdicts, the prescription does not apply.

Art. 520. Prosecutions for injuries to reputation, for rape, assault with intent to ravish, assault aggravated by injury to pudicity, are prescribed by one year.

Art. 521. Prosecutions for an attempt to commit a crime, if no other offence is committed by the attempt, are barred by one year.

Art. 522. The prescription is barred in two cases :

1. If complaint was made of the offence within the time prescribed, although it was not followed by further prosecution, if the offender was either unknown or could not be found, or was rescued, or escaped.

2. Where the party injured, or the person whose duty it was to prosecute, was absent from the state, or was prevented by force or imprisonment, or debarred by threats, from prosecuting ; in either of which cases the prescription begins from the time the party shall return, or the disability shall cease.

Art. 523. When the defendant shall, according to the rules hereinbefore prescribed, except to the form of any act of accusation, that the time at which the offence is alleged to have been committed is beyond the time limited by the prescription, such exception shall not be allowed if the public prosecutor shall undertake to show, on the trial, either of the circumstances (designating which) that are in the last preceding article declared sufficient to rebut the prescription ; and if he shall fail so to do on the trial, or to show that the offence was committed within the time limited, the defendant must be acquitted.

Art. 524. Although there is no prescription for prosecutions for offences not enumerated in this chapter, yet provision will be found in the Code of Evidence to check any attempts to oppress, by delaying the accusation.

TITLE III.

OF THE MODE OF PROCEDURE IN CERTAIN CASES NOT IMMEDIATELY CONNECTED WITH PROSECUTIONS.

CHAPTER I.

Of inquests on dead bodies.

Art. 525. Whenever death shall be caused by violence, or a dead body of any person shall be found, and it is not known in what manner he came by his death, notice shall be given to the coroner of the parish, or, in his absence or inability to serve, to a magistrate.

Art. 526. Immediately after receiving such notice, it shall be the duty of the coroner, or magistrate, to summon a jury of inquest, consisting of eighteen persons qualified to serve as petit jurors, to meet at the place where the dead body is.

Art. 527. Officers of justice, and deputies whom the coroner may appoint, are bound to execute all his legal warrants for summoning the jury of inquest, and for making arrest and serving such orders as he is authorized to make.

Art. 528. When twelve or more of the jury are assembled, they shall be sworn, in the form hereinbefore prescribed, diligently to inquire into the cause and manner of the death of the person whose body is before them, and to make a true inquisition according to the evidence offered to them, or arising from the inspection of the body.

Art. 529. A surgeon or physician shall also be summoned and sworn, if any can be found within ten miles, as a witness, who shall, in the presence of the jury, inspect the body, and give a professional opinion as to the cause of the death.

Art. 530. The coroner shall also summon and examine as witnesses, on oath, all such persons as he or any of the jury shall reasonably suppose to have any knowledge of facts to be ascertained by the inquest.

Art. 531. After hearing the testimony, the jury shall determine when and in what manner, and by the act of whom it shall appear to them that the deceased came to his death ; and when a majority of such jury shall agree in making any such statement, the same shall be reduced to writing by the coroner, and signed by the jurors agreeing to the same. This statement is called the coroner's inquest.

Art. 532. If by the inquest it shall appear that any DESIGNATED person has been guilty of an offence in producing the death of the deceased, either as principal or accomplice, the coroner shall immediately issue his warrant for the arrest of such person, which shall be in the form of warrants of the like nature issued by magistrates, and shall be executed and proceeded on in the same manner.

Art. 533. The coroner has power to summon witnesses, and issue all such process to enforce their attendance and that of the jury, and to punish a refusal to attend, or to testify, in the same manner as a magistrate may in cases submitted to his jurisdiction. He has also the same power to issue a search warrant for any article necessary to the investigation before him, that is by this Code given to magistrates.

Art. 534. The inquest, together with any evidence that may have been taken by the coroner, and the return of the warrant, shall be transmitted to the clerk of the court having cognizance of the offence; and all material witnesses shall be bound over by the coroner to appear at such court ; and in relation to the arrest, examination, and other proceedings, after an inquisition, the duties of the coroner and the officers of justice shall be the same as those prescribed generally by this Code in cases of warrants of arrest issued by magistrates.

CHAPTER II.

Of the disinterment and dissection of dead bodies in cases of suspected murders.

Art. 535. Whenever a FAMILY-MEETING of the relations or friends of the deceased, convened according to law, shall determine that it is expedient to make an examination of the dead body of any person who has been already interred, in order to discover the cause of his death, and shall make application to a judge for that effect ; or whenever the judge shall himself deem it necessary, in consequence of evidence presented to him, he shall appoint two surgeons to perform any chirurgical operation that may be necessary, and shall issue his order to the sheriff to have the body disinterred and examined.

Art. 536. The surgeons shall make a VERBAL PROCESS of the whole professional proceedings, which they shall sign, and the sheriff shall also make minutes of the whole of his proceeding, which shall be signed by him, and at least three persons who were present at the operation.

Art 537. The VERBAL PROCESS of the surgeons and the minutes of the sheriff shall be returned to the judge who issued the order, and may serve as corroborating testimony to found a warrant of arrest, but shall not be evidence on the trial.

Art. 538. The FAMILY MEETING may, in like manner, apply for the examination of the dead body before interment, and when the order is granted, the same proceedings as are before directed shall take place.

CHAPTER III.

Of the proceedings in case of property found, where the owner is unknown.

Art. 539. When any one shall come by finding to the possession of any personal property, greater in value than twenty dollars, of which he has no reason to believe any designated person to be the owner, he shall be deemed to have concealed the same, and to have appropriated it to his own use, so as to incur the penalties directed by the   article of the Code of Crimes and Punishments, unless he shall pursue the directions of this chapter.

Art. 540. He must, within three days, give to the parish judge a written notice, containing a description of the property found, with its marks (if any), and the time and place of finding the same.

Art. 541. If the property be above the value of one hundred dollars, he must either deliver it to the sheriff of the parish, or give such security as the judge shall approve, to restore the same if legally claimed within six months.

Art. 542. If it be of greater value than three hundred dollars, consisting of money, jewels, gold or silver bullion, notes or other instruments in writing, or any article of small bulk, he shall deposit the same in some bank, if there be one within five miles, which will take charge of the same as a deposit for safe keeping—if there be no such bank within that distance, it shall be deposited with the parish judge, unless the finder give the security mentioned in the last preceding article.

Art. 543. A particular inventory of the property must be made by the parish judge and recorded in his office.

Art. 544. Within eight days after the report made to the parish judge, he shall cause an advertisement of the finding, describing the property particularly, to be published, with a notice to the owner to claim the same within six months from the time of finding ; which advertisement shall be continued once every month during the six months.

Art. 545. If the owner appear within the six months, and prove his property to the satisfaction of the judge, it shall be restored to him on his paying all the costs of preserving the same, all the expenses attending the procedure decreed by this chapter, and ten per cent. on the value of the property to the finder.

Art. 546. This chapter applies to property found stranded or drifting in any lake or stream of water within the state, except only that, in this last case, the owner shall be bound to pay a reasonable salvage, proportioned to the trouble and risk of saving and securing the property, over and above the ten per cent. on the value ; which salvage shall be determined by the parish judge.

Art. 547. If no owner appear to claim the property within six months, it shall be delivered to the finder, if not in his possession, and if it be, his bonds shall be cancelled, and he shall not be criminally liable for any use he may make of the same.

CHAPTER IV.

Of the mode of proceeding in cases of vagrancy.

Art. 548. A vagrant is one who, having no visible means of subsistence, lives in idleness, or in the practice of drinking, or gaming, and who, by the whole of his conduct and character, gives just reason to believe that he gains his subsistence by illegal means.

Art. 549. On the complaint of three householders to a magistrate stating that they have reason to believe, and detailing those reasons, and that they do believe that any designated individual comes within the description above-mentioned, the magistrate shall issue his warrant to bring the person before him, and shall require him to give an account of the means by which he gains his living.

Art. 550. The account required by the last article may, if the party implicated desire it, be given to the magistrate in private, but it must be on oath, and supported by at least one credible witness; and if such account show legal means of subsistence, to the satisfaction of the magistrate, the party shall be dismissed. But if the party refuse to render any account, or render one not satisfactory to the magistrate, he shall be required to report himself to the magistrate, and to show, within three days, that he has adopted some regular means of livelihood, or to leave the district, or to give security for his good behaviour.

Art. 551. If the party fail in performing one of the conditions prescribed by the last section, the magistrate shall issue his warrant to send him to the HOUSE OF IN-DUSTRY, there to be employed for sixty days, or until he shall find security for his good behaviour, or that he will leave the state, and not return within two years.

Art. 552. If, after his discharge, the party shall again be found in a state of vagrancy, either in the same or in any other district in the state, he shall, after the like inquiry, be sent to the house of industry for six months; and the same process shall be repeated as often as the same kind of life shall be resumed.

Art. 553. No person shall be deemed a vagrant, under the provisions of this chapter, who, from bodily infirmity, or infancy, or old age, is unable to gain a livelihood by labour. Persons of this description, if without the means of subsistence, are under the care of the police of the parish to which they belong.

CHAPTER V.

Of the mode of proceeding in cases of alleged insanity.

Art. 554. Insanity alleged on the trial to have existed at the time of committing the offence, must be determined, like any other ground of defence, by the jury impanneled for the trial of the cause ; but if the defendant be acquitted on that ground, it should be specially so found, that the court may make order for his safe custody, according to the provisions of the Code of Crimes and Punishments.

Art. 555. If insanity be alleged, or observed by the court, to exist at any other stage of the proceeding, it must be inquired of by a jury specially sworn for that purpose, who shall be drawn from the panel of petit jurors in the same manner as they are drawn for the trial of causes.

Art. 556. If the insanity be alleged or discovered before the trial, or after conviction and before judgment, the question to be submitted to the jury shall, in the first case, be, whether the defendant is of a sufficiently sane mind to make his defence, or give instructions for it ; in the second case it shall be, whether he have sufficient sanity of mind to show cause against the judgment, and take those other measures he is allowed to take for the diminution of the punishment.

Art. 557. If the insanity be alleged after judgment, the inquiry shall be, if it exist in such a degree as to make him dangerous to others, or unconscious of the nature and consequences of his offence.

Art. 558. Whenever, in any of the cases mentioned in the three last preceding articles, the insanity of the defendant shall be alleged, or shall be observed by the court, they shall name a physician to attend him, in order that he may be examined as a witness before the jury.

Art. 559. Counsel shall be assigned to the defendant on such inquiry, if none have before been employed or assigned.

Art. 560. The jury may interrogate the defendant on such inquiry.

CHAPTER VI.

Of the mode of proceeding in trials for adultery.

Art. 561. In order to avoid collusive attempts between the husband and a pretended adulterer to obtain a divorce, to the injury of the wife; or between the husband and wife, to injure an innocent person, charged as the adulterer; the Code of Crimes and Punishments has provided, that prosecutions for adultery shall be joint against the wife and the supposed adulterer (if he be alive); and that there can be no conviction of the one without the other, under the modifications to be contained in this code : these are the following :

1. If the defendant, who is charged with being the adulterer, shall have been either summoned or arrested, but he should not appear, an attorney shall be named for his defence, who shall enter a plea of "not guilty" for him, and the trial shall proceed in his absence.

2. If he be alive, but shall have left the state before the prosecution is commenced, a warrant or citation shall issue against him, and be renewed, from time to time, for six months, until it shall be served, and until the trial shall actually take place. If he be not found, the trial may proceed, after the expiration of the six months, against the wife alone.

CHAPTER VII.

Of the application of moneys collected for fines, and of compensations for services to prosecutor, and for losses incurred by innocent defendants.

Art. 562. The mode in which fines are to be collected, is prescribed in the chapter of punishments in the Code of Crimes and Punishments.

Art. 563. Sheriffs, coroners, and the marshal of the city court of the city of New Orleans, must, once in every three months, render to the treasurer of the state, an account of all fines either of them may have received prior to that time; or if they have received none, make a return to that effect, in writing, signed by them respectively.

Art. 564. At the time of rendering such account, the balance in the hands of the officer rendering it shall be paid to the treasurer of the state, who shall carry the same to account of a fund, called the "compensation fund"— which shall be applied, first, to the payment of warrants for recompense drawn by the governor, or by the judge and public prosecutor, in cases authorized by the second chapter, first title, first book of this Code; secondly, to such other uses as the legislature may direct.

·Art. 565. If any sheriff, coroner, or marshal shall neglect or refuse to render such account, and to pay the balance that may be due thereon, or to make such return, he shall forfeit a sum of fifty dollars.

Art. 566. It is hereby made the duty of the treasurer to cause prosecutions to be commenced for the offences against this chapter; and also, to file petitions in a court of competent jurisdiction for an account of fines that may have been received; and in such suits the defendants shall pay costs, although it may appear that no money was due to the state ; unless the defendant can show, that he had made the returns required by this chapter, before the commencement of the suit.

Art. 567. Suspicion of guilt sometimes subjects the innocent to the vexatious expense and privation of liberty incident to the measures preparatory to the trial, by which their innocence is ascertained. Justice requires that such persons should be compensated by the public, because the loss and inconvenience was caused by its officers, and in attempting to secure its peace and safety. To do full justice in the few cases where it will be found due, would expose the treasury to petitious demands in so many others, that the law can only give relief in such a manner as to aid the more needy class of sufferers, while it offers no temptation to fraudulent combinations.

Art. 568. Therefore, whenever the judge who, before trial, shall discharge a person who has been committed, or bailed, for any offence—or whenever the jury, who shall acquit any defendant—shall certify, that he did not, by any improper conduct, give reasonable ground for suspicion that he had committed the offence, he shall be entitled to such compensation for the losses he has sustained by reason of the prosecution, as the judge shall think reasonable ; but such compensation shall in no case exceed an amount of emolument which he might have made during the time that he was confined, or necessarily employed in his defence, to be ascertained according to the following circumstances :

1. If the defendant have no trade or profession, the compensation shall be calculated according to the wages of day-labourers.

2. If he be a mechanic, the average rate of wages for hired workmen of his trade shall be the measure, without any regard to the particular skill of the defendant.

3. If the defendant pursue any other calling or profession, the compensation shall not exceed twice the amount which could be allowed to a mechanic.

Art. 569. The sum allowed shall be paid by the treasurer out of the compensation fund, on the judge's warrant, countersigned by the clerk of the court, to the person in whose favour the allowance is made.

Art. 570. In such cases the acquittal shall always be published, and the expenses paid by a similar draft on the same fund.

GENERAL PROVISIONS.

Art. 571. No omission of any matter of form, prescribed by this system, nor any departure from the forms given for proceeding under it, shall render the proceeding void, unless it be so specially provided ; or unless the departure from the form has caused some injury to the party complaining of it.

Art. 572. Where a particular provision is made in any part of this system, contrary to a general provision, the particular provision must be observed.

Art. 573. All offences which are created by the Code of Procedure, or the Code of Reform and Prison Discipline, shall be tried in the same manner with those which are created by the Code of Crimes and Punishments.

Art. 574. Whenever a notice or interval of a certain number of days is directed to be given or to elapse, three whole days, exclusive of the two terms referred to, must intervene, unless the contrary be expressed.

BOOK III.

CONTAINING THE FORMS TO BE USED IN ALL THE
JUDICAL PROCEEDINGS PRESCRIBED OR
AUTHORIZED BY THIS CODE.

TITLE I.

OF THE FORMS TO BE USED IN THE PROCEEDINGS AUTHORIZED
BY THE FIRST BOOK, TITLE FIRST, FOR THE PREVENTION
OF OFFENCES.

CHAPTER I.

General provisions.

Art. 575. Where the forms given in this book are filled
up, the parts within brackets are to be changed according
to the circumstances ; the real names are to be substituted
for the letters used to represent them in the forms, and
the real dates for the blanks or the fictitious dates used in
the forms.

Art. 576. The certificate of the attestation of the magistrate to affidavits, the seals to writs, and the signatures
of parties, clerks and magistrates, are omitted in most of
these forms. The cases in which they are necessary, in
practice, are either declared by the law on the subject, or
result from the nature of the instrument.

Art. 577. Where the beginning or conclusion of any
form has been given before, it is omitted in the subsequent forms of the same nature. The part of the form
omitted in the beginning of any precedent, is to be supplied by copying the formal part that had before been

given, down to the recurrence of the word with which the new form begins. Thus, in the precedents of an indictment, the formal part must be copied in each case down to the word "did," with which word some of the forms, given for the different officers, begin in the subsequent precedents; or to the word "that," with which others begin. The formal conclusion is supplied by "&c."

CHAPTER II.

Of the forms to be used in the proceedings under the third chapter of the title and book aforesaid.

Art. 578. The honorary certificate, directed to be granted by the article, shall be in the following form :
"*State of Louisiana—certificate of merit.*
"A. B. having [here insert the act with such circumstances as in the opinion of the court rendered it worthy of recompense], the criminal court of said state [reciting the style of the court] have, according to the laws of the said state, caused this certificate to be made out, under their seal, to record the merit of his conduct, and to have the other effects provided for by law. Witness **J. T.** judge of the said court, this   day of in the year   ."
Art. 579. The certificate directed by the article to entitle the person giving information of an offence to the reward thereby directed, shall be as follows :
"We certify, that A. B. gave the first information which led to the conviction of C. D. of the offence of [here insert the description of offence]; and that, pursuant to the directions of the Code of Criminal Procedure, he is entitled to receive from the treasurer of the state, out of the compensation fund, the sum of fifty dollars. Dated the   day of   in the year   ."
Art. 580. The several proceedings for the prevention

of offences by the intervention of officers of justice, which are authorized by the third chapter of the title and book mentioned in the title of this chapter, shall be according to the following forms :

1. The form of an affidavit required by the first article of that chapter :

" I, A. B., do hereby declare, that I do fear that C. D. intends to commit an offence against my person [or property, designating which] by [designating the act which is apprehended]; and that I have just reason for this fear, because [here insert the circumstances which cause the apprehension.] "

2. Form of the warrant :

" To H. H., one of the constables," &c.

" Whereas, A. B. hath made oath before me C. D. [designating the office of the magistrate], that he has just reason to fear and does fear, that E. F. intends to [here insert the nature of the offence] : You are, therefore, ordered to arrest the said E. F., and bring him before me to answer the said allegation, and to be dealt with according to law. Given under my hand, this   day of   in the year   ."

3. The form of the bond :

" We, E. F. and G. H., acknowledge ourselves bound in solido to the state of Louisiana in the sum of   to be paid by us, or our heirs, if the said C. D. shall commit any offence against [the person] of A. B. within the term of one year."

4. The form of commitment, if the accused do not find security.

" To the sheriff of the parish, &c.   By C. D. [one of the justices, &c.]

" Keep in safe custody, until he shall be discharged by law, E. F. herewith delivered to you, charged, on the oath of A. B., with an intent to [here insert the charge]. Witness my hand, this   day of   in the year   ."

Art. 581. Any one committed by virtue of such commitment, may be brought up by order of the magistrate who committed him whenever he finds security, and on executing the bond aforesaid shall be discharged.

5. Warrant for arrest, on the view of the magistrate, under the article.

"To H. H. one of the constables," &c.

"Whereas, E. F., in the presence of C. D., one of the justices [insert his style of office], did commit illegal violence on the person of A. B. : You are, therefore, commanded to arrest the said E. F., and bring him before me to answer for the said offence, and to be dealt with according to law. Given under my hand this   day of   in the year   ."

6. Application for a summons, in case of an intended libel.

"To C. D. one of the justices," &c.

"A. B. complains that E. F., as he is informed and believes, is now printing a libel against him, which he intends to publish [or that he has written and intends to print, or continue to sell and circulate, some such libel, or some such publication as is forbidden by the Penal Code, as the case may be]; he, therefore, prays that the said E. F. may be summoned, for admonition according to law."

7. Summons on the above complaint.

"To I. K. one of the constables," &c.

"Summon E. F. to appear before me, [one of the justices, &c.], on the   day of   next, at   o'clock in the morning, at my office, to hear complaint of A. B. against him, for intending to publish [or for continuing to circulate, &c., as the case may be] a libel against him [or other publication forbidden by the Code of Crimes and Punishments, as the case may be.] Witness my hand, this   day of

C. D."

Art. 582. If the person summoned do not appear, and the officer to whom it was directed shall return, that it was duly served, such summons and return shall have the same effect as to the punishment, in case of conviction, that the admonition would have had.

CHAPTER III.

Form of proceeding authorized by the fourth chapter respecting search warrants.

Art. 583. The forms to be used for proceedings authorized by this chapter are as follows :

1. Affidavit for procuring a search warrant for stolen goods, or goods taken on false pretences or fraud :

" A. B., being duly sworn before me, C. D., one of the justices, &c. [insert the office of the magistrate], doth depose, that the following property, viz. [describing it], the property of [insert the name of the owner], has been stolen [or has been taken by false pretences, or has been forcibly and fraudulently appropriated, as the case may be], in the parish of   ; and that the deponent believes, that the said property is concealed in the house of I. K. [or as the case may be, in a particular chamber, or in a barn, or other place, describing it], in the said parish; and he so believes because [here state the circumstances on which the belief is founded.]

2. Affidavit for procuring a search warrant for seizing forged instruments in writing, or counterfeit coin, or the instruments and materials for making them.

" A. B., being duly sworn before me, C. D., [insert the magistrate's office], doth depose, that he believes that certain forged bank notes [or counterfeit coin, or instruments, or materials for making them, as the case may be] are concealed in the house of [describing the place] with the fraudulent intent of passing the same [if it be bank notes or coin] or of [employing the said instruments or materials in committing the crime of forgery or counterfeiting, as the case may be] ; and he also believes [state the circumstances on which he founds his belief.]

3. Affidavit for procuring a search warrant for arms and munitions prepared for insurrection or riot.

" A. B., being duly sworn before me, C. D., [insert the magistrate's office], doth depose, that he believes certain arms [or munitions, as the case may be] consisting of [describe of what kind the arms or munitions are], are concealed in [describe the place] ; and that they are intended to be used for the purpose of a riot [or insurrection, as the case may be], which he also believes certain persons have conspired to make [or have actually made, if such be the case] ; and that his reasons for believing as aforesaid are [insert the reasons for believing in the insurrection, or riot, or the conspiracy, to effect them, as well as the concealment of the arms for that purpose.]

4. Affidavit for a search warrant for some article, the production of which may be necessary on a trial :

" A. B. being duly sworn, &c. [as before] doth depose, that on the trial of E. F. now under examination, [or lately committed or bailed, as the case may be], on an accusation of [state the offence], a certain silver-mounted pistol [or any other article, describing it], will, as he believes, be necessary to be produced, and that the same, as he believes, is now in the house occupied by G. H., situate in [describing the place] ; and that his reasons for believing that the production of the said article will be necessary are [here state the circumstances.]

5. Warrant to search for goods stolen, taken under false pretences, or forced :

" To the sheriff of the parish of   , [or to A. B., one of the constables of the parish of   .]

" Whereas, affidavit hath this day been made before me, C. D. one of the justices, &c. [insert the office of the magistrate] by A. B., that certain property belonging to   was stolen [or obtained by false pretences from him, or had been fraudulently appropriated, as the case may be], and that he had good reason to believe and did believe, that the said property was concealed in the house of   , situate in   [or other place, describing it] : you are therefore required, without delay, to make search in the said house [or other place] in the daytime for the said property ; and if you find the same, or any part thereof, that you bring the same, with the person in whose custody the same was found, before me without delay, to be examined and dealt with according to law. Given under my hand and seal, this day of in the year

6. Search warrant for seizing forged instruments in writing, or counterfeit coin, or the instruments and materials for making them.

" To the Sheriff, &c.

" Whereas, an affidavit has been made, &c. [as in the preceding form] that certain forged bank bills [or counterfeit coin, or instruments or materials for making forged bills or counterfeit coin, as the case may be, reciting the affidavit], are concealed, &c. [as in the affidavit, describing the place particularly], with the fraudulent intent of passing the said bills or coin [or employing the said materials or instruments in committing the crime of forgery or counterfeiting, as the same may be stated in the affidavit] : You are therefore required," &c. as in the last form.

7. Search warrant for seizing arms and munitions prepared for insurrection or riot.

" To the Sheriff, &c.

" Whereas, &c. [the direction and recital as in the preceding forms] affidavit has been made before me, &c. by A. B. stating that he believes, and has good reason to believe, there are certain arms [or munitions, describing them as in the affidavit] concealed in [describing the place as in the affidavit], and that they are intended to be used for the purposes of an insurrection, [or riot, as the case may be] which certain persons have conspired to make [or have made], as he also believes, and has good reason to believe : You are therefore required," &c. as in the preceding forms.

TITLE II.

OF THE FORMS TO BE USED IN THE PROCEEDINGS AUTHORIZED BY
THE FIRST BOOK, TITLE SECOND, FOR SUPPRESSING
PERMANENT OFFENCES.

CHAPTER I.

*Forms of proceeding to be used for giving effect to the
directions for suppressing permanent offences against
public tranquillity, public safety, public health, public
property, morals, and decency, and reputation.*

Art. 584. Affidavit of the existence of an unlawful
assembly or riot :

" A. B. and C. D. of the parish of [New Orleans],
being sworn, say, that E. F., G. H., and I. K., and others
to the deponent unknown, to the number of more than
twenty, are now assembled in [the public square of the
city of New Orleans] with the intent to aid each other in
violently and illegally [rescuing from the sheriff one J. S.
who has been legally committed on an accusation of murder, which intent was openly expressed by numbers of the
said assembly in the presence of these deponents.]"

Art. 585. In case of a riot, this clause is to be added,
"and that the said persons have begun to execute their
purpose [by assaulting and beating the officers of justice
who have the custody of the said J. S.]"

Art. 586. Proclamation and order of a magistrate for
the dispersion of an unlawful assembly or riot.

The magistrate shall, according to the directions of the
Penal Code, display a white flag, which shall be carried
either by him or by an officer of justice, or other person

appointed by him. The flag bearer shall then proclaim "Silence! while [F. T. judge of the criminal court] speaks in the name of the law!" The magistrate shall then make his order in the following form: "In the name of the state of Louisiana, and by virtue of the powers vested in me by law as [the judge of the criminal court,] I order this assembly to disperse; and I warn each of you, that by remaining he makes himself liable to imprisonment at hard labour for any riot that may be committed by himself or his associates, and to fine and imprisonment for not retiring in half an hour after this warning, even if no other offence be committed; and if any or other crime should be committed in the prosecution of the illegal purpose for which you are assembled, all of you will incur the guilt and punishment. Again I command you, in the name of the law and the state, to disperse."

Art. 587. All the consequences of not dispersing are incurred if the magistrate is by violence prevented from making the proclamation, or displaying his flag; or if he should not make the proclamation in the form prescribed, provided (if not prevented by violence) he shall display the flag, cause his office to be known, and give the order to disperse. But the magistrate is guilty of a neglect of duty who does not pursue the forms above directed.

Art. 588. After making the proclamation and order, the magistrate shall take notice of the precise time at which such order was given, and as soon as possible shall make a minute thereof in writing, signed by himself and other witnesses.

Art. 589. If the proclamation be made to those actually engaged in a riot, the magistrate shall cause those to be arrested who shall persevere in the unlawful act after the proclamation has been made.

Art. 590. If the proclamation be made to an unlawful assembly, but before any riot has been committed, he shall arrest those who remain in the said assembly after the expiration of the half-hour from the time of the order to disperse, as well as those who, before the ex-

piration of that time, shall commit any act that amounts
to a riot.

Art. 591. Application to procure an injunction against
any trade, or continuing any act or cause injurious to public
health.

Such application must be made in the following form :

" To the [judge of the criminal court] :

" The petition of A. B., C. D., and E. F., inhabitants of
[the Bayou St. John in the city of New Orleans], showeth,
that G. H., of the same place, hath lately been indicted in
this court for [suffering the blood which he uses in refining
sugar to putrefy] in a manner injurious to the health of
the inhabitants in the vicinity ; that notwithstanding such
indictment, the said G. H. continues the said practice to
the great danger of your petitioners and others in the
vicinity : they therefore pray, that the said G. H. may
be enjoined from continuing the said unhealthy process."

Art. 592. Citation on the above petition to be served
on the defendant :

" G. H., you are cited to appear before [the criminal
court of the state of Louisiana] on the   day of
            next, at ten o'clock in the morning, to show
cause, if any you have, why the prayer of the petition, a
copy whereof is annexed, should not be granted.   Dated
the   day of   in the year eighteen
hundred and   ."

Art. 593. Injunction on the above petition :

" The state of Louisiana to G. H.

" Whereas, an indictment hath been presented against
you in the criminal court, charging [that in carrying on
the business of refining sugar you suffer the blood used in
that process to putrefy] so as to injure the health of
persons residing in the vicinity ; and whereas it hath been
represented to our said court, that notwithstanding such
indictment, you still continue the said [process] to the
great injury of the persons in the neighbourhood of your
works : you are, therefore, commanded to desist from continuing such [mode of carrying on the said business] as is

complained of, under the penalty of fine, imprisonment, and sequestration of your [works]. Witness, F. T. judge of the said court, the   day of   in the year   ."

Art. 594. If it shall appear to the court that this injunction is wilfully disobeyed, they may order the works, or other cause of injury to public health, to be sequestered until the trial of the indictment, or until the defendant shall give security to obey the order of the court.

Art. 595. In all cases where any one shall wilfully disobey any lawful writ of injunction, issued by a competent court in a criminal cause, he may be fined not exceeding fifty dollars, and imprisoned not exceeding ten days, by the court, on hearing, in a summary manner, without the intervention of a jury.

Art. 596. Writ of sequestration for disobedience to the injunction.

"The state of Louisiana to the sheriff of [the parish of the city of New Orleans :]

"You are commanded to take into your possession [the buildings situate at the Bayou St. John's, in which G. H. now carries on the business of refining sugar, and that after causing the putrid blood to be removed therefrom], you safely keep the said [building] until the further order of this court. Witness," &c.

Art. 597. The form hereinbefore prescribed shall be used in cases of manufacturing or storing articles, dangerous from their explosive nature to human life, except that in the petition, the injunction and the sequestration, the charge shall be according to fact of the manufacture carried on, or the article stored, and that it endangers the lives of the inhabitants in the vicinity, instead of their health, as is stated in the forms above prescribed.

Art. 598. Petition for the removal of a building or obstruction of public property, held for the common use of all the inhabitants :

"To F. T. [judge of the criminal court.]

"A. B. complains that C. D. has lately erected a [house]

which permanently obstructs the free use of [a street called Lafayette-street, in the city of New Orleans]; that the said [street] is public property, held for the common use of all the citizens, and that the part thereof on which the said [house] is erected has been in such common use for twelve months next preceding the time of erecting the said [house,] of all which the said A. B. is ready to make proof, and he prays that the said C. D. may be cited, and that the said obstruction may be removed."

Art. 599. The citation shall be in the following form :

" C. D., you are cited to appear before me, at [my dwelling-house in the suburb of St. Mary,] on the day of   at ten o'clock in the morning, to show cause, if any you have, why the prayer of the petition, a copy whereof is annexed, should not be granted.   Dated the   day of   in the year   ."

Art. 600. The order for removal shall be in the following form :

" By [F. T. judge of the criminal court.]   To the sheriff of the parish [of the city of New Orleans.]

" Whereas, complaint has been made to me that C. D. has lately erected a [house] which permanently obstructs the free use of a [street called Lafayette-street, in the city of New Orleans] ; that the said street is public property, held for the common use of all the citizens ; and that the part thereof on which the said [house] is erected has been in such common use for twelve months next preceding the time of erecting such [house] ; all which allegations have been clearly proved, and the inconvenience to the public being, in my opinion, so great from the obstruction aforesaid as to render it improper to wait the event of a trial for the offence, I do therefore, by virtue of the powers vested in me as judge of the court of the highest criminal jurisdiction in this district, command you, that you cause the said [house] to be removed, so that it may no longer obstruct the said street."

Art. 601. Complaint of an intended libel, or of publication injurious to morals and decency :

" To A. B., one of the justices of the peace for the parish of Plaquemine :

" C. D. of the said parish, complains that E. F. of the said parish, hath written or printed a false and malicious libel concerning the deponent, which he is continuing to sell or publish, [or has written a false and malicious libel against the deponent, which he intends to publish, as the case may be] [or that the said E. F. has prepared and intends to publish an obscene print (or picture) or a written composition called, as the case may be] which manifestly tends to corrupt the morals of youth ; all which the complainant has good reason to believe and does believe : wherefore he prays, that the said E. F. may be cited before you, and that he may receive the admonition in such case directed by law."

Art. 602. Citation in the above complaint :

" [E. F., of the parish of Plaquemine,] you are hereby cited to appear before me [A. B. one of the justices of the peace for the said parish,] on the   day of   at ten o'clock in the forenoon, to hear such things as may be addressed to you in relation to a libel against C. D. [or a publication contrary to morals and decency, as the case may be.] Dated the   day of   in the year   ."

Art. 603. Admonition on the above citation :

" E. F., affidavit having been made before me, that there is good reason to believe that you intend to publish or sell a libel against C. D. of this parish, [or as the case may be, a publication against decency, manifestly tending to corrupt the morals of youth] or [that you have prepared and intend to publish some work of that description,] it is made my duty to admonish you, which I hereby do, that although no restraint can be laid on the liberty secured to every one by the constitution, "freely to speak, write, and print on any subject," yet the same constitution makes you liable for the abuse of that liberty, and the laws have empowered and directed me to warn you that if, after this admonition, you should commit the offence that is apprehended, you will suffer the highest punishment that can be inflicted, that is to say [if the apprehended offence be a libel purporting the accusation of a crime] imprisonment for twelve months and a fine of three thousand dollars ; [if the apprehended libel does not import the accusation of a crime, then say, imprisonment for nine months and a fine of two hundred and fifty dollars,] [and if the apprehended offence be one against decency, then say, imprisonment for six months and a fine of one thousand dollars.]"

CHAPTER II.

Of the forms to be used in the suppression of permanent offences against personal liberty.

Art. 604. The suppressive remedy for offences against personal liberty is the writ of *habeas corpus*. The directions for obtaining and proceeding under that writ are minutely detailed in the first book of this Code, title second, chapter seventh. The forms are herein given to preserve uniformity in practice ; but no part of such forms are essential but such as are declared to be so in the chapter above referred to.

Art. 605. Petition for a writ of *habeas corpus* by the party imprisoned, where the imprisonment is under colour of judicial process, but irregular in form :

"To J. L. [district judge of the state of Louisiana for the first district.]

"The petition of A. B., of the city of New Orleans, showeth, that he is imprisoned in the prison of the city of New Orleans, in the custody of the sheriff of the said city, by virtue of [an order purporting to be a commitment made by C. D., one of the justices of the peace for said city,] a copy of which [order] is hereunto annexed, [or if the copy has been refused to be given, say, a copy of which commitment is not hereunto annexed, because, on application to the keeper of the prison, the same was refused to be given]; and your petitioner is advised and believes, that his imprisonment, or under colour of the said [order], is illegal. Your petitioner, therefore, prays, that a writ of *habeas corpus*, directed to said sheriff or the keeper of the said prison, may be granted, ordering him forthwith to bring your petitioner before you, that he may be discharged according to law."

Art. 606. When the petition is made by any other than the person imprisoned, it may state the fact of imprisonment and illegality, according to the best of his information and belief.

Art. 607. Petition when the imprisonment is by virtue of judicial process, regular in form but illegally obtained, and where a third party is interested in the discharge.

As in the last form to "in the custody of the sheriff of the said city, by virtue of a writ purporting to be a writ [of capias ad satisfaciendum, issuing out of the parish court for the parish of the city of New Orleans, at the suit of C. D., to satisfy a judgment pretended to have been obtained in the said court, for the sum of one thousand dollars; but in truth no such judgment was ever entered, nor is there any judgment, order, or decree to authorize the said process.] Wherefore he prays, that the said C. D. may be cited according to law, and that a writ of *habeas corpus* be granted," &c.

Art. 608. On the above petition, the judge issuing the *habeas corpus* shall indorse these words, "the withinnamed A. B. must be brought up, notwithstanding the [execution] within mentioned," otherwise the sheriff need only send up the [execution], as is provided by the third section of the seventh chapter of this Code, above referred to.

Art. 609. Citation to the plaintiff at whose suit the execution mentioned in the preceding petition was taken out, conformably to the directions in the said chapter, regulating proceedings on *habeas corpus*.

" By J. L., district judge of the state of Louisiana for the first district. To C. D., of the city of New Orleans.

" You are hereby cited to appear before me, at the court house of the district court, at nine o'clock to-morrow morning, to show cause, if any you have, why A. B., confined illegally, as is said, at your suit, in the prison of this city, should not be discharged on a writ of *habeas corpus.* Dated," &c.

Art. 610. Petition where the imprisonment is not under colour of any judicial process.

" That he is illegally confined by J. W. [in the fort of Plaquemine, in this district] ; he therefore prays that the said J. W. may be cited according to law, and that a writ of *habeas corpus* be granted," &c.

Art. 611.*

Art. 612. The form of the writ of *habeas corpus* is set forth in the   article of this code in the chapter relating to " the suppression of offences against personal liberty."

Art. 613. Proof of the service of a writ of *habeas corpus* when a copy has been kept.

"A. B. being duly sworn, doth depose, that on the day of   , about the hour of ten before noon, he delivered to C. D. the original writ of *habeas corpus,* of which a true copy is hereunto annexed."

Art. 614. Proof of service where no copy has been kept.

As above. " That on the   day of   , at about the hour of ten in the forenoon, he did serve on C. D. a writ of *habeas corpus,* allowed by J. L., district judge, directed to the said C. D., by which he was ordered [forthwith] to produce A. B., said to be in his custody, before the said judge, at the court room of the first district court, in this city ; that the said service was made by delivering the said writ to the said C. D."

Art. 615. Affidavit in cases where the person to whom the writ is directed refused to receive it.

* Art. 611, referring to slavery, happily being no longer required, is omitted.

As above. " That he offered the writ which is hereunto annexed, on the   day of   at about the hour of ten before noon, to C. D., to whom the same is directed, but that he refused to receive the same, whereupon the deponent verbally informed the said C. D. of the contents of the said writ."

Art. 616. Proof in cases where the person to whom the writ is directed conceals himself, or refuses admittance to the person charged with the service.

As above. "That he went to the dwelling house of C. D., to whom the writ of *habeas corpus*, of which a copy is hereunto annexed, was directed, with the said writ in his possession, but that he was refused admittance into the said house [or that having entered the said house he sought for the said C. D. in order to serve the said writ, but that the said C. D. was not there to be found, and the deponent believes that he conceals himself to avoid the service thereof ; whereupon the deponent proclaimed aloud his business, and fixed up the said writ on the outside of the said house, on the outer door thereof, where he left the same]."

Art. 617. In this last case, if the deponent have kept no copy, he must, instead of saying "a writ of *habeas corpus* of which a copy is annexed," describe the same as in the form above prescribed for proof of service when no copy was kept.

Art. 618. Form of a return when he to whom the writ is directed, has not the person he is directed to produce in his custody, or under his control.

"I, C. D., to whom the within writ is directed, do return, that I have not now, nor within three days before the date of the said writ, have not had the within-named A. B. within my power, restraint, or control.

(Signed)   "A. B.

" Sworn before,

" E. F., justice of the peace," &c.

Art. 619. Form when he had the custody or control of the party within three days, but has transferred him to another.

"I, C. D., to whom the within writ is directed do return, that I have not the within-named A. B. now in my custody, or under my restraint or control ; but that on the   day of   [the said C. D. was delivered to me as a deserter from the first regiment of United States infantry, by J. S. a sergeant in the first company of said regiment, I being at that time commander of the fort of St. Phillips in this state, and that I afterwards, to wit, on the   day of   transferred the custody of the said A. B. to L. M., a captain in the said regiment, before the issuing of the said writ, and before I had any notice of an intent to apply for the same.]"

Art. 620. Form when a party is in custody on judicial process.

"I, C. D., to whom the within writ is directed, do return, that in obedience thereto I have the within-named A. B. at the time and place within mentioned in my custody, and that the cause of his detention is a certain [order or commitment] which is annexed to this writ, to me directed as [keeper of the prison of the city of New Orleans.]"

Art. 621.*

Art. 622. Form of return when the party is too sick to be produced.

"I, C. D., to whom the within writ is directed, do in obedience thereto return, that the said A. B. is detained in my custody by virtue of [an order of commitment to me directed as keeper of the prison of the city of New Orleans, which is hereunto annexed], and that I have not produced the said A. B. because it could not be done without danger to his life from the sickness which he now suffers, as appears by the testimony of the physician and witnesses hereunto annexed."

* Art. 621, referring to slavery, being no longer required, is omitted.

Art. 623. Certificate of physician.

"I, D. H., a physician regularly admitted to practice, certify, that I have visited A. B. now in custody of [the keeper of the prison of New Orleans] and found him suffering with a [bilious fever], and that, in my opinion, he cannot be brought before the judge on the annexed writ without danger of his life."

"We, I. K. and L. F., being duly sworn, do depose, that we have seen the within-named A. B., and believe, from the state of his health, that he cannot be produced in obedience to this writ, without danger to his life. In witness whereof, as well we the said witnesses as the said A. B. have signed this deposition."

Art. 624. Form of a warrant to bring up the prisoner when the writ of *habeas corpus* has not been obeyed.

"By J. L. [district judge of the first district court.] To A. B. [one of the constables of the city of New Orleans.]

"Whereas, a writ of *habeas corpus* was lately allowed by me, directed to C. D., of the city of New Orleans, directing him to bring before me A. B. in his custody, as was said illegally detained, and the said C. D. having disobeyed the said writ,—These are to command you, to take the said A. B. out of the custody, or from under the restraint or control of the said C. D. or of any person to whose custody he may have transferred him, and to bring him before me without delay, to abide such order as I may make in the case. Witness my hand, this day of   in the year   ."

Art. 625. Warrant to arrest the person to whom the *habeas corpus* was directed, for not bringing up the prisoner.

Direction and recital as in the preceding form. "These are to command you, that you arrest the said C. D. and bring him in safe custody before me without delay, to be dealt with for his said default according to law. Witness," &c.

Art. 626. Commitment, where the party on being brought before the judge, on the preceding warrant, refuses to return the writ or to produce the prisoner.

"By J. L., district judge, &c. To [the keeper of the prison of the city of New Orleans.]

" Receive in your custody C. D., herewith sent to you for refusing obedience to a writ of *habeas corpus*, by me issued, directing him to produce A. B. in his custody as was alleged, and him the said C. D. safely keep until discharged by due course of law. Witness, &c."

Art. 627. Petition for a warrant to bring up the prisoner when there is danger of his being carried out of the state, or of irreparable injury, and to arrest the person in whose custody he is.

"To J. L., district judge, &c.

"The petition of A. B. showeth, that C. D. is now in the custody or power of one J. S. [who has put him on board of a vessel called the Tartar, lying at the levee of this city, now ready to sail ; and that the said J. S. intends, as the deponent is informed and verily believes, forcibly to convey the said C. D. against his will and without any legal authority, out of this state ;] and the deponent verily believes, that if a writ of *habeas corpus* issue it will be disobeyed, and the said C. D. will, notwithstanding such writ, be conveyed out of the state, [or suffer irreparable injury, as the case may be ;] and the petitioner shows, that the said J. S. hath knowingly and illegally deprived the said C. D. of his liberty, with intent to [convey him out of the state ;] wherefore he prays, that a warrant may issue to bring before you the said C. D. to be discharged according to law, and to arrest the said J. S. to answer for the said offence.

" Sworn," &c.

Art. 628. Warrant on the above petition.

" By J. L. &c. To the sheriff, &c.

" Whereas proof has been made before me, that [one C. D. is illegally confined on board a vessel called the Tartar, lying at the levee of this city, and by one J. S. who intends illegally and forcibly to convey the said C. D. against his will out of this state, before he can be relieved by the due course of law :] these are, therefore, to command you to take the said C. D. out of the custody of the said J. S., or of any other person to whose custody he may have transferred him, and to bring him before me, [at the court-room of the first district court,] without delay, to abide such order as I may make in the case; and you are also commanded to arrest the said J. S. and bring him before me, without delay, [at the said court-room,] to answer for the said offence. Witness," &c.

Art. 629. When the petition does not expressly charge, that the person in whose custody the prisoner is has committed an offence, in the arrest and detention of the person detained, then the part of the warrant ordering his arrest is to be omitted.

Art. 630. Return when the party ordered to be produced has died in imprisonment, with record of the inquest.

" I, C. D., to whom the within writ is directed, do in obedience thereto return, that the within-named A. B. was committed to my custody [as keeper of the prison of the city of New Orleans] on the   day of last, by virtue of [a warrant of commitment] which is hereunto annexed, but that I cannot produce him, as I am directed, because on the   day of   last he departed this life [by the visitation of God,] as appears by the proceedings herewith returned."

Annex the inquest.

Art. 631. Notice to the coroner of the death of the prisoner.

" To the coroner of the parish of New Orleans.

" Please to take notice, that last night, about the hour of twelve, C. D. a prisoner, confined in the prison under my charge, departed this life, that his body now remains in the said prison in the situation in which he died, and that I request you will summon a jury of inquest to perform the duties in such case required by law."

Art. 632. The summons for the jury and the inquest shall be in the form hereinbefore prescribed for inquests on dead bodies.

Art. 633. Discharge when no sufficient cause of detention is shown by the return.

" By J. L. judge of the district court, &c.   To the keeper of the prison of the parish of New Orleans.

" Discharge out of your custody C. D. of the said city, if detained for no other cause than that shown by your return to the writ of *habeas corpus,* allowed by me on the   day of   last, and for your so doing this shall be your sufficient warrant.   Dated the   day of   in the year   ."

Art. 634. Order to remand when sufficient cause of detention is shown.

" To the keeper of the prison, &c.

" C. D. brought before me on a writ of *habeas corpus,* dated the   day of   instant, is remanded to your custody, the cause shown by you, in your return to the said writ, being sufficient in law for his detention."

TITLE III.

OF THE FORM TO BE USED IN THE PROCEEDING AUTHORIZED BY THE FIRST BOOK, TITLE THIRD, FOR CALLING FOR AND EMPLOYING MILITARY FORCE.

ONLY CHAPTER.

Forms of information and requisition.

Art. 635. Information of the existence of a riot or insurrection.

" To J. L., district judge, and I. K. and L. M., justices of the peace.

"A. B. and C. D., inhabitants of the city of New Orleans, being duly sworn, say, that a number of men, consisting of more than twenty, [that is to say, one hundred and more,] according to the best estimate the deponent can make of their numbers, are now assembled [in Chartres-street in this city, many of them armed with swords and pistols, and others with clubs, and bricks, and other missiles, with the intent, as avowed by many of them, to break into the prison of the said city in order to liberate the persons legally confined therein; that they have already begun to execute their threats by breaking the outer door of the said prison, and] that they have refused to disperse, although they were ordered so to do by proclamation, solemnly made in the manner directed by law by a magistrate; and the deponent further says, that the said rioters cannot be arrested or dispersed by the ordinary form of civil authority, such arrest having been attempted by the officers of justice, who were always resisted by force and with deadly weapons, [and some of them wounded and others killed in the attempt."]

Art. 636. Application of the judge and other magistrates to the governor for the employment of a military force.

"To his excellency H. J. governor of the state of Louisiana·

"We, J. L., judge of the district court, and I. K. and L. M., justices of the peace for the city of New Orleans, being convinced by the affidavits of two inhabitants of this state, that a riot has taken place in the parish [of the city of New Orleans,] where they reside, and that the persons engaged therein cannot be arrested or dispersed by the ordinary force of civil authority; all which, as well as the object of the said riot, appears by the affidavit aforesaid, which is hereunto annexed and to which we refer; we therefore request, that you will be pleased to order a military force of at least two hundred men, to repair to the place where the said rioters are assembled, and to act under our direction, according to law."

TITLE IV.

OF THE FORMS USED IN THE PROCEEDINGS AUTHORIZED IN THE SECOND BOOK, FOR PROSECUTING OFFENCES.

CHAPTER I.

Special forms of complaints, accusations, citations, and warrants of arrest.

Art. 637. Form of a complaint where the complainant is not sufficiently acquainted with the circumstances to make oath of the fact.

" Be it remembered, that on this   day of before me, P. B., associate judge of the city court of the city of New Orleans, personally appeared A. B. of the said city, who made complaint, that [his store, situate in Royal-street, was broken open last night between the hours of ten and twelve, and that ten pieces of Irish linen were stolen and carried away] by some person or persons to him unknown, but that he believes [his opposite neighbour C. D.] can give testimony that may designate the offenders.
                    (Signed)   " A. B.
" Sworn this day before me."

Art. 638. Citation for witnesses to appear before the magistrate.

" Mr. C. D., you are commanded to appear forthwith before me, [G. P., one of the associate judges of the city court of the city of New Orleans, at my office in the city-hall,] to testify what you know relative to a complaint made by A. B., of [house-breaking]; and hereof fail not under the penalties imposed by law of fine, imprisonment, and constraint. Given under my hands, this day of   in the year   ."

Art. 639. Return of the service.

"I, H. R., one of the constables of the city of New Orleans, certify, on my oath of office, I did on this day deliver a copy of the within citation to C. D. therein named, about the hour of ten in the morning."

Art. 640. If the witness does not appear according to the citation, the magistrate is authorized to impose a fine not exceeding five dollars, and to issue a warrant of attach-ment to constrain his appearance; and if he appear and refuse to give testimony, he may commit him to prison until he shall submit to be examined.

Art. 641. Warrant of attachment to compel the appearance of a witness before the magistrate.

" By G. P., associate judge of the city court of New Orleans. To any officer of justice of the said city.

" You are commanded to take into your custody C. D., and bring him forthwith before me, that he may be ex-amined as a witness in the complaint of A. B., entered before me of the [crime of house-breaking;] and for so doing this shall be your warrant. Witness my hand this day of   in the year   ."

Art. 642.*

Art. 643. Ex-officio complaint by the public prose-cutor.

" Be it remembered, that on the   day of in the year   , before me, J. P. &c. came J. P., attorney-general of the state, who gave me to understand, that he had reason to believe that [A. B. and C. D. would, if examined, prove that the offence of giving and

---

* Art. 642, referring to slaves, is omitted, for reasons stated in former notes.

receiving a challenge to fight a duel had been lately committed by E. F. and G. H. of the city of New Orleans, respectively]; he therefore required, that a citation should be issued to the said A. B. and C. D. to appear and testify what they know in the premises."

Art. 644. Form of an accusation where the defendant's name is not known.

" Be it remembered, that on the   day of in the year   , before me, G. P., one of the justices of the peace, &c., personally appeared A. B. of the said city, who on his oath declared, that on [this day, at nine o'clock in the morning, he was attacked in the high road in this parish, and by violence was robbed of ten dollars in silver and a gold watch, which were taken from his person by a man unknown to the deponent, with red hair, and a large scar over his left eye, marked with the small pox, and appearing to be about six feet high, and dressed in a sailor's jacket and trousers.]"

CHAPTER II.

Forms of proceeding in offences against the sovereign power of the state, from the complaint to the indictment; but applicable in the former parts to the other offences mentioned in this title.

Art. 645. Form of an accusation of sedition.

" Be it remembered, [as in the above form], who on his oath declared, that J. S. [of the parish of St. Mary's, now in this city, hath enlisted in this city more than one hundred men, and arrayed and furnished them with arms], for the purpose of subverting and changing the constitution of the state by force of arms, [so as to abolish the senate and make other changes in the said constitution ; that the deponent was applied to by the said J. S. to enlist for the purpose aforesaid, and saw him enlist ten other persons, to whom he gave arms in the presence of the deponent.] "

Art. 646. Form of complaint for exciting sedition by a writing.

——" That J. S. of this city has confessed himself as the author and publisher of a writing, published in hand-bills in this city on or about the   day of   last, a copy of which is hereunto annexed, by which he excites the people of this city, to resist, by *force*, the execution of a constitutional law of the state, that is to say, [to resist the execution of an act imposing a tax on the real estate in this city, passed the   day of   .]"

Arts. 647 and 648.*

Art. 649. Warrant of arrest in sedition, for exciting insurrection.

" By G. P., one of the associate judges of the city court of New Orleans. To the sheriff of the said city.
" You are commanded forthwith to arrest, and bring before me, J. S., of the parish of St. Mary's, charged on oath with sedition in enlisting men and furnishing arms, for the purpose of subverting the constitution of the state by force—that he may be examined and dealt with according to law. Given under my hand, the day of   in the year   ."

* Arts. 647 and 648,—providing forms of complaints for exciting slave insurrections,—are omitted, for the reasons mentioned in an earlier part of this work.

Art. 650. Examination of the prisoner.

" Be it remembered, that on the   day of
in the year   J. S. being brought before me, on my
warrant, issued on the complaint of A. B. on a charge of
[sedition in attempting to subvert the constitution of the
state by force of arms,] I did, according to law, inform
him of the nature of the accusation against him, and read
to him the examinations of the witnesses which had then
been taken ; who, that is to say, I. K. and H. H., were at
his request summoned and were cross-examined by him,
as appears by the said examinations hereunto annexed ;
and I did then inform him, that although he was at liberty
to answer the questions I was about to put to him in what
manner he thought proper, or not answer them at all,
yet a departure from the truth, or a refusal to answer
without assigning a sufficient reason, must operate as a
circumstance against him as well on the question of commitment as of his guilt or innocence on the trial.   I then
put to him the following interrogatories :

1. What is your name and age ?
To which he answered, ['My name is J. S. and I am
twenty-five years of age.]'

2. Where were you born ?
To which he answered, ['in the city of New Orleans.]'

3. Where do you reside, and how long have you resided there ?
[Insert answer.]

4. What is your business or profession ?
[Insert answer.]

5. Do you know the persons who have been sworn as
witnesses on the part of the accusation, or any, and which
of them, and how long have you known them ?
To which he answered, &c.

6. Where were you at the time the act of which you
are accused is stated by the witnesses to have taken place?
To which he answered, ['I was at the town of Natchez.]'

7. Give any explanation you may think proper of the
circumstances appearing on the testimony against you,

and state any facts that you think will tend to your exculpation.

To which he said, [state the answers of the defendant.]

G. P., Judge," &c.

Art 651. If, after examination and hearing evidence, the magistrate shall think there is no reasonable ground for committing the defendant, he shall write on the warrant, immediately after the return, "Let the within named J. S. be discharged, the evidence, on examination, not being sufficient for commitment," and shall then sign the same.

Art. 652. Commitment when the evidence warrants it.

"By G. P., one of the associate judges of the city of New Orleans. To the keeper of the prison of the city of New Orleans.

" Receive into your custody, J. S., herewith delivered to you, charged, on oath before me, [with the crime of sedition, by enlisting men and furnishing them with arms for the purpose of subverting the constitution of the state by force of arms;] and him safely keep until he shall be legally discharged. Witness my hand this   day of   in the year   ."

Art. 653. When the offence is bailable of right, or the proof in a case not bailable of right is not evident, nor the presumption strong, the defendant must be bailed, if he offer good security ; which is done in the following form :

"We, J. S. as principal, and G. P. and I. D. as securities do acknowledge that we are indebted, in solido, to the state of Louisiana in the sum of   to be paid if the said J. S. should not appear at the next [criminal court,] to be held at [the city of New Orleans,] on the   day of   next, to answer those things that shall be objected to him, and particularly to a charge of [sedition] whereof he is accused, and to abide the orders of such court; but if he should so appear and abide, then this recognizance to be void. Witness our hands, this day of   in the year   ."

Art. 654. The witnesses are also to enter into recognizance in the following form:

"I, A. B., acknowledge that I am indebted to the state of Louisiana in the sum of   to be paid if I should not appear at the next [criminal court,] to be held in the city of New Orleans, on the   day of next, to give testimony in an accusation against J. S. for sedition, and to abide the order of the court; but if I so appear and abide, this recognizance to be void. Witness my hand, this   day of   in the year ."

Art. 655. If any witness should refuse to sign such recognizance, he may be committed by the magistrate in the following form:

"By G. P. &c. [as above]. To the keeper, &c. [as above].

"Receive in your custody, A. B. herewith delivered to you, he having refused to enter into recognizance to appear and give testimony [against J. S. on a charge of sedition,] and him safely keep until he shall enter into such recognizance before me, or some other magistrate, or shall be otherwise released by law. Witness," &c.

Art. 656. If any one shall make oath, that another is a material witness on behalf of the prosecution in a case of CRIME, and that there is good reason to believe that he intends to depart the state, or otherwise to avoid attendance on the trial, the magistrates may direct him to find security to be recognized with him for his appearance to testify; and on his refusal, or inability to do so, may commit him by an order in the form of that prescribed by the last article, altering only the cause of commitment according to the circumstances of the case.

Art. 657. Any one committed under the last article, for inability to find security, shall receive out of the recompense fund, on the warrant of the judge, a compensation for the time he is imprisoned, to be calculated according to the rules established for compensation to persons acquitted.

Art. 658. The forms and the provisions of the ten last preceding articles apply to all prosecutions, (changing the description of the offence where it occurs in any of the said forms).

Art. 659. Form of indictment for sedition.

The beginning and conclusion shall be according to the form prescribed in the chapter of this code, entitled " *Of indictments and informations.*"

The charge in this offence shall be " did [design and attempt to subvert the constitution of this state by force of arms ; and did, on the day and year and at the place aforesaid, enlist one hundred men, to the jurors unknown, and furnish them with arms, for the purpose of changing and subverting the constitution by force of arms," &c.]

Art. 660. Another charge for the same.

——" Did design and attempt, by force of arms to dismember the state by [forming a government, in defiance of the authority of the state, in that part of the same lying west of the Mississippi river, and for that purpose, on the day and year and at the place aforesaid, collected an assemblage of men armed and arrayed], with the intent of carrying such design into effect by force of arms, and so the jurors say," &c.

Art. 661. The form of commitment on the accusation

for exciting the people to resist the execution of the laws or commit sedition, is the same as that given above for sedition, except the charge, which is "charged on oath, before me, of having published a writing exciting the people of the city of New Orleans to [resist the legal execution of a constitutional law of this state for the levying a tax in the said city] ; or, [to dismember the state by force of arms] ; or, [to subvert the constitution of the state by force of arms.]"

Art. 662. The form of examination, summons, and proceedings against witnesses, and recognizance, are the same, for this offence, and for the offences hereafter mentioned in this chapter, as those before contained in this chapter, changing only the names and description of the offences where they occur.

Art. 663. Form of the charge of the indictment for exciting the people to commit sedition.

The formal parts are the same in all cases.

"That J. S. on the   day of   in the year   , at the parish of New Orleans, did excite the people of the city of New Orleans to resist, by force, the legal execution of a constitutional law of this state, entitled 'an act for levying a tax on the real property in the city of New Orleans,' by a certain writing printed and published by him, of which the following is a copy, [insert the particulars] ; contrary," &c.

Art. 664. When the charge is of a verbal excitement, instead of "by a certain writing," in the indictment insert "[by using these expressions, addressed to a number of inhabitants of the said city assembled to prepare a petition against the said tax, ' We are fools to think of petitioning. Let us do ourselves justice. Take arms and put any officer to death who will attempt to levy the tax. I will be the first to set the example.' Thereby verbally counselling and exciting the people of the city of New Orleans, a part of the people of the state, to resist the legal execution of the said constitutional law]; contrary," &c. And in the commitment, instead of the words "having published a writing," &c. insert "having used a verbal discourse," &c.

Arts. 665 and 666.*

CHAPTER III.

Of the forms of complaint, warrant of arrest, commitment, and indictment, on prosecution for offences against the legislative power.

Art. 667. Complaint for preventing the house of assembly from meeting, &c.

" Be it remembered, &c. [as in the preceding forms of complaint] that A. B. [on the first day of February now last past, at nine o'clock in the morning, came to the government house of the state, situate in the city of New Orleans, followed by a guard of soldiers, and placed a soldier at each door of the chambers usually occupied by the house of representatives of the said state, and gave orders to such soldier not to permit any one to pass into the said chamber ; and this deponent further saith, that the house of representatives had adjourned on the twenty-ninth day of January last to meet on the said first day of February, at ten o'clock in the morning ; and that this deponent being a member of the said house, as well as a majority of the members thereof, presented

* Arts. 665 and 666,—giving forms of indictments for slave insurrections,—have been omitted ; the occasion for legislative enactment thereupon having passed away.

themselves about the said hour to enter into the said
chamber, but that they were by force of arms prevented
by the said soldiers under the command of the said J. S.,
and that the said house of representatives did not and
could not meet that day."

Art. 668. In like manner when the complaint is of any
of the offences created by the third title of the second
book of the Code of Crimes and Punishments, relating
to "Offences against the legislative powers," state the
circumstances thereof in the complaint particularly.

Art. 669. Form of charge in the warrant of arrest on
the above complaint.

——"Charged on oath, before me, with [having
designedly and by force prevented the house of representatives of this state from meeting.]"

Art. 670. The charge in the commitment for this
offence, is the same as that directed for the warrant of
arrest.

Art. 671. Charge in the indictment.

——"[Did designedly and by force prevent the house
of representatives, being one of the houses composing the
general assembly of this state, from meeting] ; or according to the fact stated in the complaint, [did with intent
to prevent the meeting of the house of representatives of
this state, being one of the houses composing the general
assembly of this state, by the use of personal violence
offered to A. B., C. D., and E. F., members of the said
house of representatives, prevent them from attending
the said house] ; or, [did by force and the threats thereof
force the senate] [or the house of representatives], being
one of the branches of the general assembly of the state
of Louisiana, then and there in session, to adjourn [or

disperse], or [to pass a law, entitled an act, &c.] giving
the title ; or [to reject an act, entitled an act, &c. which
they constitutionally might have passed] ; or, [did
threaten A. B. then a member of the house of representatives, that he, the said J. S., would beat and otherwise
ill-treat him, unless he voted for the passage of a bill then
before the said house, entitled an act, &c. with intent to
influence his official conduct as a member of the said
house of representatives] ; or, [did make an assault upon
A. B. late a member of the house of representatives, and
did beat and ill-treat him in consequence of the conduct
of the said A. B., while he was a member of the said
house] ; or, [did offer to bribe A. B., then a member of
the house of representatives of this state, by promising
that if the said A. B. would vote for the passage of a
certain law then under consideration in the said house,
entitled, " an act for incorporating an insurance company
called the Safety Company," he the said A. B. should
have ten shares in the stock of the said company] ; or,
[did bribe A. B., a member of the house of representatives
of this state, by transferring to him ten shares in the
stock of an insurance company called the Safety Company,
as an inducement to the said A. B. to vote for an act then
before the said house for continuing the charter of the
said company] ; or, [did offer to one C. D. the sum of one
thousand dollars, (or the right to subscribe ten shares in a
certain bank, called the Fog Bank, when the said bank
should be incorporated), for the purpose of securing his,
the said C. D.'s interest with the general assembly, or
with some members thereof, in order to procure an act
incorporating the said bank] ; or, [that the said J. S.,
on the   day of   in the year   ,
at the parish of New Orleans, did receive from A. B. the
sum of   or the promise of ten shares in the
Fog Bank, as a compensation for exerting his influence
with the general assembly to pass an act incorporating
the said bank] ; or, [that A. B. being a member of the
house of representatives of the state of Louisiana, did on

the　　　　day of　　　　　　in the year　　　　　, at the
city of New Orleans, receive from J. S. a transfer of ten
shares in a certain bank called the Specie Bank, as the
consideration for a promise then and there made by him
the said A. B. to vote for the passage of a law then
pending before the said house, entitled an act, &c.] contrary to the laws, &c.

CHAPTER IV.

*Forms for prosecution of offences against the executive
power.*

Art. 672. Complaint against officers.
" To A. B. justice of the peace, &c.
" C. D., being duly sworn, says, [that E. F. lately
appointed to the executive office of inspector of flour in
the City of New Orleans, on the　　　　day of
in the year　　　　, at the city of New Orleans, performed an official act by inspecting and marking one
hundred barrels of flour for G. H. of the said city,
merchant, he the said E. F. not having then taken the
oath of office required by law.]"
" Sworn," &c.
Art. 673. Citation to E. F.
" You are cited to appear before me A. B. justice of
the peace, &c. on the　　　　day of　　　　next, at
ten o'clock in the morning, to answer to a complaint
entered against you for having, as inspector of flour for
the city of New Orleans, inspected and marked one
hundred barrels of flour, before you had taken the oath
of office required by law."
Art. 674. Charges in indictments for offences under
this title.
—— " Did offer the sum of one hundred dollars to
A. B., register of mortgages, to induce him to give a
certificate that a certain parcel of land, belonging to him,

the said   , was free from incumbrance, when, in fact, the same was incumbered to a large amount."

—— "Did by threats of violence to the person of A. B. [one of the constables of the city of New Orleans,] force him [to make an arrest of one A. B. without any warrant or other legal authority," &c.]

—— "Did attempt to force," [as in the preceding form.]

—— "Did by force resist and attempt to prevent A. B. [a notary public, from entering on his minutes an act of sale legally made by I. K. to L. M." describing it.]

—— "Did, he being then a [notary public,] receive the sum of [one hundred dollars] from A. B. as a bribe for [making an entry in the register of his office of a sale made to him the said A. B. by C. D. as of a date prior to the true time of recording the same.]"

—— "Did, he being then legally appointed and exercising the office [of inspector of tobacco], extort and receive from one A. B. the sum of [ten dollars for inspecting five hogsheads of tobacco, being more than is allowed by law for performing such service]; or [for doing any act (describing it) which he was by law obliged to perform, and for which no remuneration is given by law]—that he did extort and receive ten dollars when, in fact, he had not made such inspection ; or [did receive the sum of ten dollars for inspecting five hogsheads of tobacco], being more than the sum allowed by law for that service, which were voluntarily given to him by one A. B. for [making such inspection.]'

—— "Did receive [the sum of ten dollars] from one A. B. for refraining from [condemning ten hogsheads of tobacco], which he was not authorized by law to [condemn], and which sum the law did not authorize him to receive."

—— "Being an executive officer, to wit, a notary for the city of New Orleans, he negligently [or intentionally as the case may be] omitted [to enter on his register a certain act of sale, under private signature made, &c. (describing it) which was acknowledged and left with him for that purpose], by which omission such an injury accrued to the said   as would entitle him to a civil action against the said E. F."

—— " Being [sheriff of the city and parish of   ] did, under pretence of performing the duties of his office, [arrest one A. B. and keep him in prison from the said   day until the   day of the same month], he the said E. F. falsely pretending that he had a [writ or other process for arresting and detaining the said A. B.]"

CHAPTER V.

Forms relating to offences against the judiciary power.

Art. 675. Form of information against a judge or juror for receiving a bribe.

" That J. S. had a cause pending in the   court of this parish, against the deponent, which was tried by [the court or a jury, as the case may be], and that the said J. S. on the   day of   , during the pendency of the said suit, gave to A. B. [the judge of the said court, or a juror summoned to try the said cause] a promise in writing to pay to the said A. B. the sum of one thousand dollars when he the said J. S. should obtain judgment (or a verdict) in the said cause]; which written promise the said A. B. then and there received, and did promise to give a judgment (or verdict) for the said J. S. against the deponent."

Art. 676. Commitment thereon.

—— " Charged on oath with having, as judge of   or as juror, received a bribe from one J. S. in a suit between him and one C. D."

Art. 677. Indictment.

——" That A. B. being appointed to the office of [parish judge of the parish of L.] and exercising the duties of that office, did on the   day of   in the year   , at the parish aforesaid, [receive from one J. S., who then had a suit pending undetermined in the said court, a written promise to pay to him the said judge the sum of   dollars in case the said suit should be determined in favour of the said J. S.] as a bribe to influence the official conduct of him the said A. B."

Art. 678. Complaint for corrupt or malicious conduct, not amounting to bribery.

———— " That A. B. being appointed [parish judge of the parish of L.] and exercising the duties of that office, on the   day of   in the year   , at the said parish of L. with design to injure this deponent, and maliciously to have him declared an insolvent debtor, and by a forced surrender to deprive him of the possession of his property, did persuade one C. D. of the said parish, a creditor of the deponent, to present a petition for a forced surrender against the deponent, to him the said C. D., alleging in such petition that the deponent had suffered his notes to be protested, and had committed other acts of bankruptcy, which petition the said C. D. did present, but, although he did not make oath to the truth of such petition, or give any other proof thereon, the said A. B., under colour of his office, ordered a provisional seizure to be made of the deponent's property, and other proceedings to be had as in case of a forced surrender, against him."

Art. 679. The same transaction may be stated to be corruptly done, alleging the motive instead of a desire to injure, to be that of securing some emolument or advantage to himself, [describing it], or to another, (by giving him the management of the estate at Syndic, or some other means.)

Art. 680. Warrant and commitment.

————" Charged on oath, with having officially as parish judge [or maliciously] granted an order of seizure, as in case of a forced surrender, against C. D."

Art. 681. Indictment.

————"That A. B. being appointed to the office of [parish judge of the parish of L.] and exercising the

duties of that office, on the   day of   in the year
, at the said parish of L., did [corruptly, for the purpose of securing emolument to himself, or to another, stating what emolument, as the case may be], or [maliciously, for the purpose of injuring one C. D., grant, under colour of his office, but in a manner unauthorized by law, an order of seizure, as in a forced surrender, against one C. D.]"

Art. 682. Complaint of an offer to bribe.

——" That the deponent is, and since the   day of
last, has been clerk of the parish court of the parish of L., and that C. D. of the said parish, on the
    day of   in the year   , in the parish aforesaid, offered to the deponent that if the deponent would permit him the said C. D. to alter a certain record of a judgment obtained in the said court, and then in the official custody of the deponent, [describing it,] by erasing the word ' hundred,' and inserting the word ' thousand ' instead thereof, he would give to the deponent the sum of three hundred dollars, which the deponent refused to do."

Art. 683. Warrant of arrest and commitment.

——" Charged on oath, with having offered to bribe A. B. clerk of the parish court of the parish of L."

Art. 684. Indictment.

——" That one A. B. having been before the
day of   in the year   , legally appointed clerk of the parish court of the parish of L., and being on that day in the legal exercise of the duties of the said office, one C. D. of the said parish, on the day and year and in the parish aforesaid, did offer to give to the said A. B. three hundred dollars as a bribe, if he would permit him the said C. D. to alter the record of a judgment entered in the said court in favour of the said C. D. against one E. F., for five hundred dollars, by erasing in the said record the word ' hundred ' and inserting in the place thereof the word ' thousand,' so as to falsify and forge the said record, and make it appear to be a judgment for five thousand dollars.]"

Art. 685. Complaint of forcible opposition to an officer of justice.

——" That the deponent is [sheriff of the parish of L. and was so on the   day of   last, that having in his hands a warrant in due form of law, issued by G. P. one of the justices of the peace for the said parish, to arrest one E. F. charged with the crime of forgery, and being about to execute the said warrant on the said E. F., who was then in the house of G. H. in the said parish, he was by force of arms opposed by I. K. and L. M. in the lawful execution of the said official act, and prevented by force from entering the said house to search for and arrest the said E. F., they the said I. K. and L. M. knowing, at the same time, the office of the deponent and his authority to make the said arrest.]"

Art. 686. Warrant for arrest and commitment.

——" Charged with having forcibly opposed A. B. sheriff of the parish of L. in the lawful execution of an official duty."

Art. 687. Indictment.

——" Did by force oppose A. B. then being sheriff of the said parish of L. in the lawful execution of an official act, that is to say, by forcibly preventing him from making the arrest of one E. F. by virtue of a warrant in due form of law, issued by G. P. one of the justices, &c. commanding the said sheriff to arrest the said E. F. and bring him for examination, on a charge of forgery, they the said I. K. and L. M. well knowing that the said A. B. was sheriff of the said parish, and had legal authority to make the said arrest."

Art. 688. Complaint where the opposition was made in a case when the arrest was authorized to be made without warrant.

——" That on the   day of   last, A. B. was murdered in the said parish, by a blow with an axe on the head of the said A. B., of which he instantly died, given by C. D. of the said parish ; that the said C. D. immediately fled, and that the deponent having good reason to believe that he would effect his escape before a warrant could be obtained, and there being no magistrate present, the deponent pursued the said C. D. with the intent to arrest and bring him before a magistrate for examination and commitment, but that I. K. and L. M. well knowing all that is above stated, forcibly opposed the deponent in the lawful execution of the said duty."

Art. 689. Warrant for arrest and commitment.

——" Charged on oath with having forcibly opposed E. F. legally acting as an officer of justice, in the lawful execution of the official act of arresting C. D., who fled after having committed murder, the circumstances under which the said E. F. acted being then known to the said I. K. and L. M."

Art. 690. Indictment.

——" That on the   day of   in the year   , in the parish of L. the crime of murder was committed on one A. B. by a certain C. D., who instantly endeavored to make his escape, and there being good reason to believe that he would effect it before a warrant could be obtained, and there being no magistrate present, E. F. pursued the said C. D. with the intent to arrest him ; but that I. K. and L. M. well knowing the premises, on the day and year and at the place aforesaid, forcibly opposed the said E. F. in making the said arrest," &c.

Art. 691. Complaint of rescue.

——" [That the deponent being sheriff of the parish of L, had on the   day of   last a warrant in due form of law, issued by G. P. one of the justices, commanding the deponent to arrest A. B. charged on oath with the crime of forgery ; on which warrant the said A. B. was lawfully arrested and in the custody of the deponent, who was proceeding with him to the said justice as by the said warrant he was commanded, and that] I. K. and L. M. did on the day and year and the place last aforesaid, by force of arms, rescue the said A. B. from the deponent's custody and set him at liberty."

Art. 692. Warrant and commitment.

——" Charged with having rescued from the custody of the sheriff of the parish of L. one A. B., lawfully arrested by the said sheriff on a [warrant for forgery," &c.]

Art. 693. Indictment.

The same as the complaint, substituting the name of the sheriff for the words "the deponent," whenever they occur.

Art. 694. Complaint of escape.

——"That A. B., being lawfully arrested and in the custody of the deponent [by virtue of a warrant to him directed and delivered, issued in due form of law by G. P., one of the justices, &c., commanding the deponent to arrest the said A. B., charged on oath with assault and battery upon G. H.,] and being so in custody the said A. B. privately escaped therefrom without being legally discharged," &c.

Art. 695. Warrant and commitment.

——"Charged on oath with having escaped from a lawful arrest," &c.

Art. 696. Indictment.

——"Did, after being lawfully arrested, on a charge of [assault and battery committed upon one G. H.], escape from the custody of the sheriff of the parish of L., without being legally discharged."

Art. 697. Complaint for breach of prison.

——" That he is the keeper of the public prison of the parish of L., and that A. B. was legally committed to his custody in the said prison on the   day of   last, by a commitment in due form of law, issued by G. P. one of the justices, &c., charging the said A. B. [with the crime of house-breaking ; and that in the night of the   day of   last, the said A. B. broke the said prison by taking out two of the iron bars which formed the window-grates of the said prison], and escaped [or attempted to escape] out of the said prison by the breach he had so made."

Art. 698. Warrant and commitment.

——" Charged with breach of prison and attempt to escape [or with having escaped.]"

Art. 699. Indictment.

——" That on the　　　　day of　　　　in the year　　　, [being legally] confined in the public prison of the parish of L. in the said parish, and in the custody of the keeper thereof, on a charge of [house-breaking,] he did then and there forcibly break [the bars which formed the window grates thereof], and escape through the breach he had thus made."

Art. 700. Indictment for aiding the prisoner to attempt an escape.

——" That one A. B. was on the　　　　day of　　　　in the year　　　, lawfully confined in the public prison of the parish of L. by virtue of a commitment made by a magistrate, for the [crime of theft], and that I. K. and L. M. did, on the day and year and in the parish aforesaid, furnish the said A. B. with [a hammer and saw] for the purpose of attempting his escape, by breaking the said prison with the instruments aforesaid."

Art. 701. Warrant and commitment for the above offence.

——" Charged with having furnished to A. B., a prisoner legally confined in the public prison of the parish of L., instruments for attempting his escape by breaking the prison."

Art. 702. In all the proceedings under this chapter, if the defendant be an attorney at law or a counsellor at law, these words must be inserted after his name in the charge of the offence, " he being at that time an attorney at law," or " counsellor at law," or both, as the case may be.

Art. 703. Complaint against an attorney, for malpractice.

——" That A. B., being on the　　　　day of　　　　last, an attorney and counsellor at law, duly admitted to practise in the parish court of the parish of L., and having been charged with the prosecution of a suit brought by the deponent in that court against one C. D. for the recovery of a tract of land, on the day and year and in the parish aforesaid, during the pendency of the said suit, did designedly divulge to the said C. D.. to the injury of the deponent, a circumstance that came to his knowledge by virtue of this trust, to wit [that I. K., under whom the defendant claimed the land in question, had resided for two years in this state, the knowledge of which fact enabled the said C. D. to avail himself of a plea of prescription against the deponent's] title; or, [did give counsel to the said C. D. to plead prescription against the deponent's title;] or, [did, after having been consulted on the merits of the case for the deponent, under pretext that the deponent had not paid his fees, (or, under some other pretext, stating it,) appear for the said C. D. as his counsellor in court in the said cause] —[or secretly as his adviser, as the case may be]; or, [did in the prosecution of the said cause, with intent to injure the deponent, (agree to put off the trial of the said cause) when he was not obliged by law so to do, by which the deponent suffered great injury]; or, [did with intent to injure the deponent, omit to bring on the trial of the said cause, which he lawfully might have done, by which the deponent suffered great injury] : or, [did receive from the said C. D. the sum of one thousand dollars, under colour of a fee for advice to be given for services to be rendered by the said A. B., but in reality as a bribe for betraying the trust reposed in him as attorney and counsellor to the deponent."]

Art. 704. In the warrant and commitment, it will be sufficient to say, in either of these complaints—

——" Charged with malpractice as an attorney at law, or a counsellor at law, or both, [or charged with receiving a bribe], as the case may be.

Art. 705. Indictment.

The same charge as in the complaint, substituting the name of the complainant for the words " the deponent," whenever they occur.

Art. 706. The above forms will serve for all prosecutions against attorneys or counsellors, changing only the charge according to circumstances, retaining in all cases the words of the article, under which the prosecution is made, where the sense will admit.

Art. 707. Complaint for personating any officer of justice.

——" That one A. B., not being an officer of justice, but fraudulently pretending to be [one of the deputies of the sheriff of the parish of L., in such assumed character on the   day of   in the year   , in the parish of L., made an assault on the deponent and kept him in custody and imprisonment for the space of two hours]; or, in such assumed character, exacted and received, [or attempted to receive, as the case may be], the sum of five dollars from the deponent, for fees due to the said sheriff."

Art. 708. Warrant and commitment.

——" Charged on oath with falsely and fraudulently personating an officer of justice."

Art. 709. Indictment.

The same charge as in the complaint, substituting the name of the complainant for the words " the deponent," whenever they occur.

Art. 710. Complaint for falsely personating another in a judicial proceeding.

——" That A. B. without having received any authority from the deponent, falsely personated him, and in such assumed character, [on the   day of in the year   , in the parish of L., put in a plea of confession of judgment in a suit brought by one J. S. against the deponent, in the parish court of the parish of L. ;] or [put in bail for one C. D. in a suit brought against him by one J. S. in the parish court of the parish of L.]"

Art. 711. Complaint for perjury in a court of justice.

" Be it remembered, that on   this day of   in the year of our Lord   , before me, G. P. judge of the city court of the city of New Orleans, came I. K. and L. M. who being sworn, do say, that [on the   day of   last, they were present in the district court of the first district of this state then sitting in this city, and that they saw and heard J. S. sworn as a witness in the said court in a cause then and there pending, between A. B. plaintiff, and C. D. defendant, and that the said J. S. did then and there, under the sanction of the oath so administered, falsely, deliberately, and wilfully assert and give in evidence in the said cause, that he heard the defendant acknowledge on the first day of January last, in the city of New Orleans, that he owed the sum of one hundred dollars to the plaintiff in the said suit, which assertion the deponents declare to be a falsehood, because they say that on the said first day of January the said J. S. was not in the city of New Orleans, but was seen by both the deponents on that day in the city of New York."]

Art. 712. Warrant and commitment.

—— " Charged on oath with the crime of perjury."

Art. 713. Indictment.

—— " That J. S. being, on the ⸻ day of ⸻ in the year ⸻, at the parish of New Orleans, sworn as a witness, on oath legally administered to him ⌊in the district court of the state of Louisiana for the first district⌋, in the suit pending in the said court between A. B. plaintiff and C. D. defendant, did under sanction of the said oath declare and assert as evidence in the said cause, that [here insert the particular part of the evidence which is found to be false]; which evidence and assertion so given and made the jurors present, was a deliberate and wilful falsehood, inasmuch as [the said J. S. was not at New Orleans at the time asserted in his said evidence, but at the city of New York, and did not hear the defendant acknowledge that he owed the said sum to the plaintiff.]"

Art. 714. In proceedings for perjury on a written instrument, such as an accusation before a magistrate, an examination before commissioners, or answers to interrogatories, the whole instrument need not be copied in the complaint or the indictment, but only that assertion which is alleged to be false ; the whole instrument must, however, be produced and shown to the defendant previous to the arraignment in the manner herein before directed with respect to forged instruments, with the modifications contained in a subsequent chapter prescribing the forms of proceeding on prosecutions for forgery.

Art. 715. Complaint for perjury, in answer to interrogatories put by a plaintiff.

—— " That the deponent on the   day of in the year   , presented a petition to the parish court of the parish of L. against J. S., for the recovery of a sum of money due to him, by promise, for goods sold ; that, according to the forms prescribed by law, he annexed to his said petition certain interrogations to be answered by the said J. S. on oath : among which interrogations was the following : ' First interrogatory—did you not on the   day of   , or at any other time, acknowledge that you had purchased the goods mentioned in the petition, and promise to pay the amount to the plaintiff ? '—which interrogatories were allowed, and ordered by the judge of the said court to be answered, and that the said J. S. made answers thereto in writing ; and in answer to the interrogatory herein before set forth, on the   day of   last, in the parish of New Orleans, under the sanction of an oath legally administered, that is to say, by G. P. one of the judges of the city court of the city of New Orleans, did deliberately, and wilfully, and falsely allege and declare, in writing, as follows : ' In answer to the first interrogatory the respondent [meaning the said J. S.] answers—that he never made such acknowledgment as set forth in the said first interrogatory ' —which allegation *the deponent declares* is a falsehood, inasmuch as the said J. S. did make such acknowledgment as is stated or inquired of by the interrogatory above recited."

Art. 716. The charge in the indictment is the same as the complaint, inserting the name of the complainant instead of the words " the deponent," and the words " the grand jury present," instead of the words " the deponent declares," in the conclusion of the statement.

Art. 717. Complaint for false-swearing.

——" That J. S. on the   day of   in the year   , in the parish of New Orleans, made a volun tary affidavit under the sanction of an oath, administered by H. P. one of the justices, to the following effect, [recite the part of the affidavit alleged to be false]; and the *deponent declares*, that the allegation aforesaid contained in the said affidavit, is a falsehood, deliberately and wilfully made, inasmuch as in truth [insert the true statement as above."]

Art. 718. The indictment pursues the complaint, changing as is above directed in the last precedent.

Art. 719. Complaint for subornation or perjury.

——" That [as in the case of perjury by a witness in court]; and that W. S. of the said parish, did, by means unknown to the deponent, procure the said J. S. to make the false declaration and commit the perjury aforesaid."

Art. 720. Indictment.

——" That [the same as the indictment for perjury by a witness in court ; and add,] and the jurors aforesaid do further present that W. S. of the said city, did, on the said   day of   in the year   , at the parish of New Orleans, by means to the said jurors unknown, induce the said J. S. to make the false declaration and commit the perjury aforesaid."

Art. 721. Complaint for endeavouring to suborn.

——" That J. S. on the   day of   in the year   , in the parish of L., by offering a reward of one hundred dollars to him, endeavoured to persuade one W. S. to commit perjury by declaring, under the sanction of an oath as a witness in a certain cause then pending and to be tried before the parish court of the parish of L., brought by this deponent against A. B., that he the said W. S. had [insert the fact endeavoured to be proved,] he the said J. S. well knowing that [if the said W. S. had wilfully and deliberately made the said declaration, under the sanction of an oath lawfully administered in the said court,] he would have been guilty of perjury."

Art. 722. Indictment.

——" That J. S. on the   day of   in the year   , at the parish of L., by offering a reward of one hundred dollars to one W. S., did endeavour to persuade him the said W. S. to commit perjury by declaring, under the sanction of an oath to be legally administered to him the said W. S. as a witness in a certain cause then pending and to be tried in the parish court of the parish of L. between one I. K. plaintiff and A. B. defendant," &c. as in the complaint.

Art. 723. Complaint and indictment for obstructing the proceedings of a court of justice.

——" That J. S. during the session of the parish court of the parish of L. on the ___ day of ___ in the year ___, in the parish of L. did [by loud speaking or making a clamour and noise] wilfully obstruct the proceedings of the said court; or [that the parish court of the parish of L. on the ___ day of ___ in the year ___, made a legal order for the maintenance of order (or to preserve regularity of proceedings therein), which order directed [insert the purport of the order;] and that the said order was signified to one J. S. for his government, but that he the said J. S. did refuse to obey the same, and did," [insert the act of disobedience.]

Art. 724. Indictment for using indecorous expressions, &c.

——" That J. S. on the ___ day of ___ in the year ___, in the parish of ___ in the [parish court of the said parish] then open and in session, did verbally use the following [indecorous,] [contemptuous,] or [insulting] expressions, addressed to the judge of the said court, [of,] or [to,] the [judge of the said court,] or said [court,] that is to say, [recite the expressions complained of."]

Art. 725. Indictment for indecorous expressions in writing.

——" That J. S. on the ___ day of ___ in the year ___, in the parish of New Orleans, in a written argument or pleading, addressed to the [judges of the supreme court of the state of Louisiana,] in a suit then pending in the said court between A. B. plaintiff and C. D. defendant, did use the following [indecorous, | [contemptuous,] or [insulting] expressions of or [to] the said court, or [the judges thereof,] that is to say," [insert the language complained of.]

Art. 726. If the party complained of be an attorney or counsellor, and the indictment be on a third offence, the circumstances of his being an attorney or counsellor must be set forth in the indictment.

Art. 727. Indictment for obstructing the proceedings of courts.

——" That on the   day of   in the year , at the parish of L. the parish court of the said parish being then open, J. S. [by threats of violence] or [by violence] offered to A. B. the [judge of the said court,] or [summoned to attend the said court as a juror,] or [as a witness,] or attending the said court to [prosecute] or defend a suit as a party or [as an attorney or counsellor,] obstructed the proceedings of the said court."

Art. 728. If the person accused in the above indictment be an attorney or counsellor, that fact must be stated.

CHAPTER VI.

Forms of proceeding on prosecutions for offences against public tranquillity.

Art. 729. Indictment for an unlawful assembly.

——" That A. B., [together with C. D., E. F., &c.] or together with three or more persons, to the jurors unknown, did, on the   day of   in the year , in the parish of L. assemble with intent to aid each other by violence illegally to [pull down a house erected by G. H. in the said parish,] or [to do any other illegal act, reciting it.]"

Art. 730. For a riot.

——" That A. B. [as in the preceding form to the end]; and that being so assembled, the said A. B. and the others of the said assembly, did actually, by violence and illegally, [pull down the said house, or do any other illegal act, reciting it.]"

Art. 731. When the original assembly was not unlawful.

—"That A. B. together with three or more persons, to the jurors unknown, having assembled on the   day of   in the year   , in the parish of L. for a lawful purpose, did, afterwards and before the said assembly was dispersed, on the same day and year and at the place aforesaid, proceed to aid each other in committing, and did commit the unlawful and violent act of [recite the unlawful act.]"

Art. 732. An unlawful assembly for the purpose of witnessing a boxing match.

——"That A. B. with three or more others, to the jurors unknown, on the   day of   , at the parish of L., assembled together for the purpose of being present at and witnessing a boxing match, made up and agreed to be fought between [C. and D.] or [between two persons to the jurors unknown.]"

[If the fight actually takes place, add,] "and the jurors further present, that a single combat with fists, or a boxing match, was then and there fought in the presence of the said assembly, whereof the said A. B. was one, and that he and the other persons composing the said assembly witnessed the boxing match; and [if wagers were laid, add,] that the said A. B. then and there laid a wager on the event of such combat or boxing match."

Art. 733. Indictment for public disturbance.

——"That A. B. and C. D. on the   day of   in the year   , in the parish of L., did meet in the public highway, near to the houses of I. K., and J. S., and G. H., and other inhabitants of the said parish, and being so met [by vociferation, quarrelling,] or fighting with each other, greatly disturbed the said inhabitants of the said place in the prosecution of their business; [or if at night, say,] in their necessary repose."

Art. 734. The enumeration of the names of the inhabitants in the above, is made only to designate the place, but is not necessary if the neighbourhood be otherwise designated, as a square or street in a city.

CHAPTER VII.

Forms used in prosecutions for offences against the right of suffrage.

Art. 735. Indictment for bribing at an election.

—— "That A. B. on the day of in the year , at the parish of L., was an inhabitant of the said parish entitled by law to vote at public elections for members of the and for governor of this state, and that J. S. on the day and year and at the place aforesaid, for the purpose of influencing the vote of the said A. B. at the public election then about to be held on the day of then next thereafter, for the election of [a governor of the state of Louisiana], did offer to the said A. B. [the sum of ten dollars, or any other advantage or emolument which would constitute bribery, according to the definition of that term in the Book of Definitions, describing what such advantage or emolument is], as a BRIBE, if he would consent to vote at such election for C. D. as governor."

If the charge be for giving a BRIBE, insert " did give " instead of " did offer ; " and instead of the words, " if he would consent to vote," insert " for consenting to vote."

If the charge be for receiving a BRIBE, add at the end of the last form, " which the said A. B. received, and promised, in consideration of such bribe, to vote for the said C. D."

Art. 736. Indictment for offering or giving a bribe to a judge or clerk of the election, or the officers attending it.

——" That A. B. being [parish judge of the parish of L., is by virtue of his office constituted by law one of the judges of the public elections for members of the general

assembly and governor of the state, in the said parish of
L.]; and that J. S. desiring to influence the said A. B.
to betray the said trust reposed in him by law, on the
day of   in the year   , at the
parish aforesaid, proposed and offered to the said A. B.
[to procure for him by the influence of him the said J. S.
the place as cashier of the bank of   in the city of
New Orleans, as a bribe, if he the said A. B. would, at a
public election for governor of the state, then about to be
held in the said parish, on the   day of
then next, put into the ballot-box one hundred ballots
with the name of X. Y. written thereon, and take out an
equal number that had been legally deposited therein,
containing the name of some other person."

If the charge be bribery against the judge, clerk, or
other officer, add, "which proposal the said A. B. did
then and there accept, and promised to perform the illegal
act so requested to be done as a consideration for the said
bribe."

Art. 737. The above form will serve for indictments
against clerks and other officers of elections, changing
only the allegation of the office.

Art. 738. Indictment for hiring persons to procure
votes.

——" That J. S. on the   day of   in the
year   , in the parish of   did offer or [give,
as the case is], to one A. B. [the sum of fifty dollars] as
a reward for his services in persuading or procuring
persons qualified to vote as electors for [governor] to vote
at an election then about to take place for X. Y. as
[governor], or, as the case may be, [to vote against
A. Z.]"

Art. 739. Indictment for endeavouring to procure
votes by threats.

——" That A. B. of the parish of L. on the
day of   followed the business of a grocer, and in
the way of his business, then and for a long time before,
had the custom of one J. S. and made lawful gains by
supplying him with groceries for his family, and that the

said A. B. on the   day of   last aforesaid,
was entitled to vote at a public election for members of
the general assembly of this state then about to be held
on the   day of   then next in the said
parish ; and the jurors further present, that J. S. of the
said parish, being desirous of procuring the vote and
influence of the said A. B. at the said election in favour
of C. D., E. F., &c. as members of the house of representatives, on the day and year and at the parish first aforesaid, threatened the said A. B. to withdraw his custom
or dealing from him in his said trade of grocer, if he the
said A. B. did not, at the said election, vote for the said
C. D. and E. F., as members of the house of representatives."

Art. 740. Indictment against a clerk of election for
making a false entry.

——"That J. S. being appointed clerk of the public
election began to be held on the   day of
in the year   , at the parish of L. for members of
the house of representatives of the state of Louisiana, and
being in the exercise of the duties of the said office on the
     day of   in the year aforesaid, did knowingly
make a false entry on the list of voters at the said election,
by inserting thereon [insert the false entry.]"

Art. 741. If against a judge.

——"That J. S. being a judge of the public election,
began to be held, &c. [as in the above form] did knowingly put into the ballot-box a ballot not given by an
elector, or [did permit a ballot, not given by an elector,
to be put into the ballot-box ;] or [did take, or permit to
be taken, out of the ballot-box, in a manner not prescribed
by law, a ballot deposited therein ;] or [did designedly
change the ballots given by the electors;] or [did
designedly destroy the ballots given by the electors at
such election by burning the same ;] or [did designedly,
by omitting to seal the box, or any other omission or
act, describing it], destroy or change the ballots given
at the said election."

Art. 742. The other offences under the second chapter

of the seventh title of the Penal Code, may be indicted according to the above form, stating in the same manner the offence of the defendant, and the act or omission as nearly as possible in the words of the article creating the offence.

Art. 743. Indictment for bringing armed men within a mile of the place of election.

—"That A. B., having under his orders [as colonel of the militia of the state, or other military office, if he hold one, stating it], a body of troops or armed men, did, on the   day of   in the year   , at the parish of L., order and bring [or did keep, according to the fact], the said troops within one mile of the [courthouse] of the said parish, where a public election for [members of the general assembly] of the state of Louisiana was on that day held, and [if such be the charge, add] with intent to influence the said election."

Art. 744. Indictments for riots at elections must be in the form of indictments for riots on other occasions, only adding to the charge that such riot was within half a mile of the place at which a public election was then held.

Art. 745. Indictments for other offences committed at elections must state the holding of the election in the form above given, and the offence as nearly as possible in the words of the article which forbids the offence.

CHAPTER VIII.

Of forms used in prosecutions for offences against the liberty of the press.

Art. 746. Indictment for preventing any one from publishing by threats, &c.

—"That A. B. having the intention, according to the right secured to him by the constitution, of freely speaking, writing, and printing on any subject, to write, or to publish, or verbally to make [an investigation into the public character and conduct of J. S. as governor of the state of Louisiana, (or as judge or member of the general assembly, or as any other officer, stating the office), or any other speech, or publication, or writing, describing its nature], J. S. of the parish of L. on the   day of   in the year   , in the parish aforesaid, in order to prevent, or endeavour to prevent the said A. B. from exercising the right secured to him as aforesaid, did threaten him, that if he printed, [wrote or spoke, as the case may be], the said investigation, [or other matter, according to the fact], he the said J. S. would beat him the said A. B. [or do some other injury to his person, property, or credit, describing the nature of the injury,]" &c.

If the offender be a member of the general assembly, or a judge, or judicial or executive officer, then add, if his intent will warrant the charge, "he the said J. S. being [state the place or office], and having made the said threats, in order to prevent an investigation of his official conduct, [or if he be a member of the general assembly, the investigation of the branch to which he belongs, stating it,"] &c.

If the offence be committed by a judge, and the publication be prevented by an official act, or the threat of one, follow the above form down to and including the words "that he the said J. S. would," after which insert "he being then [state his office] by virtue of his office, arrest [or state any other official act that was threatened.]"

If the publication was prevented, or attempted to be prevented, by the actual exercise of the official act, state, —— " did by virtue of his office, he being then [state the office], arrest or [state the official act] the said A. B., and did thereby prevent, or attempt to prevent, the said A. B. from speaking, [printing, or writing, as the case may be], what he so intended."

Art. 747. Indictment against a judge for granting an

injunction against a publication, under an allegation that it was a libel.

——"That J. S. being judge and [state the office] did [insert the date and place] issue an injunction commanding A. B. to desist from publishing a writing which he intended to publish, entitled or purporting to be [describing the writing] under pretext [that the same was a libel or a seditious writing on,]" [stating the cause for granting the injunction.]

Art. 748. Indictment for preventing the investigation of legislative, judicial, or executive proceedings.

——"That J. S. [being a judge, and state his office if he have any], intending to restrain the right, given by the constitution, to examine the proceedings of the legislature, or of any branch of the government, and intending also to give effect to an act of the general assembly, entitled 'an act,' [insert the title], passed in contravention of that clause in the constitution which declares that no law shall be made to restrain the right aforesaid, did," [here insert the act done in obedience to the unconstitutional law.]

CHAPTER IX.

Of the forms to be used in prosecutions for offences against public records.

Art. 749. Indictment for forging a public record.

——"That A. B. on the   day of   in the year   , at the parish of L. forged a public record, purporting to be the record of an act of the general assembly of Louisiana, of which forgery the following is a copy [insert an exact copy of the forged record,] with intent to injure or defraud, and so the said jurors say, that the said A. B. hath committed the crime of forgery, contrary," &c.

Art. 750. When the forgery consists in altering a record, the indictment shall be :

———"That among the records of conveyances and other authentic acts, kept in the notary's office now under the care of A. B. notary public, in [state the place] there was prior to the   day of   in the year   , a certain [act of sales,] made by I. K. to L. M. of which the following is a copy [insert a copy of the record as it was before the alteration,] and that J. S. on the   day of   in the year   , at the parish of L., without any legal authority, and with intent to injure or defraud, made such alterations in the said record as to make it appear to be ot the following tenor [insert a copy of the record as altered,] and so the said jurors say, that the said J. S. hath committed the crime of forgery."

Art. 751. When, from obliterations made in the original record it is difficult to prove what its exact tenor was before the alterations, the form shall be :

———" That among the records [designating them as above] there was one purporting to be [describe the nature of the altered record as it was before the alteration,] and that J. S. on the day [state the date] at the parish of L., without lawful authority, and with design to injure or defraud, made such alterations in the said record as to make it appear to be of the following tenor," [insert a copy of the record as altered.]

Art. 752. Indictment for forging an official certificate of an officer having the custody of public records.

———" Did make and forge a false certificate, of which the following is a copy, [insert an exact copy of the forged certificate,] with the design to injure or defraud, and so the said jurors say, that the said J. S. hath committed forgery, contrary," &c.

Art. 753. Indictment for carrying away, defacing, or destroying a public record.

———" That J. S. on the   day of   in the year   , in the parish of   did fraudulently [carry away,] [deface,] or [as the case may be, destroy,] a public record, that is to say, the record of [the death of A. B. kept by the recorder of births and deaths in the city of New Orleans,] [or any other public record," describing it.]

Art. 754. If either of the above offences be committed by the officer having the custody of the record, in relation to which the crime was committed, it must be thus stated, after describing the offence : " with design to injure or defraud : he the said J. S. being at that time the officer entrusted with the custody of the said public record."

Art. 755. If the offence be concealing or carrying away the record by an officer, the description of the offence must be, " did [conceal] or carry away a public record, [describing it,] so that persons interested therein could not have access to it ;" or, as the case may be, " did advise or counsel such [forgery,] [destruction,] or [carrying away,]" according to the case.

Art. 756. Other forms against officers for offences affecting public records.

——" That J. S. being an officer entrusted with the custody of public records, that is to say, [describe the office,] did, knowingly and fraudulently, certify the entry of an act on the said records, in the name of one A. B. who was not present at the time such act purports to have been passed ; or [who did not consent to such act,] which act is in the words following, [insert copy of the act.]"

Or, ——" did intentionally and fraudulently place on the said register or records, an act in words following, [copy the act,] under the date of the   day of
        in the year   , which was not the date at which the said act was, in truth, registered or recorded, with intent to give an illegal advantage to [naming the person favoured by the fraud ; or say, to some one to the jurors unknown.]"

Or,——" did fraudulently permit A. B. or some person to the jurors unknown, to personate one I. K., and in his name and without his authority, in the execution of an act, entered or intended to be entered on such record or registry."

Or,——" did undesignedly, and for want of proper

care, suffer the said records, so entrusted to his care, [or some part of the records, describing it,] to be [defaced,] or [taken away,] or [lost,] or [to be altered,] so that a certain [act] which was truly entered on the said record or registry, in the following words, [insert a copy of the original (act),] appeared, after such alterations, to be an [act] in the words following, [insert the (act) as altered;] by reason of which [alterations,] [defacement,] [obliterations,] or [loss,] one A. B. was injured in his [property,] [condition,] or [reputation,]" according to the case.

Or, ——did, in his official capacity, certify as true that [insert the act falsely certified] when, in fact and truth, the part so certified was false; by reason of which false certificate one A. B. was injured," &c. [as in the last charge.]

If in the last case the accusation be, that the falsehood was fraudulently certified, it must be so stated; but need not, unless specially intended, inasmuch as the mere falsehood is a misdemeanor, and the doing it fraudulently is a crime.

Art. 757. Indictment for using a record so forged, or fraudulently made, or entered.

—— Charge the offence according to the circumstances, as set forth in one of the preceding forms of this chapter, and then add, "and the jurors aforesaid do further present, that Y. Z. well knowing the premises, afterwards, on the   day of   in the parish of L. [used the said record or act, so (forged,) or fraudulently entered,] or [made,] or [registered,] or [recorded] the said [false declaration,] [as the case may be,] producing the same in a court of the parish of L. [stating the court] as testimony, or by, [state the means by which advantage was endeavoured to be derived from the fraudulent act.]"

CHAPTER X.

*Of the forms used in prosecutions for offences against the
current coin and public securities.*

Art. 758. Indictment for counterfeiting.

——"Did counterfeit [two gold coins of the United
States, called eagles; or one silver coin of the Kingdom
of Spain or of the Republic of Mexico, called a dollar;
or one gold coin of Portugal, called a half-johannes; or
any other gold or silver coin, according to the case,
describing them only by their popular names, without
adding their value or any other description.]"

Art. 759. Indictment for passing or offering to pass.

——That J. S. one, &c. [as in the form] having in his
possession one counterfeited gold coin of the United
States, called an eagle, or one [describing the counterfeited coin as above,] and knowing the same to be
counterfeited, did, on the day and year last aforesaid, at
the parish of L., pass or offer to pass the same [as the
case may be] to one I. K. or to some person to the said
jurors unknown," &c.

Art. 760. Indictment for having in possession dies or
other instruments.

——"That J. S. on the　　　　 day of　　　　 in the
year　　　　, at the parish of L., had in his possession
a die [or some other instrument, describing it as a punch,
screw, or other implement, by name,] such as is usually
employed solely for the coinage of money, with the intent
of committing the crime of counterfeiting, or of aiding
therein."

Or, ——"did, on the　　　　 day of　　　　 in the
year　　　　, at the parish of L., repair a die [or other
instrument, describing it, as a *punch, screw,* or other

implement, by name,] such as is usually employed solely in the coinage of money, with the intention of committing the crime of counterfeiting, or of aiding therein."

Or, ——"had in his possession and did conceal certain base metal prepared for coinage, with the intention," &c. [as above.]

Art. 761. Indictment for having counterfeit coins in possession with intent to pass them.

——"That J. S. on the   day of   in the year   , at the parish of L., had in his possession [three counterfeited gold coins of the United States, called half eagles, and ten counterfeited silver coins of the Republic of Mexico, called dollars,] with intent to pass them as true, or cause them to be passed as true, contrary to the laws," &c.

Art. 762. For diminishing the weight of coins.

"That J. S. having in his possession [ten gold coins of the United States, called eagles,] with intent to profit, did, on the   day of   in the year   , in the parish of L., diminish the weight of the said coins, and did afterwards, on the same day and year, at the place aforesaid, pass [or attempt to pass, according to the case,] the same for the value the said coins had before the weight was so diminished." [Or, after the charge of diminishing the weight, as above stated, insert,] "did send or carry the same to [stating the place] to be passed for the value the said coins had before they were so diminished in value," &c.

CHAPTER XI.

Forms used in prosecutions for offences against the public receivers.

Art. 763. Indictment against receivers of public money for the fraudulent appropriation thereof.

——" That J. S., being a person legally empowered

to receive money or [security for money] for the state, or for the corporation of [giving the title of the corporation], by virtue of his office [state the description or name of the office] did, on the   day of   in the year   , and on sundry other days between that time and the day of commencing the prosecution for this offence, illegally appropriate certain large sums of money [or certain securities for money, describing them], amounting in all to one thousand dollars, which he had before that time received for the state of Louisiana, [or for the public corporation, naming it]; and did, on the   day of   in the year   , last aforesaid, at the said parish, by rendering a false account, or [as the case may be] by producing false vouchers [describing them], or by other means [describing those means,] endeavour to conceal such illegal appropriation, with intent to defraud the state of Louisiana, [or the corporation of (naming it)], of the said moneys [or securities, as the case may be.]"

Art. 764. Indictment for illegal appropriation with intent to restore the same.

As in the preceding form, omitting the charge of rendering a false account and all the subsequent part of the charge, and instead thereof state, " and the jurors further present that on the   day of   in the year   , at the parish of L., demand was made by A. B. a person legally authorized for that purpose by the state [or the corporation] from the said J. S. of the sum [or of the securities] so illegally appropriated by him; but that he did not, within three days after such demand, pay the same."

Art. 765. Indictment for not depositing public money.

——" That J. S. being a person legally empowered to receive money or securities for money for the state, [or for the corporation of (naming it)] by virtue of his office [state what it was], did, on the   day of   in the year   , at the parish of   receive a sum [or sums, as the case may be], of money [or securities] to the amount of three hundred dollars and upwards, and did not, within three days after having so received the said sum of money or securities, deposit the same in an incorporated bank, according to the directions given by law, although a bank of that description, to wit, the bank of L., was within three leagues of the place of abode of the said J. S."

If the bank was more than three leagues and not more than twenty from the receiver's abode, then the charge must be, " that he did not make the deposit within fifteen days after receiving the same, and that the treasurer of the state did not enlarge the time allowed for making the said deposit."

Art. 766. Indictment for extortion by a receiver.

——" That J. S. being a person legally appointed, by virtue of his office [state the office] to receive taxes for the state [or for the corporation of L.] on the [state the date and place], did, under pretence of collecting the said tax, extort from one A. B. the sum of   , which was not due for such tax ; or [did attempt to extort from A. B. a sum of   more than was really due for such taxes] ; or did demand a sum of   or an emolument of [describing the nature of the emolument], or [a service or a favour, describing the nature thereof particularly,] from A. B. as a consideration for granting a delay in the collection of a sum of   then due from the said A.B. for taxes to the said state [or corporation] ; or as a consideration [stating any other consideration in relation to the collection of such money, for which the said sum was paid, or such emolument, service, or favour was granted, unless it were paid or given for the emolument allowed by law for such collection,]" &c.

Art. 767. Indictment for preventing the collection of public moneys by force.

——" That on the   day of   in the year   , at the parish of   one A. B. was duly authorized as [sheriff of the said parish, or other office, designating it], to enforce the payment of taxes [or other debt, stating of what kind], due to the state [or to a public corporation, naming it], and J. S. on the day and year and at the place aforesaid, did, by force, attempt to prevent, or [did, by force or threats of force, prevent] the said A. B. from seizing the goods of one C. D., [or state any other act which he was prevented from doing], with intent to enforce the payment of a sum of ____ due from him the said C. D. to the state, [or to the corporation, naming it], for taxes, [or for any other debt, stating it], which seizure [or other act in which he was obstructed, stating it,] was a duty required of the said A. B. by law relative to the collection of taxes [or debt.]"

CHAPTER XII.

Forms of indictment for offences which affect foreign commerce.

Art. 768. Charge for exporting flour without inspection.
——"Did export from this state [or ship for the purpose of exportation] on board the ship called the [Andrew Jackson] [one hundred barrels of flour] without having caused the same to be inspected, according to the directions of the laws of the state in such case provided."

Art. 769. For counterfeiting the mark of an inspector.
——"Did COUNTERFEIT the [mark], or [brand], or [stamp], directed by the laws of this state to be made or placed on all flour exported from the port of New Orleans, and made or placed such counterfeit [mark, or brand, or stamp,] on [one hundred barrels of flour,]" &c.

Art. 770. For placing articles of inferior value in a package, with intent to defraud.
——"Did, with intent to defraud, put into a [hogshead] apparently filled with [tobacco], or [a bale apparently filled with cotton], or [a box apparently filled with spermaceti candles], or [a package apparently filled with cochineal], or [any other cask, bale, box, or package, describing it, with apparent articles], being merchandize

usually sold by weight, a quantity of [rubbish], [or any other article, describing it], being of less value than the said tobacco [or other article], with which the said hogshead, or [bale], or [package], or [box], was apparently filled," &c.

Art. 771. For selling merchandize with articles of inferior value concealed therein.

——" Did [sell], or [barter], or [give in payment], to A. B., or [expose for sale], or [ship for exportation in a certain ship called A. J.] a [bale apparently filled with cotton, or other articles as above], being merchandize usually sold by weight, with a quantity of [rubbish] concealed therein, with intent to defraud, contrary," &c.

Art. 772. For destroying or injuring a vessel, with intent to defraud.

——" That J. S. within the limits of this state, that is to say, in the river Mississippi, below the Balize, in the parish of Plaquemines, he being then and there the owner, [part owner], [freighter], of a certain [schooner] called the [Bee], or being then and there employed as [master], [supercargo], [seaman], or as [state any other capacity], on board a certain schooner called the [Bee], with intent to defraud or injure A. B. who was [or some person or persons, to the jurors unknown, who was or were] the [owner or owners of the said vessel] or [of the cargo on board, or of any part thereof], or [the underwriters on the said vessel, or the cargo on board, or some part thereof,] or those interested in the said schooner, or the said cargo, [or in the voyage], [freight], or [profits] of the said [schooner] ; did [destroy the said schooner], or did injure the said [schooner,] by [running her on shore], or [cutting away the masts], or [doing other injury, describing it.]"

If the offence be committed on the high seas, it must be so stated, and it must be averred that the offender, at the time, was a citizen of this state, or domiciliated within it.

Art. 773. For fraudulent insurance.

——" That J. S. on the   day of   in the

year   , at the parish of New Orleans, caused insurance to be made for one thousand dollars, by the
insurance company called the New Orleans Insurance
Company, on one hundred hogsheads of rum, which he
represented to the said insurance company as shipped [or
about to be shipped] at Jamaica in the West Indies, for
New York, and pretended that the said hogsheads contained Jamaica rum of the first proof, with intent to
defraud the said New Orleans Insurance Company, had
actually shipped one hundred hogsheads containing water,
[or rum of less than one half the value of Jamaica rum
of the first proof], instead of one hundred hogsheads of
Jamaica rum of the first proof, contrary," &c.

If the insurance were made at some place not within
this state, the goods must be stated as having been represented as shipped, or about to be shipped, within the
state of Louisiana, and goods of inferior value to have
been actually shipped there.

Art. 774. Against àn inn-keeper for concealing a
seaman.

——"That J. S. being the keeper of a tavern, or
[lodging-house, or boarding-house], did, on the   day
of   in the year   , at the city of New Orleans,
entertain, [lodge], or [conceal], A. B. a seaman who had,
within one month previous to the day last aforesaid,
DESERTED from a merchant vessel called the D. in the port
of New Orleans, he the said J. S. knowing that the said
A. B. had so deserted."

Art. 775. Against a master of a vessel shipping a seaman who has deserted.

——"That J. S. being the master of a ship called
the D., lying in the port of New Orleans, on the [insert
the date and parish], did SHIP as a mariner on board the
said ship, one C. D. who did not produce his discharge
from the master of the vessel in which he last sailed, he
the said C. D. having deserted from a ship called the
Bee, in the said port of New Orleans, within one month
before he was so shipped by the said J. S."

Art. 776. For using false weights and measures.

——"That A. B. in the weighing of a quantity of sugar sold to C. D. on the   day of   in the year   , in the parish of L., did use a false weight, knowing the said weight to be false, with a design to defraud."

The same form as to a false balance.

Art. 777. For a false measure.

——"That J. S. on the   day of   in the year   , at the parish of   , in the measuring a quantity [of whiskey], or [of cloth], sold on that day to C. D., did use a false measure, knowing the same to be false, with intent to defraud."

Art. 778. Warrant of arrest and for the seizure of false weights, or measures.

"By A. B. [one of the judges, &c.]   To the [sheriff of the city and parish of New Orleans.]

"You are commanded to arrest J. S. charged on oath before me, with having fraudulently used a false weight in the weighing of a certain quantity [of sugar] sold to C. D., knowing such weight to be false; and you are also commanded to seize the weights used by the said J. S. in weighing the articles sold by him in his trade of [a grocer, or other trade, as the case may be]; and to bring as well the said weights as the said J. S. before me, on [insert the return of the warrant], to be dealt with according to law."

Art. 779. When the weights, or balances, or measures, are brought before the magistrate, in pursuance of the above warrant, he shall cause the measures and weights to be compared and tested in his presence, by the officer appointed to keep the standard of weights and measures ; and if it be a balance that is the subject of prosecution, he shall examine it, and shall retain all those that appear to be false, to be used on the trial, and afterward destroyed according to law.

Art. 780. The above forms are to serve for purchases by false weights, measures, or balances, changing the words "*sold to*" for the words "*purchased from.*"

Art. 781. For altering marks.

——" That J. S. having [one hundred barrels of flour, which had been inspected by the officer appointed for that purpose by virtue of the laws of this state, and which barrels had been marked by the said officer with a mark, denoting that the flour contained in the said barrels was of inferior quality, did, on the   day of   in the year   , at the parish of New Orleans, falsely alter the said marks, so as to make it appear that the said officer had put on the said barrels a mark denoting that the flour contained in the said barrels was of the best quality,]" &c.

Art. 782. Form of indictment for counterfeiting a mark or brand.

——" Did, with intent to defraud, counterfeit the brand or mark used by the public officer appointed to inspect tobacco, [and by him to denote that tobacco was of a good quality] by marking the said counterfeit brand or mark on one hundred hogsheads of tobacco."

Art. 783. Fraudulently using a marked cask, or box, &c.

——" That J. S. having in his possession [ten pipes marked, by one of the officers of the customs of the United States in the port of New Orleans, as containing French brandy], did, on the   day of in the year   , at the parish of L. fraudulently use the same for the sale of liquor of an inferior quality to that denoted by the said mark,]" &c.

Art. 784. Forging a written instrument.

——" Did make a false instrument in writing, of which the following is a copy, [insert copy of the instrument], with intent to injure or defraud," &c.

Art. 785. For forging by altering.

——" That J. S. on [insert the date and place] having in his power a certain instrument in writing in the following words and [figures], to wit, [insert copy of the instrument as it was before it was altered], made such alterations in the said instrument as to make it appear to be of the following tenor [insert copy of the instrument as altered] with intent to [injure] or [defraud,]" &c.

Art. 786. When from obliteration in the original instrument it may be difficult to prove its exact tenor, it will be sufficient, instead of inserting the copy of the original instrument, to state, "that having in his possession a certain instrument in writing, by which, among other things, [he promised to pay to A. B. at the time mentioned in the said instrument the sum of one thousand dollars], [or insert any other part of the instrument that was altered], but of which the other contents are not sufficiently known to the jurors to enable them to set the same literally forth, the said J. S. on the   day of   in the year   , in the parish of L., altered the said instrument so as to change the same into an instrument of which the following is a copy, [insert the copy of the instrument altered], with intent to [injure] or [defraud,]" &c.

Art. 787. For forgery by writing over or on the back of a true signature.

——" That J. S. having in his possession a paper on which was written a true signature of A. B., without any legal authority and with intent to defraud, wrote over the said signature, [or on the other side of the paper that contained such signature], the words following, to wit, [insert the instrument], with intent to injure or defraud."

Art. 788. For forgery by adding a signature.

——" That J. S. on the   day of   in the year   , at the parish of L., having in his power an instrument in the following words, [insert the copy of the instrument], written by A. B. [or by some person to the jurors unknown, as the case may be], altered the same by adding thereto the false signature of the name of A. B. with intent to injure or defraud."

Art. 789. For forgery by altering an instrument made by the offender himself.

——" That J. S. having before that time made a certain instrument in writing, of which the following is a copy, [insert the copy], delivered the same to A. B., and that on the   day of   in the year   , at the parish of L., the said instrument then

being the property of [insert the name of the holder] he
the said J. S. with intent to defraud [or injure], altered
the said instrument so as to make it appear to be one
of the tenor following, [insert copy of the instrument as
altered,]" &c.

Art. 790. When the forgery consists in making an
instrument in the name of a fictitious person, the indictment must be in the form above prescribed, for "forging
a written instrument" without any special avowal that
the name of the person was fictitious, and it may be
proved on the trial without such special averment.

Art. 791. Form of the charge for making an instrument with a false date.

——"That J. S. on [insert the date and place] made
a certain instrument in writing, of which the following
is a copy, [insert it], which instrument was falsely dated,
with intent to [injure] or [defraud] a certain A. B.
[insert the name of the person whose interest would
have been affected by the false dating of the instrument
if the same had been true,"] &c.

Art. 792. Form of charge for uttering an instrument
under pretence that it was the act of another.

——"That J. S., on the   day of   in the
year   , at the parish of L., made a certain instrument in writing, of which the following is a copy, [insert
it], and with intent to defraud [uttered or passed it, as
the case may be], to A. B. as the act of another person
bearing the name of J. S."

Art. 793. Form of a charge for making a note in the
offender's name on the other side of a paper containing
a blank signature.

——"That J. S. having in his power a paper containing
the true signature of one A. B. on the   day of
      in the year   , at the parish of L., wrote on
the other side of the paper, containing such signature, a
[promissory note or bill of exchange, as the case may
be], purporting to be the bill [or note] of him the said
J. S. and signed with his name [or firm, as the case may
be], so as to make the said signature appear as the

indorsement of the said [bill or note], without any lawful authority and with intent to defraud [or injure.]"

Art. 794. Form of charge for uttering or passing illegal instruments in writing.

——" That J. S. on the [insert date and place] having in his possession, or under his control, an instrument in writing, of which the following is a copy, [insert it], and knowing the same to be [forged] [or to have been *fraudulently made*, if it be not a forgery, but is one of those instruments the making or uttering of which, by any disposition of the Penal Code, are declared to be an offence], [uttered] or [passed] the said instrument to one C. D. with intent to defraud."

Art. 795. For engraving a plate, or preparing implements or materials for the purpose of forging bank notes.

——" That J. S. on [state the date of time and place], did engrave [or as the case may be, had in his possession] a plate, or [did prepare paper], [a rolling press], or other implements or materials, [declaring what they were], for the purpose of [their or its] being employed in forging the notes of a bank [called the Bank of New York, doing business in the city of New York], or [called the Bank of Canada, doing business at Montreal], or [any other bank wherever situated], knowing such purpose, and with intent to defraud."

Art. 796. For having a forged or fraudulent instrument in possession, with intent to utter.

——" That J. S. on the   day of   in the year   , at the parish of L., had in his possession a certain instrument in writing, of which the following is a copy [insert it], and knowing the same to have been forged, [or to have been *fraudulently made*, if it be not a forgery, but is one of those instruments the making or uttering of which, by the Code of Crimes and Punishments, is declared to be an offence], with intent to utter or pass the same, and to defraud or injure."

Art. 797. For procuring a signature by a false reading or false interpretation of the instrument.

——"That one A. B. being a person who from infirmity or ignorance [as the case may be] could not read,
[or who was ignorant of the language, naming that in
which the instrument was written], J. S. on the
day of   in the year   , at the parish of L.,
with intent to defraud, induced the said A. B. to sign
as his act a certain instrument in writing, of which the
following is a copy [insert it], by falsely pretending to
[read, or to interpret the said instrument, or by misrepresenting its contents, as the case may be], so as to
cause the said A. B. to believe that the said instrument
purported to be materially different in this, to wit, [state
the misrepresentation, or the false reading, or the false
interpretation], contrary," &c.

Art. 798. If in the case provided for by the last preceding form, the act was not signed but assented to in
a manner that would, if there had been no error, have
made the instrument the act of the party, it must be so
stated, instead of charging that it was signed.

Art. 799. Charge for falsely substituting an instrument instead of the one intended to be signed.

——"That A. B. having the intention of signing or
giving his legal assent to a certain instrument in writing,
so as to make it his act, which was prepared by him or
by his direction, and purported to be [insert copy of it
if it can be procured, if not, state the general purport
thereof, and particularly the parts in which it differed
from the substituted instrument], one J. S., falsely and
without the knowledge of the said A. B., substituted
for the instrument so intended to be signed, or legally
assented to, another instrument in the following words,
[insert copy,] and by means of such false substitution
induced the said A. B. to sign [or assent to, as the case
may be], the said last-mentioned instrument, with
intent to defraud," &c.

Art. 800. If either of the offences, charged by the
two last forms, shall be committed by a public officer
whose duty it is to record public acts, or by a counsellor
or attorney-at-law, that circumstance must be charged.

Art. 801. Charge in an indictment for falsely personating another.

——" That J. S. of the city of New Orleans, broker, pretending to be [J. S. of the parish of St. Francisville, planter], or [pretending to be A. B.] on the   day of   in the year   , at the parish of L. before [I. K., being parish judge of the said parish, acting as notary public], in the name of the said [J. S. of St. Francisville, or of the said A. B.] gave his assent to an act of which the following is a copy [insert it], and declaring that he could not write, authorized the said notary to record his assent, he personating the said [J. S. of St. Francisville, or the said A. B.] to the said act, with intent to defraud."

Art. 802. Indictment for making a false schedule in case of insolvency.

——" That J. S. having presented to the [district court of the first district] a petition praying for a meeting of his creditors, in order [that they might receive a cession of his effects], or [grant him a respite] made a false account of his [credits], [property] or [debts] in the schedule annexed to his petition, in this, that the said J. S. omitted to place on the said schedule [a tract of land or other property, describing it,] or [a credit of a debt due to him from A. B. of one hundred dollars], or [a debt due from him to C. D. for one hundred dollars], or [did place on his said schedule a sum of one hundred dollars as due by him to I. K. when in fact no such sum was due], and did exhibit the said false account, in such court, as true, with intent to defraud," &c.

Art. 803. For fraudulently destroying or concealing books of account in cases of insolvency.

——" That J. S. having presented his petition to [state what court], in order to procure a meeting of his creditors, for the purpose of making to them a cession of his property, [or obtaining a respite], and obtaining the relief in such cases granted by law, did fraudulently destroy [or conceal] a certain book of accounts [or papers] relative to his estate, which, by law, he was bound to produce for the use and inspection of his said creditors, that is to say, one book of account called a ledger, containing accounts from the   to [or otherwise, describing the book or papers destroyed or concealed.]"

Art. 804. Making simulated conveyances.

——"That J. S., not having property of sufficient value to pay his debts, did on the   day of in the year   , in the parish of L., in order to prevent the property hereinafter mentioned from becoming liable to the payment of his debts, make an act of which the following is a copy [inserting it], which act the jurors present was simulated, and intended for his own use, or for that of his family."

Art. 805. If the property was personal property, and no written conveyance was made, say, "made a verbal sale and delivery of [describing the property], which sale the jurors present was simulated," &c.

Art. 806. Form of indictment for receiving a simulated conveyance.

Follow the preceding form, and at the end add, "and the jurors further present, that I. K., knowing the purposes for which the said [conveyance,] [mortgage,] or [disposition,] was made, and that it was simulated, received the same for the purposes aforesaid, contrary," &c.

Art. 807. For suffering fraudulent judgments.

——"That J. S. not having sufficient property to pay his just debts, on the   day of   in the year   , with intent to defraud his creditors, or some one or more of them, did voluntarily suffer a judgment to be entered in the [parish court of the parish of L.] in favour of one I. K. for the sum of   by which the [real property of the said J. S. in the said parish was bound] and [personal property belonging to him was seized], which judgment the jurors present was for a sum not due, or for a larger sum than was really due, contrary," &c.

Art. 808. For recovering such judgment.

——"That one J. S., being on the   day of

in the year   , at the parish of L., not having sufficient property to pay his debts, I. K. in collusion with the said J. S. and with intent to defraud the creditors of him the said J. S., or some one or more of them, did recover a judgment in the parish of L. for the sum of   which was voluntarily suffered to be entered by the said J. S. with intent to defraud his creditors, or some one or more of them; and the jurors further present, that the said I. K. recovered the said judgment for a sum not due, or for a sum larger than was due from the said J. S., and that [real property of the said J. S. has been incumbered], and [personal property belonging to him has been seized], under the said judgment."

Art. 809. For conveying without consideration to defraud creditors.

[Beginning as in the last form.] "Did without any consideration [or for an inadequate consideration,] [convey,] [mortgage,] or [affect by an onerous condition, stating it,] all that [describe the property sold, mortgaged, or affected,] to one I. K."

Art. 810. For receiving such conveyance.

[Add to the last preceding form, " which [conveyance,] [mortgage,] or [onerous condition,] the said I. K. did on the day and year last aforesaid, at the place aforesaid, receive, he then well knowing the said fraudulent intent."

CHAPTER XIII.

Forms of indictments for offences affecting public property held for common use.

Art. 811. Form of indictment for maliciously breaking levees.

——" Did maliciously break down the levee, or embankment of the river Mississippi, opposite to the plantation of A. B. in the said parish."

Art. 812. For impeding navigation by embankments, &c.

——" Did make a certain wharf [or other construction, describing it,] in the bed of the river Mississippi, opposite to the lands of A. B. in the said parish, by which the navigation of the said river was impeded, [or which was made contrary to an ordinance of the police, being legally made on the   day of   in the year   ,] contrary to the laws," &c.

Art. 813. For erecting obstructions in a street or public road.

——" Did erect a [fence,] [or dig a ditch,] [or make any other obstruction, describing it,] in the public road, [or street] [or square] in the said parish, [near to or opposite the house or land of A. B., or otherwise describing the place,] by which the public use of the said [street,] [or road,] [or square,] was obstructed ; [or did unlawfully destroy a bridge erected on the street or public road, at (describing the place,)] in the said parish."

Art. 814. For obstructing the banks of navigable rivers.

——" Did on the [bank,] [or on the embankment,] [or the space set apart by the police regulation on the banks of the river Mississippi for a tow path,] erect a house, [or any other obstruction, describing it,] by which the public use of the said [bank, embankment, or tow path, as the case may be,] was prevented [or rendered less convenient.]"

CHAPTER XIV.

Forms of indictments for offences against public health and safety.

Art. 815. Indictment for illegally carrying on a manufactory of gunpowder.

——" Did carry on a manufactory of gunpowder, [or did keep more than ten pounds of gunpowder at one time] within three hundred yards of a public road, [or of a dwelling house, to wit, the dwelling house of A. B. in the said parish,] [or of land of A. B. he the said A. B. not having permitted the said manufactory to be carried on,] contrary to the laws," &c.

Art. 816. For carrying on trade in a manner dangerous to health.

——" That J. S. [being a manufacturer of parchment in the parish of L., did on the   day of
in the year   , in the parish aforesaid, suffer the water, in which the skins used in the said manufactory are soaked, to remain and putrefy,] in a manner injurious to the health of those who reside in the vicinity of the said manufactory, contrary," &c.

Art. 817. For adulterating liquors in a manner injurious to health.

——" Did adulterate, for the purpose of selling the same, [one pipe of wine intended for drinking,] by mixing therewith a substance called [sugar of lead] which rendered the said wine injurious to the health of those who should drink thereof."

Or ——" Did sell to one A. B. [one pipe of wine which had been adulterated with (as in the foregoing form)] knowing the same to be adulterated."

Art. 818. For adulterating drugs.

——" Did fraudulently adulterate, for the purpose of selling the same, a certain quantity, to the jurors unknown, of a drug [called quinquina or Peruvian bark, or jesuit's bark,] by mixing therewith a quantity of bark of the oak tree in the said drug, [or to make the same injurious to health.]"

Art. 819. For selling adulterated drugs.

——" Did sell to one A. B. one ounce of a drug or medicine called quinquina or jesuit's bark, or Peruvian bark, which had been fraudulently adulterated by mixing therewith a quantity of bark of the oak tree, in such manner as to lessen the efficacy [or change the operation] of the said drug, [or to make the same injurious to health.]"

CHAPTER XV.

Charges in indictments for offences against morals and decency.

Art. 820. Keeping a disorderly house.

—— "That J. S. on several days between the day of   and the   day of   in the parish of L., did keep a disorderly house for the purpose of public prostitution."

Or —— " Did [keep a public tavern, or a house for the sale of spirituous liquors, without having the license required by law.]"

Or —— "That J. S. having a license for keeping a tavern in the parish of L., [or for the sale of spirituous liquors by retail,] did on the   day of   in the year   , and at divers other times afterwards, in the parish of   permit [here insert the act forbidden by the license or by law to be done in the town,] in the said tavern."

Or —— " That J. S. having a license to keep a gambling house in the parish of L., did on the   day of   in the year   , and at divers other times afterwards, permit [insert the act forbidden by the license or the law to be done in the gambling house.]"

Art. 821. For publishing obscene prints or pictures.

—— " Did [make, publish, or print, as the case may be,] a certain obscene [print] [or picture] which [was shown to the said J. S. on his examination, if the defendant was arrested or summoned previous to the finding of the indictment,] is now exhibited to the said jurors and will be produced on the trial of this indictment, but which cannot be decently described in words, and which was manifestly designed to corrupt the morals of youth."

Art. 822. On the examination of any one accused of this offence, the print or picture must be exhibited to the defendant on his examination, and marked by the magistrate and others, so as to be identified, and shall also be exhibited to him in court previous to his arraignment.

Art. 823. Form of charge on an indictment for an obscene written or printed composition.

——" Did [make,] or [publish,] or [print] an obscene composition [of which the following is a copy,] which composition the jurors present was manifestly designed to corrupt the morals of youth."

Art. 824. For making an obscene exhibition of the person in public.

——" Did in the public-highway to a number of persons then present designedly make an indecent exhibition of his person, or [of the person of A. B.] whereby the modesty of those present was offended, contrary," &c.

Art. 825. For uttering obscene expressions with intent to insult one of the female sex.

——" Did in the presence and hearing of one or more persons of the female sex, with design to insult them, utter divers obscene expressions as follows, [repeating them,] contrary," &c.

Art. 826. For seducing a woman under promise of marriage.

——" That A. B., being a woman of good chaste reputation, at the parish of L. one J. S. addressed her with proposals of marriage, which the said A. B. received favourably, and the said J. S. thereupon made a promise that he would marry the said A. B. ; and under the faith of that promise, on the   day of   in the year   , at the parish of L., seduced her, and afterwards failed to comply with his said promise."

Art. 827. For soliciting prostitution.

——" Did for hire received from one A. B. procure the means of illicit connexion between him and a certain woman named C. D. [or a certain woman to the jurors unknown]"

Or, when all the parties are unknown, state, "did for hire procure the means of illicit connexion between two persons of different sexes, to the jurors unknown."

Or, "did for hire [solicit] [or procure] a woman [named A. B.] or [a woman to the jurors unknown,] to prostitute her person to a man named C. D. [or to a man to the jurors unknown.]"

Art. 828. For adultery against the wife and the person with whom the crime is committed.

——"That Anne B., being the lawful wife of C. D., on the   day of   in the year   , at the parish of   , committed adultery with J. S., and so the jurors present the said Anne B. and C. D. did together commit the offence of adultery."

Art. 829. For adultery by the husband.

——"That A. B., being the lawful husband of C. D., did on the   day of   in the year   , at the parish of L., commit adultery with one E. F., and did during the time he so committed the said offence, keep the said E. F. as his concubine in the house with his said wife ; [or did, by ill-treating his said wife, force her to leave the house in which he resided, and did, after her departure, keep the said E. F. as his concubine in it.]"

Art. 830. For violating a place of interment for the purpose of stealing.

——"Did open the [grave,] or [vault,] or [tomb,] in which the dead body of one A. B. had been interred, with the intent of stealing the coffin or vestments with which the said A. B. had been interred, [or some article, describing it, which was interred with the said body.]"

Art. 831. For removing a dead body for the purpose of exposure or dissection.

——"Did, without legal authority, remove from the [grave,] or [vault,] or [tomb,] in which it had been interred, the dead body of one A. B. for the purpose of selling, or exposing, or dissecting the same."

Art. 832. For purchasing, selling, or dissecting a dead body before interment.

——" Did purchase the dead body of one A. B. from C. D., or from certain persons to the jurors unknown ; [or did sell the dead body of one A. B. to C. D., or to a certain person to the jurors unknown,] before the said body was interred."

Art. 833. For dissecting a dead body before interment.

——" Did, without being authorized in any manner provided by law, dissect the dead body of one C. D. which had not been interred."

CHAPTER XVI.

Of the forms of indictments for offences which affect persons in the exercise of their religion.

Art. 834. For restraining the free exercise of religion by force or threats.

——" Did by FORCE [or THREATS, stating of which kind,] prevent A. B. from attending Divine service in the Protestant Episcopal Church, which attendance was a lawful act required by the Protestant Episcopal religion, which the said A. B. professed."

Art. 835. For maliciously preventing the free exercise of religion.

——" That A. B., being a person professing the [Roman Catholic religion, and being confined by sickness to his bed, was desirous of having the sacraments of that religion administered to him by C. D., a priest of that church, and had a note written to him requesting his attendance for that purpose, but that one J. S. maliciously destroyed the said note before it was delivered to the said C. D. with intent to prevent the said A. B. from doing the lawful act of receiving the said sacraments, which was required by the religion professed by the said A. B.]"

Art. 836. For forcibly obliging another to perform religious rites.

——" Did by force [or threats of injury to person or property, stating what the threats were,] oblige or endeavour to oblige one A. B. [to receive the communion according to the rites and ceremonies of the church.]"

Art. 837. If the offender be a judicial or executive officer, and the act be done under colour of his office ; or if he be a priest, or minister, or preacher of any religious sect or congregation, the fact must be stated in either of the preceding forms in this chapter.

CHAPTER XVII.

Of the forms of indictments for offences affecting reputation.

Art. 838. Charge for slander, charging a crime.

——" Did in the presence of sundry persons make the following false and defamatory allegation of one A. B.— ' he is the man who murdered C. D.'—intending thereby to convey the idea that the said A. B. had committed the crime of murder."

Art. 839. For slander, by signs, imputing the vice of habitual drunkenness.

——" That J. S. being in company with A. B., I. K., and others, on the   day of   in the year   , at the parish of L., [a discourse arose of and concerning persons addicted to the vice of habitual drunkenness, whereupon the said J. S., in order to make it falsely be believed that the said I. K. was guilty of the said vice, raised his right hand to his mouth, as if in the act of bringing a glass to his lips, and at the same time, unperceived by the said I. K., with the other hand pointed him out to the observation of the persons there present ; and the jurors further present, that the said

A. B., one of the said company, asked the said J. S. whether the said I. K. was a drunkard, to which question the said J. S. nodded his head in the manner usually done to give an assent,] and that by the said signs the said J. S. did falsely impute to the said I. K. the vice of habitual drunkenness] in order to cause his society to be avoided by people in general."

Art. 840. For a libel, by painting, imputing a crime.

——"Did make and publish a certain engraved and printed picture, by and in which a figure, intended to represent one I. K., was represented as [picking the pocket of another of a purse, thereby intending to convey the idea and make it be believed that the said I. K. had committed the crime of stealing from the person], which picture or engraving is annexed to this indictment."

Art. 841. To every indictment for libel by a PICTURE, the same shall be annexed to the indictment, and shown to the party accused before his arraignment, in the manner and for the purpose set forth in the chapter of this Code respecting indictments, unless such picture was painted on a building, or on some article too bulky to be brought into court, or has been destroyed by some other means than the act of the prosecutor, or by his procurement.

Art. 842. For a libel charging moral guilt.

——"Did make and publish [or circulate, as the case may be,] a certain writing of and concerning one I. K. in the words following, [' of the character of this Mr. K. you may judge from this circumstance, that he was treasurer of a charitable society in New Orleans last year, and that a Flemish account was given of the funds ;' meaning thereby that the said I. K. had appropriated to his own use the funds of some charitable society that were entrusted to him as treasurer thereof.]"

Art. 843. For a libel imputing a mental defect that would cause the society of the party to be avoided.

——"Did make, publish, and circulate a certain writing concerning one I. K., printed in the public paper [called the Daily Gazette,] in the words following, to wit : [' To

Mr. I. K.—I should be surprised at your conduct if I did not know the unhappy state of your mind; that no intimacy can render any man safe in your society; that you abuse and defame, according to your caprice, every man who has the misfortune to associate with you, without provocation and without mercy.']"

Art. 844. Where the charge is direct, as in the last form, there is no need of any explanatory allegation; where the words, inporting the charge, are not perfectly clear, or their application is not apparent, the meaning must be alleged. The Code of Evidence gives rules as to the cases and manner in which those allegations are to be proved.

Art. 845. Injury to reputation by exhibiting an effigy.

——"Did, with the intent to bring I. K. into contempt, and to excite ridicule and indignation against him, exhibit [or make with intent that it should be exhibited] an effigy or figure intended to represent the said I. K."

Art. 846. If more than twelve persons are collected to witness the exhibition and refuse to disperse, they may be indicted as an unlawful assembly, by adding to the above form, "And that the said J. S. [the person above indicted] and A. B., C. D., and others to the jurors unknown, were unlawfully assembled to aid each other in making the said unlawful exhibition. And in case they refuse to disperse, the indictment may be for a riot, by adding to the charge of an unlawful assembly the following: "And the jurors further present, that the persons so unlawfully assembled, then and there committed a riot, by remaining together for the purposes aforesaid half an hour and more after they had been warned by a magistrate to disperse in the form required by law."

Art. 847. For injury to reputation by dramatic performances.

——"Did, with intent to bring one I. K. into contempt, and to excite ridicule and indignation against him, perform [or cause to be performed] a certain dramatic work, called 'the Tartuffe,' in which the said I. K. was represented or personated by an imitation of his person, dress, manners and gestures, in such a manner as made it apparent to those who were present, and who knew the said I. K., that he was the person intended by such personification."

Art. 848. For combining to make a false accusation of a crime.

——"That J. S. and C. D., on the   day of   in the year   , at the parish of L., did combine falsely to accuse one I. K. of the crime of stealing ; and in pursuance of such combination, they the said J. S. and C. D. [or one of them stating which,] did declare [state whether verbally or in writing] that [the said I. K. had stolen ten sheep from him the said J. S.]"

If the combination should be to extort any pecuniary advantage, then insert, " Did, for the purpose of extorting some pecuniary advantage from one I. K., combine falsely to accuse [or to threaten to accuse] the said I. K. of the crime of stealing, and in pursuance of such combination, did, for the purpose aforesaid," &c. as above.

Art. 849. For false accusation with intent to extort.

——" Did, with intent to extort money or procure some other profit, [threaten one A. B. that he the said J. S. would accuse him the said A. B. of the crime of rape ;] or [did falsely accuse one A. B. of having committed the crime of rape ;] or [did falsely accuse or threaten to accuse, as charged in the preceding form,] one A. B. of [having sold the favours of his wife, or other act that would bring him into contempt.]"

Art. 850. For fabricating defamatory papers.

——" Did, without any lawful authority and with intent to injure the reputation of one I. K., publish or circulate, or make with intent that it should be circulated, a false writing, purporting to be a letter written by the said J. S. in the words following, to wit, [insert copy.]"

CHAPTER XVIII.

Of the forms of indictments for offences affecting the person of individuals.

SECTION I.

Simple assaults and batteries.

Art. 851. Form of indictment for a simple assault.

——" That J. S. on the   day of   in the year   , at the parish of L., upon one A. B. did make an assault by striking at the said A. B. with a cane, [or in any other manner that by law will constitute an assault, describing it.]"

Art. 852. For a simple assault and battery.

——" Did, with intent to injure, make an illegal assault on one A. B. and struck him with his fist in the face, [or with a cane on the head,] [or by throwing water in his face,] [or by pushing another person against him,] [or by firing a pistol and wounding him with the ball, or in any of the various ways in which this offence may be committed, describing the act without fiction or exaggeration.]"

SECTION II.

Assault and battery in relation to the person.

Art. 853. For an assault and battery against a public officer in the execution of his office.

——" Did, with intent to injure, make an illegal assault on one A. B. [one of the constables of the city of New Orleans, at the time of the said assault being in the legal execution of his office, to wit, distraining certain goods of the said J. S. by virtue of a warrant legally issued by G. P. one of the judges of the city court,] he the said J. S. well knowing the office of the said A. B. and that he was in the legal exercise of them."

Art. 854. For assault and battery committed by an officer under pretence of executing his office.

——" That J. S. on the   day of   in the year   , in the parish of L., he being then and there [sheriff of the said parish,] under pretence of executing his office by [serving a summons on one A. B. to appear as a witness in the parish court of the parish, did make an illegal assault on the said A. B., and with intent to injure, did seize him by the collar and drag him in the street towards the said court.]"

If in a case where the officer had authority to use force but exceeded the necessary degree, say, " then being sheriff of the said parish, by virtue of his office arrested one A. B. on a warrant, [describing it,] and although no resistance was offered to the said arrest, yet the said J. S., under pretence of executing the said warrant, illegally assaulted and beat the said A. B. by," [describing the assault.]

Art. 855. For assault against an ascendant—against a woman—a tutor.

——" Did, with intent to injure, make an illegal assault on A. B. the [father,] [mother,] [grandfather,] [grandmother,] [tutor,] of him the said J. S." &c.

In the indictment for assault and battery by a man against a woman, no particular averment is necessary, the names, and the relative personal pronouns used in the indictment are a sufficient indication of the sex.

SECTION III.

Assault and battery in relation to the place.

Art. 856. Assault and battery in a court of justice.

——" Did in the parish court of the parish of L. make an assault."

Art. 857. Assault and battery committed in the house of another.

——" Did go to the house of one I. K. with the intent of committing an assault and battery on one A. B. then residing in the said house as [a guest,] and did then and there, in pursuance of such intent, illegally and with design to injure, make an assault on the said A. B." &c.

Art. 858. Assault and battery in a church during the celebration of public worship.

——" Did, during the celebration of public worship in the [Catholic church,] with intent to injure, make an illegal assault in the said church upon one A. B. &c. whereby the congregation of [Catholics] was disturbed in the performance of their worship, or religious rites and ceremonies."

SECTION IV.

Assault and battery in relation to the intent.

Art. 859. Assault and battery with intent to murder or ravish.

——" Did, with intent to commit the crime of [murder] or [of rape,] make an assault," &c.

Art. 860. With intent to dismember or inflict a permanent injury.

——" Did, with intent to dismember one I. K. by

cutting off his ears, make an assault on him the said I. K., and with a penknife made several cuts in his head and cheeks."

Art. 861. If the intent be to disfigure, say :

——" Did make an illegal assault upon one A. B. with intent to disfigure him by slitting open his nostrils, and in attempting the said injury did wound the said A. B. in several parts of his face."

Art. 862. If the intent be to do a permanent injury, not amounting to dismembering or disfiguration, say :

——" Did make an illegal assault upon one A. B., and with design to inflict a permanent injury by [laming the said A. B. in the right leg, did attempt to cut the tendons of the said leg with a knife.]"

Art. 863. If the design of the assault and battery, or the assault alone, be to commit any other crime than murder or rape, such intent must be specified in the same form as is given above for an assault with intent to commit those crimes.

Art. 864. For assault and battery with intent to force another to commit an offence.

——" Did make an illegal assault on one A. B. with intent to force him to commit the crime of theft by stealing the horses of a certain C. D., and did beat and wound the said A. B. and threaten to kill him unless he would consent to commit the said crime."

Art. 865. For an assault and battery on a woman, attended with immodest words or actions.

——" Did make an illegal assault upon one Anne B., and did accompany the said assault by words and gestures calculated to wound the modesty of the female sex, and by violently laying his hands on the said Anne."

Art. 866. If, in the case stated in the last form, the offender was tutor or curator and the person injured was his ward, or if the offender was schoolmaster and the person injured was his scholar, those circumstances must be stated, thus :

——" That J. S. on the   day of   in the year   , at the parish of L., was the tutor [or curator] of Anne B., a minor; [or was the schoolmaster of Anne B., employed to teach her reading and writing,] [or music,] [or any other art or any science,] and that on the day and year and at the place aforesaid, the said J. S. made an assault upon the said Anne," &c. as in the last form.

Art. 867. For an assault or battery with intent to dishonour or provoke a duel.

——"Did make an illegal assault and battery upon one A. B. by pulling his nose with intent to dishonour the said A. B. [or to force the said A. B. to accept or to give a challenge to fight a duel.]"

SECTION V.

Forms in assaults aggravated by the degree or the manner.

Art. 868. For assault by design and with a deadly weapon.

——" Did, in consequence of a premeditated design to [wound and otherwise ill-treat one A. B.] [or to disfigure, or to dismember, or to inflict a permanent injury, stating particularly the design,] make an assault upon him the said A. B. with a deadly weapon, to wit, [with a sword,] and did wound the said A. B. in the arm."

Art. 869. For assault and battery by premeditated design, but not with a deadly weapon.

——" Did in consequence of premeditated design to beat and ill-treat one A. B. [or to disfigure, or dishonour, stating the intent particularly,] make an illegal assault upon the said A. B. [and with a cane struck and bruised him in his face and head.]"

Art. 870. If the offences, described in the preceding forms of this section, be committed by lying-in-wait, that circumstance must be charged, thus:

——" Did, in consequence of a premeditated design

[to beat and ill-treat, or to disfigure or dismember, or
to dishonour, &c.] lie-in-wait for the said A. B. and
make an illegal assault," &c.

Art. 871. Assault and battery, attended by disfiguration, dismembering, or other permanent injury, when no
design to inflict that degree of injury is proved.

——" Did make an illegal assault upon one A. B.
and with design to injure him did [strike,] or [thrust,] or
[cut the said A. B. with a sword, state the nature of the
injury and the weapon,] so that the said A. B. in consequence of such battery was dismembered by the loss
of [or losing the use of] an [eye, a leg, or other member, stating which;] or was [disfigured by a large
wound, leaving a scar under the right eye, which drew
it from its natural position, or otherwise, stating how;]
or [did receive such injury in his right leg as makes it
certain that he will, for the rest of his life, be lame,]
or [such bruises in his chest as render it probable that
he will labour for the rest of his life under the infirmity
of weakness in the lungs, or other permanent bodily
hurt, describing it.]"

SECTION VI.

Forms of indictment for false imprisonment.

Art. 872. Form of indictment for false imprisonment
by assault.

——" Did illegally and intentionally detain one A. B
in [the high-way, or other place, describing it], by
making an assault on him with a drawn sword opposed
to his breast, by which the said A. B. was illegally
prevented from moving from the place where he then
was, by the just fear of death or great bodily injury, for
the space of one hour."

Art. 873. By actual violence.

——"Did illegally and intentionally detain one A. B. in [describe the place] by [violently seizing him by the collar with his hands, or by binding him with a rope,] [describing the manner of the detention], and kept the said A. B. so detained as aforesaid, for the space of [two hours.]"

Art. 874. By some material impediment to the power of locomotion.

——"Did illegally and intentionally detain and imprison one A. B. in [a [chamber] or cellar, or other place in the said parish], by locking or barring the doors and windows of the said [chamber] when he the said A. B. was therein, in such a manner as to prevent him from leaving the said place, and kept him so imprisoned for the space of [ten days.]"

Art. 875. By threats.

——"Did illegally and intentionally detain one A. B. in [describe the place] by threatening, that if he should leave the said place [naming it] he would [describe the threat], and by means of such threats did detain the said A. B. in the said   for the space of [six hours,]" &c.

Art. 876. False imprisonment may be charged to have been inflicted when such is the case, by a combination of all the means stated in the preceding forms; and may also be joined in the indictment with all the different kinds and degrees of assault and battery, stating them in the forms above given.

SECTION VII.

False imprisonment aggravated by the purpose or the degree.

Art. 877. Indictment for false imprisonment and conveyance out of the state.

——"Did illegally and intentionally detain one A. B. [by making an assault on him with a drawn sword or other weapon, or by seizing him with his hands, or any of the other modes above described] and did forcibly convey the said A. B., so imprisoned, out of this state to [the city of Natchez], or [to some place to the jurors unknown.]"

Art. 878. If the charge be an intent to convey out of the state, after stating the imprisonments as above, add :

——" Did keep the said A. B. in form aforesaid during the space of [two days] with intent to convey him by force out of this state, [to the Havanna,] or to some place without this state to the jurors unknown."

Art. 879.*

Art. 880. For false imprisonment used as the means of forcing another to commit an offence.

——" Did illegally and intentionally detain one A. B. [for the space of   ] by [insert the means] with the intent to force the said A. B. to [aid the said J. S. in forging bills of the bank of B. or any other offence, describing it.]"

Art. 881. For false imprisonment with intent to commit an offence. — After the charge of the false imprisonment, as in the above form, say, " with the intent to [rob the said A. B., or to murder, or any other crime, describing it.]"

Art. 882. If the intent of the imprisonment is to force a woman to do an immodest act, after the charge of the imprisonment, as above, add, " with intent to force the said A. B. to do some act, or submit to some treatment, injurious to the modesty of her sex."

Art. 883. In the case provided for by the last form, if the person accused be the tutor, curator, or schoolmaster of the party offended, it must be specially so stated in the form prescribed in the fourth section of this chapter.

Art. 884. Form of indictment when the imprisonment was legal, but used with the intent set forth in the two last forms.

---

* Art. 879, referring to slaves, is omitted.

——" That Anne B. on the   day of   in
the year   , in the parish of   , having been
guilty of a [misdemeanor, or crime, stating it], or [having
threatened injury to any one, or done any other act
[stating it] which would justify a complaint and accusation,] one J. S. procured a warrant to be issued against
the said Anne B. by G. P. one of the justices, &c., for
the said offence, and caused her to be arrested and
imprisoned thereon, with intent and for the purpose of,"
&c. as in the last form.

SECTION VIII.

Forms of indictment in cases of abduction.

Art. 885. Indictment for false imprisonment and
abduction.

——" Did, [state the false imprisonment according to
the forms in the preceding section, and add,] with the
intent to force the said A. B., by means of such detention, to consent to a marriage with the said J. S. or with
a certain I. K.]"

Art. 886. Abduction of a female under fourteen years.

——" Did take and carry away from the care, superintendence, and custody of her [father,] [mother,] [tutor,]
[or other person having legal charge of the minor, stating
his quality with respect to her,] one Anne B. a female
minor, under the age of fourteen years, without the
consent of the said [father, &c., or other person having
legal charge of the said minor], and [without the consent
of the said Anne B., if such be the case], with the intent
of marrying the said Anne B., [or keeping her as a con-
cubine], [or inducing her to prostitute her person to
others.]"

SECTION IX.

Forms of indictment in cases of rape.

Art. 887. Rape by force.

———" Did make an assault upon one Anne B., and her, against her consent, did by force and violence carnally know."

Art. 888. Rape by menace.

———" Did ravish one Anne B., and against her will did carnally know her by threatening her with instant death, [or with putting out her eyes, or other great bodily harm, stating it.]"

Art. 889. Rape by fraud.

———" Did approach one Anne B. she then being asleep, [or the room in which she lay, she being in bed, being dark, or state such other circumstances as favoured the fraud,] and causing the said Anne B. to believe that he the said J. S. was her husband, the said Anne B. thus fraudulently did ravish and carnally know."

Or, ———" Did designedly administer to one Anne B. a certain drug or substance, to the jurors unknown, [or called   ,] by which an unnatural sexual desire was produced in the said Anne B. [or by which she was thrown into such stupor or weakness as weakened or prevented resistance], and while she was under the influence of the said drug or substance, her the said Anne did ravish and carnally know."

SECTION X.

Forms of indictment for procuring a miscarriage or abortion.

Art. 890. For procuring without the consent of the woman, by violence.

——" That on the   day of   in the year
          , at the parish of   , one Anne B., being
pregnant, J. S. of the same place, with intent to procure
the said Anne to miscarry of the child with which she
was then pregnant, without her consent or knowledge,
did cause her to swallow a certain drug or substance
called   , or [did apply to her body a certain
substance called   ,] or [did by violence and against
her consent forcibly compress the body of the said Anne],
and by those means caused the said Anne to miscarry of
the child of which she was then pregnant."

Art. 891. If done with the consent of the woman, the
above form may be used, substituting only the words
" with her consent," for the words " without her consent
or knowledge."

Art. 892. For furnishing the means, knowing the
purpose.

The same form as above. Instead of charging that
he " did cause her to swallow," &c. say, " did furnish to
her [to be taken with her consent], [or to I. K. to be
administered to the said Anne B., without her consent or
knowledge,] a certain drug or substance called
which was taken [or applied] by [or to] the said Anne B.,
and caused her to miscarry of the child of which she
was then pregnant, he the said J. S. knowing the
purpose to which the said drug or substance was intended
to be applied."

Art. 893. For furnishing the means when they fail in
their effect.

As in the last preceding form to the words " which
was taken [or applied] by [or to] the said Anne B.,"
after which add, " for the purpose of causing her to miscarry of the child with which she was then pregnant, but
which failed in producing such miscarriage, he the said
J. S. well knowing, at the time of furnishing the said
drug or substance, the purpose to which it was intended
to be applied."

Art. 894. If the offender be a physician or surgeon, or
midwife, or practise as such, that fact must be charged.

SECTION XI.

Form of indictment for maliciously giving a potion injurious to health.

Art. 895. ——" Did maliciously cause one I. K. to swallow, or inhale, without his knowledge, a drug called , or some drug or substance to the jurors unknown, which caused a violent change in the usual functions of his body, [or injured his health.]"

SECTION XII.

Forms of charges in indictments for homicide.

Art. 896. Indictment for negligent homicide in the first grade.
——" That J. S. on the   day of   in the year   , in the parish of L., being about to repair the barrel of a musket, believing the same not to be loaded, but without examining whether it was loaded or not, negligently put the breech of the said musket-barrel into a heated furnace ; and the jurors present, that the said musket-barrel was, unknown to the said J. S., loaded with powder and ball, and that owing to the heat of the furnace the powder exploded and drove the ball through the heart of one I. K. who was accidentally passing, and inflicted a mortal wound, of which wound, made by the said ball, the said I. K. instantly died : therefore the said jurors present, that the said J. S. is guilty of negligent homicide in the first grade."

Art. 897. Negligent homicide in the second grade.
——" That J. S. on the   day of   in the year   , at the parish of L., [caused one of his servants to mount on the back of an unbroke colt, for the

purpose of breaking him, in the public street or high-way, where, at the time, a number of persons were passing on their lawful business, to the evident danger of the lives of such persons, without taking any precaution to avoid the danger to which the said persons were exposed ; and the jurors present, that the rider of the said colt being unable to govern it, the said colt ran violently against one I. K. then passing in the said [high-way] or [street], and inflicted on him the said I. K. a mortal bruise on the breast, of which the said I. K. afterwards, that is to say, on the   day of   in the same year, in the parish aforesaid, died : therefore the said jurors present, that the said J. S. is guilty of negligent homicide in the second grade.

Art. 898. For negligent homicide, in the first grade, in the attempt to do an unlawful act.

——" That J. S. on the [insert date and place], intending unlawfully [and maliciously to kill an ox belonging to one I. K. in an unfrequented field, fired with a rifle loaded with ball at the said ox, without having previously examined whether any person was concealed by a bush which grew in the said field ; and the jurors present, that the said I. K. was concealed from the view of the said J. S. by the said bush, and that the ball discharged from the said rifle, as aforesaid, after killing the said ox, entered the right side of the said I. K. and inflicted a mortal wound] of which the said I. K. afterwards, on the same day and year, at the place aforesaid, died : wherefore the said jurors present, that the said J. S. has committed the first grade of negligent homicide in the commission of an unlawful act."

Art. 899. Negligent homicide, in the second grade, in the commission of an unlawful act.

——" That J. S. on the [insert date and place] [intending and attempting to kill and steal a turkey belonging to I. K. then feeding near the door of the dwelling-house of the said I. K., negligently fired a fowling-piece, loaded with powder and small shot, at the said turkey, but in the direction of the window of the said house, and that some of the shot, so fired from the said fowling-piece, passed through the window and inflicted a mortal wound on the right temple of A. K., a female child of the said I. K., aged five years or thereabouts, of which wound the said A. K. afterwards, on the same day and year, and at the place aforesaid, died] : therefore the jurors present, that the said J. S. hath committed the second grade of negligent homicide, in the [attempt] to do an unlawful act."

Art. 900. In all indictments for homicide, in doing or attempting to do an unlawful act, the circumstances of such unlawful act must be detailed with as much precision as if the indictment were for doing such act ; and also, it must be stated whether the unlawful act were accomplished, or only attempted, because it is from a knowledge of these circumstances only that the court can determine the degree of the offence and the manner of punishment."

Art. 901. Indictment for manslaughter.

———" That J. S. on the   day of   in the year   , at the parish of L., under the immediate influence of sudden passion, arising from an adequate cause, did [strike one I. K. on the head with a bar of iron, and did thereby inflict a mortal wound, of which the said I. K. afterwards, on the same day and year, and at the parish aforesaid, died] : wherefore the said jurors present, that the said J. S. the said I. K. then and there unlawfully did kill and slay."

Art. 902. Charge in an indictment for murder.

———" That J. S. on the   day of   in the year   , and in the parish of L., with a premeditated design to kill one I. K. made an assault upon the said I. K. and with a dirk inflicted a mortal wound on the left breast of him the said I. K., of which wound he the said I. K. afterwards, on the   day of   in the year aforesaid, at the place last aforesaid, died : wherefore the said jurors present, that the said J. S. the said I. K., in manner aforesaid, with a premeditated design, did kill and murder."

Art. 903. Indictment for infanticide.

——"That J. S. on the [insert date and place], in order to conceal the birth of a male child, born on the   day of   in the year   , of [insert the name of the mother], or [if the person accused is the mother, say, of the said J. S.] did, with a premeditated design to kill, expose the said child to the inclemency of the weather in an unfrequented field in the said parish, on the night of the said   day of   , and left the said child so exposed during the whole of the said night, of which exposure the said child, on the same night, died : wherefore the said jurors present, that the said J. S. the said male child did, in manner aforesaid, with premeditated design, kill and murder."

Art. 904. For assassination to conceal a crime.

——"That J. S. [insert date and place] having committed the crime of robbery by violently and fraudulently taking from the person of A. B., against his will, one gold watch and fifty Mexican dollars, in order to conceal the said crime, with premeditated design to kill, did make an assault on the said A. B. and by discharging a pistol, loaded with powder and ball and buckshot, against the head of him the said A. B. with the said ball and buckshot, inflicted a mortal wound under the right eye of the said A. B., of which wound the said A. B. afterwards, on the   day of   died : therefore the jurors say, that the said J. S. the said A.B. did, in manner aforesaid, with a premeditated design, kill, murder, and assassinate."

Art. 905. Assassination in the commission of a crime.

——"That J. S. on the   day of   in the year   , at the parish of L., for the purpose of committing the crime of robbery of one I. K. by violently and fraudulently taking from the person of the said I. K. against his will, one gold watch, did, with premeditated design to kill, make an assault upon one A. B. who then and there endeavoured to prevent the said robbery, and with a sword inflicted a mortal wound on the right side of the said A. B." &c. [as in the preceding form.]

Art. 906. Assassination for the purpose of obtaining an inheritance, and by hiring to murder.

——"That J. S. being the next of kin to one I. K. for the purpose of obtaining the inheritance of the said I. K. on the   day of   in the year   , did hire P. L. and N. O. for a reward promised to them by the said J. S. to kill the said I. K., and that the said P. L. and N. O. agreed to murder and assassinate the said I. K. for the said hire, and in pursuance of such agreement on the night of the day last aforesaid, entered the bed-room of the said I. K. and did make an assault upon him the said I. K. there lying in his bed, and the said I. K. with a pillow pressed by them on his face did suffocate, of which suffocation the said I. K. then and there died : wherefore the said jurors present, that the said J. S. and the said P. L. and the said N. O. the said I. K. with a premeditated design then and there, in manner aforesaid, did kill, murder, and assassinate."

Art. 907. Assassination by the means used to murder; lying-in-wait, arson, poison.

——"That J. S. on [set forth the date and place] with a premeditated design to kill one I. K. did lie-in-wait for him in a wood through which the said J. S. expected that the said I. K. would pass, and did then and there make an assault on the said," &c. [as in the preceding form.]

Art. 908. By arson.

——" With a premeditated design to kill one I. K., did set fire to the dwelling-house of the said I. K. in which he the said I. K. then was, and by means of such fire did burn and consume the said dwelling-house, and by the fire and smoke caused by the burning of the said house, the said I. K. was suffocated and burned, and of which burning and suffocation the said I. K. then and there died : wherefore the said jurors present, that the said J. S. the said I. K. with a premeditated design then and there did kill, murder, and assassinate."

Art. 909. By poison.

——"That J. S. having the premeditated design to kill one I. K. on the   day of   in the year

, did, in order to effect such design, mix a certain poison, called opium, in the soup prepared for the dinner of the said I. K., and the said I. K., having, on the same day and year, at   , without any knowledge of such mixture, swallowed a portion of the said soup with the said poison mixed therein, by the effect of the said poison became disordered in his body, and afterwards of such disorder, caused by the said poison, to wit, from the day last aforesaid until the   day of   now last past, languished, and then of the said disorder, so caused as aforesaid, in the parish aforesaid, died : wherefore the jury present," &c. [as in the last.]

Art. 910. In charging murder and assassination by poison, it is necessary to state that the poison was taken by the deceased without knowing that it was poison, otherwise it might amount only to a charge of aiding in suicide, which is another offence. It is also necessary to state the time of giving the poison and the time of death.

Art. 911. If the indictment state one kind of poison, and the proof is death by another, it will support the indictment.

Art. 912. When any circumstance in the situation or the condition of the person killed gives to murder the character of assassination, it is sufficient to state that circumstance in the indictment, after the name of the person killed. The same rule applies as to murder under trust, where the trust arises from the relative conditions or relationships of the murderer with the person murdered ; such condition or relationship being stated after the name of the person accused. When the trust arises under a special or implied promise, it must be stated thus :

——" That J. S. on [inserting the date and place], being [the master of a vessel called the Fly, then bound on a voyage from New Orleans to Havanna, took on board the said vessel, as a passenger, one I. K. and promised to convey him (the danger of the seas excepted) from the said port of New Orleans to the

Havanna ; but the jurors present, that the said J. S. violating the trust so reposed in him, and with premeditated design to kill, did, on the   day of   last, on board the said vessel called the Fly, then lying in the river Mississippi, within the parish of Plaquemines, make an assault upon him the said I. K. and by force threw the said I. K. from the deck of the said vessel into the water in the said river, where the said I. K. sunk and was suffocated by the said water, and then and there, in consequence of such suffocation, instantly died and was drowned] : wherefore," &c.

Art. 913. Attempt to kill by poison.

The charge is the same as that of assassination by poison, omitting only the latter part which charges the death.

Art. 914. Charge for aiding in suicide.

——"That A. B. on the   day of   in the year   , at the parish of L., committed suicide by [swallowing a quantity of poison, which then and there killed him]; and that J. S. before that time, that is to say, on the   day of   in the parish aforesaid, [procured the said poison and gave it to the said A. B. for the purpose of enabling him to commit the said suicide, he the said J. S. well knowing that it was the intention of the said A. B. to destroy his own life [by swallowing the said poison.]

SECTION XIII.

Forms of indictments and other proceedings against the provisions of the Penal Code respecting duels.

Art. 915. Using insulting words or gestures, or making an assault to provoke a duel.

——"That J. S. on [insert date and place], intending to provoke one I. K. to fight a duel, or if the said I. K. should not fight a duel in consequence of such provocation, that the said I. K. should be dishonoured, did use the following words, speaking to the said I. K. ['you are a coward']; or did use an insulting gesture, by [snapping his fingers in the face of the said I. K.]; or did make an assault upon the said I. K., by striking him in the face with the palm of his hand, or other insult, assault, or insulting gesture," [describing it,] &c.

Art. 916. Answers and explanations of the defendant.

"To the district court of the second district of the state of Louisiana.

"The answer and explanation of J. S. to the indictment [or information] filed against him for using insulting words [or gestures] to [or of] I. K., [or assaulting him, as the case may be,] with intent to provoke the said I. K. to fight a duel, or as an alternative to dishonour him—this defendant saith, that the [words or gestures, as the case may be,] charged in the said indictment were used [in the heat of passion, that he is truly concerned for having used them, and that he has the highest respect for the said I. K., and never seriously intended to impeach his courage"]—[or any other denial or explanation that he may deem satisfactory.]

Art. 917. Certificate when the court is satisfied with the explanation.

"By the district court of the second district, &c.

"Whereas an indictment was filed in this court, on [insert date,] charging [insert the charge]; and whereas the said J. S. afterwards presented to this court an answer and explanation [or acknowledgment] [or denial] hereunto annexed, which answer and explanation, in the opinion of this court, ought to satisfy the honour of the said I. K. It is therefore ordered, that the said answer be recorded and published, together with this judgment."

CHAPTER XIX.

Forms of indictments in offences against civil and political rights and conditions.

Art. 918. Against a nurse for substituting a child.

——" That A. B. on the   day of   in the year   , at the parish of L., confided an infant male child of him the said A. B., aged one month or thereabouts, to J. S. of the said parish, for the purpose of suckling and nursing the said child ; and that the said A. B. having been absent from the state for a long time, to wit, for five years and upwards, the said J. S. afterwards, on the   day of   in the year   , and at the parish aforesaid, with intent to deceive the said A. B. the [father, or mother, or tutor, or curator], of the said child, substituted [or attempted to substitute] another child for the one confided to her."

Art. 919. For exposing an infant, under the age of six years, with intent to abandon it.

——" That A. B. having on the   day of   in the year   , at the parish of L., confided a [female child, named C. B., aged two years or thereabouts, the daughter of the said A. B.,] to J. S., of the said parish, for the purpose of having the said child nursed and educated ; [and that the said J. S. afterwards, to wit, on the   day of   in the year   , in the parish afore said, exposed and deserted the said child in a wood in the said parish], where the life of the said child was greatly endangered, with the intent the said child then and there wholly to abandon," &c.

Art. 920. Against the father or mother for exposing an infant, with intent to abandon it.

——" That J. S. being the [father] [or mother] of an

illegitimate male child, born of the said J. S. [or, if the indictment be against the father, born of one I. K.] on the   day of   in the year   , at the said parish, did, on the day and year and at the place aforesaid, expose and desert the said child in a certain highway where the life of the said child was endangered, with intent wholly to abandon the said child."

Art. 921. For fraudulently producing a child with intent to intercept an inheritance.

——" That A. B. of the parish of L., long before and on the   day of   in the year   , was the owner and possessor of a large real and personal estate in this state, and that the said A. B. on the day aforesaid, had only two descendants, to wit, C. and D. his sons ; and that the said C. on the day last aforesaid died without leaving any legitimate descendants, whereby the said D. became the presumptive heir to the said A. B. ; and the jurors present, that one J. S. afterwards, to wit, on the   day of   in the year   , at the parish aforesaid, with design to intercept half of the inheritance of the said A. B. from the said D. fraudulently produced an infant male child, falsely pretending that the said infant was the legitimate child of the said C. deceased, and which child would, if he had really been the legitimate child of the said C., have stood in the order of succession to the inheritance of the said A. B. equally with the said D."

Art. 922. If the offence be committed against a collateral presumptive heir, and the child produced be alleged to be a descendant, the charge must be " of a design to intercept the whole inheritance."

Art. 923. For making a false entry on register of births.

——" That J. S. on [insert date and place] being then minister of the Protestant Episcopal Church in the parish of L. and charged with keeping the register of marriages for the members of the said church, did fraudulently make a false entry on such register, falsely registering therein that on the   day of   in the year   ,

A. B. was married to C. D. by him the said minister, [or by I. K. formerly minister of the church], with intent to injure one E. F. in her condition and civil rights [as legitimate wife of the said A. B.]"

Art. 924. For bigamy.

——" That J. S. on the   day of   in the year   , at the parish of   , being then married to Anne, the daughter of J. B., and the said Anne being then living, contracted another marriage with C. D. of the said parish, according to the form required to give validity to marriages in this state, he the said J. S. having, at the time of his contracting the said second marriage, no reasonable cause to believe the said Anne, his wife, to be dead."

CHAPTER XX.

Forms of indictments for offences affecting private property.

SECTION I.

Forms of indictments for burning and other malicious injuries to property.

Art. 925. For maliciously setting fire to a dwelling-house or other property.

——" That J. S. on the   day of   in the year   , at the parish of L., did maliciously set fire to a dwelling-house belonging to [or inhabited by] one I. K., with intent to destroy the same," &c.

Art. 926. If the house be not a dwelling-house, but contains property of the value of one hundred dollars, it must be thus described : "a certain house belonging to [or occupied by] I. K., situated in the same parish, containing personal property of the value of one hundred dollars."

If the house be empty, and be not a dwelling-house, it must be described as a " house."

Art. 927. For destroying a house with gunpowder or other explosive matter.

——"Did maliciously place gunpowder [or other explosive matter, designating it,] under [or in] a certain house, [or a house containing personal property of the value of one hundred dollars,] [or a dwelling-house] belonging to [or occupied by] I. K. situated in the said parish, and put fire to the said gunpowder [or other explosive matter] thereby causing the same to explode, with intent to destroy the said house," &c.

Art. 928. The above forms answer for the offence of setting fire to the other objects which the Code of Crimes and Punishments makes it an offence to set fire to, adding a charge of the value.

Art. 929. When bodily injury is suffered by any one, by the commission of the offence of malicious burning of a house or other property, or the offence be committed in the night, or if the buildings contain any domestic animals, those circumstances must be added to the charge.

Art. 930. For the destruction of a ship or other vessel, or raft, by fire.

——"Did, designedly and with intent to injure, illegally set fire to [or destroy by explosion of gunpowder, stating the manner,] a certain boat, [raft, schooner, or other vessel, describing it,] with the cargo on board, [if any, describing it,] being, together with such cargo, of the value of one hundred dollars."

Art. 931. For the malicious destruction of property by other means than by fire.

——"Did maliciously destroy a certain boat, commonly called a pirogue, with the cargo, consisting of fifty hogsheads of sugar, being then and there in the exclusive possession of one I. K., and being, together with such cargo, of greater value than ten dollars, by boring a hole in the bottom of the said pirogue and sinking it in the river Mississippi."

Art. 932. For fraudulently removing a land-mark.

——"That J. S. on the   day of   in the

year   , at the parish of   , did fraudulently [or maliciously, as the case may be,] remove a [cypress post] which had been placed to serve and did then serve as a land-mark to designate the boundary between two parcels of land in the said parish, the one in the possession of [the said J. S.] and the other of the said tracts in the possession of one A. B."

SECTION II.

Forms of indictments for house-breaking.

Art. 933. House-breaking by force, in the night.

——"That J. S. on the night of the   day of   , in the year   , in the parish of L., about the hour of eleven, by force, entered into a house occupied by I. K. in the said parish, with intent to steal, [or burn the said house, or to commit murder, or any other crime, naming it.]"

Art. 934. For entering in the day and concealment until night.

——"That J. S. on the   day of   , in the year   , at the parish of L., entered, in the day-time, secretly and fraudulently into the house of one I. K. situated in the said parish, and concealed himself in the said house until the night of the same day, with the intent to steal," &c.

Art. 935. For entering by discharging fire-arms or throwing a stone.

——"Did, with intent to do a bodily injury to one I. K. then being in a certain house [occupied by him the said I. K.] in the parish aforesaid, discharge a pistol, loaded with gunpowder and a ball, into the said house, through the door thereof; [or throw a stone through the window of the said house, or other missile, as the case may be.]"

SECTION III.

Forms of indictments for the forcible or fraudulent acquisition of property.

Art. 936. For a fraudulent breach of trust.

——" That J. S. on [insert date and place] having before that time, at the parish of Point Coupee, received [ten bales of cotton, belonging to one I. K.] of the value of fifty dollars each, [to be carried by him the said J. S. from the said parish of Point Coupee to the parish of L., to be there delivered to one A. B.] did, on the day and year and at the place first above mentioned, fraudulently appropriate the said [ten bales of cotton] to his own use."

Art. 937. When the property was received on a contract of loan, or letting or hiring.

——" That J. S. on [state the date and place] received from one I. K. on a contract of letting and hiring a certain [bay horse with a gig, of the value of   ], to be used by him the said J. S. for the purpose of conveying him to the Bayou St. John's in the said parish, and to be returned to the said I. K. on the same day; and the jurors further present, that the said J. S. did not on the said day return the said [horse and gig] to the said I. K., but did, on the day and year and at the parish aforesaid, fraudulently appropriate the said [horse and gig] to his own use."

Art. 938. For the fraudulent appropriation of property found.

——" That J. S. [insert date of time and place] found a certain [red morocco pocket-book, containing bank-notes to the value of   ,] which had before that time been casually lost by one I. K., and that the said J. S. then and there knowing, or having good reason to believe, that the said I. K. was the owner of the said [pocket·

book and its contents,] fraudulently did then and there appropriate the same," &c.

Art. 939. Where the finder has no reason to believe any designated person to be the owner.

[As before to the words "lost by one I. K."] "and that the said J. S. did then and there conceal and appropriate the same to his own use."

Art. 940. For opening and reading a sealed letter.

——" That J. S. [insert date and time of place] did open and read [or cause to be read] a sealed letter, written by I. K. to A. B., he the said J. S. not being authorized so to do by the said I. K. or the said A. B. or by law."

Art. 941. For malicious publication—add,

——" And that the said J. S. [or one C. D.] did maliciously and without authority publish the said letter [or a part of such letter] by printing the same in the words following, [insert the printed letter,] which publication is hereunto annexed, he the said J. S. [or C. D.] knowing the manner in which the said letter was obtained."

Art. 942. If, in the preceding form and that immediately following, the publication was in any other mode than by printing, there is no necessity of inserting a copy of the published letter in the indictment, or giving any other declaration of the letter than the names of the writer and of the person to whom it was addressed.

Art. 943. For taking and publishing a letter.

——" Did take from the legal possession of I. K., without his consent, a certain letter written by one A. B. to him the said I. K., and did maliciously publish the same by printing it in the following words, [insert copy of the published letter,] which printed letter is hereunto annexed."

Art. 944. For obtaining property by false pretences.

——" That J. S. [insert date of time and place,] did, with a fraudulent intent, and by the consent of one I. K., obtain from him one pair of silver candlesticks, belonging to him the said I. K., by falsely pretending that he the said J. S. was the servant of one A. B., a person well known to the said I. K., and that the said A. B. had sent him the said J. S. to borrow the said candlesticks for him the said A. B. ; and the jurors further present, that the said I. K. would not have consented to deliver the said candlesticks to the said J. S. if he had not made use of the said false pretence.

Art. 945. For false pretences by personification.

——"That one J. S. with a fraudulent intent, and under the false pretence that he was G. H. of the parish of Point Coupee, planter, a man of great wealth and credit, on the   day of   in the parish of L., induced one I. K. to deliver to him the said J. S. thus personating the said G. H. five hundred yards of raven's duck and ten pieces of Scotch plaids, which he falsely asserted were wanted as supplies for the plantation of the said G. H. whom he falsely personated, and the jurors present," [as in the last form.]

Art. 946. If the false pretence be that he is another person of the same name, instead of charging the false pretence as above, say, "falsely pretending that he the said J. S. was another person, also named J. S. of," &c. [as in the last form.]

Art. 947. Charge for obtaining goods on the false pretence of immediate payment.

——"That J. S. on [insert date of time and place] with a fraudulent intent, induced one I. K. to deliver to him [describe the goods] under the false pretence that he would immediately pay the sum of   dollars· for them in cash ; and the jurors further present, that the said J. S. refused to return the said goods or to pay the said sum, although he was afterwards on the same day and year, at the parish aforesaid, within one hour after the delivery of the said goods, required so to do." [If the demand was made after one hour, state, "although he was afterwards, to wit, on the   day of   in the same year,] [stating some time within three days of the delivery] required so to do, the said goods then being in the possession of the said J. S. ; and the jurors

further present, that the said I. K. would not have consented to deliver the said goods if the said J. S. had not
made the said false pretence of immediate payment in
cash," &c.

Art. 948. For giving a check of no value in payment.

——"That J. S. on [insert date of time and place]
purchased from one I. K. [insert description of property]
and with intent to defraud, did give to the said I. K.
in payment for the said property a check or draft,
drawn by him the said J. S. [or by A. B.] on the
bank of   payable on demand for the sum of
          , which he the said J. S. falsely pretended
and affirmed would be paid at sight, he the said J. S.
then and there well knowing that the said check or
draft was then of no value; and the jurors further
present, that the said check was of no value : and that
the said I. K. would not have delivered the said property
if the said J. S. had not made the said false and fraudulent
pretences, contrary," &c.

Art. 949. For false pretences by producing false
papers.

——"That J. S. being desirous of purchasing one
hundred bales of fair Louisiana cotton from one I. K.,
with a fraudulent design to induce him to sell the said
cotton at a low price, produced a writing which he falsely
pretended was a Liverpool price current [or letter from
C. & Co. of Liverpool] dated the   day of
last, in which false paper [or writing] it was stated that
the price of fair Louisiana cotton, on the day of the date
thereof, was seven pence sterling per pound ; and the
jurors present, that the said paper [or writing] was false
and fraudulent, and that giving credit to the false pretence of the said J. S. he the said I. K. sold and
delivered to him one hundred bales of cotton at the
price of fourteen cents a pound, which he would not have
done if the said J. S. had not made the false pretences,
and by which the said I. K. was defrauded of the sum
of   dollars."

Art. 950. False pretences by cheating at cards.

———"That J. S. on [insert date of time and place] fraudulently obtained from one A. B. the sum of
dollars at a game of [skill and chance called whist] by means of packing the cards in such a manner [as to keep in his own hand all the court cards, or other means, describing them,] which means the jurors present were other than those which would have been given to the said J. S. by the regular chances of the said game, or by the fair exercise of his skill therein, he the said J. S. falsely pretending that the said sum of money was won by the regular chances of the said game, and the fair exercise of his skill therein ; and the jurors further present, that the said A. B. would not have delivered and paid the said sum of   dollars if the said J. S. had not made the said false and fraudulent pretences."

Art. 951. Charge in indictment for theft.

———"That J. S. on [insert date of time and place] one piece of lace, of the value of   dollars, the property of A. B., from his possession fraudulently did take without his assent."

Art. 952. Theft by effraction.

———"That J. S. [insert date of time and place] in the day time, with a fraudulent design, did enter into a certain house occupied by A. B. [or ship called the Bee] and one piece of lace of the value of   dollars the property of A. B. and in his possession then and there being, fraudulently did take without the assent of the said A. B."

Art. 953. Breaking into a ship or house with intent to steal.

———"That J. S. on [insert date of time and place] with intent to commit a theft, a certain house belonging to [or occupied by] one A. B. did break and enter," &c.

If theft be committed, add, "and one piece of linen of the value of   , belonging to the said A. B. from his possession fraudulently did then and there take, without the assent of the said A. B."

If any one were in the house or ship, then add, "and the jurors further present, that C. D. was at the time of the said entry in the said house [or ship,] and did resist the said J. S. [or was prevented by fear from resisting him, as the case may be.]"

Art. 954. For entering a house and stealing by breaking a chest or box, &c.

——"That J. S. on, &c. in the day time, with a fraudulent intent, into a certain house belonging to [or in the occupation of] one A. B. did enter, and a certain box [or chest, or other enclosed place] did forcibly break, and a piece of gold coin, then in the said box, belonging to A. B., being found, did fraudulently take, without the assent of the said A. B."

Art. 955. For fraudulently appropriating property taken from a wrecked vessel.

——"That a certain ship or vessel, of which the name and the owners are to the jurors unknown, was wrecked [or stranded] [or burned] on the west shore of the Lake Pontchartrain, in this state, on the   day of   in the year   , in the parish of New Orleans; and that J. S., on the day and year and at the place last aforesaid, ten bales of cotton, driven on shore from the said wreck, did fraudulently appropriate, knowing them to have proceeded from the said wreck."

Art. 956. For privately stealing from the person.

——"That J. S. on [insert date of time and place] one [gold watch of the value of fifty dollars, belonging to and in the possession of I. K.,] privately from the said I. K. did fraudulently take, without his assent."

Art. 957. For robbery.

——"That J. S. [date, &c.] from the person of one I. K. by force and against his will, one gold watch of the value of fifty dollars, belonging to him, did fraudulently take."

Art. 958. For robbery by threats of violence.

——"That J. S. [date, &c.] from the person of one I. K. one hundred gold coins of the United States, called eagles, belonging to him the said I. K. did fraudulently take, and did force the said I. K. to deliver by threatening the said I. K. [to accuse him of the crime of rape];

or [to burn the house of the said I. K.] ; or [to assassinate him] or [to do any other injury to his person, property, or character, describing it]."

Art. 959. For receiving property, knowing it to be fraudulently obtained.

——" That J. S. on [date &c.] did fraudulently receive [or did fraudulently conceal or endeavour to conceal] one gold watch, belonging to one I. K. of the value of fifty dollars, which had been fraudulently taken [or obtained] from him by [theft,] or [fraudulent breach of trust,] or [by the fraudulent appropriation of property found,] or [by false pretences,] he the said J. S. well knowing that the said property had been so fraudulently taken [or obtained]."

Art. 960. For attempts to defraud by threats.

——" That J. S. with a fraudulent intent did, on [insert date &c.] threaten one I. K. that he would [set fire to the dwelling-house of] him the said I. K. if he the said I. K. did not [give him a sum of one hundred dollars,] or [did not procure for him the place of undersheriff of the parish], as the means of avoiding the execution of the said threat."

Art. 961. If the threat be of injury to person or reputation, or any other injury to property than the one above specified, it must be particularly set forth.

Art. 962. If the threat be in writing, it must be in the following form :

——" That J. S. on [insert date &c.] did, with a fraudulent intent, make an instrument in writing, and send the same to one I. K., which instrument is in the words following, to wit : [' Mr. I. K. if you wish to avoid the burning of your house, or the infamy of having made an attempt to suborn a witness, you will do well to enclose a bank-note for one hundred dollars, by post, addressed to A. B. at L.']—meaning thereby to demand of the said I. K. the sum of one hundred dollars as the means to avoid the destruction of the house of the said I. K. or an accusation of having attempted to suborn a witness to commit perjury, contrary," &c.

Art. 963. For writing a malicious threatening letter, without any design to defraud.

——"That J. S. [insert date], maliciously intending to vex and disquiet one I. K., wrote [or caused to be written and sent or delivered, as the case may be,] to the said I. K. a certain writing, in the words following, to wit, [insert the letter.]"

CHAPTER XXI.

Forms of indictments for conspiracy.

Art. 964. Conspiracy to rob and murder.

——"That J. S. and N. O. on [insert date] fraudulently intending to rob and murder one A. B. agreed together, or with other persons to the jurors unknown, [according to the fact] [that the said N. O. he being then and there a domestic servant of the said A. B. should admit the said J. S. at midnight, on some subsequent day into the house of the said A. B., and that they should then and there strangle and kill the said A. B. in his bed, and should carry off and steal all the money and other valuable property found in the said house.]"

Art. 965. Conspiracy to make a false accusation.

——"That J. S. and N. O. on [insert date] intending maliciously to injure one A. B. agreed together, or [with others as above,] that they the said J. S. and N. O. would accuse the said A. B. of having committed the crime of rape upon one C. D., they the said J. S. and N. O. well knowing that the said A. B. was innocent of any such crime."

Art. 966. Conspiracy to lower wages.

"That J. S., N. O., and L. M., on [insert date], being master-shoemakers in the said city of New Orleans, entered into an agreement and combination with each other, and with other master-shoemakers in the said city to the jurors unknown, that they would give to the journeymen-shoemakers, whom they should severally employ, no more than [the sum of   for each day's work, or for each pair of shoes, &c., stating the substance of the agreement; and if any penalty be imposed by the agreement for a breach of it, state the same particularly.]"

Art. 967. Conspiracy to raise wages and abridge the time of labour.

"That J. S., N. O., and R. P., being persons usually working as journeymen in the trade of shoemaking, did, on [insert date] enter into an agreement and conspiracy to and with each other, and to and with divers other persons to the jurors unknown, that they would not work at their said trade unless they were paid at the rate of   for each pair of shoes, and   for each pair of boots, or   for each day they should work at their said trade; [or that they would work only ten hours for a day's work;] [state, as above, the substance of the agreement, and if it contained any penalty for a breach of it, or any proceeding to oblige others to enter into the conspiracy, state the same.]"

Art. 968. The agreement is the offence, but if any thing be done in consequence of it to carry it into execution (as if the penalty imposed by the agreement be enforced, or any injury be offered to others to force them to join in the conspiracy,) it should be stated, that the court may apportion the punishment.

Art. 969. Conspiracy to raise the price of flour.

"That J. S. and I. K., being merchants dealing in the purchase and sale of flour, on [insert date] did enter into a conspiracy and agreement to and with each other, and to and with other persons to the jurors unknown, that they would purchase each of them one thousand barrels of flour, and would not sell the same for less than twelve dollars for each barrel, [insert the conditions of the agreement and the penalty, if any, for its breach.]"

CHAPTER XXII.

Forms of indictments against principals who become such by aiding or encouraging the act, against accomplices and accessaries.

Art. 970. Whenever any one, who hath not himself committed the offence, hath made himself a principal by any of the acts enumerated in the third article of the fifth chapter of the first book of the Code of Crimes and Punishments, he is a principal in the second degree, and he may be indicted jointly with the one who personally committed the offence, or separately ; but, in either case, the commission of the offence and the act which made the abettor liable, must be stated according to the truth ; but if he be present at the act, it will be sufficient to state that he was so, and that he aided or encouraged the others, without stating in what manner particularly.

Art. 971. The person becoming liable, as a principal, under the provisions of the above recited article, may be indicted, tried, and punished, although the one who personally committed the offence should have escaped, or be acquitted, or pardoned, but the commission of the offence must be proved.

Art. 972. Indictment against principals in the first and second degree, jointly for murder.

——" That J. S., on the   day of   in the year   , at the parish of L., with a premeditated design to kill one I. K., made an assault upon the said I. K., and with a dirk inflicted a mortal wound on the left breast of him the said I. K., of which wound he the said I. K. afterwards, on the same day and year, at the place aforesaid, died : and that L. M. during the time that the said J. S. was committing the said offence stood at a short distance from the place where the said murder was committed, knowing that the said J. S. was engaged in the perpetration thereof, and with the intent to keep watch and give notice to the said J. S. of the approach of any one who might interrupt the commission of the said offence ; whereupon the jurors aforesaid present, that the said J. S. and L. M. the said I. K. in manner aforesaid did kill and murder, contrary," &c.

Art. 973. Indictment against the principal in the second degree alone.

"That, &c. [insert the charge against the person who actually committed the offence, according to the forms prescribed for such offence, then add,] and the jurors aforesaid do further present, that L. M. at the time the said offence was committed was present [and by words and gestures did encourage the said J. S. to commit the said offence, he the said L. M. well knowing the unlawful intent of the said J. S. in committing the said offence.]"

Art. 974. Indictment against an accomplice for having committed the offence, &c.

"That, &c. [state the offence, according to the proper form, and then add,] and the jurors further present, that L. M., before the said offence was committed, to wit, on the   day of   in the year aforesaid, at the parish aforesaid, did unlawfully advise, command, and encourage, [or did agree to aid,] or [did promise the sum of   dollars to,] or [offer his interest in procuring the office of sheriff of the county of L. for,] or [did prepare and furnish the pistol to, &c. as the case may be,] the said J. S. in order to induce him to commit the said offence."

Art. 975. Indictment against an accessary.

"That, &c. [state the offence, according to the proper form, after which add,] and the jurors aforesaid do further present that L. M., well knowing the said J. S. to have committed the said offence as aforesaid, afterwards, to wit, on the   day of   in the year aforesaid, at the parish of L., did conceal the said J. S. or aid him, in order that he might effect his escape [from arrest, or trial, or the execution of his sentence, as the case may be.]"

CHAPTER XXIII.

Of informations.

Art. 976. Form of an information by the attorney-general, or district attorney.

"Be it remembered, that on the   day of
in the year   , in the criminal court of the state of
Louisiana, came J. P., attorney-general of the state of
Louisiana, and gives the said court to be informed, that,"
&c. [as in an indictment.]

Art. 977. After an information has been filed, the
prosecution cannot be dismissed but by leave of the
court, on motion of the public prosecutor, who must
state his reasons for such motion, which motion with the
reasons must be entered on the minutes of the court,
together with the decision of the court on such motion,
whether it be allowed or rejected.

Art. 978. All the provisions respecting indictments in
this Code apply to informations in cases where by law
they may be filed, unless the contrary is expressed or
results from the nature of the two modes of proceeding.

CHAPTER XXIV.

Of joining different offences and persons in the same indictment, and of different courts, for the same offence.

Art. 979. No indictment can contain a charge for more
offences than one, under the modification hereinafter in
this chapter contained.

Art. 980. The practice of inserting different charges

or counts in an indictment for the same offence, is abolished; but where there is evidence before a grand jury sufficient to prove a fact which is an offence, and the evidence renders it doubtful whether it was done with one or the other of several intents, either of which would aggravate the offence, the jury may charge the intent in the alternative, and the accused may be convicted on the proof of either on the trial.

Art. 981. Form of indictment charging the intent in the alternative.

"That J. S. on &c. [insert date] at the parish of L., upon one A. B. did make an assault by seizing the said A. B. by the throat with his hands and striking him, &c. with the intent either to murder the said A. B. or to disfigure him, or to do a permanent injury by laming him," &c.

Art. 982. In cases of libel it will be sufficient to charge in the indictment that the defendant *"made," "published,"* or *"circulated,"* the libel: and proof of either, according to the definition of those terms in the Penal Code of Crimes and Punishments, will be sufficient. In like manner, an indictment will be good which charges that the defendant either made the counterfeit coin, or a forged instrument, or had the same in possession, with intent to pass (in cases where such possession is made an offence); or that he knowingly uttered or passed the same, naming the person to whom.

Art. 983. In indictments for all offences against private property in which, according to the forms hereinbefore prescribed, it is necessary to aver the name of the owner or possessor of the property, it will be sufficient to state in the alternative that either A. B. or C. D. was such possessor or owner; and in like manner, proof of either will be sufficient.

Art. 984. The several persons may be joined in the same indictment in the following cases:

The person who gives and he who receives a bribe.

The principal, the accomplice, and accessary.

The suborner and the perjurer.

The employer and the actual assassin, (in cases of assassination for hire.)

The adulteress and her paramour.

Joint rioters, conspirators, and all others who jointly commit an offence.

Art. 985. Although several be joined, yet each defendant may demand and have a separate trial, except in case of adultery, as is before provided for.

CHAPTER XXV.

Of the mode of making the charge in cases of repetition of the offence.

Art. 986. That the party accused has been before convicted of an offence of the same nature may be stated in the indictment according to the following form : after the charge of the offence add, " and the jurors do further present, that the said J. S. was heretofore in the court of [state the court] in or about the year   convicted of [state the offence, and if he was more than once convicted, state the same in like manner, and conclude,] wherefore the said jurors present, that the said J. S. hath [a second or third time] committed an offence affecting [private property, according to the nature of the offence.]"

Art. 987. If the prior convictions are discovered after the time of finding the indictment, but before the trial, the public prosecutor may give notice to the defendant, at any time before the trial, that he will give evidence of such conviction, specifying the offence and the time as is above set forth, and shall then be allowed to give such evidence.

Art. 988. If the prior conviction be discovered after conviction, whether sentence be passed or not, the record of the conviction shall be received by the court, and the defendant shall be brought up and required to show cause why the additional punishment should not be inflicted, which he may do by denying that he is the person formerly convicted. If the identity is denied, it shall be tried by a jury, and the burthen of proof shall be on the public prosecutor.

A CODE OF EVIDENCE.

INTRODUCTORY TITLE.

Art. 1. The Code of Evidence, which is applicable as well to civil as to criminal cases, will direct judges, other magistrates, ministers of justice and jurors, what proof is sufficient to commit, to indict, and to convict an offender, against the Code of Crimes and Punishments.

Art. 2. Where, in this Code, examples are given to illustrate certain rules of evidence, they are never intended as an enumeration of all the cases coming within such rules. When a limitation to certain enumerated cases is intended, it is unequivocally so expressed.

Art. 3. The substantive word *judge* in this Code means the power which has the right of deciding on the subject matter to which the article in which it is used applies; it may, according to the subject, mean either the magistrate, the jury, or the arbitrator or referee.

Art. 4. All the rules of evidence which are laid down to regulate the introduction and declare the effect of proof adduced on the principal matter in dispute in judicial investigation, apply also to the introduction and effect of the same kind of proof on any incidental question, except when it is otherwise expressly provided.

Art. 5. Particular provisions in this Code control general rules, but in the particular case only in which they are introduced.

Art. 6. By the expression "immoveable estate," or "immoveables," is meant all that is made such by destination or provision of law, as well as by nature.

Art. 7. When the word "*evidence*" is used in this Code, it always means "*legal evidence*," as herein defined.

Art. 8. In all cases whatever where anything is

declared to be legal evidence, it must be understood to be with the proviso that it is applicable to the issue or fact in litigation. Whether so applicable or not (when there is no express provision) it is left to the discretion of the court to determine. But in the exercise of this discretion great liberality must be used, and no legal evidence excluded that has even a remote application to the question.

Art. 9. If in any criminal case the provisions of this Code, for the admission or exclusion of evidence, shall in the opinion of the court be found to have operated unjustly; and in consequence thereof any one is convicted, judgment shall not be be pronounced until after the report has been made to the legislature, in the manner hereinafter provided. But if such provision shall operate, in the opinion of the court, in favour of the accused, who shall, in consequence of evidence admitted or excluded conformably to such provision, be acquitted, judgment of acquittal shall be rendered : and in either of these cases (as well as in civil cases, where a verdict has, in the opinion of the court, been unjustly given in consequence of evidence admitted or excluded conformably to such provision) a full report shall be made to the legislature of the case, together with the reasons of the court for thinking the particular provision unjust or inexpedient; and if the legislature shall, at the first session after the report, make the alterations, in substance as suggested by the court, a new trial shall be given in the civil suit, and to the party convicted in a criminal cause ; otherwise judgment shall be given on the verdict.

Art. 10. If in the trial of any cause a question shall arise, relative to the admission of evidence for the decision of which no provision is made in this Code, the court shall decide according to such principles as they believe the legislature would have been guided by had the case been foreseen ; and shall, in like manner, report the case and their decision, with the reason thereof, to the legislature. And although the legislature should amend this Code in consequence of such representation, or should omit so to do, it shall not affect the decision if it be made in a civil cause.

Art. 11. But if the case provided for by the last preceding article be a criminal one, and the principle adopted by the court shall have admitted or excluded evidence, to the prejudice of the accused, which evidence would not have been so excluded or admitted as the Code now stands, and the accused shall, in consequence thereof, be convicted, no judgment shall be had on such conviction, but the defendant shall be discharged.

Art. 12. The last three preceding articles relate only to questions on the admissibility of evidence; all questions, as to its credit and weight, when admitted, must be decided by the judge or the jury, to whichever the fact is submitted, except in cases of evidence declared by law to be conclusive.

BOOK I.

OF THE NATURE OF EVIDENCE, AND OF ITS SEVERAL KINDS.

TITLE I.

GENERAL PRINCIPLES AND DEFINITIONS.

Art. 13. Evidence is that which brings or contributes to bring the mind to a just conviction of the truth or falsehood of any fact asserted or denied.

Art. 14. From the above definition it results that judges of fact, except in cases of proof declared to be conclusive, are not bound to decide in conformity with the declarations of any number of witnesses, which do not produce conviction to the mind, against a less number, or against presumptions which do satisfy the mind.

Art. 15. A conviction produced by evidence, which ought not, according to the rules of true reason, to have that effect, is not a just conviction. But different minds may have different conceptions of what is true reason; the law, in order to secure uniformity of decision on this point, declares what evidence ought, in given cases, to produce, or contribute to produce such conviction, and that evidence is called legal evidence.

TITLE II.

DISTRIBUTION OF THE SUBJECT.

Art. 16. LEGAL EVIDENCE, in relation to its nature, is of two kinds: that which the judge receives from his own knowledge, and that which he derives from other sources; the latter is either testimonial, scriptory, or substantive.

TESTIMONIAL EVIDENCE is that which is offered by the relation of any other person, whether communicated to the judge orally or in writing.

SCRIPTORY EVIDENCE comprehends all written evidence other than the declarations of witnesses reduced to writing.

SUBSTANTIVE EVIDENCE is that which is produced by the exhibition of any object which from its nature, situation, or appearance, creates a belief of the truth or falsehood of the allegation in dispute.

Art. 17. Evidence being different in the degree of effect which it ought to produce, is therefore divided into three kinds: presumptive evidence, direct evidence, and conclusive evidence.

Art. 18. Presumptive evidence is that, which by directly proving one fact, renders the existence of another fact probable.

Art. 19. Direct evidence is that, which if true, conclusively establishes or destroys the proposition in question.

Art. 20. Conclusive evidence is that, which by law is declared to be such proof of that which it asserts, as cannot, while it exists, be contradicted by other testimony.

The law does not and cannot in this case command belief; but on the exhibition of certain evidence it does command such decision, as would be the result of a belief in the existence of the fact which such evidence purports to prove.

Art. 21. These degrees may be produced by either of the kinds of evidence above enumerated; the actual inspection or perception of the judge, the declaration of witnesses, the exhibition of written proof, or of substantive evidence. The law under each of these divisions is declared in the subsequent titles.

Art. 22. Every offence being in this system clearly defined and directed to be distinctly charged in the act of accusation, all rules of evidence applicable to one, are applicable to all ; therefore, in criminal cases, whatever constitutes the offence, whether act, omission, or intent, must be supported by such LEGAL EVIDENCE as proves the allegation.

Art. 23. So in civil cases, all fictions being in like manner discarded, and the demand and defence being required to be set forth according to the truth, the same rules of evidence are applicable to all actions.

Art. 24. It results from the two preceding articles, that no provisions are necessary in this Code to designate what evidence is required or permitted in each kind of action or division of offence.

BOOK II.

OF THE RULES APPLICABLE TO THE SEVERAL KINDS OF EVIDENCE.

TITLE I.

OF THE EVIDENCE OFFERED TO A JUDGE FROM HIS OWN KNOWLEDGE.

Art. 25. Under some circumstances the judge is allowed to frame his decision upon the conviction brought to his mind by means of his own senses without the intervention of any other proof. But he can do this only in cases particularly provided by law ; these are especially designated in the different codes of this system.

Art. 26. In all other cases than those so specially provided for, the judge hears the testimonial, sees the scriptory, or the substantive, evidence, and must decide (not from his knowledge, but) from the conviction produced on his mind by this evidence.

Art. 27. The power given to a magistrate to arrest when an offence is committed in his presence ; to a judge, to determine on the authenticity of a record, to order the removal of a person who interrupts the proceedings of a court, and the authority given to the magistrates to determine when the military may be directed to act in support of the civil power, are examples of cases in which the judge is empowered to act on evidence derived from his own knowledge.

Art. 28. In all other cases where facts material to the decision of the cause have come to the knowledge of the judge, and he is not specially authorized to act on such knowledge, he must state the facts in open court under oath, and is liable to cross-examination like any other witness. When there is but one judge, and the fact is to be tried by the court, if the testimony of the judge is necessary, the cause shall be tried by the judge of an adjoining district in the manner provided for in cases where the judge is interested.

Art. 29. Jurors are not permitted to act on the evidence of their own knowledge. Whatever has come to the knowledge of either of them, must be stated under oath in open court.

TITLE II.

OF TESTIMONIAL EVIDENCE.

Art. 30. Rules for procuring the personal attendance or the written testimony of witnesses, are contained in the Codes of Civil and of Criminal Procedure. This chapter directs what persons may be produced as witnesses ; to what points they may be examined, and the mode of conducting the examination.

CHAPTER I.

What persons may be examined as witnesses.

Art. 31. The only persons who, under all circumstances, are excluded from giving testimony are :

1. Those who are of INSANE MIND at the time of examination.

2. Children under fourteen years of age, whose faculties do not appear to be sufficiently developed, to receive correct impressions of the fact relative to which they are interrogated, to relate those impressions correctly, and to feel the obligations of doing it truly.

Art. 32. Whether a child under the age of fourteen has attained the intellectual powers required by the preceding article, or whether the person offered as a witness be of sane mind or not ; must be determined by those who are to decide on the principal fact in question between the parties, and to come to such determination, they must examine the person who is offered as a witness, and other witnesses if it be deemed necessary. If the trial is by a jury, a majority shall determine whether a witness objected to for either of these causes shall be examined.

Art. 33. The circumstances and cases in which certain persons otherwise permitted to testify, are excluded from giving testimony, are the following : *

2. A counsellor or attorney-at-law shall not be interrogated to disclose any fact that has come to his knowledge by communication from his client. But this rule is subject to the following limitations and explanations : viz.—It shall apply only to facts which were

---

* Specification 1—relating to slaves as witnesses—being happily no longer requisite, has been omitted.

communicated to the counsellor or attorney for the purpose of conducting or defending some judicial proceeding pending, or apprehended. It shall not apply to any other person than a licensed counsellor or attorney, although the purpose of the communication may be the defence or prosecution of a suit.

3. A priest of the Catholic religion shall not be forced to reveal any thing which he knows only by its being confided to him in religious confession by his penitent.

CHAPTER II.

Of the different modes of taking testimonial evidence.

Art. 34. Testimonial evidence may be exhibited in three different forms :
By affidavit.
By oral examination.
By written deposition or interrogation.

SECTION I.

Of testimony by affidavit.

Art. 35. In all cases in which the affidavit of the party or a witness is by the Code of Civil or Criminal Procedure, allowed as a sufficient ground for the issuing of any process order, or other judicial proceeding, the party making such affidavit may be cross-examined by the party opposed in interest before the judge of the court from which such order or process issues, and evidence may be produced to disprove the facts stated in such affidavit.

Art. 36. In order to carry the preceding Article into effect, if no injustice will in that particular case be suffered by the delay, the judge shall require reasonable notice to be given to the opposite party of the time and place of examination, together with a copy of the affidavit before the order or process shall issue.

Art. 37. If the judge shall be of opinion that the ends of justice will be defeated by delay or by giving the notice required, he may, if the proof warrants it, give the order required ; but shall, at a proper time, cause the notice required by the last article to be given, and if by the cross-examination of the deponent or the production of opposite proof, the alleged facts shall be disproved, the order shall be rescinded, and the party who has obtained it shall pay the costs and damages sustained by the other party in consequence thereof, to be awarded by the court, or by a jury if either party require it.

Art. 38. Notice shall be given to every person making an affidavit, or swearing to the truth of any pleading or paper whatever to be used in any judicial proceeding, before the oath is administered, that he will be liable to cross-examination, and that he subjects himself to the penalty of perjury if the statement be designedly false ; and the magistrate who administers the oath shall give such notice and insert in the certificate of attestation the words "after the notice required by law," or words to that effect, under the penalties prescribed by law for a neglect of duty.

Art. 39. It is the duty of every magistrate who shall administer the oath of attestation to any affidavit, to inquire of the deponent whether he has read the same ; and if the answer be that he has not, or cannot read, then to cause him to read, or to have it read to him distinctly, and after giving the notice required by the last article, to cause him to sign his name, if he can write, and if he cannot, then to make a mark at the foot of the said affidavit, opposite to which the magistrate shall write the name of the deponent.

Art. 40. The oath or affirmation to all affidavits shall be according to the form prescribed by the Code of Procedure, with additions required by this section.

SECTION II.

Of the examination and attestation of those who are parties to judicial proceedings in civil causes.

Art. 41. All fictions being expressly discarded from the judicial proceedings of this state, no party to a suit shall be permitted to make any allegation of fact in a court of justice of which he is not willing to declare his knowledge or belief under oath. Therefore, all petitions, or answers intended to be used in any suit, and containing any allegation of fact, or the belief of any fact by the party in the suit on whose behalf such petition or answer shall be exhibited, shall be sworn to in the form prescribed for affidavits by the preceding section, and the same notice shall be given that the party is liable to cross-examination, and the penalties of perjury in case of wilful falsehood.

Art. 42. In addition to the discovery directed to be mutually furnished by the parties in answer to interrogatories, as provided by the laws regulating the practice of the courts in civil cases, (or in lieu thereof) any party to a suit may summon another party or any one having an adverse interest and being within the state, to attend the trial in order to be examined touching the matters in controversy ; and if such party be not within the state, or do not attend, the same proceedings shall be had either to procure the deposition of the said party, or to put off the trial, as are directed with respect to witnesses who are absent or refuse to attend.

Art. 43. The deposition of any party to the pleadings, or his answers to interrogations or on oral examination in court, shall have no other force than the judge or jury who try the fact shall deem it entitled to ; therefore, that part of the present law which directs that to countervail such testimony drawn from the party, the oath of two witnesses, or of one witness with circumstantial evidence, shall be necessary, is repealed.

Art. 44. In every trial where the parties, or either of them, have appeared, whether in pursuance of such provisions or not, he or they, at the request of the opposite party, or of any juror, or by direction of the judge for his own satisfaction, may be sworn to answer such proper questions as shall be put to him or them relative to the matter in dispute.

Art. 45. On the trial of any cause, if the judge or a majority of the jury shall deem it necessary to form a true decision after hearing the testimony, that any party not present shall be examined, the trial shall, at the discretion of the court, be postponed, and the usual measures taken for obtaining the attendance or the deposition of the party upon interrogatories, to the point deemed to be important by the judge or the jury as aforesaid. All questions pertinent to the matter in dispute may be put to a party examined in the manner aforesaid, which might be put to a witness.

Art. 46. When any party to a suit shall be examined in pursuance of the provisions of this section, the same rules shall be observed for conducting the examination as are laid down for the examination of witnesses by the third section of this chapter.

Art. 47. This section relates exclusively to civil causes.

SECTION III.

To what points and in what manner witnesses may be examined.

Art. 48. If the witness be a Catholic priest, he shall not be interrogated for the purposes of revealing any thing that has been confided to him by confession; but he may be examined as to knowledge obtained from any other source.

Art. 49. The counsellor or attorney employed by the

defendant or assigned to him by the court, shall not be interrogated for the purpose of revealing any thing that he knows only by its being communicated to him by his client in relation to the cause in which he is employed, and for the purpose of conducting or defending the same, or for the purpose of procuring professional advice on some lawful occasion. What he knows in any other manner, although it may also have been communicated by his client, or what he knows by communication from his client, before he became his counsellor or attorney, or at any time, if the fact so communicated have no relation to the cause or matter in which it was communicated to him, he shall be obliged to declare whenever the question is otherwise pertinent.

Art. 50. If it should become material in any suit to require information of a fact which it would be dangerous to the public safety to disclose at the time of trial, this is a good cause for postponing the trial until such danger shall cease.

Art. 51. No witness shall be obliged to answer any questions but such as are immediately pertinent to the issue between the parties, or which may elucidate or establish some incidental fact necessary to be inquired into in the cause. Questions as to the character of a witness, and questions which, though unconnected with the merits of the case, may be put to test the veracity of a witness, are examples of such incidental inquiry. But of the pertinency of any question, the court, in its discretion, must judge according to the circumstances of the case.

Art. 52. The constitution having provided "that in criminal prosecutions the accused shall not be compelled to give evidence against himself," the legislature feel themselves bound to extend the same protection to witnesses in all cases, and to declare that no witness shall be compelled to answer any interrogatory, if the answer he would give would furnish evidence to justify a prosecution against him for a CRIME.

Art. 53. With the exceptions contained in the five last

preceding articles, and the restrictions hereafter put upon leading questions, all other interrogatories may be put to any witness.

Art. 54. The rule that no one shall discredit his own witness is abolished. The party calling a witness may cross-examine him to test his veracity, and call witnesses to his character in the same manner as if he had not been called at his instance.

Art. 55. Leading questions are not permitted to be put. Such only shall be deemed leading questions as suggest to the witness some statement (inconsistent with the truth) which the party proposing the question wishes to prove. This is a matter left to the sound discretion of the court. But it must be so exercised as not to prevent suggestions necessary to recall the facts in question to the memory of the witness, when the transaction is remote, when from its nature it was not likely to have made a strong impression on the mind of the witness, or when from age or indisposition, timidity, or other cause, the mind of the witness is weakened or disturbed.

Art. 56. The witness may, on his examination, refer to written notes made by himself or by his direction for the purpose of refreshing his memory as to events mentioned in them ; he may refer to writings made by others for the same purpose, but in that case he must speak from his own recollection of the fact thus revived by the writing—not from the evidence of the writing itself; and he must in all cases declare when, and by whom, and for what purpose, the writing to which he refers was made ; and he shall not be permitted to refer to them if they appear to have been made by either of the parties in the suit, or by their direction, for the purpose of suggesting to the witness what he ought to say.

Art. 57. In all cases where a witness is examined to prove or disprove any matter of account or calculation, he must be permitted to refer to the papers or books containing such account or calculation.

Art. 58. It is the duty of the judge to prevent any harsh or threatening language to be used towards a witness for the purpose of confusing or intimidating him. Reasonable time shall be given to the witness to recollect himself before he is urged to answer. After his testimony has been given, he may rectify any mistake in his answers within a like reasonable time, to be judged of by the court.

Art. 59. Whenever the testimony of a witness is reduced to writing he may, before signing it, correct any inaccuracies which may have been made in reducing it to writing, or any error which he himself may have made ; and such correction may be made even after signing the deposition within a reasonable time, to be judged of according to circumstances by the court.

Art. 60: He who judicially alleges a litigated fact must produce evidence to support it, whether it be a fact in charge or discharge.

Art. 61. No fact judicially alleged by one party and in the same manner confessed by the other need be proved by other evidence.

Art. 62. A fact judicially alleged by one party and neither confessed nor denied by the other, must be proved by the alleging party ; but the oath of the party alleging shall be presumptive evidence to have such weight as the judge or jury, to whichever the fact is submitted, may think it deserves.

Art. 63. The evidence required by the preceding articles, is any of the several kinds specified in the Code as legal evidence.

Art. 64. The judicial allegation above mentioned means the affirmative declaration made in the course of judicial proceeding, that a fact or state of things exists or has happened, on which the one party relies to support his charge, or the other to exonerate himself from it. An affirmative assertion of innocence amounts only to a negation of a charge made, and is not, therefore such an affirmative declaration as the party making it is bound to support by proof.

Art. 65. The rule of evidence which required that the best evidence, or, as it is sometimes stated, the best attainable evidence, shall be produced, shall hereafter operate to the exclusion of other evidence only in the following cases :—

1. When the law shall have declared that to give validity to a contract, it shall be made in writing, no other proof shall be admitted of such contract, unless it be proved that the writing required by law was made, and that it has been casually lost or destroyed, or has been placed, without the default of the party offering the inferior evidence, out of his reach.

2. When it is proved that SCRIPTORY EVIDENCE of the matter in question has been made, and was in possession of the party offering the inferior proof, unless he show that it has been casually lost or destroyed, or without his default has been placed out of his reach.

3. When the legislature shall have declared certain evidence necessary for the proof of designated facts.

4. When the fact alleged is one which, if true, must have appeared by AUTHENTIC ACT.

Art. 66. In all other cases where evidence is offered, which the judge or jury shall deem of an inferior nature to other evidence which is not produced, such inferior evidence, if legal, shall be admitted, and the non-production of the other shall operate only as presumptive proof against the party failing to produce it, to have such effect as such judge of the fact shall, according to circumstances, give to it.

Art. 67. In all cases where a writing is proved to be in the possession of the opposite party, who, on proper notice being given, does not produce it, evidence may be given of its contents.

Art. 68. The rule established by the Civil Code, that parol evidence shall not be admitted against or beyond what is contained in the acts, nor what may have been said before or at the time of making them, is to be taken with the following modifications :

1. It applies exclusively to writings, containing obligations or donations, and to testamentary dispositions.

2. Parol evidence, in all cases of written instruments,

shall be admitted to prove error, fraud, violence, threats, or any other circumstance which, by the Civil Code, would avoid or modify a contract.

3. It may be admitted to remove any ambiguity, whether apparent on the face of the instrument, or arising out of the application of its terms.

4. Any one of the parties to a written instrument may be called on by another to explain, on oath, either by parol evidence on the trial, or by answer to interrogatories, at the option of the party making the inquiry, any point in litigation between them, arising out of such instrument, and that, whether the interrogation goes to contradict, explain, or add to, or diminish the obligation specified in the writing.

Art. 69. Whenever error, fraud, violence, or threats are alleged as reasons for setting aside a contract, the following points must be inquired into by the judge, and considered, if he is to decide or give in charge to the jury, in addition to the evidence of the direct fact alleged :

1. If error is the reason alleged, the character as to caution and prudence in conducting his affairs, of the party alleging that he was deceived; his knowledge of the particular business which formed the subject of the contract; the deliberation or haste with which it was effected.

2. If the objection be fraud, violence, or threats, the character of both parties must be the subject of inquiry, as presumptive evidence of the fraudulent or violent practices on the one side, or of a submission to them on the other.

3. In all cases of this kind, the time that has elapsed after the error or fraud was discovered, or the violence or threats had ceased, before the proceedings were had, or complaint made for redress, and the reason for the delay, if any.

Art. 70. Parol evidence is not admitted unless the witness be under the sanction of an oath. Therefore the witness is only to be interrogated as to his own knowledge or belief, and not as to what he has heard from others, upon whom none of the sanctions to secure veracity could operate. This is a general rule, to which there are the following exceptions :

1. A witness may declare what a party has said, if the testimony be called for by the opposite party; and this extends not only to the declarations of the actual parties to the suit, but those of the persons under whom they claim; and also to the declarations of such agents or other persons as could have bound them by their contracts in the matter in contest; but no declaration of one under whom the party claims shall be given in evidence unless it was made while such person was interested, or of the agent except while he was in the employ of the party.

2. What has been said relative to the matter in dispute by others, in the presence and hearing of one party to the suit, may be given in evidence by the other as a foundation for presumption to be drawn from what was said or done by the party, or from his silence; but in all such cases the party implicated may require that he be allowed to explain upon oath.

3. What a witness has said before he was sworn, may be shown to prove that it was consistent, or inconsistent, with his declaration on oath.

4. What a witness has declared on a former trial between the same parties for the same cause, if the witness be dead, or his testimony cannot be procured.

5. When the declarations of a party, or a witness, are admitted under the first or second exceptions above mentioned, any thing said by another person in the same conversation, which is necessary to counteract or explain what was said by such party or witness may be given in evidence.

6. Proof of the handwriting of a subscribing witness to an instrument who is absent or dead, may, in certain cases, be admitted, on the presumption that he would not have signed if he could not prove the execution. To rebut this presumption, any material declaration of such witness may be given in evidence.

7. In cases not depending on scriptory evidence, a party

may give as evidence what he himself said or did in relation to the matter in litigation at the time of the transaction on which it is founded, in order to explain the intention with which any thing was said or done, that he is charged with in the proceedings or by the evidence ; but in this case he may himself be examined under oath by the adverse party.

Art. 71. When the fact inquired of is one of which the knowledge is generally acquired by information of others, or by information joined to personal observation, forming what is usually called facts of public notoriety, they may be stated on such information by parol evidence : of this nature are — pedigree, boundary, births and deaths, cohabitation, residence, profession or trade, possession with reputation of ownership, general reputation, custom, course of trade, prescription, public historical events. In all these cases, and others of the same description, the witness may testify, not only as to the public notoriety of the fact, but may specify the persons from whom he has derived his information.

Art. 72. What a person, who is dead at the time of trial, has said or done in relation to the subject in controversy, may be given in evidence, if such act or declaration was, at the time of making it, contrary to his pecuniary interest.

Art. 73. In prosecutions for homicide, the deposition of the deceased may be given in evidence, or what he was heard to say after receiving the wound, if he do not live long enough to have his deposition taken, or if circumstances prevent its being taken.

SECTION IV.

Of evidence to the character of parties and witnesses.

Art. 74. In all criminal prosecutions the general character of the party accused may be shown by evidence, but to such points only as would evince a disposition or indisposition to commit the offence with which he is charged. Thus, if the prosecution be for a battery, the defendant may show that his general reputation is that of mildness and forbearance ; and on the part of the prosecution, the reverse may be proved.

Art. 75. The general character of witnesses for veracity, or the contrary, may be also shown, both on the part of those who introduce them and on the opposite part.

Art. 76. Evidence of general character may be introduced to discredit a witness, by showing that he is habitually addicted to any vice that evinces a disregard to moral character ; such as intoxication, or that he is a common vagrant ; or if the witness be a woman, that she is a common prostitute.

Art. 77. Particular facts may also be given in evidence ; but they must be of a public and notorious nature, such as conviction for a CRIME ; but this must be proved, either by the production of the records or the oath of the witness himself ; or if the conviction took place out of the state, by testimonial proof.

Art. 78. All facts which would show the incapacity of the witness, either to perceive accurately, or correctly to relate, what he states, may also be shown ; such as a natural imperfection in any of the senses, want of memory or of skill, usual inattention to subjects of the nature of that in question, or general ignorance of them, or a temporary disability arising from disease or intemperance.

Art. 79. Any particular bias, arising from interest, affection, relationship, from fear, enmity, favour, or affection, or intimate friendship to or with either of the parties, or having had disputes with them, or being under their control or influence in the relation of ward, servant, tenant, debtor, or obligated by past favours.

Art. 80. The examinations of the witnesses, taken before the examining magistrate, may be produced to contradict what they may say on the trial, or to show that they have been consistent.

Art. 81. The depositions of such witnesses, taken in the presence of the defendant, pursuant to the directions of the Code of Criminal Procedure, may be read as evidence, if the witness is since dead or cannot be found in the state.

Art. 82. The examination of the defendant, taken before the examining magistrate, if made according to the directions of the Code of Criminal Procedure, may also be produced.

SECTION V.

Of written depositions on interrogatories.

Art. 83. All the rules for receiving the oral declarations of witnesses, apply to their examination taken in writing on interrogatories.

Art. 84. When the oral testimony of witnesses is taken down in writing, in the cases provided by law for regulating the practice of the courts, the question shall be taken down as well as the answer, and the answer recorded as it is given.

TITLE III.

OF SCRIPTORY EVIDENCE.

Art. 85. Scriptory evidence is of two kinds—AUTHENTICATED and UNAUTHENTICATED.

CHAPTER I.

Of authenticated acts.

SECTION I.

Of the different kinds of authenticated acts.

Art. 86. Authenticated acts are such instruments in writing as are attested by a public officer, legally authorized for that purpose, in the form prescribed by law. They are evidence of that which is attested to have been done in his presence by the officer whose attestation gave them validity ; but of nothing more.—Thus, the joint attestation of the speaker of the house of representatives, of the president of the senate, and of the governor, is authentic evidence that a bill has become a law of the state. The attestation of the governor and secretary of state, under the seal of the state, is authentic evidence that the copy to which it is affixed is a true copy of the statute. The signature of the governor to a proclamation issued by him, under the seal of office, to apprehend a person accused of murder, is authentic evidence that such proclamation was issued on the day it bears date, that complaints were made to him of the commission of the crime and of the flight of the defendant, or of any other fact which he certifies to have been done in his presence ; but it is not evidence that the crime was committed or that the party fled.

Art. 87. They are of several kinds :

1st. Legislative acts, passed by the constitutional authority, and attested in the manner prescribed by law.

2d. Records of courts.

3d. Such records of the different branches of the executive government as are made in the legal administration of their different departments, and as are declared to be authentic acts.

4th. Written instruments, made in the presence of and attested by such public officer, as is for that purpose commissioned according to law, and purporting to testify what is said, done, or contracted, by those whose act it is.

SECTION II.

Of legislative acts.

Art. 88. Legislative acts are proved, either by a production of the original act deposited in the archives of the state : by a copy attested by the signature of the person exercising the executive authority of the state, and by the secretary of state, or other proper officer having the custody of the said archives, under the seal of the state ; or, by the printed copy contained in the statute book, or the gazette printed by the printer of the state. Provided, that on the production of either of the said copies of a legislative act, it shall be lawful for any party, alleging a mistake in the printed or other copy, to prove it by producing the copy under the seal of the state, or in such attested copy, by collating it with the original archives, and procuring, in this last case, a correction of the attested copy ; but the party alleging such mistake must prove it ; and, until the error be shown, such copy shall be deemed a true one, and shall have its full and entire effect.

Art. 89. There is no distinction in the mode of proof between public and private legislative acts. The court, however, is bound to take notice of and carry into effect all public acts which apply to the facts before them, whether they are pleaded or offered in evidence or not ; but a party claiming a right or exemption, under a private act, must produce it.

Art. 90. A private legislative act is one that concerns certain designated individuals only. All other legislative acts are public.

Art. 91. All acts of incorporation made for regulating the police or local government of any particular part of the state, for the establishment of banks, for authorizing the imposition of a toll, tonnage, wharfage, or other duty, for the establishment of hospitals, or other purposes of charity, or for the promotion of education, religion, or science, are public acts. All other acts of incorporation are private acts.

Art 92. The enumeration contained in the last article relates solely to the purpose of this title : it does not affect the nature or definition of corporations established by law.

SECTION III.

Of judicial records.

Art. 93. Judicial records are all the written proceedings in a court legally constituted and directed to record its decrees. They comprehend, not only the orders and judgments of such courts, but the written pleadings and allegations of parties; the proofs and documents they have produced, when the same are made part of the written proceedings ; and the certificates and returns of the officers of such courts ; the verdict of jurors, and all other proceedings, which are entered on the minutes or preserved among the records of such court.

Art. 94. Judicial records of courts, within this state, are proved by a production of the original record, or by a copy attested to be a true copy by the clerk of such court, under the seal of the same, to which must be annexed a certificate signed by the presiding judge of such court, declaring that the person who has attested the same is clerk of such court ; but any error or omission in such copy may be rectified by a collation with the original record ; but, unless such error be shown, the copy is a conclusive evidence. All records from other states, must be authenticated in the manner directed by the laws of the United States, in order to be received as proof in this state. Legislative acts from other states may be proved by the production of such printed statute books as are proved to be received in the courts of such state.

Art. 95. Records of judgments on proceedings in foreign countries, other than the states of the Union, are proved by the certificate of officers, whose duty it is, by the laws of the country in which such court is situated, to give such certificates, together with such other attestation as is required by the laws of such country, to make such copy evidence in other courts of the same country ; which fact, to wit, that the attestation is in such form, must be certified by the minister for the proper department of such government, and his signature and office must be certified by the minister of the United States, if there be one in such country ; or, if there be none, by some consul of the United States for that district of such country in which the decree was given, under his hand and consular seal ; and in countries where there is neither American minister nor consul, the substance of such certificate must be proved by two witnesses, examined on commission or in open court.

Art. 96. Whenever a foreign judgment is made the

foundation of a suit or of a defence, and the party wishes to produce the copy, whether authenticated in the manner set forth in the last preceding article or only by the certificate of the clerk or judge, he must, at the time he files his petition or answer, deposit in the court the said copy, and give notice to the opposite party that he intends to produce such copy in evidence; and if the opposite party shall, within ten days, give notice, in writing, that he will oppose the introduction of such copy, then the party offering the same must prove such record by an examination of the proper officer on a commission; but, in such case, all reasonable expenditures, made in the execution of such commission, whatever may be the event of the suit, shall be borne by the party opposing the introduction of the copy; provided such copy should, by the return to the commissioner, be proved to have been complete and correct. But if no such notice of opposition be given, the copy certified as aforesaid shall be evidence of such judgment.

Art. 97. If such foreign judgment be not the foundation of the suit or of the defence, but may be necessary to be produced on some collateral point arising in the cause, then the copy, authenticated as is before mentioned, must be deposited at least fifteen days before the day appointed for the trial of the cause; and notice must be given as is set forth in the last preceding article, and the same proceedings must be had by the parties as is provided for in the said article.

Art. 98. Nothing in the preceding articles shall prevent the admission of the copy of any foreign record certified by the recording officer of the court in which it was given and by the judge, as itself good evidence when proved to be a true copy by the oath of a competent witness, taken according to law, who has collated it with the original.

Art. 99. As evidence, a judgment rendered in either of the United States or in a foreign country has the same effect, and is subject to the same rules, as are established in the section on *res judicata* for judgments rendered in this state; but no judgment rendered in any court whatever in a suit *in rem*, whether by attachment or otherwise, shall have any other of the effects of the *res judicata*, except so far as respects the thing, the seizure whereof was the first process in the cause; unless the party appeared and defended such suit either in person or by attorney.

Art. 100. If the only object be to prove a condemnation in a foreign court of admiralty, it is not necessary to produce copies of any other part of the proceedings than the libel and the final decree of condemnation; and none of the evidence taken in such court shall be evidence even between the same parties to prove any other point than the one in contestation in the original cause.

SECTION IV.

Of records of the executive branches of government.

Art. 101. The following are the acts of the different departments of executive government which have the force of authentic acts:—

1st. Commissions, or special authority to perform any civil duty, given by the governor, pursuant to law, or any proclamation issued by him. They must be under the seal of the state, and must be signed by the governor, and attested by the secretary of state.

2d. Certificates of election directed by law to be given to persons chosen to fill any place in office, signed by the persons who are authorized to determine the result of such election.

3d. Certificates of the administration of oaths of office, and other oaths necessary to be taken previous to the performance of the duties of any place or office, signed by the persons authorized to administer such oaths.

4th. Entries in the proper books of the registry and cancelling of mortgages. Donations and other acts directed by law to be registered, and such certificate as by law the officer appointed to make such registry is entitled to give.

5th. Entries in the proper book of the registries which may be made of births, baptisms, marriages, and deaths, by any officer who is or may be appointed by law to enregister the same.

The commissions, proclamations, special delegations of authority, certificates of election, and certificates of administration of oaths, are themselves the original authentic acts; and those given by the proper officers in this state, and in the form prescribed by law, need no additional proof, it being the duty of all judges in this state, *ex officio,* to know the seals and signatures of the officers whose acts they purport to be. Where the original of these acts cannot be produced, a copy of the record of the commission or certificate of election, under the seal of the state, certified by the secretary of the state, is authentic evidence. With respect to the certificate of the administration of oaths of office, if the original cannot be produced, the fact may be proved by other testimony, which may be or may not be authentic according to its nature.

Art. 102. Entries in the proper books of the register of mortgages, or other officers appointed to enregister any description of acts of baptisms, marriages, births, or deaths, are proved by the official certificates of such officer, with the addition of his seal of office where he is authorized to keep such seal; and such copy is an authentic act, as are also all such official certificates as he is by law authorized to give.

Art. 103. The registry of a mortgage, or of any other act which is directed to be registered for the purpose of giving notice to those who may be interested, or the authenticated copy of such registry, is not evidence of the act itself; it is evidence only that the law which directs the registry has been complied with. Therefore, the registry, or an authenticated copy of it, does not dispense with the introduction of the act itself, or other legal evidence of its having been made.

SECTION V.

Of notarial acts.

Art. 104. Written instruments, made in the presence and attested by a public officer duly appointed and commissioned for that purpose, purporting to testify what is said, done, or contracted by the parties to such act, are authentic acts, as are the copies of such acts attested by such officer in the form prescribed by law. These acts are called "notarial acts;" but they have the same effect when passed before any other officer authorized by law, although not a notary ; and whenever the term notary is used in this chapter, it includes all such officers as are empowered by law to authenticate private contracts.

Art. 105. All acts passed before a notary shall be written in his registry, and signed by the contracting party, by the notary, and two witnesses at least. This written instrument is called the original notarial act ; it remains as a record in the hands and on the books of record of the notary. A copy of this notarial act, certified to be a true copy by the notary or his successor in office, and under his official seal, is full proof of such act in any court within the jurisdiction of which such officer exercises his functions ; but in any other court the signature of the notary must be certified to be true, either by the judge of the court of highest original civil jurisdiction within which the notary resides, or by the governor under the seal of the state.

Art. 106. In order to give to any notarial instrument the form of an authentic act, it must have the following requisites, the want of either of which destroys its authenticity :

1st. It must contain in the body of the act the name and office of the notary, or other officer, before whom it is passed, and the place for which he is appointed.

2d. The place at which, and the day, month, and year when it was made.

3d. The names and places of abode of the parties ; or, if they have no fixed residence, the last place of their permanent abode.

4th. It must appear that the act was passed within the district of country for which the notary was appointed.

5th. It must be stated to be passed in the presence of at least two witnesses, citizens of this state and inhabitants of the place for which he is appointed.

6th. It must be signed by the party obligated if it be an UNILATERAL contract, or by the declarant if it be a protest or declaration, and by all the parties if it be a SYNALLAGMATIC contract ; and if either of the said parties cannot sign his name, either from want of knowledge, accident, weakness, or disease, he must declare his incapacity and from which of the said causes it proceeds, and such declaration must be inserted in the act. It will not be sufficient for the notary to certify such incapacity, he must certify the declaration of the party.

7th. It must be signed by the notary, and by the witnesses who are named as such in the act. No person is a competent witness for this purpose who cannot write.

8th. Where either of the parties to an act cannot read, the notary must certify that he has read the act to such party in the presence of the witnesses, and that he consented thereto ; and when the party incapable of writing can make a mark, he shall do so, and the notary, or one of the witnesses, shall write opposite thereto the name of such party, stating that it is his mark. When, from whatever cause, the party cannot make the mark, it must be stated in the instrument.

9th. All signatures, as well of parties as of witnesses and of the notary, must be at the end of the instrument ; but for the approval of any correction in the instrument, the signature may either be put in the margin or at the end of the instrument, and a signature by initials will be a sufficient approval of a correction which creates no material change in the instrument; but every material correction must be approved by a full signature.

10th. All interlineations, erasures, obliterations, or apparent changes, in any part of the act which is necessary to give it validity, in the names of the parties or witnesses, in the expression of any sums, or the description of the thing which is the object of the act, in the date, in the time of any payment, or in any other part of the act, which alters the obligation, or increases or lessens the responsibility of either party, must be enumerated and approved by the signatures of all the parties.

11th. The act must appear to have been passed before one duly authorized by law to give authority to such acts.

Art. 107. All the matters and forms set forth in the last preceding article, are necessary to give to any act, passed before a notary, the force of an authentic act; but there are some notarial acts, such as testaments, to the validity of which other formalities are specially required, in addition to those above enumerated.

Art. 108. A notarial act is also invalid, as an authentic act, if, on its face, it appears to have been executed by a married woman, without the assent of her husband, or of the judge in cases where such assent is required; or by a minor, or other person incapable of contracting, without the assistance of a tutor or curator, if such curator or tutor be no party to the act.

Art. 109. Signature, in this title, means the name of the party, written by himself; as evidence of his assent to an instrument as a party, or to attest it as a witness : the family name must be written at length—the baptismal or prenominal name may be abbreviated, or indicated only by the initial letter, or altogether omitted, if such has been the usual mode in which the signer has subscribed his name.

Art. 110. No party to an instrument shall avoid any obligation created thereby, by showing that he has not signed it in his true name, or in the manner in which he usually signed the same, provided the signature be made by him.

SECTION VI.

Of the effect of notarial acts.

Art. 111. Notarial acts, passed in the form required by law before an officer duly authorized, are authentic acts, and have the following effects :

1st. As to all persons, even those not parties to the act, it is conclusive evidence that everything which the notary certifies to have been declared, acknowledged, or done in his presence, and in that of the witnesses, was so declared, acknowledged, and done by the parties ; but against any but the parties and those who succeed to them or to their rights, it has no other effect. Thus, a *bona fide* purchase made by an authentic act from a person in possession, who has no title, although it can give no right against the true owner, who was no party to the sale, is yet conclusive evidence against him, for the purpose of establishing a prescription and giving a title to the fruits during the time that the purchaser possessed in good faith.

2d. As to all who were parties to such act, and those who succeeded to them, or to their rights, it is conclusive proof of that, which is the object of such act ; and also of everything relating immediately to the object of the act—which is therein acknowledged by both parties—or which is recited or enounced by one party and acknowledged by the other, either expressly or by necessary implication. That recital or enunciation by one party shall be said to be acknowledged by necessary implication, which the other must, from the nature of the transaction, have known, and which it would be his interest to deny if untrue, which is suffered to remain uncontradicted by the act.

That recital or enunciation relates immediately to the object of the act, which, if omitted, would make a material change in the obligations incurred, or rights acquired by either of the parties.

Thus, for the illustration of the different parts of the last rule :—If a sale is made by a notarial act for a certain price, which is promised to be paid in a given time, (this purchase and sale being the object of the act,) it is conclusive proof of that transaction between the parties, so that the purchaser needs no other proof of the sale, nor the seller of the promise to pay the price, than the production of the act itself.

If the thing sold was subject to a yearly rent or charge, and the seller declare that he has deposited the money in the hands of a third person for the payment of the arrears up to the day of sale, this enunciation is not the immediate object of the act ; yet it relates immediately to it, because the omission of it would have made a change in the rights and obligations of the parties ; but it is not conclusive against the purchaser, unless he expressly acknowledge that it is true, because it is not a fact which he is supposed to know. If he expressly acknowledge it, it is conclusive, and he can never afterwards call in question the truth of such deposit. But if, in the last example, the rent-charge had, before the sale, been due to the purchaser himself, and the seller had, in the act, declared that all the arrears were paid, this declaration, if uncontradicted by the buyer, would of itself, without any express acknowledgment, by necessary implication, be conclusive evidence that the declaration was true ; because the fact, from the nature of the case, was within the knowledge of the purchaser, and it was an enunciation which, if not true, it was his interest to contradict.

If in the sale the vendor declare that he had acquired the property as instituted heir of A. B., and the legal heir of A. B. should bring a suit for the property against the purchaser, alleging that the will, under which the vendor claimed, was void—this enunciation in the act would not be conclusive evidence that it belonged to the estate of A. B., for this enunciation did not immediately relate to the object of the act, which was the sale ; nor was it a matter either within the knowledge of the purchaser, or which he was interested in denying if it was untrue.

3d. Any enunciation made in a notarial act is evidence against the party making the enunciation in favour of the person who is no party to the act, whether it relate to the object of the suit or not ; but it is not conclusive evidence; it amounts to an extrajudicial confession only, and, as such, is ranked in the class of presumptions, which have more or less weight, according to the circumstances under which the declaration was made.

4th. A declaration or enunciation made by one party to an act, and either expressly or by necessary implication acknowledged by another, forms the same kind of proof against both, as set forth in the last preceding article.

5th. An act signed by the parties, intended for a notarial act, but not valid as such for want of some formality required by law, is still good as an act under private signature, if it have the requisites to give it force as a private act ; nor can the defect of its not being signed in as many copies as there are parties in interest, be opposed to its validity as a private act.

6th. The mention in an inventory, made by notarial act, of any obligation or other paper, forms no such proof against one not a party to the inventory, as to dispense with the production of the original. The entry in the inventory proves that a paper purporting to be such an obligation was produced, but it is not conclusive evidence that it was the act of the party. Where the original has, by other proof, been shown to have existed, and has since been destroyed, and there are circumstances to prove its identity with the paper mentioned in the inventory, it may be admitted as presumptive proof of the contents of such obligation.

7th. Although the enunciations made by the parties are, in the cases above stated, sometimes conclusive and sometimes presumptive proof between the parties, and are sometimes presumptive proof in favour of third persons ; they form no species of proof whatever against third persons, and cannot injure their rights or obligate them.

To this rule there is one exception : an enunciation in an act, made many years before it is offered, may at the discretion of the judge, under the limitation hereafter expressed, be admitted as presumptive evidence between those who are not parties to it in questions of age, relationship, descent, affinity, filiation, absence, or death ; but in no other questions.

Thus, an ancient notarial act of a family assembly may be admitted as presumptive proof between third persons, that the parties who composed it stood in the various degrees of relationship which they severally enounced. So, too, the enunciation of the deceased, in an authentic and ancient certificate of burial, of the age of the child ; in the like certificate of baptism, the time of a death of a person in the act of partition between his heirs, may be permitted as presumptive proof of the enunciations therein contained.

But the discretion of the judge, to admit the testimony mentioned in the exception of the rule, is limited to cases in which, from the date of the act and from other circumstances, he is convinced that the parties making the enunciation had no motive to declare a falsehood.

8th. Notarial acts take effect immediately after their signature. Therefore, no alteration of an act, once perfected, is lawful even if done with the consent of the parties ; any modification they desire must be made by a separate act ; but such an act cannot affect any rights acquired by third persons by the act itself, or derived from one of the parties after such act.

SECTION VII.

For what causes and in what manner a notarial act may be declared
not authentic.

Art. 112. No notarial act, which contains on the face
of it any omission of any of these things which have been
herein before enumerated as necessary to give it validity,
shall be considered as an authentic act; and the evidence
of this shall be the inspection of the authenticated copy,
or of the original in cases where it is required to be
produced, or of other evidences taken according to the
directions of the following article.

Art. 113. When, on the presentation of the copy of a
notarial act duly certified, if the party against whom it
is produced will declare, on oath, or otherwise make
appear to the court that there are defects in the original
of the said act, which do not appear on the copy, it shall
be the duty of the judge, if the facts are material, and
also in all cases where the handwriting of the parties,
witness, or notary, may be legally brought in question,
to cause the original to be brought into court, if the
same be within the jurisdiction of the court, but if otherwise, then to appoint three proper persons to make a
collated copy of such original, and to report specially
whether there are any, and if any, what variations
between the original and the copy which had been produced, and also between the handwriting of the notary,
parties, or witnesses, in question—to compare the
acknowledged handwriting of the party whose hand is
disputed with that which is in dispute, and to report
thereon ; which persons shall be sworn before some
magistrate to perform the duty faithfully ; and their
report, or that of a majority of them, shall be a legal
presumption of the truth of what it contains. After

hearing the report of the persons commissioned as aforesaid, and such other legal proofs as may be adduced by the parties, the judge shall determine on the validity of the original act, in cases where it is not within the jurisdiction of the court, in the same manner as he would by inspection if the original had been produced.

Art. 114. There are cases in which a notarial act, although it may contain apparently all the requisites to make it an authentic act, ought not be admitted as such. These are :

1st. Where the signature of the notary, parties, or witnesses, or either of them, are forged.

2d. Where the act has been altered, or a material part, since the execution.

3d. Where either the notary, or either of the witnesses, were not present when the act was signed by the parties or by either of them.

4th. Where the act was falsely read in a material part to a party, who could not read; or falsely translated in a material part to a party who could not understand the language in which it was written.

5th. Where it was executed out of the limits for which the notary was appointed.

6th. Where the act is signed by one personating the party whom it purports to bind, whether the one so personating him bears the same name or not.

7th. Where the act purports to create any obligation upon, or to dispose of, or affect the property of any person incapable by law of contracting without the aid of a curator or tutor, and no such tutor or curator was party to the act.

8th. Where the act was made in fraud of creditors.

9th. Where it was made without consideration or for an inadequate consideration, in order to avoid any law regulating successions.

10th. Where it is made under any other circumstances, which, by the laws in force at the time of making the act, shall be declared to render it void.

11th. Where any of the requisites necessary to give

validity to the act, have been falsely certified by the notary.

12th. Where the act wants any of the parts or clauses which are necessary by law to give effect to such contract as it purports to be. But this shall not prevent an act, invalid as to one intent, from being operative in another, in cases where it is otherwise allowed by law.

13th. Where either of the parties was in a state of mind, either from bodily weakness, derangement of intellect by intoxication, or other cause, which rendered him incapable of understanding the nature and consequence of the act, and such incapacity must have been apparent to the notary and witnesses.

14th. Where the witnesses have not the qualifications required by law.

15th. Where the consideration, declared to have been paid by the act, has not been paid ; and this whether there is a renunciation of the exception of *non numerata pecunia*, or not.

16th. Where the act contains any disposition of property, or any pecuniary obligation in favour of the notary, or any of his relations, by affinity or consanguinity in the ascending or descending line, or collaterally to the relationship by consanguinity or affinity, of uncle or nephew, inclusively ; and this extends to the case where the disposition is made in the name of a person interposed for the benefit of the notary or any such relation.

17th. Where the act purports to dispose of property which cannot, by law, be conveyed—such as the dotal property of a married woman.

Art. 115. For any one of the causes mentioned in the last preceding article, or for any of the defects apparent on the face of the act, which are in this title declared to destroy its authenticity, a suit may be brought by any one interested in having the said act declared invalid ; in which suit the objections made to the same shall be particularly set forth ; and all persons, interested in supporting the validity of the act, must be made parties.

Art. 116. Whenever a notarial or other authentic act

is the foundation of any suit, or of the defence to any suit—that is to say, whenever, to support the claim for which the suit is brought, or the defence which is made to the suit, it is necessary to produce such authentic act—in all such cases, a copy of the act, intended to be relied on, shall be filed with the petition, answers, or other pleading in which a reference is made to the same ; and if the party against whom it is produced intends to object to the same, he must do so specially and in writing, specifying the particular cause of nullity on which he intends to rely ; otherwise no such objection, other than those apparent on the face of the act, can be heard on the trial.

Art. 117. Wherever it may be necessary to introduce an authentic act in evidence, on some collateral matter, not being the foundation of the suit ; or, if introduced by the defendant, of the defence, the party, if he can reasonably be supposed according to the circumstances of the case to have foreseen the necessity of producing such act, shall file a copy thereof ten days at least before the trial, and shall give notice to the opposite party, who may then make his objections in the manner directed by the last article.

Art. 118. If the party who ought, according to the preceding articles, to file the copy of a notarial act on which he means to rely, do not file it, the court may force its production, on the application of the opposite party ; or at his option, he may make his objections verbally at the trial ; and if they are supported either by inspection or evidence, the act must be rejected as evidence, and the party whose duty it was to have filed the act, cannot in such case object to the want of notice of the objections.

Art. 119. If it appears that the party could not reasonably have foreseen the necessity of producing such authentic act, and an objection be taken to its authenticity for any cause not apparent on the face of the act, the court, if they think the act material evidence, and if the objection be supported by affidavit either of the party or other person, may, according to circumstances, give the necessary time to make and answer the objections.

Art. 120. In all cases of objections to the validity of any act, which appears on the face of it to have all the formalities required by law to give it authenticity, the burthen of proving the defects lies on the party objecting to the validity of the act.

Art. 121. On the question of the validity of an authentic act, the persons whose names are subscribed as witnesses, when not otherwise incompetent, are competent witnesses.

The notary is also a good witness in all cases where no objection has been made to the act in any point that implies a want of integrity, misconduct, or inattention on his part; or where, if made, they are entirely unsupported.

Art. 122. Authentic acts, not notarial, may be declared invalid for either of the following causes:

1st. Forgery of the signatures, or either of them, or of the body of the act.

2d. Want of legal authority in the party making such act.

3d. Making the act out of the limits for which the officer was appointed.

4th. If the authentic act be a commission, or other authority given under a law, the want of the qualifications required by law in the person commissioned or designated to perform the duty, including the objection to the want of security, and the taking of the oaths of office where they are required.

5th. Fraud in obtaining the act by a false personification, or such other false pretence as would make the party practising it liable to punishment if they had been used to procure the delivery of goods or money, under such penal laws as may be in force at the time of using such false pretences.

6th. Bribery, either to the officer making the act, or any other person, to do any thing necessary to procure the act to be made.

Art. 123. Suits for invalidating all authentic acts (not

notarial) and oppositions to their introduction as evidence, shall be governed by the same rules as are laid down respecting notarial acts.

Art. 124. Forgery and bribery, mentioned as causes for invalidating a notarial or other authentic act, shall be construed according to the definitions of those offences given in such penal law as shall be in force at the time such acts were made.

Art. 125. When a notarial act, or other authentic act, shall, by final sentence of a court, be declared void for any cause, the court pronouncing such sentence shall direct that it shall be noted in the margin of the original of such notarial act, and of the record of such other authentic act, if any such record shall have been kept, and on the certified copy which was produced in court.

CHAPTER II.

Of unauthenticated scriptory evidence.

SECTION I.

Of the different kinds of unauthenticated scriptory evidence.

Art. 126. Unauthenticated scriptory evidence is of two kinds :

1. That which is attested by the signature of the party whose act it purports to be, called an act under private signature.

2. All other written evidence not so attested.

SECTION II.

Of evidence under private signature.

Art. 127. All written instruments, signed by the party whose act they purport to be, which are not authentic acts, are called acts under private signature.

Art. 128. Independent of positive law, no written instrument is, in its nature, evidence of the truth which it contains. It shows that certain covenants are written, and that certain names are subscribed to them; but in itself it contains no proof, not even of the presumptive kind, that those names were subscribed by the parties, or that the covenants were made by them. In authentic acts this proof is supplied by the credit which the law declares shall be given to the attestation of a sworn officer. To acts under private signature, no such credit is given; the production of them does not raise even presumptions of their validity.

Art. 129. But although the law creates no presumption from the production of such an act, yet to avoid unnecessary delays and expenses, it permits the party against whom it is produced to be interrogated whether the signatures are true. From this permission result the different effects produced by the confession, the denial, or the ignorance of the fact, stated in the answer of the defendant, or of his refusal to acknowledge or deny the writing.

Art. 130. In every case where any party to a suit finds it necessary to produce a writing under private signature, either to support his action or maintain his defence, and wishes to have the answer of the opposite party, as to the truth of the signature, he must annex the original instrument to his petition or answer, and must pray that the opposite party may declare whether the signature be true or false.

Art. 131. If the signature which a party is thus called on to confess or deny, purports to be his own, the answer must be explicit, either that he confesses it to be his, or that it is forged. An answer which does not directly deny the signature, shall be deemed to be a confession.

Art. 132. If the signature purports to be, not that of the party himself, but of some other person, for whose obligation the opposite party endeavours to make him liable, either personally or by virtue of some office, duty, or trust, then the party interrogated is not obliged to answer explicitly, as in the former case. If he have seen the party write whose signature is in question, or is, from other circumstances, acquainted with his hand-writing, he must say so, and declare whether he believes the signature to be true or false. It is only when he declares himself utterly ignorant of the handwriting that he is dispensed with declaring his belief.

Art. 133. The answers to these interrogatories need not be on oath, unless it is required by the opposite party; and when it is, the effect is regulated by special provisions for that purpose.

Art. 134. The recognition or denial of a signature must be made by the party himself, who is interrogated. A wilfully false answer, not only incurs the civil effects herein provided, but is considered as an offence, and is punishable by the Penal Code.

Art. 135. The following are the effects produced by the answers, or by the refusal to answer, to the interrogatory demanding the recognition of a signature:

1st. If the party avow the signature, whether it be his own or that of another for whose obligation he is responsible, it makes the act, as to him and his representatives, an authentic act, and judgment may be immediately rendered thereon, without any other proof or trial—if such avowal be not accompanied by some legal defence, in the manner hereinafter provided; and it has, with respect to third persons, the same effect that an authentic act in any other form has by law.

2d. If it purport to be the act of one for whose obligation the respondent is liable, and he say that he is acquainted with the signature and believes it to be true, it creates a legal presumption in favour of the act.

3d. If the signature be denied, or if in cases where he is permitted to say so, the respondent answers, that he is ignorant whether the signature be true or false ; then no presumption is to be raised on either side. But the burthen of proving the signature true lies on him who asserts it.

4th. If the party interrogated do not answer in the time prescribed by the rules of court, the default is equivalent to a confession, and gives authenticity to the act.

5th. If the party avowing the signature have a legal defence to make against the operation of the instrument, supposing the signature to be true, he may set forth the same in his answer, and then the obligation of the act shall not be carried into effect until such defence be decided on. A legal defence, in the meaning of this article, is any such as might be made on an ordinary trial, after the signature to the instrument has been proved.

Art. 136. In all cases, whether under this section or not, when it becomes necessary to prove handwriting, it shall be done in the manner following :

§ 1st. If there be one or more subscribing witnesses, one of them at least must be examined, if he be within the state, and his testimony that he saw the party sign, is direct evidence, as is also the testimony of a witness to the same fact, although he was not a subscribing witness.

§ 2d. If the names of subscribing witnesses appear to the act, and they are dead or not within the state, the handwriting of one at least of the said witnesses, and of the party to the act, must be proved in one or all of the modes following, that is to say—by a witness who has seen the party write, or who has acquired a knowledge of his handwriting by correspondence, (by which is meant, writing letters and receiving answers, under such circumstances as give no suspicions of deception.)

Handwriting may also be proved by a comparison with

some authentic act, or other instrument acknowledged by the party, or positively proved by witnesses in the same cause to be his. This mode of proof may be resorted to at the request of either party, and the comparison is made by the judge on his own inspection ; but he may at the like request, be assisted by persons, skilled in the knowledge of handwritings, named by the court, and sworn to compare the papers, and truly to give their opinion to the judge. But no writing can serve as an instrument of comparison which has been judicially denied by the party, although it may have been proved to be his.

§ 3d. If there are no subscribing witnesses to the act, and none who can give direct evidence of the signature, then the handwriting may be proved in either or all the modes set forth in the last preceding paragraph.

§ 4th. An act, under private signature, may also be proved by an authentic act, if it be therein either recited or referred to in such a manner as that its identity is clearly established. Thus, if in a notarial act of inventory, a promissory note, given to the deceased, by a person who signed the inventory, as executor or tutor, is particularly set forth, and the note itself is referred to by a mark at the time of making the notarial act; this sufficiently identifies the note, and renders no other proof necessary. But if the act, under private signature, be merely recited in an authentic act to which the maker of the note is party, but the note be not produced and marked at the time of making the authentic act, then other proof must be resorted to, to identify the act under private signature which is in dispute, with the one recited in the authentic act.

§ 5th. None of the above modes of proving an act under private signature exclude the admission of the testimony of witnesses, who, although they were neither present at the making of the act, nor are acquainted with the handwriting, yet testify to facts to prove or disprove the act, which could not reasonably be supposed to have happened if the signature were in the one case, and in the other were not that of the party.

§ 6th. The proof by comparison of hands alone, unsupported by other circumstances, is not a sufficient evidence of the validity of an act under private signature, where the signature has been denied.

Art. 137. No suit can be brought for the purpose of making the party to an act, under private signature, acknowledge or deny it, so as to give it the effect of an authentic act, before the time limited in the obligation for it to become due has elapsed, unless in cases where by law it is made exigible before, except as is provided in the following section.

SECTION III.

Of copies.

Art. 138. It is a general rule of evidence, that copies are not evidence when the original can be resorted to. Copies of certain authentic acts are modified exceptions to this rule. There is no exception as to acts under private signature. There are, however, different kinds of copies of such acts entitled to different degrees of credit, in cases where the original cannot be produced. There are formal and informal notarial copies, and unattested copies.

Art. 139. If the holder of an act, under private signature, thinks the original is exposed to risk of loss, or fears that the evidence may not be procured when wanted, he may, at any time at his own expense, present a petition to any court of competent jurisdiction, and pray that the party who has signed the act may be summoned to attend at the office of some notary, at a given time, in order to witness the registry of such act, a copy whereof must be annexed ; and the party shall be summoned to attend accordingly.

Art. 140. If the party summoned shall file his answer to such petition, and deny the signature to the act, then that fact shall be tried as in ordinary cases, and if found in favour of the petitioner, judgment shall be rendered for him with costs, directing that the instrument shall be registered.

Art. 141. If the party summoned does not deny the signature, but (in cases where such answer is permitted) shall say that he is ignorant whether it be true or false, then evidence must be produced as in common cases; and if it be found that the act is valid, it shall be ordered to be registered.

Art. 142. If the party make no answer, and shall attend at the time and place directed for the registry, whether he then acknowledge the act or not, the notary, on production of a certified copy of the petition and the judge's order, of the return of the proper officer certifying that the party was duly summoned, or in cases where, after proof of the act in court, it shall be ordered to be registered, on production of that judgment, shall register the act in his ordinary register, and shall annex thereto the certified copies of the previous judicial proceedings.

Art. 143. If the party, after having been summoned, do neither answer nor attend, the notary shall, in like manner, proceed to copy the act and annex the proceedings. Authenticated copies of records thus made are called copies in form, and they have the same force and effect as the originals, if the said originals should be lost or destroyed; but if not proved to be so lost or destroyed, they must be produced in any suit brought thereon. The said copy and proceedings shall be authentic evidence of the signature; but this shall not entitle the plaintiff to prompt execution thereon—it only dispenses him with the proof of the signature and with the production of the original, in case it be lost or destroyed.

Art. 144. Proof of the destruction of an original act has a different effect from that which is produced by showing that it is lost. In the first case the court may, on production of the formal copy or other legal proof, give immediate effect to the obligation of the act. In the last, they must direct that security shall be given to repay the money, if the original should be produced in the hands of a bonâ fide holder, within such time as the court in their discretion shall direct, or order that the judgment shall not be executed until public notice shall have been given for such a time and at such places as the court shall direct, describing the instrument, setting forth the judgment, and calling on all persons to allege any reasons why it should not be carried into effect. The provisions of this article apply to all cases where judgment is given, or evidence of the contents of an instrument lost or destroyed, as well as in cases coming under this section.

Art. 145. Acts may also be recorded without any judicial proceeding if done in the presence of the party obligated, testified by their signature, and attested in the common form by the notary. Authenticated copies of such records are also copies in form, and have the force and effect with the copies mentioned in the preceding article.

Art. 146. Acts under private signature may also be transcribed on the registry of a notary without any judicial order, and out of the presence of the parties. This registry, and notarial copies thereof, are called informal copies. They do not fully replace the original, in case of its loss, as the formal copies do. They have, however, the following effects :—

1. They serve as the foundation of a prescriptive right from the time of the registry only.

2. They verify the existence of the act back, at least, to the period of its registry, where the time of the execution is in question.

3. Where the party has enjoyed or exercised the right given, or possessed the property purported to be conveyed, by such act, for ten years from the time of registry, without interruption, it has the force of an authentic act.

4. Connected with other proof of the execution of the original act and its loss, and of the identity of the paper which was registered with such original, they may form,

according to circumstances, presumptive evidence of the contents of such original.

Art. 147. An informal copy, without the intervention of a justice or of a public officer, is called an unattested copy, and it may, when the loss of the original is proved, be admitted as presumptive evidence to show what were its contents in cases where it can be established by legal proof that the copy is correct, and that the original from which it was taken was executed by the party against whom it is produced.

Art. 148. In case it is proved that the original was purposely destroyed by the party offering the copy, or by him under whom he claims, no copy, not even a formal one, shall be admitted in evidence.

Art. 149. When the original is proved to be in the possession of the opposite party, an informal copy is presumptive evidence of the contents, if the original is not produced after due notice. In such case, even parole proof may be resorted to for that purpose in the manner hereinafter provided.

Art. 150. Original acts, under private signature, may also be deposited in the office of a notary, who must enter in his register an act of deposit.

Art. 151. The act of deposit must declare at whose request it is made, and designate the parties to the act who were present at such deposit ; it must be signed by those parties, by the notary, and two witnesses, in the form of other notarial acts. The notary must annex thereto the act deposited, having first made his paraph at the foot of every page of writing contained in such act, and carefully noted all interlineations, erasures, or obliterations, appearing thereon.

Art. 152. Acts thus deposited, and copies thereof duly attested, have the force of authentic acts against the parties who have signed such act of deposit, from the date of the act deposited. Against third persons they have the same effect which authentic acts are declared to have, only from the date of the deposit.

Art. 153. Acts deposited by one party alone have no

effect as authentic acts, except against him; but they have all the other effects which, in a preceding article, are ascribed to informal copies.

Art. 154. The *ex parte* depositions of witnesses to the execution of an act, under private signature, give it no additional validity, nor are they a sufficient warrant for a notary to make a copy in form.

SECTION IV.

Of the form and effect of acts under private signature.

Art. 155. GENERAL PROVISION.—All the rules contained in the succeeding section apply exclusively to acts under private signature, unless the contrary be expressed.

SECTION V.

Of the requisites to an act under private signature.

Art. 156. An act under private signature may be made the evidence of all kinds of obligations or declarations, excepting those which by law are directed to be made by authentic act only; it must be signed with the names of those whom it purports to obligate, or by the declarant if it be a mere declaratory act.

Art. 157. The signature must be made at the end of the act in the proper handwriting of the party, if he can write; it must consist of the name commonly subscribed by such party to his other writings; but no act shall be invalidated because the party has falsely pretended that he could not write, or has made his signature differently from his usual manner.

Art. 158. If the party cannot write, his signature shall

consist of a mark made by him at the end of the act, in the presence of two witnesses, and of his name written by one of them, with a declaration that it is the mark of the party. This signature must be attested by that of the two witnesses.

Art. 159. If the party can read, but from whatever cause, is unable to write, he must, before affixing his mark, declare in the presence of the witnesses that he has read the instrument, or that it has been read to him. If he cannot read, the instrument must be read to him intelligibly by one of the witnesses in the presence of the other.

Art. 160. No instrument, purporting to be the act of a person who has not himself signed the same with his name, shall have any validity against such person, unless the requisites prescribed by the last two preceding articles have been complied with, or the party shall judicially avow the validity of the act, after having the same read to him by an officer of the court.

Art. 161. If an act be defective, for the want of any of the formalities above described, its execution is no bar to a suit founded on the obligation of which it was intended as the evidence, if such obligation can be sustained by other proof.

Art. 162. It is not necessary to the validity of such an act, that any part but the signature should be in the handwriting of the party obligated.

Art. 163. In an instrument containing an obligation respecting money, or any other article of which the sum, quantity, or number, is expressed in words in the body of the instrument, and repeated elsewhere on the paper in figures, if there be any difference between such a repetition and the body of the instrument, the latter shall be esteemed the true numeration, unless an error of calculation appears on the face of the act. If the numeration, both in the body of the instrument and out of it, be in figures, other evidence may be admitted to prove the intent of the parties.

Art. 164. Acts containing no other than communicative, or other synallagmatic contracts, must have the legal signatures of all parties who, by the terms of the act, are obligated to each other thereby ; if any of the signatures of such parties are wanting, the act is invalid as to the others.

Art. 165. If the act purports to contain communicative, or other synallagmatic contracts, between certain parties, and also a unilateral contract, relative to the same thing, by which they are jointly bound to another, it need not be signed by the party to whom the obligation is made by the unilateral contract.

CHAPTER III.

Of scriptory evidence not attested by the signature of party.

SECTION I.

Of the different kinds of unattested scriptory evidence.

Art. 166. Evidence, coming under this division, is of two kinds :

1. Writings which, from their form and nature, show that they were intended to receive the signature of a party, and are therefore imperfect without it. Of this kind are unsigned contracts of any kind, declarations of trust, testaments, and codicils.

2. Writings which, from their nature, do not appear to have been intended to be attested by any signature. Such are entries in account books, family records of births and deaths, and memoranda of other events.

SECTION II.

Of writings intended to be signed by the parties.

Art. 167. Writings of the first kind are never to be admitted as direct proof of the contract, or disposition of which they would have been the evidence, if they had been perfected. They may be admitted as presumptive evidence—

1st. Of the intent to make the contract, or disposition in case where such intent is material to the issue.

2d. Of the truth of any other enunciation contained in the writings.

3d. Of the knowledge which the party making such writing had of any fact therein stated.

But such writing cannot be admitted at all, unless it is in the handwriting of the party whose act it purports to be, or is proved to have been made by his direction, or to have been approved by him after it was made.

SECTION III.

Of writings not intended to have been signed by the parties.

Art. 168. Writings of the second kind may be admitted (against the party making them) as presumptions of the fact they purport to state, when they are proved to be in his handwriting, or to have been made by his direction, or to have been read and approved by him.

Art. 169. The party against whom either of the two kinds of unattested writings is produced, may be admitted to give an explanation, on oath, of the circumstances under which the same were made, and the intent of making them—subject to cross-examination.

Art. 170. These kinds of written evidence can be admitted for the party who made them, only when it appears that they were made at a time and under circumstances which show that they were not intended to create legal evidence for the party making them.

Art. 171. When any written evidence is produced, under the preceding article, the opposite party may demand that the other be examined on oath.

SECTION IV.

Of writings not made by the parties to the suit.

Art. 172. All the previous provisions of this chapter relate to writings made by one of the parties to the suit, or by some one under whom he claims, or by the direction of one of them. Writings made by others, in which are included those which are printed, and maps and plans, can be introduced in the following cases :

1st. Historical works—to elucidate any historical fact that may become material in a litigated cause.

2d. Books of art or science—when any thing, appertaining to the branch of learning of which they treat, is in dispute.

3d. Maps or plans—to elucidate questions of locality,

When made by persons who had no interest in making erroneous representations to the prejudice or advantage of either of the parties, and who are either dead or so situated that their testimony cannot be procured. Or,

When legally attested to be accurate by the persons who made them, or by others who have verified the delineations they contain.

4th. Accounts stated or calculations made by persons who prove them to be accurate.

5th. Nautical and other almanacs—whenever the calculations they contain are material to the issue.

TITLE IV.

OF SUBSTANTIVE EVIDENCE.

Art. 173. Substantive evidence being that which arises from the existence or position of an object in relation to the fact in dispute, it follows that, unless it comes within the scope of that evidence which is offered to the senses of the judge in the situation and under the circumstances which make it material to the cause, it requires other evidence for its introduction. A bloody dagger is substantive evidence : if the judge saw it in the hand of an assassin immediately after the blow was struck, it would be the foundation of evidence coming within his own knowledge; otherwise, it must be supported by testimony to show when and where it was found, and the instrument itself forms the substantive evidence.

Art. 174. The following are examples of substantive evidence :—The mark on a tree coinciding with that stated by testimonial or scriptory evidence in cases of disputed boundary is substantive evidence of a land-mark. The number of concentric circles in the wood that has grown over the mark is substantive evidence of the number of years that have elapsed since it was made.

The inscription on a monument or tombstone is presumptive evidence of the time of birth or death, and the other material facts it commemorates.

TITLE V.

Art. 175. Presumptions are of two kinds : such as are the result of the reason only of the judge, exercised on the circumstances which are proved, without any express direction of law to guide him in his conclusions, which are called simple presumptions ; and legal presumptions, which are such as the law expressly directs to be drawn from certain circumstances.

Art. 176. The difference between a simple and a legal presumption is this—that the first is an inference drawn by the judge, from the circumstances by the unrestrained exercise of his reason; the last is a deduction made by the law itself, which the judge is forced to adopt, whatever may be his own conclusions from the facts.

That a man of good character will not tell a falsehood ;

That other things being equal, a man will do that which is most conducive to his interest and happiness;

That a mother will not abandon her infant ;

Are examples of simple presumptions, drawn from the structure of the human mind.

That if the obligation is delivered to the debtor, the debt has been paid ;

That the rent due from former years has been paid, when a receipt is produced for the last year ;

Are other instances of simple presumptions, drawn, not like the former from nature, but from the common course of business and affairs. All these, although natural conclusions, are simple presumptions, because there is no positive law directing them to be drawn.

That the person who has been in the peaceable possession of real property for more than a year, is the owner ;

That, when no time is expressed for the duration of a lease of a predial estate, it shall be for a year ;

Are examples of legal presumptions, which the law expressly orders to be drawn.

Art. 177. The effect of a presumption, whether simple or legal, in favour of any affirmative or negative proposition, is, that the proof of such proposition is considered as established, until the contrary is shown by direct proof, or rendered doubtful by other presumptions.

Art. 178. When the party, who alleges a fact, brings no evidence of any kind to support it, the want of such evidence creates a presumption in favour of the party who denies.

Art. 179. When the existence of one fact necessarily supposes the existence of another, so that, if one be true the other cannot, in the nature of things, be false, the induction drawn from the establishment of the first fact is not a presumption, but conclusive evidence.

Art. 180. The division of presumptions heretofore known in our law, under the name of *presumptiones juris et de jure*, is abolished. Evidence, heretofore arranged under that head, will be found in its proper division in this title.

Art. 181. A legal presumption (unless declared by law to be conclusive) has no greater force of itself than a simple presumption, and may be counteracted by one if sufficiently strong.

Thus, the lease of a predial estate, when no time is expressed, creates a legal presumption that it is to continue for a year ; but if the lessor, at the time of making the lease, with the knowledge and assent of the lessee, makes another to a third person, to commence at the end of three months from the time of making the first, the first presumption is counteracted by the second.

Art. 182. Presumptions can only be raised from facts, which appear by legal testimony; therefore a matter that cannot be given in evidence, cannot be a legal foundation for any presumption.

Art. 183. Simple presumptions must be founded :

First, on the establishment of some fact by legal testimony.

Secondly, by such deduction from that fact as is warranted by a consideration of the usual propensities or passions of human nature ; by the usual course of business ; by the particular habits or passions of the individual, whose act is in question ; or by the course of nature.

TITLE VI.

OF DIRECT EVIDENCE.

Art. 184. Direct evidence being that which, if true, conclusively establishes the proposition in question, it follows that this kind of evidence gives rise to one inquiry only, to wit —Whether the fact be true ? The mind once convinced of this, has no other operation to perform, in order to arrive at the truth of the proposition asserted, which must be true, if the evidence be true. In all cases, therefore, where any doubt remains of the fact in question, after the mind of the judge is fully satisfied that the evidence, offered in support of it, is true ; such evidence is not direct, but presumptive only.

Art. 185. Although the effect of direct evidence, when established to be true, is conclusive of the fact in question ; yet the truth of such evidence (in cases where it is not declared by law to be conclusive) depends on presumptions more or less strong. The declaration of a witness, that he saw the act in controversy done, is direct evidence, and (if the judge have no doubt that the witness tells the truth) is conclusive. But whether the judge will give credit to the witness, must depend on the pre sumptions in favour of, or against his veracity, arising from character and other circumstances. Thus, too, the authority of written testimony, even of records, (independent of positive law,) depends on the presumption.

that the witnesses who prove, or the public officer who recorded them, would not attest a falsehood.

Art. 186. It results from the preceding articles, that direct testimony (when not declared by law to be conclusive) may be counteracted, not only by other direct contrary evidence, but by presumptions.

TITLE VII.

OF CONCLUSIVE EVIDENCE.

CHAPTER I.

Definition and division of the different kinds of conclusive evidence.

Art. 187. Proof of any kind may produce conviction in the mind of the judge of the truth or falsity of any proposition; but no evidence is called conclusive in this code, but that which is declared to be such by it or by anterior law.

Art. 188. When the law has declared that certain proof forms conclusive evidence of any fact, the judge, whatever may be his own conclusion, can make no other than such as has been drawn by the law. He can admit no presumptions or direct proof to weaken the effect of evidence, so declared to be conclusive; but in the manner prescribed by law, in particular specified cases, he may admit evidence to disprove its existence.

Art. 189. Conclusive evidence is classed under several heads:

First—Such as arises from the uniform course of nature.

Second—That which is expressly declared to be such by law.

Third—That which is produced in the mind of the judge by the clear and unequivocal exercise of his senses.

That, where maternity is proved, there must have been cohabitation, is an example of the first class.

Where there is no personal incapacity, cohabitation is conclusive proof of the second class, that the issue of the wife is the issue of the husband.

And an example of the third class may be given in the case where the issue is, record or no record, and the judge decides it by inspection.

Art. 190. In order that the course of nature should be the foundation of conclusive proof, it must be the invariable course of nature ; its general course only gives rise to presumptions. Proof that an absentee was born two hundred years ago, is conclusive proof that he is dead, because no instance has been known of human life extended to that period. If it be shown that he was born one hundred years before, the law creates a presumption of his death, which may, however, be counteracted by proof, because though it be the general course of nature for men to die before that age, it is not invariable.

Art. 191. When the law, by the enactment of positive rules, declares certain evidence to be conclusive, it is done to avoid litigation or fraud, and prevent the temptation to perjury.

Some of these rules are declaratory of the conclusion drawn from the invariable course of nature, mentioned in the preceding articles ; others are positive provisions, established by legislative wisdom, for the object above stated in this article.

The birth of a child more than three hundred days after the death of the husband is conclusive proof that such child is not his, and is an example of the declaratory rule above mentioned, as the same is contained in our law as it now stands.

The authority given to a judgment between the parties, to an authentic act, and to a judicial confession, are examples of the positive rule.

CHAPTER II.

Of res judicata.

SECTION I.

What judgments are valid as *res judicata.*

Art. 192. *Res judicata* is whatever has been finally decided by a court of competent jurisdiction—proceeding according to the forms of law—by a valid sentence—on a matter alleged, and either denied or expressly or impliedly confessed by the other; and it is conclusive evidence of that which it decides, between the same parties or those that represent them, litigating for the same thing, under the same title, and in the same quality.

Art. 193. Such judgment may be used, either as a plea (in which case it bars any other suit brought for the same cause) or as evidence, and is then conclusive of that which it decides, under the modifications contained in the following articles.

Art. 194. The decision must be final that is to say, it must be such as the court, rendering it, could not alter, on the application of either party, or reconsider it of its own accord; therefore, an interlocutory order that a party account; a judgment that needs confirmation; the verdict of a jury, or even a final judgment, before it is signed, and before the time has elapsed within which it may be set aside on a motion for a new trial or rehearing, has not the force of *res judicata.* A judgment appealed from has not the force of the *res judicata*, and is not even presumptive proof; but a final judgment, although the time for appealing may not have elapsed, is conclusive proof until the appeal be made.

Art. 195. By appeal, in this title, is meant any legal

process whatever, by which the judgment of an inferior court may be reconsidered and modified or annulled.

Art. 196. The judgment, to form conclusive proof, must have been rendered by a competent tribunal. A sentence having all the other requisites, is no proof, if the person who rendered it had no power to decide on the subject matter in dispute between the parties; but this want of jurisdiction must appear by an examination of the proceedings in the court in which the judgment was rendered, and of the law by which the court rendering it was empowered to act : and no allegation of any matter not appearing from the said laws and proceedings shall be admitted to show a want of jurisdiction, although such allegation would have deprived the court of its jurisdiction, had it been pleaded and proved in the original cause.

Thus, a judgment given for more than one hundred dollars by a justice of the peace under our present laws is no evidence that the defendant owes that sum, because the court has no jurisdiction; or that he owes any smaller sum, because the whole judgment is void.

But a judgment rendered in a court of the United States, in a suit brought by a person styling himself an alien against a citizen of the state, would be conclusive evidence, although in fact he was not an alien; nor can any evidence of that fact be admitted in opposition to the judgment.

Art. 197. Where the court in which the judgment relied on as evidence has been given is one of limited jurisdiction, either as to sum, person, place, or the nature of the suits of which it can take cognizance, its decisions are no proof, unless the circumstances necessary to confer jurisdiction appear on the record of the suit.

Art. 198. The courts of this state will *ex officio* take notice of the jurisdiction given to the different tribunals within the same ; but where a judgment given in another state, or in a foreign country, is relied on, the production of the judgment, duly authenticated, is presumptive evidence that the court had a competent jurisdiction, unless the contrary appear on the record; but such presumption may be removed by showing the want of jurisdiction by such evidence as is allowed by law.

Art. 199. Whenever a judgment is offered, either as presumptive or conclusive evidence, all the proceedings in the suit, in which such judgment was rendered, must be produced.

Art. 200. Every judgment to operate as evidence of the thing judged must have been rendered in the forms which are prescribed by law, in order to give validity to the judgment, unless the matter which is alleged as want of form has been either impliedly or expressly assented to by the party who alleged it.

Thus the want of a citation is a defect that would render the judgment void; but if the party has expressly acknowledged service of the petition, or impliedly waived the necessity of a citation, by putting in an answer, this shall not be made an objection.

Art. 201. The want of form, prescribed by law for the validity of a judgment, must (in order to bar its operation as *res judicata*) be such as is apparent on the face of the record. No other evidence can be resorted to, in order to prove any such defect.

Art. 202. A sentence to produce the effect of *res judicata*, must not only have been rendered, but must be in itself valid, according to the forms of law.

Art. 203. Judgments may be erroneous and unjust without being invalid, within the purview of the last article. Whether the error be in the construction of law, or the deduction from fact, the judgment is valid, unless appealed from; but an invalid judgment is one that appears on the face of it to be void.

SECTION II.

What judgments are invalid to produce the effect of *res judicata.*

Art. 204. Judgments, under the following circumstances, are not valid under the preceding articles :

1st. When the judgment is uncertain, and is not rendered certain by some part of the record. Thus, a judgment that the defendant pay the damages which the plaintiff sustained, is uncertain; but if the judgment had been to recover what the plaintiff demanded, it would be rendered certain, by referring to the plaintiff's demand. If it were to recover damages as A. should determine, it would not be void, but could not operate as *res judicata* for another reason, because such judgment would not be final.

2d. When the judgment pronounces something expressly contrary to the law; by which is meant, when it declares that what is acknowledged by all to be law, shall not be observed : as if on a plea of infancy, to avoid a contract, it should declare, that because the defendant was twenty years of age, he should be bound. But a decision on the construction of law is still binding, although the judge may have been wrong in his construction. Nor is the force of a judgment lessened, although the evidence should not warrant the conclusion drawn by the judge.

3d. When there is an evident error of calculation appearing in the judgment itself : as if in a suit for the value of three hogsheads of sugar, the sentence should be, that the defendant pay, at the rate of $70 per hogshead, the sum of 250 dollars.

4th. Where the judgment is contrary to the judicial confession of the party in the same suit : as if the decree should declare, that a defendant should go quit of a debt demanded by the plaintiff, and which the defendant had confessed in his answer to be due.

5th. Where the decree is given against one not a party to the suit.

6th. Where the judgment has been rendered against one who appears in the suit to be a minor, or other person who is not, by law, competent to defend his own interests without the intervention of his curator or tutor, or other person designated by law to watch over his interest. This rule includes married women, who appear without being authorized by their husbands, or by the court, in cases in which authorization is required.

7th. Where the party can show, in the manner hereinafter prescribed, that the judgment has been obtained by forgery or fraud, and the party had no notice in time to avail himself of the objection in the court where the judgment was rendered.

Art. 205. The judgment must also be in a matter alleged by the parties in the suit in which it is given. Thus, if the demand be for one acre of land, and the judgment is that the plaintiff recover three acres, this judgment would be neither conclusive evidence of his title to the two additional acres, nor a bar to the defendant if he should sue to recover them.

Art. 206. It is not sufficient that the matter on which the judgment is given be alleged by one party ; it must also be denied or admitted by the other party : but a general denial of all facts alleged is sufficient for this purpose, without specially negativing the several facts alleged.

Art. 207. The denial or admission, referred to in the last two preceding articles, may be either express or implied. A denial of the fact in question is implied when it is a necessary consequence from the denial of another fact. Thus, a denial that the party was ever indebted is an implied denial of the charge of a sum alleged to be due for interest ; but an allegation that the principal sum has been paid, is no negative of the interest being due.

Art. 208. A refusal or neglect to answer in the time prescribed by the rules of procedure, creates an implied admission of the allegations to which the answer is required. Therefore, a judgment by default, rendered definitively, is *res judicata*, although the fact, on which it is pronounced, was neither expressly denied or admitted.

Art. 209. A judgment absolving a party from that which he has judicially confessed to be due in the same suit (provided such confession has not been set aside) is not *res judicata* in favour of the person making the confession.

Art. 210. Such judgment as is described in the foregoing articles is conclusive ; that is, it is a bar when pleaded, and conclusive proof when offered in evidence, of that which it decides ; but of nothing else contained in such judgment : therefore, nothing alleged by way of inducement, illustration, argument, or example, in giving the judgment, has the force of a judgment.

Art. 211. The pleadings in each cause are the only evidence of what was alleged, and denied or confessed, and the decisory part of the judgment of that which was decided.

SECTION III.

Against whom the *res judicata* may be given in evidence.

Art. 212. The effect of *res judicata* is confined to the parties in the suit, or to those who succeed to their interest. There are, however, exceptions to this rule, which will be particularly noticed.

Art. 213. Parties are those only who appear in the suit and allege or answer ; who have been cited in the manner prescribed by law, although they do not appear or answer, or who have intervened in the suit to contest or prosecute the same.

Art. 214. No person can be concluded by a judgment although a party to it, unless for the amount of the interest, which, at the time of rendering such judgment, he had or claimed in the matter in controversy. No interest accruing after such judgment by any party is affected by it. Thus, if the heir or executor sue one for effects belonging to the succession, and it should appear that the defendant had no property belonging to the estate, and judgment be thereupon rendered in his favour, this judgment shall be no bar to a subsequent suit against the same defendant, who may afterwards have got possession of part of the estate.

Art. 215. But every person cited to show what right he has in any matter in controversy is, as to the other parties in such suit, and as to any claims he may then have, bound by the judgment rendered therein, although he do not set forth his right.

Art. 216. Not only the parties, but those who succeed to the interests in the subject in controversy, are bound by the judgment ; but they must succeed to them—that is, they must hold or claim under them. Thus, the sentence against the ancestor binds the heir—against the seller binds the purchaser; but a sentence against or in favour of the possessor does not bind him who recovers the property from such possessor, or acquires it in any other manner, which does not suppose the property to have been in him at the time of such judgment.

Art. 217. Every one is a party to a suit who appears as such, either in person, by a mandatory duly constituted, or by an attorney-at-law duly licensed to practise in the court in which the suit is pending and employed by him ; and it shall be presumptive evidence that such attorney-at-law was employed by the party, if he had in his hands the papers necessary for the prosecution or defence of the cause, or if the party knew that such suit was prosecuted or defended in his name, and did not disavow the attorney in such court.

Art. 218. To be bound by a judgment, it is not sufficient to have been a party to the suit only, but to the judgment ; therefore, a party who, before the judgment, is allowed to discontinue—whose name is struck out of the proceedings—who is otherwise dismissed before a hearing on the merits—or who, on the hearing, is dismissed as having improperly been made a party—is not bound by a judgment afterwards rendered ; but if the order of dismissal be appealed from and reversed, and such party's name is afterwards reinstated in the pleadings, he shall be bound by the judgment.

Art. 219. A judgment on an appeal against the party in the original suit, who has neither cited, nor appeared, nor in any manner waived a citation in such court of appeals, is not *res judicata* against such party.

Art. 220. The exceptions to the rule that none but parties to a judgment are bound by it, are the following :

1st. Where a suit has been brought for the purpose of determining a right of common or servitude claimed by several persons, either by one or against one or more of the persons claiming such right, the judgment shall be conclusive for or against all the other commoners or persons claiming the same servitude or right of common, under the same title ; but not if they claim under a different title.

2d. When a public or private corporation, or body politic, shall claim a right of laying or receiving any toll, tax, duty, wharfage, tonnage, or any other contribution or imposition whatever, a judgment rendered in a suit to try the legality of such claim, between the said corporation or body politic and any individual interested therein, shall be conclusive as to the right of such public or private corporation or body politic.

Provided that, in the two cases above mentioned in this article, the decision shall not be conclusive, except against those who are individually made parties, unless two concurring judgments have been pronounced on the same right ; in which case the judgment shall be *res judicata* as to all ; but if the servitude claimed be indivisible, a single judgment is conclusive.

3d. A judgment against a principal debtor shall bind his surety, although he be no party to it ; and, in like manner, a judgment in favour of the principal shall be conclusive evidence for the security.

4th. If one who has acquired by purchase, donation, exchange, or any other contract, suffers the former proprietor to prosecute or defend a suit affecting such property, the person so acquiring such property, having notice of such suit, he shall be bound by the judgment, if it be given against the former proprietor, although he, the purchaser, be no party; but a judgment given in favour of the former owner in such suit, shall not prejudice the title of the true owner. The same rule applies to the creditor who suffers the owner of property, who has pledged or mortgaged it to him, to litigate respecting it with his knowledge. In this case the creditor shall be bound to the amount of his interest by the judgment given against the owner; and, in like manner, if the owner of the property pledged or mortgaged suffers the creditor to litigate respecting it, he shall be bound by the sentence.

Provided that the said judgments, mentioned in this article, be rendered on a fair contestation of the right, and not collusively, or by default or confession; and, therefore, in any such case, the party against whom any such judgment is opposed, either as an exception or evidence, may show that it was entered by collusion, and defeat its effect.

Art. 221. There are no other causes than those expressed in the last preceding article, in which one who is not a party to a judgment, or who does not succeed to the rights of those who were parties to it, is bound thereby.

Art. 222. Where, in a suit brought by one plaintiff, judgment has been given against him, and he afterwards brings another suit for the same cause of action jointly with another, the former judgment shall be conclusive against the former plaintiff, if his interest be a divisible one, and under the same title with that brought in question in the former suit. If his interest be indivisible, or if the last claim is under a different title, the former judgment is not conclusive.

Art. 223. To give a judgment the force of *res judicata,*

when pleaded or offered in evidence in another cause, it must appear that the subject matter in controversy in both causes is the same. If it be essentially the same, although demanded in a different form, the judgment is conclusive. Thus, if a personal action is brought on a debt due by mortgage, and it be decided that nothing is due, this judgment is a bar to a subsequent hypothecary suit for the same debt. In like manner, if the first suit be a hypothecary action, and the decision is that nothing is due to the plaintiff, such judgment shall bar a personal suit for the same thing.

Art. 224. There are, however, exceptions to, and modifications of, the rule contained in the last article, as follows :

1st. Where the matter in dispute is an aggregate body, of which the parts are changeable by nature, without changing the character of the whole. Thus, a judgment relative to a flock is conclusive between the parties, although the individual animals composing the flock may not be the same at the time of both suits.

2d. Where the party who has failed in a demand for the whole shall afterwards bring a suit for a part, the first judgment is a bar ; and this, whether the controversy be for a certain piece of property, a sum of money, or an incorporeal right. Thus, if a judgment be brought for a tract of land, and judgment be rendered for the defendant, the judgment will be a bar to an action brought under the same title for any part of the same land, either for an undivided part or for a certain designated portion. The same rule applies where a suit is brought for two separate pieces of property and judgment be rendered for the defendant, the plaintiff cannot afterwards sustain a suit for either of them separately. The rules laid down under this second head also apply to the defendant ; if the judgment be rendered against him for the whole, he can never sustain an action for any of the parts separately.

3d. Where a suit has been brought for a distinct part and under a PARTICULAR TITLE, and a demand is afterwards made for the whole, the judgment, in the first suit, is *res judicata* only for that part which was in controversy in the first suit. But if the first judgment were for a demand for a part, under a UNIVERSAL TITLE, such judgment, if against the plaintiff, is no bar to the suit for the whole.

4th. There is an exception to the second rule of this article, in the case of a suit brought in the cases allowed by law for the materials which have been employed in the construction of a house.   This demand is not barred by a judgment given against the plaintiff in a suit brought by him for the house.

Where what is demanded by the second suit, although not the same with that which was the subject of litigation in the first, yet is incident to, or grows out of it, or by law belongs to him who is the owner of that which was the object of the first suit.   Then the first judgment is a bar to the second suit.   For example :

If, in a demand for a principal sum, it has been adjudged that it was never due, and the same plaintiff should sue for the interest of such sum, the first judgment would bar the second suit, although the demand was not for the same thing.   In the example given, if the judgment in the first suit had been, not that the capital had never been due, but only that it had been paid, then the first judgment is no bar to the second suit, under the law relative to *res judicata;* but it is a bar under another principle, that to avoid circuity of actions the right to interest shall always be determined in the same suit by which the principal is demanded.   Thus, too, a judgment settling the title to land, is a bar to a subsequent suit for alluvial soil added to it since, or to a claim for trees which have been cut, demanding them as the growth of the land, by virtue of the same title under which the land was claimed.

5th. Whenever the thing demanded by a second suit is so included in that which was decided by a former judgment, that the decree rendered must confirm or annul that which was given in the first, then, although the same thing be not nominally demanded, yet the first judgment shall be considered as *res judicata* between the parties.

For example—If, in one suit respecting a servitude of view, it has been determined that the party has no right to raise his wall ten feet, this judgment will bar a claim to raise his wall twenty feet ; for, if the second judgment should be against the right claimed in the second suit, it affirms the judgment given in the first ; if it allows the right, it annuls the first decision.

6th. In determining whether the same thing be demanded by a second action, courts must determine by the substance, not the form of the demand. Thus, if judgment be rendered on a written obligation for the payment of money, this judgment shall be a bar to a subsequent suit for money lent, founded on the same transaction, unless, in this case, the obligation be declared void for some reason not affecting the original cause of action.

7th. But if a plaintiff fails in a suit, because he has mistaken the manner in which it ought to have been brought, such judgment is no bar to a suit brought in the proper form for the same thing.

Art. 225. A judgment on a claim of ownership, or for possession of property, is no bar to a suit for a usufruct or servitude, or use on the same land. Nor is a judgment on a claim for such usufruct, servitude, or use, any bar to a suit for the property or possession.

Art. 226. A judgment in a suit for possession is no bar to a suit for the property ; but a recovery in a suit where both property and possession are claimed, is a bar to a subsequent suit for possession.

Art. 227. A judgment in a suit for one species of servitude is not a bar to a suit for different servitude, although that which was first demanded may include the last. Thus, a suit for a right of footway is not barred by a judgment that the party claiming it had no right to a servitude for the passage of cattle.

Art. 228. Another requisite to the conclusiveness of a

judgment is that the thing demanded must, in both suits, be not only the same, but demanded under the same title.

Art. 229. The last requisite to give effect to a decision as *res judicata* is that the parties should, in both suits, prosecute or defend in the same quality; if in the first suit the party against whom the judgment is opposed or defended, sued as executor, curator, tutor, attorney-in-fact, or garnishee, and in the second appeared in his own name, the judgment can neither be a bar nor evidence for or against him, although the same thing be the object of the suit, and it be against the same party.

Art. 230. Yet if a quality be assumed or given in either suit which would make no alteration in the party's right, the judgment shall have its effect as a bar or as evidence. As if a man bring a suit, on a promise made to him personally by another, or for personal injury done to him, and in such suit call himself heir or executor of another, or give other of those qualities to the defendant, judgment in such suit would be conclusive in another which might be brought for the same cause, unless the first judgment were given as an exception taken to the quality assumed, and not on the merits.

CHAPTER III.

Of confession.

Art. 231. Confession in relation to the manner in which it is made, is either judicial or extra judicial. In relation to its nature, it is either full or partial only.

Art. 232. A judicial confession is that which is made by a party in some writing forming part of the proceedings in a cause, or which is made before a person authorized by law to receive the same, and reduced to writing by him, or under his authority, in the manner prescribed by law. Extra judicial confessions are those which are made in any other manner.

Art. 233. Full confession is that which acknowledges the fact alleged, with all its material circumstances, so as to leave nothing to be supplied by other evidence. Partial confession is that which acknowledges some circumstance from which an inference may be drawn to operate as presumptive evidence.

Art. 234. In civil cases, every proceeding being usually made with due deliberation and a knowledge of facts, a judicial confession, whether full or partial, is conclusive evidence of what is so confessed, but with the following provisions to guard against error.

1. Whenever a judicial confession has been made by the party himself, which on reflection he deems to be erroneous, he may on application within a time which the judge shall deem reasonable, and on showing cause to his satisfaction, obtain leave to amend such confessory proceeding.

2. When the confession has been made by an attorney or agent, such amendment shall be of course, if the party shall without unnecessary delay, after the proceeding comes to his knowledge, state the error on oath, and apply to have the same amended.

3. The condition of such amendments shall always be, that the adverse party shall be paid all costs and expenses he may have incurred in consequence of the error, and have time allowed him, if he require it, to supply other evidence of the facts at first confessed.

Art. 235. In criminal cases, no confession, whether full or partial, is conclusive evidence to the jury on a trial. The answer of "guilty" to the charge, if persevered in after the admonition and inquiry hereinafter directed, is such evidence as justifies the court in pronouncing sentence, without the intervention of a jury.

Art. 236. When the accused, on his arraignment, shall plead "guilty," it shall be the duty of the court to admonish him of the consequences of such answer, and to inquire, as well from him as from others, and particularly if he be in custody from the officer having charge of him, whether his acknowledgment has been produced by any threat or promise; and also when there is any reason to suppose insanity or imbecility of mind, to inquire into that fact.

Art. 237. In all other cases of a full or partial confession, whether judicial or extra judicial, the accused may show, to avoid the effect of such confession, not only by other evidence that it was not true, but that it was produced by error, by threats, promises, false hopes, confusion of mind, or any other efficient cause. And in every such case, the confession is to have such weight as the judges of the fact shall, in their discretion, give to it, under a consideration of all the circumstances of the case.

Art. 238. In all cases the whole confession must be taken together; that is to say, every thing said, done, or written, at the time of the confession, tending to enlarge, restrict, or modify it, must be received as part of the evidence.

CHAPTER IV.

Of estoppels.

Art. 239. There being no other conclusive evidence than in the cases especially provided for by the legislative authority of this state, that species of conclusive evidence known in the English law of evidence by the name of "Estoppel," is abolished, and can operate as direct, or, according to its nature, presumptive, evidence only.

GENERAL PROVISION.

Art. 240. Nothing in this Code contained shall be so construed as to dispense with the proof required by the Civil Code, or other statutes, to give effect to certain contracts, or testamentary or other dispositions, or to enforce the registry or recording of certain acts, or to prove legitimacy or filiation, legitimation, or civil condition.

A CODE OF REFORM AND PRISON DISCIPLINE.

INTRODUCTORY TITLE.

CHAPTER I.

Design of the code of reform and prison discipline.

Art. 1. The Code of Reform and Prison Discipline will regulate the manner in which prisoners of different descriptions are to be confined and treated, as well before as after judgment.

Art. 2. This Code is intended not only to direct the structure and police of the prison for the confinement of convicts, but also of those which are rendered necessary for the detention of the accused before trial, for the education of juvenile offenders, and of a House of Refuge and employment for those who have undergone the sentence of the law. All these objects are necessarily connected : no one part can be abstracted without materially injuring the effect of the others.

Art. 3. Safe custody is an object common to the prisons ; but reform is the intent of all the institutions. Punishment also enters into the design of the Penitentiary, the School of Reform, and that department of the House of Detention destined to receive those convicted of misdemeanors ; but forms no part of the system, so far as it applies to the custody of the accused before trial, and to their relief and employment after having suffered the sentence of the law.

Art. 4. In all these establishments the means by which reformation is expected, are, reflection, instruction, habits of industry, and religion. To promote these is one of the first duties of the men who are charged with the important and honourable task of superintending the different departments of these institutions.

Art. 5. Reformation cannot be expected while the vicious are permitted to associate with each other or with the innocent. This kind of seclusion, therefore, is a protection not a punishment; and is consequently necessary in the House of Detention and Refuge, as well as in the Penitentiary and School of Reform.

Art. 6. All the officers appointed under this Code, from the inspector to the under-keeper, have a moral as well as a legal duty to perform. In no department of the government is there a greater call for the best qualities of the mind—a strong moral sense and unfeigned belief in religion (for they must be teachers of both), firmness in preserving order, moderation and temper in enforcing it, close attention to discover the evil propensities that have led to the crimes of the convicts, and a knowledge of human nature to apply the proper correctives. The officers of a prison are no longer jailors and turnkeys charged with the custody of the body only : they must minister to the diseased minds and correct the depraved habits of their patients. The law raises them to their true station. They have higher functions, and on the manner in which they shall perform them depends the success of the whole system to which this Code is intended to give vigour and effect.

Art. 7. This view of the intent of the law and of what it expects from the ministers who are to execute it, are placed at the introduction of the Code to impress them with a true view of the spirit which dictated it, and direct them, in those points in which the law may be made more efficacious, by a zealous and enlightened performance of their several duties.

Art. 8. From the magistrates and others, who are constituted visitors, much also is expected ; the right given by this Code is not intended as a complimentary privilege, conferred only to satisfy curiosity. Publicity and the superintending care of upright magistrates and intelligent men, is the best incentive to a zealous performance of duty. Faithful and active officers will court their investigation ; those who are negligent or corrupt, will fear it.

Art. 9. The progress of reform in the female department will depend chiefly on those of their own sex, who may accept the invitation given by the law, to carry their example and precept and persuasive exhortation to the place of punishment, and convert it into a school for religion, industry, and virtue.

CHAPTER II.

Division of the work.

Art. 10. This Code is divided into three books. The first treats of the different places of confinement, their construction, and officers ; the second directs the treatment of the persons confined ; and the third contains the regulations for the House of Refuge.

BOOK I.

PLACES OF CONFINEMENT—OF THEIR CONSTRUCTION AND OFFICERS.

TITLE I.

OF PLACES OF CONFINEMENT.

CHAPTER I.

Of the different denominations of places of confinement.

Art. 11. There shall be provided at the expense of the state, in such place in the first judicial district as the general assembly shall direct, three separate and distinct places of confinement.

Art. 12. One of them shall be called the House of Detention. In this shall be confined :

1. Persons who, in the cases allowed by law, are detained in order to secure their attendance as witnesses on criminal trials in the first district.

2. Those who are committed for trial on an accusation of MISDEMEANOR in the first district.

3. Persons sentenced to simple imprisonment (whether in close custody or not) for any period, whether in the first district, or in any other district, for more than sixty days.

4. Those who may be committed for a disturbance in court, for any such disobedience to the orders of a court or a magistrate as may be punished by imprisonment, for the non-payment of a fine, or for the breach of a recognizance, or any other engagement entered into in the course of a prosecution for an offence, in the first district, in the cases where such confinement is authorized.

5. All those who may, in the first district, be committed for trial on an accusation of CRIME.

Art. 13. Another of the said places of confinement shall be called the Penitentiary ; in which shall be confined all those convicted of crime in any part of the state, who, at the time of conviction, had attained the age of eighteen years.

Art. 14. The third shall be called the School of Reform. In it shall be placed :

1. All those convicted of crime (not punishable by imprisonment for life) who have not attained the age of eighteen years, in whatever part of the state the conviction may have been had.

2. All persons under the age of eighteen years who shall be sentenced to be placed in the said prison, on conviction, for misdemeanor, in cases where power for that purpose is specially given by law.

3. All young vagrants whose commitment shall, under that denomination, be permitted by law.

Art. 15. Prisoners committed before trial, and offenders sentenced to simple imprisonment for a term less than sixty days, in any of the other judicial districts, except the first, shall be confined in the jail of the parish in which they shall be committed, or in which they shall be sentenced.

Art. 16. Offenders sentenced to simple imprisonment in any part of the state, for any term exceeding sixty days, shall be confined in the House of Detention.

Art. 17. While imprisonment for debt continues to be authorized by the laws of the state, it must be regulated by the CIVIL LAW, and this Code contains no other provision in relation to it than that contained in the following article.

Art. 18. No person shall be imprisoned in any of the three places of confinement directed to be provided by this chapter, in pursuance of a final judgment, or for want of bail, in a civil suit.

CHAPTER II.

Of the construction of the different places of confinement.

Art. 19. The House of Detention shall be so constructed as to keep in four divisions, entirely separate the one division from the other, the prisoners comprehended in the following classes :

1. The first class shall consist of the male persons described in the first, second, third, and fourth numbers of the enumeration contained in the second article of the preceding section.

2. The second class shall consist of female prisoners of the above description.

3. The third class shall consist of male persons committed for trial on an accusation of CRIME.

4. And the fourth class shall consist of female prisoners confined for trial on an accusation of CRIME.

Art. 20. This building must also contain separate accommodations for each individual of the third and fourth classes, and for each of the persons who shall be sentenced to simple imprisonment in close custody ; and two enclosed yards—the one for the male and the other for the female prisoners of the other classes, in which they may take exercise and pursue such employment as is hereby permitted.

Art. 21. The Penitentiary shall be so constructed as to contain :

1. Cells for those sentenced to solitary confinement for murder.

2. Ranges of separate cells, one for each convict, with an enclosed court for each cell.

3. A hydraulic or other machine, to be put in operation by manual labour, so disposed that a convenient number of prisoners may work at it, separated from each other by a wall.

4. School-rooms sufficient for the instruction of a class of persons.

5. An infirmary.

6. All other necessary buildings for the safe-keeping and support of the prisoners, and for the preservation of their health.

Art. 22. The Penitentiary shall also have a separate enclosure, containing similar cells for female convicts, so disposed as to prevent all means of communication with the male convicts.

Art. 23. The School of Reform shall contain :

1. Separate divisions for the sexes.

2. A separate dormitory for each prisoner.

3. Proper courts or shops for the employment of the prisoners.

4. A school-room for each division.

5. An infirmary.

Art. 24. Each of the three places of confinement described in this section shall be so constructed as to be separate from the others ; and if for the convenience of building they should be contained in the same outer wall or enclosure, they must be so arranged as to give the prisoners in the one no means of communication with those in any other.

Art. 25. All the prisons must be so constructed as to be at all times completely ventilated, and in winter warmed by flues communicating with the different cells.

TITLE II.

OF THE OFFICERS AND ATTENDANTS OF THE SEVERAL PLACES OF
CONFINEMENT AND THEIR SEVERAL DUTIES.

CHAPTER I.

Of the appointment of the officers.

Art. 26. There shall be appointed by the governor, for the several places of confinement before mentioned, the following officers and attendants :

Art. 27. For the House of Detention, a warden and a matron. The warden, with the approbation of the inspectors hereinafter mentioned, shall name so many under-keepers, and the matron, with the like approbation, so many assistants, as by the inspectors shall be deemed necessary for the safe-keeping of the persons committed to their charge, and for the necessary attendance on them.

Art. 28. For the Penitentiary, a warden, a matron, a teacher, a physician, two chaplains, and a clerk.

Art. 29. The warden and matron shall respectively appoint so many assistants as the inspectors shall deem necessary.

Art. 30. For the School of Reform, a warden, a matron, and a female teacher ; and the keeper and matron shall respectively appoint so many assistants as the inspectors shall deem necessary.

Art. 31. The physician and the chaplains appointed for the Penitentiary shall also attend the two other places of confinement ; and the teacher of the Penitentiary shall instruct such of the persons confined in the House of Detention as choose to receive lessons, at such times as shall be directed by the inspectors.

CHAPTER II.

Of the board of inspectors and their duties.

Art. 32. The governor shall appoint five persons to form a board of inspectors.

Art. 33. The duties of the inspectors shall be to visit the House of Detention, the Penitentiary, and the School of Reform, at least once in every week, to see that the duties of the several officers and attendants are performed—to prevent all oppression, peculation, or other abuse, in the management of the several institutions; and to report to the legislature such means as may suggest themselves for their improvement.

Art. 34. They shall also, with the approbation of the governor, form rules for the government of the several places of confinement and the employment of the persons confined therein, not inconsistent with this Code. They shall direct the purchase of all implements and materials for the manufactures carried on therein, and the sale of the articles manufactured which are not wanted for the use of the prisoners, and they shall direct the manner in which all purchases of provisions and other supplies for the prisoners shall be made.

Art. 35. The inspectors shall cause accurate accounts to be kept in separate sets of books of all expenditures and receipts in each of the places of confinement.

Art. 36. They shall, on or before the first day of December, in every year, make a report in writing to the legislature, of the state of the said places of confinement and of the House of Refuge. The report shall contain the name, age, sex, place of residence and nativity, time of commitment, term of imprisonment, profession or trade prior to commitment, and employment in prison, of each person who has been committed during the preceding year to either of the said places of confinement : noticing also those who may have escaped, or died, or who were pardoned, or discharged, designating the offence for which the commitment was made, and whether for a first or repeated offence, and when and in what court, or by whose order ; and in such return the inspectors shall make such observations and give such information as they may deem expedient for making the said institutions effectual in the punishment and reformation of offenders.

Art. 37. The inspectors have power to examine any person on oath, relative to any abuse in the said places of confinement, or other matter within the purview of their duties.

Art 38. They have power to make rules for the preservation of prison discipline and for promoting industry, morals, and education, in the said several institutions, which shall not be contrary to any provisions of this Code or of other law, and to impose and cause to be inflicted the punishments they shall have ordained for the breach of such rules, and for all such infractions of prison discipline, as are made punishable by this Code.

Art. 39. They shall direct in what manner the rations for the subsistence of the prisoners shall be composed, in conformity with the general directions on that subject hereinafter contained.

Art. 40. They shall also perform such duties as are required of them in the subsequent parts of this Code.

Art. 41. Each inspector shall have the right to visit and inspect the said places of confinement and the House of Refuge whenever he shall deem it expedient ; and the keepers, wardens, clerks, and other officers of the several prisons are bound to submit to them, or either of them, whenever called on, the books, papers, and accounts, belonging to the prisons, to which such officers belong, and to admit them to the prisoners therein confined.

Art. 42. It is the duty of the inspectors to call at least once in every three months upon the proper officers of each place of confinement for an exhibition of the accounts, to examine the same, and compare the entries with the vouchers; to examine the persons employed in the said places of confinement on oath, whenever it shall be deemed necessary, and to report any abuses or oppressions that may come to their knowledge, to the governor, if any of the officers appointed by him are implicated therein, or themselves to reprimand or dismiss any other person employed when it is found necessary.

Art. 43. The inspectors in their weekly visits to the several places of confinement shall speak to each person confined therein; shall listen to any complaints that may be made of oppression or ill conduct of the persons so employed; examine into the truth thereof, and proceed therein according to the directions of the last preceding article when the complaint is well founded; and on such visits they shall have the actual calendar of the prisoners furnished to them by the warden, and see by actual inspection whether all the prisoners named in the said calendar are found in the said prison in the situation in which by the said calendar they are declared to be.

Art. 44. They shall also hear and determine all charges of breach of prison discipline that shall be reported against any prisoner, when the punishment to be inflicted is close confinement for more than twenty-four hours.

Art. 45. A majority of the said inspectors shall constitute a board, and may do any of the acts required of the said inspectors by this Code. Two of the inspectors shall be a quorum for the weekly visitations hereby directed to be made.

Art. 46. The governor, the president of the senate, the speaker of the house of representatives, the mayor of the city of New Orleans, the judges of the supreme court, of the criminal court, and of the first district, the attorney-general, and the directors of the Asylum for Orphan Boys, are authorized to attend the meetings of the inspectors, to take part in their deliberations, but not to vote, to attend their weekly inspections ; and each of the persons undermentioned may do any act which the said inspectors individually are authorized to perform.

Art. 47. Each of the directresses of the Poydrass Asylum, and the members of any female society that shall be formed for that purpose, are permitted and requested to exercise all the powers and perform all the duties with respect to the female prisoners in either of the establishments, that any individual inspector is hereby authorized to perform.

Art. 48. Each inspector shall receive for every day's attendance in the performance of the duties required by this act the sum of   dollars, provided the same shall not amount, in any one year, to more than dollars.

Art. 49. It is made the important and special duty of the inspectors, in their individual or joint visits to the convicts, to enter into friendly conversation with them, to impress on their minds the importance of moral and religious instruction, of industry, and orderly conduct, to encourage them to a perseverance in this course by a promise of aid and patronage, in the manner hereinafter directed on their discharge.

Art. 50. The inspectors shall have power to make contracts for the labour of the convicts in the Penitentiary and School of Reform with such mechanics as will teach them a useful trade, under the restrictions prescribed in the title concerning the treatment of the convicts.

Art. 51. No inspector, nor any officer or other person employed in any of the said places of confinement, shall sell any article for the use of either of them, or of the persons confined therein during their confinement, or shall purchase any of the manufactures made therein, or derive any emolument from such purchase or sale either to himself or to any relation in the ascending or descending line, or any collateral within the third degree, other than such emolument as is hereinafter expressly allowed ; and any offender against this provision shall be fined five hundred dollars and imprisoned in close custody thirty days.

Art. 52. No work shall be performed nor any article manufactured by any of the prisoners for the use of any of the inspectors or officers of either of the prisons, or of any of the attendants employed therein, or for the use of the families of either of them ; nor shall they or either of them receive, under any pretence whatever, from either of the said prisoners, or anyone on his behalf, any sum of money or gift of any assignable value, under the penalty of five hundred dollars fine, and six months' imprisonment in close custody.

Art. 53. The inspectors have power, in case of the necessary and temporary absence or disability of either of the wardens, or of any of the officers employed in either of the prisons, to employ a substitute during such absence or disability ; which substitute shall, for the time being, perform all the duties, have all the authority, and be liable to all the penalties as the officer himself.

CHAPTER III.

Of the duties common to the wardens of the Penitentiary, House of Detention, and of the School of Reform.

Art. 54. Each of the said wardens shall reside in the prison over which he presides.

Art. 55. Each of them shall visit every cell and apartment, and see every prisoner under his care, at least once every day, and when he visits the female prisoners, he shall be accompanied by the matron.

Art. 56. They shall each keep a journal, in which shall be regularly entered the reception, discharge, death, pardon, or escape, of any prisoner ; and also, the complaints that are made and the punishments that are inflicted for the breach of prison discipline. as they occur, the visits of the inspectors, the chaplain, and the physician, and all other occurrences of note that concern the state of the prison, except the receipts and expenditures, the account of which are to be kept in the manner hereinafter directed.

Art. 57. On the commitment of a prisoner accused of CRIME in the House of Detention, and when convicted of a crime on his entrance in the Penitentiary or School of Reform, there shall be entered on the journal the sex, age, apparent height, and accurate description of the person, last place of abode, and nativity of the prisoner.

Art. 58. On the death of any prisoners, the warden shall immediately give notice to the board of inspectors, and shall take the measures directed by the Code of Procedure for summoning a jury of inquest.

Art. 59. The wardens shall severally make a report in writing to the governor every six months of all the persons in custody, specifying the times of commitment and discharge, by pardon or expiration of sentence, or acquittal, and the escape or death and removal from the one prison to another of each person who has been in their custody, severally, during the preceding six months, together with the general state of the prison, and such observations and information as the warden may think necessary, or as the governor or inspectors shall direct.

Art. 60. The wardens shall appoint the under-keepers, and dismiss them at their pleasure.

Art. 61. They shall see that the duties required by this Code in their respective prisons are performed by the several officers thereof, and shall report any default both to the governor and to the board of inspectors.

Art. 62. The wardens severally have power to arrest and conduct before a magistrate for commitment any person who shall make himself liable to any penalty under this Code.

Art. 63. Each warden shall put up in every apartment and cell of the prison under his care a printed copy of the rules for the government thereof, and shall cause them to be explained to those who cannot read or are unable to understand them.

Art. 64. He shall report all infractions of the rules to the inspectors, and with the approbation of one of them, may punish the offender in the manner directed in the chapter concerning the treatment of prisoners.

Art. 65. No warden shall absent himself from the prison under his care for a night, without permission, in writing, from one of the inspectors, or in the execution of some duty that requires such absence, or by reason of some unforeseen accident which renders it necessary; and whenever such accident occurs, it is to be noted on the journal.

Art. 66. The warden shall not be present when the inspectors make their stated visits to the prisoners under his care.

Art. 67. The further duties and powers of the wardens in their respective prisons, are detailed in the chapter relative to the reception and treatment of prisoners, and in other parts of this Code.

CHAPTER IV.

Of the duty of the under-keepers in the Penitentiary and House of Detention.

Art. 68. The under-keepers must be men of sobriety, honesty, and industry. They must understand reading, writing, the first rules of arithmetic, and must speak, for the common purposes of life, the French and English languages.

Art. 69. It is the duty of the under-keepers to visit each prisoner three times in every day, to see that his meals are regularly delivered according to the prison allowance; to set those to work who are permitted or condemned to labour; and to see that they are instructed therein, according to the rules established by this Code, and to the further directions of the warden.

Art. 70. Whenever any convict shall complain of such illness as to require medical aid, the under-keeper shall immediately give notice to the physician.

Art. 71. Each under-keeper shall have a certain number of prisoners assigned to his care.

Art. 72. He shall make a daily report to the warden of the health, conduct, and industry of the prisoners, and a like report to the inspectors when required.

Art. 73. No under-keeper shall be present when the warden or the inspector visits the prisoners under his particular care.

Art. 74. The under-keepers shall obey all legal orders given by the warden for the government of the prison. They shall be removable by him at pleasure; and by the inspectors on proof of ill conduct in their offices. All orders to the under-keepers must be given through or by the warden.

Art. 75. They must remain in the prison night and day, and shall not be employed either by the warden or the inspectors in any other place. They shall not absent themselves without permission from the warden.

Art. 76. The under-keepers shall act also as guards; for which purpose arms and munitions shall be provided by the state, to be put into their hands by the warden when they are on guard, and at other times when circumstances require it; but in their daily occupations they are not to be armed.

Art. 77. No under-keeper shall receive from any one confined in either of the said prisons, or from any one in behalf of such prisoner, any emolument or reward whatever, or the promise of any, either for services or supplies, or as a gratuity; under the penalty of fine of one hundred dollars and imprisonment for thirty days; and when any breach of this article shall come to the knowledge of the warden or inspectors, the under-keepers offending shall be immediately discharged.

Art. 78. The compensation of the under-keepers shall be

CHAPTER V.

Of the duties of the chaplains.

Art. 79. The chaplains shall be, the one a clergyman of the Catholic church, the other of some one of the Protestant persuasions; each shall receive a salary of   .

Art. 80. The Catholic chaplain shall, at least twice in every week, visit every person of his own persuasion in the Penitentiary and School of Reform, and such persons as are confined in the House of Detention in close custody.

Art. 81. The Protestant chaplain shall, in like manner, perform the same duty to all the prisoners who are of any Protestant persuasion.

Art. 82. It is the duty of both to instruct the prisoners under their care in the duties of religion and morality; to exhort them to repentance and amendment; to show the folly and danger of vice; and to encourage those who are confined for a term of years with the hope of being reinstated in the good opinion of the world by a perseverance in the principles of honesty and the practice of industry; to impress on their minds that it is not their punishment but their crime that has degraded them, and that sincere repentance and amendment may cause both to be forgotten by man, as the sin will surely be forgiven by God. To those sentenced to confinement for life, they must hold out no fallacious hope of pardon, but teach them to fix their hopes on another world, and prepare for it by contrition and repentance.

Art. 83. The Catholic chaplain shall have free access to the cells of all the Catholic convicts; and the Protestant chaplain to those of the Protestant convicts; and either of them to the cell of any convict of any religion who requests it.

Art. 84. Any clergyman of any religion or religious sect may be admitted to see any convict who may require his attendance, or at his own request, at proper and reasonable hours, under the direction of the warden or inspectors.

Art. 85. The chaplains shall be furnished with forms of returns which shall contain the names of the prisoners, with blank columns, in which shall be entered by the chaplain the date of each visit he shall pay, and opposite to each name the observations he may make on the character and demeanour of the convict with respect to his moral and religious improvement.

Art. 86. Each of the said chaplains shall perform divine service at least once on every Sunday in the School of Reform.

Art. 87. Selections from Scriptures, and such other books of religious and moral instruction as shall be recommended by the chaplains and approved by the inspectors, shall be distributed among the convicts.

CHAPTER VI.

Of the qualifications of the teachers, and the duties of the teacher of the Penitentiary.

Art. 88. The teachers must be men of good moral characters ; they must understand the French and English languages, and be capable of teaching reading, writing, arithmetic, book-keeping, navigation, and land-surveying. They need not reside in the prison.

Art. 89. The teacher of the Penitentiary for the first six months after the convict shall be confined therein must attend at the cells and working courts of all the male convicts who cannot read and write, and give separate lessons, in turn, to as many of them as his time will permit, calculating seven hours in each day, on every day, Sundays included.

Art. 90. At the end of the said six months he may form classes, not exceeding eight in each class, of such of the convicts as shall have obtained favourable certificates of conduct during that period, as to industry, morality, and order, from the warden and chaplain, which class he shall assemble, at least, once in every two days, in the school-room for instruction for the space of one hour.

Art. 91. No convict shall be admitted into a class until after he has obtained such certificate, and shall be degraded therefrom for misconduct for a greater or less interval, according to the nature of the offence and the sentence of the inspectors.

Art. 92. Those convicts who can write and read, but who are desirous of instruction in any of the other branches taught by the teacher, may also be instructed in their cells after three months' good behaviour, certified as aforesaid, and may be admitted into a class on a like certificate of six months.

Art. 93. Convicts condemned to imprisonment for life cannot be admitted into a class. They may receive such instruction, if they need and deserve it, as will enable them to read; but it must be given in their cells or courts.

Art. 94. The teacher shall make rules for the preservation of discipline and order in the several classes, which he shall submit to the inspectors and the warden, and, if approved by them, shall be in force; but no punishment shall be inflicted greater than those directed by the rules established in this Code.

Art. 95. The individuals who are to compose the different classes shall be designated by the teacher with the approbation of the inspectors, after they shall have consulted the warden.

Art. 96. One rule of the instruction by classes shall be that no conversation shall be permitted between the individuals composing it on any other subject than that relating to the art or science in which they are instructed; and, to enforce this rule, it is made the duty of the teacher never to leave the class while they, or any two of the individuals composing it, are assembled.

Art. 97. The individuals composing the class shall be conducted by an under-keeper separately to and from the place of instruction, and shall not, on any pretence whatever, be suffered to speak to any one by the way.

Art. 98. The teacher may, with the approbation of the inspectors, select one or more of the convicts of sufficient instruction and ability, who has been committed for a term of years, to assist in the duties of his office, provided no person shall be selected who has not a certificate of good behaviour for at least two years, both from the chaplain and warden; and until the expiration of the said two years, and until such selection shall be made, the inspectors are authorized, if they deem it necessary, to employ such assistant, at a salary not exceeding two-thirds of that given to the principal teacher.

Art. 99. If any convict shall have, prior to his commitment, cultivated any of the arts of painting, sculpture, or architecture, as a profession, or, in the opinion of the inspectors, shall have a decided genius for either of them, he shall, after obtaining a certificate of six months' good behaviour, be permitted to employ a portion of the time allotted for labour, not exceeding one hour in each day, to his improvement therein ; and   per cent. of his earnings, after paying for his support, shall, if he request it, be appropriated to the purchase of implements and materials for the business ; provided, that this indulgence shall be suspended or forfeited, at the direction of the inspectors, by any breach of the rules of the prison.

Art. 100. Convicts committed for a term of years, who cannot read, write and cipher, may be punished, by order of the inspectors or the warden, for refusing to receive instruction therein. All other scientific instruction is an indulgence to be obtained only by a perseverance in good behaviour.

Art. 101. The female convicts who are uninstructed in reading and writing and the first rules of arithmetic, shall be taught by the matron, or such assistant as the inspectors may direct, and at such hours as they shall appoint.

CHAPTER VII.

Of the duties of the teacher of the School of Reform.

Art. 102. The teacher of the School of Reform must possess the same qualifications that are required in the teacher in the Penitentiary.   He need not reside in the establishment.

Art. 103. He shall instruct the male and female departments of the School of Reform in the several branches of learning, at the times and in the manner prescribed for that purpose in the chapter of this Code relative to instruction in the School of Reform.

Art. 104. He shall receive a yearly salary of dollars.

CHAPTER VIII.

Of the duties of the physician.

Art. 105. The physician shall visit every prisoner in the prisons twice in every week, and oftener if the state of their health requires it, and shall report once in every month to the inspectors.

Art. 106. He shall attend immediately on notice from the warden or keeper that any person is sick.

Art. 107. He shall examine every prisoner that shall be brought into the Penitentiary and School of Reform before he shall be confined in his cell.

Art. 108. Whenever, in the opinion of the physician, any convict in the Penitentiary or School of Reform is so ill as to require removal, the warden shall direct such removal to the infirmary of the institution in which he is confined ; and the prisoner shall be kept in the infirmary until the physician shall certify that he may be removed without injury to his health, and he shall then be removed to his cell.

Art. 109. He shall visit the patients in the infirmary at least once in every day, and he shall give such directions for the health and cleanliness of the prisoners as he may deem expedient, which the warden shall have executed, provided they shall not be contrary to the provisions of this Code, or inconsistent with the safe custody of the said prisoners ; and the directions he may give, whether complied with or not, shall be entered on the journal of the warden and on his own.

Art. 110. The physician shall inquire into the mental as well as the bodily state of every prisoner ; and when he shall have reason to believe that the mind or body is materially affected by the discipline, treatment, or diet, he shall inform the warden thereof, and shall enter his observations on the journal, hereinafter directed to be kept, which shall be an authority for the warden for altering the discipline, treatment, or diet, of any prisoner until the next meeting of the inspectors, who shall inquire into the case, and make orders accordingly.

Art. 111. He shall have power to cause any one infected by a contagious or infectious disorder to be separated from the other prisoners ; and if three other licensed practitioners of physic shall certify that the disease is infectious, and that the prisoner cannot, without danger to the others, be kept within the walls of the prison, the inspectors shall make an order for his removal and confinement elsewhere until he shall die or recover.

Art. 112. The physician shall keep a journal, in which, opposite to the name of each prisoner, shall be entered the state of his health ; and if sick, whether in the infirmary or not, together with such remarks as he may deem important ; which journal shall be open to the inspection of the warden and the inspectors ; and the same, together with the return provided for in the first article of this section, shall be laid before the inspectors, once in every month, or oftener if called for.

Art. 113. The prisoners, under the care of the physician, shall be allowed such diet as he shall direct.

Art. 114. No prisoner shall be discharged while labouring under a dangerous disease, although entitled to his discharge, unless by his own desire.

Art. 115. The infirmary shall have a partition between every two beds, and no two patients shall occupy the same bed; and the physician and his attendants shall take every precaution in their power to prevent all intercourse between the convicts while in the infirmary.

Art. 116. The physician shall select from among the young delinquents in the School of Reform two or more who have given evidence, to the satisfaction of the warden, the teacher, and the chaplain, of determination to reform, and who shall have made sufficient progress in their education, as his assistants in the two infirmaries, to whom he shall teach the art of compounding and administering remedies, and such other branches of medical knowledge as they may be capable of acquiring; which assistants shall be employed in the care and attendance on the sick, and shall be exempt from all other labour while they preserve the confidence of the physician, and are guilty of no breach of the rules of prison discipline.

CHAPTER IX.

Of the duties of the clerk of the Penitentiary.

Art. 117. The clerk shall, under the direction of the inspectors, keep regular accounts of all the expenses of the Penitentiary, of the proceeds of the articles manufactured therein, and of the purchase of materials to keep the convicts employed, when they do not work by contract, as is hereinafter provided. He shall also open an account with each convict, in which such convict shall be charged with the cost of his prosecution and conviction, and with his maintenance in prison, including only his food and clothing and such drugs and medicines as he may be supplied with ; and shall be credited with his labour at such estimation of its value as shall be equitable, according to its quantity and quality, agreeable to the rates paid for like labour in the city of New Orleans ; or (when he works by contract) according to the contract price of such labour.

Art. 118. The inspectors shall direct the mode in which the accounts shall be kept, and shall direct the agent they shall employ for making purchases and for selling the articles manufactured in the Penitentiary (which agent shall in no case be the clerk), to furnish the clerk with accounts and bills of all such purchases and sales.

Art. 119. The clerk shall deliver to the agent all such articles manufactured in the prison as are not done for manufacturers by contract, and which are not wanted for the use of the same, keeping an account as well of what is so wanted and retained, as of what is delivered.

Art. 120. The books of accounts shall be kept in the prison, and shall be open to the inspection of the warden and the inspectors.

Art. 121. The clerk shall keep a regular account of all the furniture, tools, and implements of trade provided for the prison, and shall submit the same to the inspectors.

Art. 122. He shall receive such remuneration for his services as shall be determined by the inspectors, not exceeding   dollars per annum.

CHAPTER X.

Of the duties of the matrons.

Art. 123. The matrons shall reside in their respective prisons. They and their female assistants shall, under the direction of the inspectors, have the exclusive care and superintendence of the female convicts. No male person, except the chaplain, shall be permitted to visit them but in the presence of the matron.

Art. 124. She shall employ them in making, mending, and washing the clothing for the prisoners. She shall cause them to be taught needle-work and other employments of housewifery, keeping them all apart at night, and as much as the nature of their employment will allow during the day. She shall report daily to the warden all infractions of order, or other material occurrence; and shall inflict such punishment, consistent with this Code, as the inspectors and teacher shall direct.

BOOK II.

OF THE TREATMENT OF THE PRISONERS IN THE SEVERAL PLACES OF CONFINEMENT.

TITLE I.

OF THE PRISONERS CONFINED IN THE HOUSE OF DETENTION.

Art. 125. The prisoners of the first class, that is to say, those confined in order to secure their attendance as witnesses, shall be under no other restriction than that which is absolutely necessary to prevent their escape from the prison. Good and wholesome food, comfortable bedding, and other necessaries, shall be provided for them at the public expense; or they may be allowed to provide it for themselves; and every such prisoner shall be immediately liberated on his giving the security for his appearance to testify that is required by law.

Art. 126. Those who are committed for want of bail, in the first district, on an accusation of misdemeanor:

Those who are condemned to simple imprisonment (not in close custody), in the first district, or who are removed on a like sentence from any other district:

Those who may be committed for the non-payment of a fine, or for the breach of a recognizance, or other engagement, entered into in the course of a prosecution for an offence:

Form a second class of prisoners. They need not be separated from each other during the day, but each shall be lodged at night in separate dormitories, unless the numbers in the prison shall render it impossible.

Art. 127. Those who are committed for want of bail on accusations of crime, form a third class. These shall be kept in separate cells or apartments both night and day, and shall have no communication whatever with each other.

Art. 128. All the above classes of prisoners shall be entitled to good wholesome food and drink, according to the prison regulations hereinafter provided for, and to beds and bedding, at the public expense ; or they shall be permitted to purchase or receive such food and beds, of a better quality, at their own expense, also under the restrictions contained under the prison regulations.

They may receive the visits of their families and friends, and their counsel, at all reasonable hours.

They shall be allowed the free use of books, of pen, ink, and paper, at their own expense.

Art. 129. The prisoners sentenced to close confinement shall each be confined in a separate apartment or cell, furnished with the prison allowance of bedding, and a chair and a table ; but may provide their own bedding if they think fit. They shall be restricted to the prison allowance of drink and food, unless the court shall order differently in the sentence, or the physician shall officially certify that their health will be impaired by confining them to it.

They shall not be permitted to receive any society in their places of confinement without permission of two of the inspectors in writing, and the time of such visit shall be prescribed and limited in the permission, and shall in no case exceed one hour at a time.

They shall not be debarred the privilege of consulting with their counsel, or receiving the visits of their physician and chaplain, at all reasonable times.

Art. 130. No prisoner in this house shall be forced to perform any labour. No prisoner shall be confined in irons ; but if he shall have made an attempt to break the prison, or have assaulted the keeper or other person employed in the house, he may be confined in a straight-jacket or arm straps.

Art. 131. All the prisoners in this house may be permitted to work at such trades and manufactures as they may desire and may be deemed by the inspectors proper to be carried on in the house, without infringing the rules hereinbefore laid down; and the inspectors shall provide the tools and implements, and the materials for carrying on such manufacture as they may deem expedient, and shall allow to such of the prisoners as may choose to work thereat three-fourths of the net proceeds of their labour, and shall pay the same as it is earned to the prisoner; the other fourth shall be deposited in bank in the manner hereinafter directed.

Art. 132. The daily allowance of food to a prisoner in the house of detention shall be the same as is allowed to a soldier in the army of the United States. The bedding shall be the same as is directed for the prisoners in the Penitentiary.

Art. 133. The inspectors shall make prison regulations for the preservation of order in the House of Detention, not inconsistent with this Code, and for the supply of food and other accommodations to such of the persons detained as are allowed to procure the same at their own expense; but no wine or spirituous liquors shall be introduced but by order of the physician, stating that the health of the party, in whose favour it is given, requires it.

TITLE II.

OF THE TREATMENT OF THE PRISONERS IN THE PENITENTIARY.

CHAPTER I.

Of the reception of the convicts.

Art. 134. Every convict sentenced to imprisonment in the Penitentiary shall, immediately after the sentence shall have been finally pronounced, be conveyed, by the sheriff of the parish in which he was condemned, to the Penitentiary, under secure guard; and when it shall be deemed necessary, the officer commanding the regiment of the place where the court sits, shall furnish a guard for that purpose, on the order of the court entered on its minutes.

Art. 135. On the arrival of a convict, immediate notice shall be given to the physician, who shall examine the state of his health; he shall then be stripped of his clothes, and clothed in the uniform of the prison that is suited to his offence, in the manner hereinafter provided, being first, if necessary, bathed and cleaned.

Art. 136. The convict shall then be examined by the clerk and the warden, in the presence of as many of the under-keepers as can conveniently attend; and his height, apparent and alleged age, complexion, colour of hair and eyes, and length of his feet, to be accurately measured, shall be entered in a book provided for that purpose, together with such other natural or accidental marks, or peculiarity of feature or appearance, as may serve to identify him ; an instrument shall also be provided by which the profile of his face shall be delineated, and it shall be marked with his name, and pasted in the said book, under the description of his person ; and if the convict can write, his signature shall be placed under the said description of his person.

Art. 137. All the effects on the person of the convict, as well as his clothes, shall be taken from him and specially mentioned, and preserved, to be restored to him on his discharge, or delivered to his curator, where one shall be appointed, pursuant to the provisions hereinafter contained.

Art. 138. If the convict is not in such ill-health as to require being sent to the infirmary, he shall then be conducted to the cell assigned to him, where he shall be kept in solitude for forty-eight hours, interrupted only by the necessary attendance of the keeper ; during this period, designed for reflection, neither books nor employment of any kind shall be allowed him.

Art. 139. On the third day the chaplain shall visit him in his cell, and shall endeavour to impress on his mind as well the wickedness as the danger of vicious and unlawful pursuits, and he shall exhort him to obedience and industry during the term of his service, and urge the utility of acquiring the means of an honest support by labour on his discharge. The warden shall then examine him, and put him to such labour as he shall seem fittest for, consulting his inclinations as well as his physical powers.

CHAPTER II.

Of the labour of the male convicts committed for a term of years.

Art. 140. Although labour forms a part of the sentence, it is annexed as an alleviation, not an aggravation of punishment. The punishment is imprisonment in solitude. All that the law entitles the patient to under this confinement, is food, clothing, and lodging sufficient for the preservation of health, but all of the coarsest kind; his health and life are the objects of attention, not his appetite or comfort. Other indulgences are the reward of industry, obedience, repentance, and reformation; these are the effects of labour; and labour, therefore, is permitted as the means of attaining them.

Art. 141. The advantages that are to be gained by perseverance in labour, obedience, moral conduct, and a desire of reform, are :

1. A better diet.

2. A partial relief from solitude, and the means of education by the visits and lessons of the teacher.

3. Permission to read books of general instruction.

4. The privilege of receiving the visits of friends or relations at proper periods.

5. Admission into a class for instruction, after a period of good conduct that shall evince a sincere desire to reform.

6. The privilege, after a long probation, of labouring in society.

7. A proportion of the proceeds of his labour on his discharge.

8. A certificate of good conduct, industry, and skill, in the trade he has learned, which may enable him to gain the confidence of society.

Art. 142. As these advantages are to be gained only by industry and good conduct, they are suspended and may be forfeited by idleness or irregularity; and at the expiration of the two days given for reflection, after the admission of the convict, the articles of this section are to be read to him, and he shall make his election whether he will avail himself of the indulgence they offer; should he consent, he shall be immediately set to labour; if he refuse, the offer shall not be repeated in less than six days; after the second refusal, it can only be repeated in fifteen days; and after a third, he cannot be permitted to accept it until a month's time shall have elapsed; after which, he shall be considered as having made his final election.

Art. 143. From among the convicts who have not, before commitment, worked at any trade, the warden shall select a sufficient number to perform the offices of cooking and other necessary attendance in the prison. He shall prefer for this purpose those who have the shortest term to serve ; but all these shall be locked up in separate cells at night.

Art. 144. If the convict has been used to any employment or trade that can be advantageously pursued consistent with the system established by this Code, he shall be furnished with the implements of such trade, and be allowed to employ himself at it. If his trade is one that cannot, in the opinion of the inspectors, be conveniently carried on, or is inconsistent with the system, he shall be taught an employment the most analogous to the one to which he has been bred.

Art. 145. If the convict has not been bred to any trade, the warden shall employ him at such business as is best adapted to his habits of life and his strength, consulting as much as possible the inclination of the convict; and in the selection of employment, regard is to be had more to giving him an honest mode of subsistence after his discharge than to the profit of the prison.

Art. 146. The regular occupation of each convict shall, for the first six months of his confinement, be carried on in the outer enclosure of his cell in solitude, interrupted only by the visits of the inspectors, the warden, the chaplain, the teacher, the physician, the person (if any) employed to instruct him in his trade, and the attendants with the regular meals, and by the exercise mentioned in the next article.

Art. 147. For the preservation of the health of the prisoners, each of them shall be made to labour one hour in every day at a handcrank hydraulic machine, or some other, calculated to exert the muscular powers in a manner beneficial to health. This crank, or other parts of the machine to which bodily power is to be applied, shall be so placed and divided, that each prisoner may labour without having it in his power to have any communication with the others employed in the same labour, and they shall be conducted separately to and from the place, under the care of an under-keeper, who shall prevent any person from having any communication with them by word or otherwise.

Art. 148. During the first six months of confinement the teacher shall give to the convicts who cannot read or write, a lesson to each, in regular rotation, employing himself at least seven hours in each day, until a class shall be formed, when he shall divide his time equally between the individual prisoners entitled to instruction and the classes.

Art. 149. At the expiration of six months each convict who has received the lessons of the teacher during that time, and such other convicts as are desirous of receiving further instruction, shall, provided they obtain a certificate of good conduct and industry in labour from the warden, the chaplain, and teacher, have the privilege of being admitted into a class, which shall receive instruction together in the school-room ; but no class shall contain more than eight ; no more than one class shall be assembled at a time, and the individuals composing it shall be conducted separately to and from the place of instruction.

Art. 150. The warden may, when necessary for the instruction of a prisoner in any business or trade, with the permission of the inspectors, employ a person of good character for that purpose, who shall, at proper hours, have access to such prisoner.

Art. 151. The warden may, with the consent of the inspectors, make contracts for the labour of the convicts, or any of them, with mechanics or manufacturers ; but a condition of the contract shall be, that the convicts shall be taught, and employed in, some useful trade ; and for that purpose a foreman or instructor, to be employed by the contractor, but approved by the warden and inspectors, shall be admitted to the enclosures adjoining the cells of the convicts, at convenient times during the hours of labour.

Art. 152. The first contract shall not be for a longer period than eighteen months; and all subsequent contracts shall be made by auction, and for one year; and the applicants for the contract shall be permitted, in the presence of the warden, to examine the convicts as to their skill and ability.

Art. 153. If any contractor or his agent shall give or promise to any of the convicts any article of food, drink, or other article, not permitted by this Code or by the prison regulation, the contract shall be forfeited, and each offender shall pay a fine of five hundred dollars, and be imprisoned not more than thirty, nor less than ten, days in close custody.

Art. 154. After being employed for eighteen months in solitary labour, the convict, if he can procure from the warden, the inspectors, the chaplain, and the teacher (if he have been under his instruction), a certificate of industry, good conduct, and a disposition to reform, may be admitted to a working class, not exceeding ten, to work at some useful trade; but no one shall enjoy this privilege the value of whose labour during the eighteen months shall not have exceeded the expense of his clothing and food, unless he shall have lost by sickness a number of days' labour, of which the value shall be equal to the deficiency in his account.

Art. 155. Each working class shall be separately employed in a different work-shop, without any communication the one class with another, and shall be under the direction of an under-keeper, who shall permit no communication between the individuals composing it but that necessary for the business, and any breach of this rule shall be punished by close confinement for such time as the warden shall direct, and by a return to solitary labour.

Art. 156. At the dawn of day the convict shall be made to rise and to clear out his sleeping cell, which shall then be locked; he shall then, after washing, commence his labour, which shall continue, including the hour for exercise at the machine and the attendance on the teacher and the time of receiving the visits of the other officers, from the rising to half an hour before the setting of the sun every day except Sundays, excepting one hour for breakfast and one hour and a half for dinner, and the supper shall be given when the work of the day is finished.

Art. 157. After sunset and before it is dark, all the convicts shall be locked up in their separate cells.

CHAPTER III.

Of the treatment of prisoners confined for life.

Art. 158. The convicts who are confined for life on a third conviction, for an offence which if it had been the first, would have been punishable by imprisonment for a term of years only, shall, in all respects, be treated like the prisoners confined for a term, except that the prison uniform shall be different, and shall designate by three different colours the number of their offences.

Art. 159. Those convicted of murder without any aggravating circumstances, and for rape, shall be strictly confined to their respective cells and adjoining courts; in which last they may be permitted to labour, except for two months consecutively in every year, commencing on the anniversary of their crime, during which period they shall only come into the court during the time necessary to cleanse the cell; and on the anniversary of the commission of their crime they shall have no allowance of food for twenty-four hours, during which fast they shall receive the visit of the chaplain, who shall endeavour by exhortation and prayer to bring them to repentance.

Art. 160. Murderers of all descriptions and those con-

victed of rape, shall receive no visits except from the
inspectors, the wardens, officers, and attendants of the
prison, and from those who are constituted visitors of the
prison. They shall have no books but selections from
the Bible and such other books of religion and morality
as the chaplain shall deem proper to produce repentance
and fix their reliance on a future state. Their uniform
and diet shall be such as is hereinafter directed.

Art. 161. Infanticides shall be treated in all respects
like those guilty of unaggravated murder, except that
the confinement without labour shall continue three
months consecutively in each year.

Art. 162. Assassins shall be confined without labour
for six months consecutively in every year, and treated in
the manner above directed.

Art. 163. Parricides shall not be indulged in the
performance of labour at any time, but shall be closely
confined in a cell, without a court, but of such dimensions
as shall be sufficient for their health, and in other respects
shall be treated like other murderers.

Art. 164. When any two of the crimes punishable
with imprisonment for life, such as rape and murder, are
combined, or where murder under trust is perpetrated by
assassination, or parricide by poison, the convict shall
receive the same treatment as is directed for parricides,
except that on the return in each month of the day on
which the crime was committed, they be debarred from all
allowance of food for twenty-four hours, and shall,
during such fast, receive the visits and exhortation of the
chaplain.

Art. 165. The fast shall not be suffered when the physician shall certify that it will be dangerous to the health
of the convict.

Art. 166. Those convicts for life who have not learned
to read may be instructed by the teacher.

Art. 167. No murderers, in any degree, shall have any
communication with other persons out of the prison than
the inspectors and visitors; they are considered dead to
the rest of the world.

Art. 168. The cells of murderers (in any degree) shall be painted black within and without, and on the outside thereof shall be inscribed, in large letters, the following sentence :

" In this cell is confined, to pass his life in solitude and sorrow, A. B., convicted of the murder of C. D. [by assassination, parricide, &c., describing the offence, if of an aggravated kind] ; his food is bread of the coarsest kind ; his drink is water, mingled with his tears : he is dead to the world ; this cell is his grave ; his existence is prolonged that he may remember his crime, and repent it, and that the continuance of his punishment may deter others from the indulgence of hatred, avarice, sensuality, and the passions which lead to the crime he has committed. When the Almighty, in His due time, shall exercise towards him that dispensation which he himself arrogantly and wickedly usurped towards another, his body is to be dissected, and his soul will abide that judgment which Divine Justice shall decree."

Art. 169. The same inscription, changing only the words " this cell" for the words " solitary cell in this prison," shall be made on the outside of the prison wall, in large white letters on a black ground. The inscriptions shall be removed on the death of the convicts to which they relate.

Art. 170. Inscriptions shall in like manner be made on the cells of those convicted of rape, and on the outer wall of the prison, to this effect : " In this cell" [or on the outer wall, " In a solitary cell in this prison,] forgotten, or remembered only to be detested and despised, lies A. B., condemned to solitude and abstinence during life, for a cowardly and brutal injury to a woman."

CHAPTER IV.

Of the clothing and diet of the convicts.

Art. 171. The uniform of the prison shall be a jacket and trousers of cloth or other warm stuff for the winter, and lighter materials for the summer. The form and colour shall be determined by the inspectors; but they shall be the same for all criminals condemned for a term, except those who have been convicted of a repetition of offences; these shall have distinctive marks on their dress, showing the number of their convictions.

Art. 172. Each of the convicts shall have such number of coarse linen shirts and trousers of the same material in summer as will be sufficient to give them a change twice in every week; and all shall be provided with other articles of clothing sufficient to preserve health and cleanliness.

Art 173. The convicts for murder shall be clothed in black outer garments, spotted and streaked with red. Those confined for life, for any other crime, shall wear such distinctive marks on their clothing as shall be directed by the inspectors, to designate their respective crimes.

Art. 174. The prison allowance of food is one pound of brown wheaten bread and one pint of mush morning and evening each day; the allowance of bread may be varied by giving three days in the week a pound and a half of Indian corn bread instead of wheaten. Water is the only liquor allowed in the prison ration.

Art. 175. Prisoners who labour and preserve the rules of the prison are allowed, in addition to the prison daily allowance, a gill of molasses, and for four days in the week two pounds of beef or pork without bone, daily, made into six messes, varied from salt to fresh, with vegetables, and for three other days soup.

Art. 176. Those whose labour and industry have entitled them to work in classes, shall also be indulged with a pint of small beer, or cider diluted with water, or a mixture of vinegar and water sweetened with molasses once every day.

Art. 177. No prisoner, while confined to his cell without labour, is to receive any thing but the prison allowance.

Art. 178. No tobacco in any form shall be used by the convicts ; and any one who shall supply them with it, or with wine, or spirituous or intoxicating fermented liquor, shall be fined two hundred dollars, and if an officer, be dismissed.

Art. 179. Any convict whose labour shall exceed the expense of his support, according to the account herein directed to be kept, shall have the privilege of directing one-tenth part thereof to be expended in the purchase of books, to be approved by the inspectors, or such articles, excepting food or liquors, as he may desire, and as may not be inconsistent with the prison rules.

Art. 180. Any convict, other than those convicted of murder or rape, who has been steadily employed for eighteen months, and is guilty of no infraction of the prison discipline, may, once in every six months, receive the visit of any friend or relation, of the same sex, for not more than fifteen minutes, in the presence of a keeper, on a written permission signed by two inspectors.

Art. 181. No person, who is not an official visitor of the prisons, or who has not a written permission from one of them, or from one of the inspectors, is allowed to visit the same. The official visitors are, the governor, president of the senate, members of the general assembly, the secretary of state, the attorney-general, the judges of all the courts in the state, the mayor, recorder, and members of the city council of the city of New Orleans, the directors of all the charitable incorporated societies in the city of New Orleans.

Art. 182. None but the official visitors can have any verbal or written communication with the convicts, nor shall any visitor whatever be permitted to deliver to or receive from any of the convicts any letter or message whatever, or to supply them with any article of any kind, under the penalty of two hundred dollars fine.

Art. 183. It is the duty of any visitor, who shall discover any abuse, infraction of law, or oppression, immediately to make the same known to the board of inspectors, or to the governor, if the inspectors or either of them are implicated.

Art. 184. No male visitor shall visit the female convicts but in the presence of the matron.

CHAPTER V.

Of the treatment of the female convicts.

Art. 185. The female convicts shall, as well as the male, each be lodged in separate cells.

Art. 186. Such of those confined for a term of years as are capable, by their habits or strength, shall be selected by the matron to perform the domestic services of the female division and for the washing of the clothes for the men's department. Those who are so employed shall, during the day, be kept under the inspection of the matron or her assistants, and not suffered to have any conversation but relative to the business in which they are engaged.

Art. 187. The others, not so selected, shall be employed in needlework, spinning, or other suitable occupations. They shall, on receiving the necessary certificate of order and industry from the matron and chaplain, be entitled to the same advantages of education and social labour that are directed for the male convicts. The classes for education and for labour may consist of such number as the matron, with the approbation of the warden or inspectors, shall desire.

Art. 188. The regulations with respect to diet are applicable to the female department, except that the matron may allow to the industrious and orderly, tea for their breakfast, if they prefer it to mush.

Art. 189. The dress for the female convicts shall be regulated by the matron, with the approbation of the inspectors.

Art. 190. Female convicts for life shall be treated in the same manner as the males, but under the direction of the matron.

TITLE III.

OF THE SCHOOL OF REFORM.

CHAPTER I.

Of the persons to be admitted into the school of reform.

Art. 191. All persons under the age of eighteen sentenced to imprisonment and labour (unless for life), and all vagrants under that age and above six years, shall be sent to the School of Reform.

Art. 192. All minors above six and under eighteen years of age, who have no visible means of honest subsistence and are not supported by any friend or relation ; all common beggars within the said age of eighteen ; all females under seventeen years of age, who live by prostitution in a DISORDERLY HOUSE, shall be considered as vagrants under the last article, and may, by order of the mayor of New Orleans, or the parish judge and two other magistrates, be committed to the School of Reform.

Art. 193. All minors above nine and under the age of fifteen, who shall commit an offence of which they shall be acquitted on account of the want of sufficient discretion to know the nature of the offence, may, at the discretion of the court, be committed to the School of Reform.

Art. 194. In like manner a minor, who being accused of a crime shall be acquitted by showing that at the time of the commission thereof he was under the age of nine years, may, at the discretion of the court, be sent to the School of Reform.

Art. 195. In cases of misdemeanor, committed by a minor under eighteen years of age, and punishable by simple imprisonment in close custody, the court may also, at their discretion, send the defendant to the School of Reform.

Art. 196. In exercising the discretion given by the three last preceding articles, the court must consider that the object of the School of Reform is not only to punish by restraint, but to separate the juvenile offender from the association of vice, to afford him the means of education, religious and moral instruction, and instruction in some mechanic art, so as to make him a useful member of society ; and that where, from the circumstances of the case, these objects will probably be attained without committing the defendant to the School of Reform, that this public institution ought not to be so burthened.

CHAPTER II.

Of the mode of reception.

Art. 197. Every one committed to the School of Reform shall be thoroughly cleansed, and clothed in the uniform of the house, which shall be comfortable and adapted to the season.

Art. 198. The name, age, sex, place of nativity of the

person committed, names and place of abode and occupation of his parents, the cause of commitment, and the authority by which it was made, shall be entered in a book specially provided for that purpose by the warden.

Art. 199. The chaplain, or teacher, and the matron (if the person committed be a female), or the warden (if a male), shall interrogate the party as to the course of life he has pursued, and shall make an abstract of his answers in the book above mentioned ; but no other means shall be used, but those of persuasion, to obtain the truth on such interrogatory.

Art. 200. After some time given to solitary reflection, proportioned to the age and degree of depravity of the offender, which shall not exceed, in any case, twelve hours, the advantages of industry, obedience, and attention to instruction, and the certainty of punishment for a contrary course, shall be impressed upon him by the warden, or, if a female, by the matron, and he shall then be instructed and employed as is hereinafter directed.

CHAPTER III.

Of the instruction in the school of reform.

Art. 201. The time of school instruction shall be one hour, to commence at sunrise, and one hour after labour in the afternoon.

Art. 202. The children shall be taught reading and writing in the French and English languages, and arithmetic ; and such of the boys as show an aptitude for learning, in the opinion of the teacher and warden, shall be taught geography, land surveying, and navigation.

Art. 203. Before the instruction begins, select portions of the Scriptures shall be read morning and evening.

Art. 204. Premiums of books and badges of merit shall be given by the warden, on the recommendation of the teachers, to the children who shall show the most diligence and be distinguished for orderly conduct.

Art. 205. A small collection of entertaining and instructive books shall also be provided for the use of those who have badges of merit.

Art. 206. The teacher has no greater power of correction than is given by law in ordinary schools, and it extends only to faults committed in relation to the literary instruction.

Art. 207. No punishment shall be inflicted on any of the females for faults committed in school but by the matron, or in her presence.

Art. 208. The boys and girls shall be taught separately, and the matron, or her assistant, shall always be present during the instruction of the girls.

Art. 209. Examinations of the scholars shall be had once every three months, in the presence of the inspectors and such of the visitors as choose to attend.

Art. 210. The teacher shall use the system of mutual instruction, and shall endeavour to qualify such of the children, of both sexes, as show a particular aptitude, to be themselves teachers according to the same method.

CHAPTER IV.

Of employment in the school of reform.

Art. 211. All the hours between sunrise and sunset that are not hereby appropriated to instruction, to meals, or to relaxation and exercise, must be employed in labour.

Art. 212. The labour to be performed shall be such as, in the opinion of the inspectors, shall be best calculated to procure a subsistence for the prisoners when they shall be restored to liberty.

Art. 213. Each of the boys shall be taught a mechanic art, and for this purpose the warden shall, with the approbation of the inspectors, contract with mechanics to find materials, to send foremen to the prison to superintend their work, and teach them the different trades, paying a reasonable sum for the value of their labour. The necessary tools and implements shall be provided by the institution.

Art. 214. The foremen so employed by the mechanics shall be men of good characters, approved by the inspectors; they shall remain in their respective workshops during the hours of labour, preserve order therein, and keep the boys at work, teaching them carefully all the branches of the trade; but they shall inflict no punishment, unless by direction of the warden and in his presence, and such punishment shall be such moderate correction as a master is authorized by law to inflict on an apprentice.

Art. 215. The foreman shall make daily reports to the warden of each boy under his care, for which purpose he shall keep a calendar containing the names of each of them, on which he shall make marks, denoting offences, or extraordinary diligence, or good conduct, which shall be shown daily to the warden.

Art. 216. Great care should be taken to suit the employment to the physical force and constitution of each boy; and the warden shall frequently visit the workshops, and see that unreasonable tasks are not imposed by the foreman.

Art. 217. If no such contract should be offered for the labour of the boys as the warden and inspectors shall deem advantageous, proper persons may be employed by the inspectors to instruct them in some mechanic art.

Art. 218. Besides the mechanic arts the boys shall be exercised for two periods in each day (not exceeding half an hour each time) in some laborious employment, that shall require as much as possible the exercise of all the muscular powers, to strengthen and fit them for any hard labour to which they may afterwards be called; for this purpose a hydraulic or other machine, to be moved by manual labour, shall be constructed in the enclosure of the School of Reform, and a mast, with yards and standing and running rigging, shall be erected, on which they shall be taught to climb, and prepare themselves for a seafaring life.

Art. 219. The treadmill shall not be introduced into this or any other of the places of confinement established by this Code.

Art. 220. The girls shall be taught needle-work, and be employed in washing, ironing, baking, and other works of housewifery ; and they may also be taught such trades as women are usually employed in, at the time and place in which they are confined. The matron shall superintend this part of their employment, and none but female instructors in any branch, except the school-master, shall be admitted into their department.

Art. 221. The children of both sexes shall, by turns, be employed in the menial service of the establishment to which they belong—waiting at the table, cleaning the workshops and eating-rooms, and other places for the common resort of persons confined ; but each one is bound to sweep and clean his own cell.

CHAPTER V.

Of the distribution of time in the school of reform.

Art. 222. At the dawn of day all the prisoners, except those in the infirmary and those confined to solitude for a breach of prison discipline, shall leave their cells ; each one shall put up his bed, remove everything that ought to be removed, and sweep the cell, which shall be locked.

Art. 223. Each one shall then wash, and twice every week, when the weather will permit, shall bathe. They shall then assemble in the school-room, when a select portion of scripture and prayers shall be read ; the school shall then be opened, and the instruction continue for one hour; immediately after which breakfast shall be served.

Art. 224. After breakfast half an hour shall be allowed for exercise in the court, but always in the presence of the warden, or some officer of the establishment for the boys, or of the matron or her assistant for the girls; immediately after the expiration of this half hour, the boys shall be put to labour, for another half hour, on the machine mentioned in the last preceding chapter, and the girls be allowed to continue their exercise.

Art. 225. The boys shall then be conducted to the workshops, where they shall be employed for three hours and a half; at the expiration of which time they shall wash and go to dinner, and after dinner shall have another half hour for exercise, and labour on the machine, and then be employed in the shops until an hour before sunset, when they shall again assemble for instruction in the school for an hour; after the evening school, half an hour shall be given for exercise, and then each one shall be locked in his separate cell.

Art. 226. In the summer the inspectors may dispense with the hard labour in the heat of the day, and appropriate it to instruction or relaxation, at their discretion.

Art. 227. On the certificate of the physician, that the labour, or any part of it, cannot be undergone by any one of the persons confined without danger to his health, it shall be remitted or modified by the warden.

CHAPTER VI.

Of diet, lodging, and clothing.

Art. 228. The diet shall be, for breakfast, coffee made of parched grain, and mush alternately, both sweetened with molasses, and corn bread; for dinner, beef or mutton soup, with vegetables and corn bread, and a quarter of a pound of the flesh of which the soup is made, for each, for four days in the week—three days fish or pease soup without meat ; supper, the same as the breakfast.   At all the meals there must be bread of sufficient quantity to satisfy their hunger ; and when the state of the market will permit, wheat bread may be substituted for corn. Water is the only drink allowed.

Art. 229. The inspectors may, when circumstances require it, change the ration of food, but it must always be coarse, but abundant and nutritive.

Art. 230. Each of the persons confined shall lodge in a separate cell, shut with a door having grates at the top and bottom, which, in cold weather, the occupant may cover with a sliding shutter, on the inside.   The cell shall contain a box for a night-pan, and a sheet of canvas, stretched by loops at the four corners and suspended by hooks in the corners of the cell for a hammock, with sheets and one blanket for summer, and two blankets and a corn-husk mat in winter.   This bedding shall be aired and washed at such periods as the physician or warden shall direct.

Art. 231. For the boys the clothing shall consist of a cap, a shirt and jacket and trousers of coarse linen or cotton, and shoes, for the summer ; a jacket and trousers of cloth, with socks and shoes, for the winter ; the linen to be changed once a week in winter and twice a week in summer.   The clothing for the girls shall be directed by the matron with the approbation of the inspectors.

CHAPTER VII.

Of the police of the school of reform.

Art. 232.   The warden shall see that every one confined in the male department, excepting those in the infirmary, is locked up in his separate cell, at the time for that purpose before designated, and that all fires in every part of the building are extinguished. No light, under any pretence, is permitted in the cells ; but lights shall be kept during the night in the galleries and passages leading to them.

Art. 233. A reflected light may be thrown into the cells of such as may desire to use the interval between the locking of the cell and nine at night in reading or study, but it shall be continued in favour of those only who can show the teacher on the following morning that they have used it to advantage.

Art. 234. A watch shall be kept at night by one of the under-keepers, and the warden may also employ with the keeper such of the boys, by turns, as may show by their conduct that such confidence may be reposed in them.

Art. 235. The roll shall be called of all the persons confined at the opening of the school in the morning, and at night previous to the retiring ; and the names of all those employed in the different workshops shall also be called at the hours of labour.

Art. 236. The meals shall be taken in the presence of the warden or some other officer of the establishment. The males shall be divided into classes of ten, who shall be seated at separate tables, and one of the boys, the most distinguished for his orderly conduct, in each class, to be called the captain of the class, shall preside at each table ; he shall see that silence is observed during the meal, shall designate two of the class, by regular rotation, to wait on the others, and take care that each one receives his full allowance, and he shall report all breaches of order to the warden.

Art. 237. The captain of the class may be degraded for negligence or misbehaviour ; and where several boys in a class are equally deserving, they shall have the distinction by turns weekly.

Art. 238. During the hours of recreation, no sports but those which exercise the body shall be allowed, and no wagering permitted ; but the warden may award prizes for dexterity or skill.

Art. 239. The utmost attention must be paid to cleanliness in the persons, clothing, and bedding, and every part of the establishment; and it is part of the duty of all the officers employed, of the visitors, and particularly of the physician, to report to the warden every infraction that may be observed of this rule. There shall be a bathing room for each of the sexes, and all the persons confined shall be forced to bathe at least twice in every week during the seasons that will admit of it.

CHAPTER VIII.

Of rewards and punishments.

Art. 240. The rewards shall consist of badges, prizes of books, the use of the library, and marks of distinction and confidence, such as being made captain of a class, watchmen, or monitors in the school. They shall be conferred by the matron for the female department, by the warden for the male, and by the inspectors for both; but all rewards for merit in school, shall be on the recommendation of the teacher.

Art. 241. The punishments are, deprivations of distinctions formerly obtained; such moderate personal castigation as does not draw blood, leave a permanent mark, or unfit the child for immediate attention to his instruction or labour; common diet; degradation from the class; confinement in solitude, or in a strait waistcoat or arm straps.

Art. 242. Irons or chains are not permitted under any pretence.

Art. 243. The teacher may preserve order in the school for boys by the moderate chastisement mentioned in the second article of this section; in the female school he may direct it to be done by the female teachers. None of the other punishments can be inflicted but by order of the warden ; or, if on a female, but by order of the matron, subject always to the revision of the warden.

Art. 244. All the punishments may be continued, or be directed to cease by the inspectors, or any two of them.

Art. 245. Escape or attempt to escape, violence used towards any officer of the establishment, a refusal to work or receive instruction, or an attempt to persuade others to resist the authority of the officers, shall be punished by all the kinds of punishment above enumerated, for such period as the inspectors and warden, or inspectors and matron may direct.

Art. 246. The warden and the matron, with the approbation of the inspectors, shall frame rules for the preservation of order, not contrary to any thing contained in the Code or this chapter. The said rules shall designate what breaches shall be punishable by any of the penalties above enumerated and in what degree. These rules shall be put up in the different work-rooms, schools, and cells—shall be read to every one on his reception in the house, and shall be rigidly enforced.

CHAPTER IX.

Of the discharge from the school of reform.

Art. 247. Discharges from the School of Reform may be either by the expiration of the term of service or by apprenticeship.

Art. 248. Whatever may be the term of imprisonment designated by law for the offence of which the party sent to the School of Reform is convicted, such party cannot be discharged (unless by apprenticeship), if a female, before she has attained the age of nineteen, or if a male, before twenty-one.

Art. 249. Those who are sentenced for a term that will not expire until after they have respectively attained the ages mentioned in the last preceding article, and whose conduct has not entitled them to the recommendation hereinafter mentioned for apprenticeship, shall, within six months after attaining the ages aforesaid, be transferred to the Penitentiary to serve out the remainder of the term.

Art. 250. Those who are entitled to the recommendation, and who have not been apprenticed for some other cause, shall be discharged after having attained the age of twenty-two if a male, or twenty if a female, although the term of imprisonment in the sentence be for a longer time.

Art. 251. The warden is authorized to bind out, by indentures of apprenticeship, such of the prisoners confined as come within the description contained in the next succeeding article ; and the indentures shall impose the same obligations and give the same rights and remedies as indentures of apprenticeship made by a parent or guardian, with the assent of the minors, under the civil law of the state.

Art. 252. In order to be legally bound, pursuant to the last article, the apprentice must have been two years in the School of Reform ; he must have learned to read, write, and understand the first three rules in arithmetic ; and must have obtained a certificate signed by the warden (and if a female by the matron), approved by the inspectors, declaring that the moral conduct and diligence of the party has evinced such a reformation as, in their opinion, will render it safe to receive him as an apprentice.

Art. 253. The duration of the apprenticeship shall be until the party bound shall attain the age of twenty-one if a male, or nineteen if a female, unless, at the time of making the indenture, the male apprentice shall have attained nineteen years of age, or the female seventeen ; in which case the indenture may be for three years, if the term of the sentence does not expire before ; but if the term should expire before, the apprentice cannot be bound for a longer term than the attainment of twenty-one years for a male, or nineteen for a female, without his or her consent, and then only for the said term of three years.

Art. 254. The male apprentices shall be put out, if possible, to mechanics of the same trade they have been taught in the School of Reform ; if no mechanic pursuing the same profession offers, some other demanding, as near as may be, the same species of labour shall be preferred ; but whatever trade may have been taught to the apprentice, he may, by his own consent, be apprenticed to a farmer or a mariner.

Art. 255. The conditions of the articles of apprenticeship shall be, on the part of the apprentice, obedience to lawful commands, and diligence, sobriety, and honesty ; on the part of the master, that he will perfect the apprentice in the trade he has been taught, or teach him the new business if such be the case, that he will continue his schooling at least one day in the week, that he will provide him necessary food, clothing, lodging, medical assistance, and that, at the end of the period, he will give him new clothing and a sum of money to be specified in the indenture, and such as the warden and master shall think reasonable.

Art. 256. No one shall be apprenticed to any one residing out of the state, nor shall the indenture be assignable without the assent of the apprentice.

Art. 257. The clause relating to the teaching and perfecting in a trade or business, is not indispensable in the indenture of a female.

Art. 258. No female shall be indented to an unmarried man, or to a married man living apart from his wife.

Art. 259. It shall be a condition in the indenture between the warden and the master, that a report shall be made once in every year of the conduct of the apprentice to the warden ; and if he has reason to believe that his reformation is complete, that he will permit him, if within the city of New Orleans or its suburbs, to visit the school and converse with the others still there.

Art. 260. The convict at the time of his discharge, whether apprenticed or not, shall be comfortably clad, and the inspectors, at their discretion, may make him an allowance in money, or deliver him books or tools, if they are satisfied with his conduct.

CHAPTER X.

Of visits.

Art. 261. Besides the persons created visitors of all the places of confinement by this Code, and those who may receive permission from them, the parents or those related in the second degree to the persons confined in the School of Reform, may visit them on stated days, to be appointed by the warden ; but when he is apprehensive that evil counsels may be given, it shall always be in the presence of an officer.

TITLE IV.

OF THE PECUNIARY CONCERNS OF THE SEVERAL PLACES OF CONFINEMENT.

Art. 262. The board of inspectors shall appoint an agent, who shall make all purchases and sales on account of all the several places of confinement, including the House of Refuge and Industry, keeping regular sets of mercantile books for each of the said institutions, which may be examined by the inspectors, the wardens, or any of the visitors.

Art. 263. The compensation of the agent shall be fixed by the inspectors, with the approbation of the governor.

Art. 264. The regular supplies of provisions, and of all other articles consumed or used in the said institutions in considerable quantities, shall be furnished by contract, and adjudged after advertisement to the lowest bidder; but the wardens shall examine the articles furnished, and have the right to reject such as are not of the quality contracted for. The physician shall, in like manner, inspect the medicines and hospital furniture.

Art. 265. All the articles manufactured in either of the said places which are not made for manufacturers by contract, in the manner hereinafter provided, shall be sold by the agent to the best advantage, under the direction of the inspectors.

Art. 266. Regular and minute accounts of the receipts and expenditures of each place of confinement, including the House of Refuge, shall be furnished each quarter by the inspectors to the governor, and yearly accounts to the legislature on the first day of their annual meeting.

Art. 267. All moneys appropriated by the legislature for the use of either of the said places, shall be drawn for by the board of inspectors as the same may be wanted, in favour of the cashier of the Louisiana State Bank, and shall by him be carried to the credit of the board of inspectors, in an account to be opened with them in their official capacity, for the use of the particular institution for which the appropriation is made (naming it in the account) between the bank and the inspectors.

Art. 268. Whenever the amount of money in the hands of the agent, received on account of either or all of the institutions, shall exceed three hundred dollars, he shall, within two days, deposit the same in the said bank to the credit of the account opened with the inspectors for the use of the prison to which it belongs.

Art. 269. No money shall be drawn from the bank, on either of the said accounts, but by a draft signed by a majority of the inspectors, specifying on account of which prison it is drawn, for what purpose, and to whom the amount is due.

Art. 270. All accounts or demands against the prisons shall be examined, allowed, and paid by the inspectors; and when they meet to settle such accounts, the agent shall act as their clerk and shall make regular entries in the books of all receipts and expenditures, to the account of the institution to which they belong; but a sum, not exceeding one hundred dollars, may be placed in the hands of each warden, and as much in the hands of the agent, to pay current expenses, to be accounted for monthly to the inspectors.

Art. 271. If either the inspectors or the agent shall fail in making any deposit in the manner and at the time directed by either of the three last preceding articles ; or if the inspectors, or either of them, shall draw out of the bank any moneys belonging to or appropriated for either of the said places of confinement, including the House of Refuge, in any other manner than is above directed, the person so offending shall pay a fine of five hundred dollars; and if any of the said moneys which are either not deposited when by the said articles or either of them they ought to be, or are drawn out of the bank contrary to the directions of this chapter, shall be applied to any other use than to that of the said institutions, or one of them, the person guilty of such misapplication shall be dismissed from his office, be imprisoned, in close custody, for sixty days, and pay a fine of one thousand dollars.

Art. 272. The wardens of the several prisons shall deliver to the agent all the articles manufactured in their prisons respectively, which are not necessary for the use of such prison, except those articles manufactured in the House of Detention by the prisoners there who have provided their own materials, or who have made a different arrangement with the inspectors for the disposal of the proceeds of their labour ; and excepting also the articles made for manufacturers by contract, in the Penitentiary, School of Reform, and House of Refuge and Industry.

Art. 273. The wardens of the Penitentiary and of the School of Reform shall each be allowed, in addition to their salaries,   per cent. on the gross amount of sales by the agent of the articles manufactured in their prisons respectively, after deducting only the cost of the materials employed in the articles so sold ; and also per cent. on the amount of sums paid for the labour of the convicts by manufacturers; but this allowance shall be forfeited for every year in which the wardens shall use any other means than those authorized by this Code to induce the convicts to labour, either by way of punishment or reward.

Art. 274. The average number of deaths in the principal penitentiaries of the United States having been found to be about   in every hundred annually (taking the average of the number of prisoners confined at all times during the year as the basis of the calculation for the whole number), as an encouragement to use greater care and attention in lessening this rate of mortality, if the said proportion shall be in any one year reduced in the Penitentiary of this state more than one-half of that average, the governor shall present to the physician books, surgical instruments, or plate, of the value of   dollars, which testimonial shall be doubled in value if the proportion be reduced more than three-fourths.

Art. 275. The average number of re-convictions in the principal cities of the Union having been found to be about   in every hundred annually of those committed to the Penitentiary in those cities; to lessen this proportion is the object of the reformatory part of prison discipline. To incite, therefore, the officers to a zealous discharge of this part of their duty, if in any one year, succeeding the third year after this Code shall have gone into operation, the number of re-commitments to the Penitentiary shall be less, in any one year, by one-half than that proportion, an honorary testimonial of that fact, consisting of a piece of plate of the value of   dollars, shall be presented by the governor to the inspectors, the wardens, the chaplains, and teachers, of the said prison; the value of which plate shall be doubled in any year in which the said proportion is reduced to less than three-fourths of the average above stated.

Art. 276. A similar testimonial shall be given to the matrons, if the like reduction takes place in the re-commitments of the female convicts.

Art. 277. The amount requisite for the purchase of the

testimonials aforesaid, shall be taken from the recompense fund, created by the Code of Criminal Procedure.

TITLE V.

OF THE DISCHARGE OF THE CONVICTS.

Art 278. Whenever a convict shall be discharged by the expiration of the term to which he was condemned, or by pardon, he shall take off the prison uniform and have the clothes which he brought to the prison restored to him, together with the other property, if any, that was taken from him on his commitment, that has not been otherwise legally disposed of.

Art. 279. A copy of his account with the prison, made out in the manner hereinbefore directed, shall be given to him ; and if the proceeds of his labour produce any balance in his favour, one-half of such balance shall be paid him.

Art. 280. Before the convict is dismissed, the chapter of the Penal Code, " Of the Repetition of Offences," shall be read to him.

Art. 281. If the warden, the chaplain, and the teacher, have been satisfied with the morality, industry, and order of his conduct, they shall give him a certificate to that effect.

Art. 282. One or more of the inspectors shall be present whenever a convict is discharged, who, as well as the officers of the prison, shall inquire into his future prospects and designs; shall aid him in an endeavour to procure an honest support, or to return to his friends ; shall exhort him to perseverance in habits of industry ; and if he can find no other employment, and is desirous of maintaining himself by labour, the warden shall admit him into the House of Refuge, hereinafter provided for.

Art. 283. If the warden shall discover that any discharged convict, instead of seeking to maintain himself by labour, shall associate with the idle and profligate, he shall immediately proceed against him as a vagrant, under the provisions for that purpose contained in the Code of Criminal Procedure.

TITLE VI.

HOW THE PROPERTY OF PERSONS CONDEMNED FOR CRIME SHALL BE DISPOSED OF.

CHAPTER I.

Of the property of convicts condemned to imprisonment and labour for a term.

Art. 284. The property of convicts condemned to imprisonment and labour, may be administered by curators during the term for which they are condemned. The letters of curatorship are revoked by their pardon or discharge ; but such revocation does not invalidate legal acts done by the curator.

Art. 285. Any person who would be entitled to the curatorship of the estate of the convict, had he died on the day judgment was pronounced against him, shall be entitled to the curatorship.

Art. 286. The mode of proceeding to obtain the letters of curatorship shall be the same as that prescribed in case of death, except that, instead of alleging and proving the death of the party, the record of his condemnation shall be produced to the judge.

Art. 287. The curatorship, in case of condemnation, carries with it all the consequences, responsibilities, rights, and duties, that result from a curatorship to a person deceased.

Art. 288. Curators and tutors may also be appointed to the persons and estates of the children of the convict, in the like manner and to the same persons who would have been entitled to the said offices if the convict had been dead.

Art. 289. The curatorships and tutorships, mentioned in the last article, are the same as to all rights, duties, and responsibilities, as they would have been had the appointment been made after the death of the convict; but they are revoked by his pardon or discharge, except in cases where his sentence incapacitates him from exercising those trusts.

Art. 290. Those who would have been the heirs of a convict, sentenced to imprisonment for a term, cannot take the estate out of the hands of the curator; but if he have a wife, or relations in the ascending or descending line, whom he was bound by law to support, the curator shall, out of the estate, provide for their sustenance.

Art. 291. All property given, or in any manner whatever accruing to a convict in the Penitentiary, shall vest in his curator, if he be sentenced for a term of years, to be disposed of in like manner with his other property; or if he be sentenced for life, shall vest in his heirs.

CHAPTER II.

Of the disposition of the property of convicts sentenced to imprisonment for life.

Art. 292. The same disposition shall be made of the estate of a person sentenced to imprisonment for life, as if he had died on the day sentence was pronounced; and any last will and testament or codicil he may have made prior to that time, shall take effect in the same manner as if he had died on that day.

Art. 293. But no disposition of any estate, either by will or otherwise, after the arrest for crime, of which the prisoner was convicted, in the case of any crime whether the sentence is for life or otherwise, shall be valid against the claim of the person entitled to a suit for the private injury committed by the crime, unless such disposition was made for a valuable and equivalent consideration to a person ignorant of the arrest.

BOOK III.

TITLE I.

OF THE DESIGN OF THIS ESTABLISHMENT.

Art. 294. The object of this establishment is twofold : the first, to afford the means of voluntary employment to those who are able and willing to labour, and gratuitous support to those who are not ; the second object is, to coerce those who, although capable of supporting themselves, prefer a life of idleness, vice, and mendicity, to one of honest labour.

Art. 295. As a House of Refuge, it is intended to afford to the discharged convict the means of support by voluntary labour, until, by degrees, he may regain the confidence of society ; to prevent those offences of which poverty and want of employment are the real or pretended cause ; and to relieve private charity from the unequal burthen of supporting the mendicant poor.

Art. 296. As a House of Industry, the establishment is intended to be a place of coercion and restraint for vagrants and able-bodied beggars ; for the first, because their mode of life raises a just presumption that it is sustained by illegal depredations on a society to which they do not properly belong ; for the second, because, by false pretences of inability, they impose on the charity of the public ; and for both as a measure of preventive justice, because their voluntary idleness, unless corrected will inevitably conduct them to vice, and crimes, and punishment.

TITLE II.

OF THE DIFFERENT DEPARTMENTS OF THE HOUSE OF REFUGE
AND INDUSTRY, AND OF THE DESCRIPTION OF PERSONS
ADMITTED TO, AND CONFINED IN EACH.

Art. 297. The House of Refuge and Industry shall
consist of two departments : the one for voluntary, the
other for forced labour ; both shall be under the direction
of the same warden ; and the one shall be called the
House of Refuge, andthe other the House of Industry.

Art. 298. In the House of Refuge shall be admitted
all such discharged convicts as may be desirous of gaining
a subsistence by labour ; all public mendicants who
allege a want of employment as the reason for asking
public charity, or who, from age, infirmity, and poverty,
are incapable, in part or in the whole, to support themselves, and have no relations who, by law, are bound to
support them.

Art. 299. To the House of Industry shall be committed all vagrants above the age of eighteen, and all
able-bodied beggars, above that age, who refuse to labour
in the House of Refuge, or elsewhere, when employment is offered to them.

Art. 300. In each department the women shall be kept
separate from the men, and they shall be under the
superintendence of a matron.

Art. 301. The building shall be so constructed as to
separate the two departments, and shall contain separate
sleeping cells for each of the persons confined in the
House of Industry, and for each of the discharged convicts in the House of Refuge. The paupers shall be disposed of in comfortable apartments, in the manner that
the warden (subject to the direction of the inspectors)
shall direct.

TITLE III.

OF THE OFFICERS OF THE HOUSE OF REFUGE AND INDUSTRY, AND OF THEIR DUTIES.

Art. 302.   This establishment shall be under the direction of the board of inspectors, in this Code before provided for ; who shall, in relation to this, have the same powers and be subject to the same duties that are before provided in relation to the other places of confinement.

Art. 303. The warden shall be appointed by the governor, and the warden shall appoint so many assistants as the inspectors shall deem necessary.

Art. 304. The matron shall also be appointed by the governor, and shall name such number of female assistants as the inspectors shall direct.

Art. 305. The physician and chaplains shall also attend in their professional capacities on the persons admitted or detained in the House of Refuge and Industry.

Art. 306. The agent of the inspectors shall also be their agent for the sales and purchases of this institution.

Art. 307. The accounts shall be kept by a clerk to be named by the inspectors.

Art. 308. All the above-named officers shall perform the same duties and have the same powers, with respect to the House of Refuge and Industry, and to the persons received or committed therein, as are required of and are given to them respectively, with respect to the Penitentiary and the persons confined therein, except so far as the same are modified by this title.

TITLE IV.

OF THE ADMISSION INTO THE HOUSE OF REFUGE, AND OF THE EMPLOYMENT OF THE PERSONS ADMITTED.

Art. 309. The House of Refuge and Industry shall be erected as near as conveniently may be to the city of New Orleans, not more than one league distant from the City-Hall of the said city. Annexed to it shall be a garden of at least three superficial acres. The building shall be made on a plan to -be approved by the governor, and sufficient in all respects to carry into effect all the provisions of this title.

Art. 310. Discharged convicts shall be admitted on their own application to the warden, and on their agreeing to observe and be bound by the rules of the said house, and the provisions of this title, of which, so far as respects their conduct and obligations, an abstract shall be read to them, and which they shall sign.

Art. 311. Able-bodied paupers, willing to labour but unable to find employment, shall, in like manner, be admitted on their own application, and on their signing an agreement to observe the rules of this house and the provisions of this title which respects them.

Art. 312. All paupers, unable to provide for their own subsistence, shall be admitted to the House of Refuge on the order of the jury of police of the parish to which they belong, or of the city council, if they belong to the city of New Orleans.

Art. 313. The inspectors shall provide the implements, materials, and other means of giving employment to all the persons admitted into the House of Refuge, adapted to their strength, age, sex, and skill respectively, except such as shall, on examination by the physician, be declared incapable of doing anything towards their support.

Art. 314. No person who shall be admitted into the House of Refuge shall leave the same, without permission of the warden, or without giving at least one month's notice of an intention to leave the same ; and any person absenting himself contrary to this rule, may be arrested on a warrant to be issued by the warden and one of the inspectors, and confined in a solitary cell for a term not exceeding three days.

Art. 315. Any person who shall leave the House of Refuge, either by permission of the warden or otherwise, and shall be found soliciting charity as a PUBLIC BEGGAR, may be arrested, and by the warrant of the parish judge and two magistrates of the parish, where such mendicant may be found, shall be committed to the House of Industry as a vagrant.

Art. 316. Any person admitted into the House of Refuge, who shall refuse or neglect to perform the labour assigned to him, may, if the inspectors shall think that the task assigned is not greater or more difficult than the strength or skill of the person can perform, be committed to the House of Industry for such time, not exceeding ten days for each offence, as the inspectors shall direct.

TITLE V.

OF THE POLICE OF THE HOUSE OF REFUGE.

Art. 317. The inspectors may make rules for the preservation of order and industry in the House, and may punish breaches thereof in the manner such rules may direct, either by imprisonment in a solitary cell, or by commitment to the House of Industry ; provided that such imprisonment shall not exceed three days, or such commitment be for a longer term than ten days, for any offence against such rules.

Art. 318. The two sexes shall be kept separate in the House of Refuge, in two distinct apartments; but boys, under seven years of age, may be kept with their mothers, or, if they have none, by proper nurses, under the care of the matron.

Art. 319. Children of paupers, between the ages of seven and eighteen, may be sent to the School of Reform by the inspectors, at their discretion, when the friends or relatives of such children do not provide for their education and support.

Art. 320. The matron shall apportion the tasks of the females in both departments of the House of Refuge and Industry, and shall superintend their labour, and report all delinquencies to the warden or inspectors, to be punished in the same manner as those of the males.

Art. 321. The warden and matron respectively shall appoint, from among the persons admitted into the House of Refuge, a male and female teacher, who shall give lessons in reading, writing, and arithmetic, to such of the persons admitted or confined as may be ignorant of these branches of learning, at such hours as the warden shall direct.

Art. 322. No wine, or spirituous or intoxicating liquors of any kind, shall under any pretence, be used by those admitted into the House of Refuge or of Industry, unless by prescription of the physician.

Art. 323. Permission may be given to such of the persons as are most orderly and industrious to see their friends out of the House on Sundays, or to attend Divine Service in the city of New Orleans.

TITLE VI.

OF THE HOUSE OF INDUSTRY, ITS POLICE, AND THE EMPLOYMENT
OF THE PERSONS CONFINED THEREIN.

Art. 324. The time and place of labour, and the intervals given for other purposes, shall be the same in the House of Industry as that directed by this Code for the convicts in the Penitentiary.

Art. 325. The prison ration for those who labour and for those who are idle shall be the same as in the Penitentiary. The same privations, punishments, and restraints, may be inflicted for idleness, or the breach of any of the rules established by the inspectors or by this chapter.

Art. 326. The same accounts shall be kept with persons confined, and the same allowance for excess of labour above the charges, shall be made.

Art. 327. Whatever is directed for the reception of convicts in the Penitentiary shall be observed when any one, committed to the House of Industry, shall be received, except the prison uniform, which shall not be given unless the clothing of the person convicted is not sufficient for health or cleanliness.

Art. 328. The labour of the persons confined in the House of Industry may be contracted for in the same manner as that of the convicts in the Penitentiary; or when not contracted for, it is to be carried to the account of the establishment; and the articles manufactured are to be disposed of in the same way as is directed for the Penitentiary.

TITLE VII.

OF THE PECUNIARY CONCERNS OF THE HOUSE OF REFUGE AND INDUSTRY.

Art. 329. The accounts of the two departments, the House of Refuge and the House of Industry, shall be kept in separate sets of books by the clerk, under the inspection of the warden and the inspectors.

Art. 330. In the books of the House of Refuge all the expenses of the paupers, sent by any parish or city, shall be charged to such parish or city respectively, and they shall be credited with the amount of the earnings of such paupers.

Art. 331. In the expenses, mentioned in the preceding article, shall be included, not only the food, clothing, medicine, and other articles provided for such paupers, but a just proportion of the salaries of the warden and other officers and attendants of the House of Refuge and Industry, calculated on the average of persons in the said house.

Art. 332. One-fourth part of the salaries of the inspectors, of the chaplains, and physician, shall also, in such account, be considered as chargeable to the House of Refuge and Industry, and a due proportion of that fourth (divided as is above directed by the average number of persons in the said house) shall be also included in the expenses charged to the parishes as aforesaid.

Art. 333. Whatever sum is found due on such account, if not paid on demand by the city or parish from which it is due, shall be added to the quota of the state taxes, payable by such city or parish, and be collected and paid into the public treasury in like manner with the rest of the state taxes.

Art. 334. All the expenses of the other persons admitted or confined in the said house, shall be paid by the state, without any counter charge.

Art. 335. A detailed account of all the expenditures and receipts of the said house shall be laid before the legislature, by the inspectors, on the first day of every session.

Art. 336. The salary of the warden shall be dollars per annum, and of the matron   dollars, and each of the assistants shall be paid   a day.

GENERAL PROVISIONS.

Art. 337. If any one shall, for hire, reward, or emolument of any kind whatever, or the promise of any, solicit the pardon of any one convicted of any offence, or procure any other to sign a petition for such pardon, or to apply for the same, he shall be fined five hundred dollars, and if he be a counsellor or attorney, he shall be suspended from practising as such in any court in the state for one year.

Art. 338. The inspectors, chaplains, teachers, physicians, wardens, matrons, assistants, and under-keepers, appointed by virtue of this Code, shall, before they enter on the performance of their respective duties, take an oath faithfully to perform the same.

EXTRACTS

FROM

A SYSTEM OF PENAL LAW

PREPARED FOR

THE UNITED STATES OF AMERICA

BY

EDWARD LIVINGSTON.

NOTE.

Mr. Livingston, while a Senator in Congress from the State of Louisiana, by the request of the Government, prepared a uniform System of Penal Law for the United States, similar to that which he had written for Louisiana. This System was substantially identical with the preceding, with the exception of the following Extracts, which, as will be seen, relate to matters belonging specially to the General Government.

TITLE I.

CHAPTER I.

Division of these offences.

Art. . There are five kinds of offences against the sovereign power of the United States, to wit :
Conspiracy against the United States ;
Insurrection ;
Giving aid to the enemies of the United States ;
Treason ;
Concealment of treason.

CHAPTER II.

Of conspiracy against the United States.

Art. . Any two or more persons who shall COMBINE and AGREE to make an INSURRECTION, or to cause the same to be made ; or to commit TREASON, or to procure the same to be committed, are guilty of a conspiracy against the United States, if the intended offence be not committed ; if the intended offence be committed, they are, according to circumstances, either PRINCIPALS or ACCOMPLICES.

Art. . The punishment of conspirators is one-fourth of that which would have been incurred by the offence which was agreed to be committed.

Art. . It is not necessary, to constitute the offence, that any act should be done in furtherance of the agreement; but there must be an agreement to commit the treason, or raise the insurrection. A combination for preparatory consultation is not sufficient.

Art. . If a conspirator shall give notice of the intended offence, so as to prevent its execution before the design has been discovered, he shall not incur any punishment for the conspiracy.

Art. . If the accused show that the design of the intended insurrection or treason was voluntarily abandoned by him before any act was done towards its execution (other than the agreement), and before it was discovered or defeated by some obstacle to its execution, the punishment shall not exceed a fine of three hundred dollars, or imprisonment for three months.

CHAPTER III.

Of insurrection.

Art. . Insurrection, as a general offence, may be committed either, First, by assembling with the intent of committing treason; or, Secondly, by assembling with the intent of opposing, by force, or actually so opposing, the execution of a particular law of the United States: Provided in this last case that the opposition do not amount to treason.

Art. . To constitute the offence of insurrection, the persons assembled must be those who intend to commit the treason, or to use the force in opposition to the law.

Art. . An assemblage for the purpose of opposing, by force, the execution of a law of the United States in its operation upon designated individuals, in their persons or property, and not extending the opposition to the general operation of such law, does not come within the definition of the offence designated by this chapter. Such meeting would be an unlawful assembly, and if force were actually used, a riot, as those offences are hereinafter described.

Art. . If the object of the insurrection be to commit the crime of treason, the punishment shall be fine not exceeding two thousand dollars and imprisonment in the Penitentiary not less than eight nor more than twelve years.

Art. . If the object be such opposition to a particular law as does not amount to treason, the punishment shall be fine not exceeding one thousand dollars and imprisonment in the Penitentiary not less than one nor more than five years ; and if the forcible opposition be actually made, the punishment shall be doubled.

CHAPTER IV.

Of giving aid to the enemies of the United States.

Art. . The offence intended by this Chapter is, giving aid and comfort to the enemies of the United States, unaccompanied by an intent that such aid should operate favourably to them in their hostilities against the United States ; when done with such intent, it is an *adherence* to such crimes.

Art. . If any citizen of the United States, or any person owing them allegiance, shall give aid and comfort to a foreign enemy of the United States, by supplying the subjects or citizens of such enemy, in the course of trade, with arms or munitions of war, horses, provisions, naval stores, or ships or other vessels, but without any intent that the same should be used in the war against the United States, he shall be fined not less than two thousand, nor more than five thousand dollars and imprisoned in the Penitentiary not less than one, nor more than five years.

Art. . If the supply mentioned in the last preceding article shall be of any other articles than those therein specified, furnished in the same manner, and without any hostile intent, the punishment shall be fine, not less than one thousand, nor more than three thousand dollars, and imprisonment in close custody, not exceeding one year.

Art. . Nothing in this chapter contained shall prevent the remittance of money or bills, to pay debts contracted with such enemy before the war, or to supplies given in consequence of a requisition made by an invading enemy upon inhabitants of a district in their power.

Art. . The words, *in the course of trade*, used in the second article of this chapter, are intended to exclude sales made to the government of the enemy, or its agents, of any of the supplies enumerated in the said article, such sales being evidence of adhesion.

Art. . Voluntary contributions to the enemy do not come within the intent of this chapter. They are always evidence of adhesion.

Art. . All articles forbidden by this chapter to be furnished to an enemy, may be seized, condemned, and sold, for the benefit of the person seizing the same.

CHAPTER V.

Of treason.

SECTION I.

Of the two species of treason defined by the constitution.

Art. . Treason is defined by the Constitution. It consists only in " levying war against the United States," or in " adhering to their enemies, giving them aid and comfort."

SECTION II.

Of treason by levying war.

Art.   . There are no constructive offences known to the laws of the United States. There must, therefore, under the first branch of the definition, to constitute the guilt of treason, be an actual levy of war against the United States according to the plain import of those words as they were understood at the time the Constitution was adopted.

Art.   . Of this species of treason there are two degrees. Treason in the lower degree and treason in the higher degree.

Art.   . Treason in the lower degree is a levy of war against the United States by persons owing perpetual or temporary allegiance to them, and made by a HOSTILE ATTACK upon, or HOSTILE resistance to, the military force of the United States, after it has been called in aid of the civil power, either to suppress a forcible resistance to the general operation of a particular law of the United States; or, to secure a state against domestic violence under the provision of the Constitution for that purpose. Any other forcible opposition to the general operation of a particular law is insurrection only.

Art.   . The opposition mentioned in the last preceding article, to the military force, must (in order to constitute the offence) be made with the intent to oppose the general operation of the particular law only ; if it be made with the intent to oppose the execution of the laws generally, it is treason in the higher degree ; if the opposition be made with the intent only to defeat the operation of the law upon designated persons, or property, it is a riot.

Art.   . Treason in the higher degree by a LEVY OF WAR, is when war is levied against the United States by persons owing a temporary or perpetual allegiance to them, for any other purpose than that which has been declared to be treason in the lower degree.

Art.   . It is necessary in every indictment for treason in the higher degree to state as well the purpose for which the war was levied, as the overt act by which it was shown.

SECTION III.

Of treason by adhering to the enemies of the United States.

Art.   . Treason by adhering to the enemies of the United States can only exist when there is an actual war with some foreign enemy, and to constitute the guilt there must be an adherence to such enemy, giving him aid and comfort in such war.

Art.   . The WAR intended by the last article is one either formally declared or evidenced by actual invasion.

Art.   . To constitute this offence, the aid and comfort given to the foreign enemy must be the consequence of an adhesion to them—that is, a desire to promote the success of their hostile operations against the United States; but such desire must be shown by acts which give aid and comfort.

Art.   . Serving in the army or navy of an enemy when employed against the United States; fitting-out, owning, or serving on board a private vessel of war cruizing, or commissioned to cruize, and make prize of the property of citizens of the United States, or its government; inviting such enemy to invade the United States; acting as a guide, or spy, or giving intelligence intended to promote the success of any military operation of such enemy, or supplying them with provisions, or other articles, with the intent that they should be used in some operation of war against the United States; are examples of such adhesion, and giving of aid and comfort to an enemy as amount to treason.

SECTION IV.

Of the evidence required for conviction in cases of treason, and its punishment.

Art.   . The Constitution provides that no person shall be convicted of treason unless on the testimony of two witnesses to the same overt act, or on confession in open court.

Art.   . The treason consists of two parts—the overt act and the intention.   After proving the overt act by two witnesses, the intent may be made out by other evidence.

Art.   . The punishment of treason in the lower degree is fine not exceeding five thousand dollars, and imprisonment in the Penitentiary not less than ten nor more than fifteen years.

Art.   . The punishment for treason in the higher degree is imprisonment in solitude for life.

TITLE VII.

OF OFFENCES AGAINST THE LAWS OF NATIONS.

CHAPTER I.

Of offences affecting public enemies.

Art.   . The provisions of the chapters of this Code, " Of offences affecting the person," and " Of offences affecting private property," apply for the protection of the persons and private property of prisoners of war, alien enemies who are by law permitted to remain in the

United States, or who, by the proper civil or military authorities, are received as agents for prisoners, messengers, or other public capacity, and of the non-combatant inhabitants of an enemy's country, in the occupation of the troops of the United States.

Art. . Offences coming within the purview of the preceding article, shall be punished in the same manner, as the like offence would be, if it had been committed in a place within the exclusive jurisdiction of the United States.

Art. . Nothing in the preceding articles of this section shall be construed to prevent or punish the restraint or force necessary for the safe custody of prisoners, the enforcement of the rules that are, or may be, prescribed by law, in relation to alien enemies, to the precautions which the officers of the troops, in an enemy's country, may find it necessary, consistent with the laws of civilized war, to take, for the security of their operations ; to the seizure of arms or munitions of war ; to the levying contributions in an enemy's country, in cases expressly authorized by the President of the United States ; and to the seizure of provisions and other articles necessary for the operations of war, although they may be private property, in an invaded country, paying, on giving evidences of debt, for the same.

Art. . Any citizen or inhabitant of the United States, or any other person, being in their military service, who shall use poisoned weapons against a PUBLIC ENEMY of the United States, or poison provisions or liquor of any kind, with intent to destroy the life of such enemy, shall be punished by imprisonment and labour for ten years, and if death be caused by such poison, the punishment shall be for life.

Art. . Any such person as is described in the last preceding article, who shall put a public enemy of the United States to death by assassination, shall be punished by imprisonment in the Penitentiary for life.

Art. . By assassination, in the last article, is meant death inflicted by one, who, for that purpose, has placed himself under the protection of the enemy, either as a bearer of a flag of truce, a prisoner, a deserter, or in any other character that necessarily creates a confidence of his having no hostile intentions. But nothing in this or the last article applies to the case of death inflicted by a prisoner in attempting or effecting his escape, unless such escape was effected by breach of parole.

Art. . The destruction of private or public property not used for the purposes of war, in an enemy's country, if such destruction be not made by a military officer, and by him in good faith deemed necessary for the purpose of an operation of war, is an offence against the laws of nations, and shall be punished by a fine not exceeding four thousand dollars, or imprisonment not exceeding two years.

Art. . No inhabitant or citizen of the United States shall, without being commissioned or authorized by, or under the command of, some commissioned officer, make any hostile invasion into an enemy's country, under the penalty of fine not exceeding four hundred dollars, or imprisonment not exceeding ninety days.

Art. . If any one shall commit any act during a truce or agreement with an enemy for the cessation of hostilities, contrary to the terms of such truce or agreement, he shall be imprisoned in the Penitentiary not less than one nor more than ten years.

Art. . It is not intended by the last preceding article to prevent the officer who made the agreement or truce from putting an end to the same, in cases not contrary to good faith; nor is it intended, in any case, to punish an act done in obedience to the order of a superior military chief.

Art. . Any citizen or inhabitant of the United States who shall, during a war between the United States and a foreign nation, do any act in contravention of a stipulation in any treaty made, or to be made, between the United States and such foreign nation, intended to operate in time of war between them, shall be fined not exceeding four thousand dollars, or imprisoned in close custody not exceeding twelve months, or both, unless such stipulation be expressly declared to be annulled by one of the contracting parties.

Art. . That part of the first article of this chapter which relates to the private property of enemies of the United States, does not apply to maritime captures, while such captures are allowed by law.

Art. . If any citizen or inhabitant of the United States, or any other person being in their military service, shall scalp, mutilate, or treat with wanton indignity, the dead body of an enemy of the United States, he shall be imprisoned in close custody not exceeding six months.

Art. . Nothing contained in this chapter shall be construed to prevent retaliation, in time of war, for breaches by the enemy of the rules of civilized warfare, but no such retaliation shall be made, except by the express order of the President of the United States, nor by him, without proclaiming the breach, accompanied by proof of the fact, nor until after demand and refusal of satisfaction.

Art. . No one shall be punished under this section for any offence which is punishable by the articles of war, if he has been acquitted, or punished, or pardoned, according to military law.

CHAPTER II.

Of offences against the law of nations on the sea.

SECTION I.

Of piracy.

Art. . It is piracy if any one illegally, FRAUDULENTLY, and by VIOLENCE, on the SEA, shall TAKE, or APPROPRIATE, or ATTEMPT to take, or appropriate, or to destroy, the property of another, or to do, or attempt to do, any irreparable injury to his person ; but to constitute the crime, the act must be committed or attempted by persons in or coming (with that intent) from, one vessel, upon persons or property in another vessel, or on shore, or upon persons or property in the same vessel; provided, in this last case, the intent be also to take, or appropriate, or abandon, or destroy, such vessel.

Art. . The punishment of piracy is imprisonment in the Penitentiary for fifteen years, and if attended with homicide, for life.

Art. . *Corollaries from the foregoing definition ; and illustrations thereof, by examples and explanations.*

1. The terms, "illegally" and " fraudulently," are used conjunctively, to distinguish a piratical from a legal act of the same nature ; for example, against public enemies or pirates ; and also from an act done illegally, but not fraudulently, such as a capture made, by virtue of a commission illegally issued, but supposed by the party to be good.

2. A violent taking or appropriation distinguishes the piratical from those which are made by breach of trust, which by this Code are classed as different offences.

3. To constitute piracy, the offence must be committed on the sea, but a modification is contained in the definition applying to persons IN a vessel attacking persons or property on shore ; for example, by firing from a vessel without landing, or by landing FROM such vessel, to do the injury on shore.

4. The terms " take" and " appropriate" are used in the disjunctive, to include in the definition a piratical appropriation not preceded by a taking. If the master of a vessel, having received into his possession, and given bills of lading for the cargo, should, by violence on the sea, drive out, or kill, or confine, the owner, his agent, or other person, who should oppose him, and appropriate the cargo to himself, it would be piracy within the definition, but there would be no taking, or a constructive one only ; but by this Code there are no constructive offences.

5. Violence is an essential part of the definition, and distinguishes piracy from private stealing on the sea. If the crew of a boat from one vessel should privately steal articles from on board another vessel at sea, it would not be piracy; if they were taken by violence it would.

6. It is a corollary from the definition, that the taking of provisions by the crew of a ship, in absolute and casual want of them, from another which has them in quantity more than sufficient for its use, giving or offering payment therefor, and without personal violence, is not piracy; the taking and appropriation is not violent nor fraudulent.

7. There may be piracy from wantonness or revenge; therefore, the destruction, as well as the appropriation of property, and murder, or other irreparable injury to the person, without robbery, is piracy.

8. The word "another," as descriptive of the persons and property which the law intends to protect, includes the property of the United States, of all foreign nations, except public enemies, and of all corporations, and the persons as well as property of all individuals whatever, except public enemies.

9. A citizen or inhabitant of the United States, knowingly taking a person from a foreign country, or from a vessel at sea, or detaining him when so taken, or delivering him on board another vessel at sea, or landing him, for the purpose of his being held in slavery, is guilty of piracy under this definition.

10. Every violent and fraudulent taking of property, or injury to person at sea, is not piracy; to constitute the crime, the act must be committed by a person in some one of the relative situations to the person injured, or to the property, that are set forth in the definition. Those situations are specified, in order to distinguish mere personal injuries and private depredations upon property on the sea, from piracy : for example, if one man murder another on board the same ship, in a private quarrel, or rob him, by violence, of his property, it is not piracy; but the same acts committed by going from one vessel to

another at sea, or to the shore from a vessel at sea, with the intent of doing those acts, would be piracy.

11. The injuries affecting person or property in the same vessel, which are enumerated in the definition, are piracy only when they are connected with some disposition of the vessel itself, as otherwise they may be classed, not as offences against the law of nations, but among those of a private nature, and punishable only on the return of the ship, by the municipal law of the country to which it belongs. As a consequence from this part of the definition, if the crew steal a part of the cargo, or murder a passenger, and remain afterwards peaceably on board, it is not piracy ; but if, in addition to this, they deprive the master of the command, or destroy the vessel, it comes within the definition : so, if the master, with or without the assistance of the crew, do either of the acts against person or property set forth in the definition, in his ship, and afterwards regularly proceed on his voyage, he can only be punished for the act done; but if he destroy, appropriate, or abandon the vessel, it is piracy.

12. The attempt to commit the enumerated injuries to property or person is declared to be piracy, although such attempt should not succeed; it cannot be made without offering violence and creating alarm, subversive of that security on the ocean which this branch of the law of nations is intended to preserve. Therefore, chasing, firing upon, or boarding a vessel, with intent to capture or plunder it, is piracy, although the attempt should not succeed.

13. The definition is not restrictive as to the country of the offender or the injured party. By virtue of the interest which the United States, in common with all other nations, have, in preserving the peaceful navigation of the sea, all offenders, coming within the purview of this chapter, may be tried and punished by the courts of the United States.

14. The term "SEA," used in the definition of this crime, includes navigable waters which are not within the juris-

diction of a court in any of the states or territories of the United States, or of any foreign country, having a court in which the crime of piracy can be punished ; but it is piracy if it be an act coming otherwise within the definition, and that crime be committed on any navigable waters whatever, by persons coming with that intent from the sea.

15. By the word "illegally," the definition excludes any justification of an act, otherwise piratical, committed by any one owing allegiance to the United States, against them or any citizen thereof, under colour, or by virtue of, any commission or authority from any foreign Government.

16. Acts that would otherwise be piratical, committed by persons sailing in a vessel under the flag and authority of an independent political Power, and acting under the instructions of such Power, are not piracy.

17. Citizens of the United States, sailing in foreign vessels, and committing acts that come within the definition of piracy against the United States, or its citizens, are not within the exception contained in the last preceding illustration.

SECTION II.

Of maritime offences against the law of nations which are less than piracy.

Art. . Any master of a vessel who shall voluntarily and corruptly surrender the vessel under his charge, or any part of the cargo, to pirates, shall be punished by imprisonment in the Penitentiary not less than ten, nor more than fifteen years.

Art. . Any person who shall, designedly and by force, prevent, or endeavour to prevent, any officer of a vessel which is attacked, or about to be attacked by pirates, from defending the same, without any intent to aid such pirates, shall be punished by imprisonment in the Penitentiary not less than two, nor more than five years : if done with intent to aid the pirates, it is piracy.

Art. . Whoever shall make a REVOLT in any vessel, without committing any other act that would amount to piracy, shall be punished by imprisonment in the Penitentiary not less than one, nor more than three years.

Art. . The revolt intended by the last preceding article is a combination by any two or more of the crew to disobey the master of the vessel ; and, in consequence of such combination, actually refusing to perform his legal commands.

Art. . Any two or more persons who shall, either on the land or at sea, conspire and agree to commit the crime of piracy, shall be punished by imprisonment in the Penitentiary not less than one, nor more than five years, unless the design be voluntarily abandoned before it is detected. Engaging or enlisting any one to serve in a piratical vessel, is evidence of such conspiracy.

Art. . Any one, who shall receive or conceal any property taken by pirates, knowing the same to have been so taken, and with intent illegally to deprive the owners thereof, shall be punished by imprisonment in the Penitentiary not less than four, nor more than ten years.

Art. . Whoever shall prepare, purchase, or fit out, or provide any arms, ammunition, vessels, provisions, or other things necessary for the execution of any act of piracy, with intent that they shall be employed in the commission of that crime, shall be punished by fine not exceeding five thousand dollars, and imprisonment in the Penitentiary not less than one, nor more than three years.

Art. . All the ships and other things provided or prepared for piracy, mentioned in the preceding article, may be seized and sold, by the order of a competent tribunal, and the proceeds applied to the recompense fund, created by the Code of Procedure ; as may also all vessels taken from pirates, which are not claimed, and shewn to have been piratically taken from the true owners.

Art. . The provisions in this Code, with respect to accomplices and accessories, apply to offences against the law of nations, and other offences on the sea.

Art. . Maritime offences are such as are committed on the SEA, as that term is explained in the first section of this chapter, or such as are begun or prepared on the land, with the intent that they shall be completed at sea.

Art. . All such acts or omissions as are declared to be offences in the two several titles of this Code, entitled " Of offences affecting the person," and " Of offences affecting property," shall, if they be committed on the sea, by or against a citizen or inhabitant of the United States, or in a vessel of the United States, and are not elsewhere in this Code specially described and made punishable, be punished in the manner directed by the said several titles.

CHAPTER III.

Of offences against the law of nations, committed by citizens or inhabitants of the United States against nations with which they are at peace.

Art. . If, after the commencement of a war between two foreign Powers, in which the United States shall be neutral, any citizen of the United States, residing within the same, shall, either within the United States or elsewhere, accept of any appointment in the army or navy, or enlist or engage himself to serve as a soldier or mariner in the army or navy of either of the said Powers against the other Powers, he shall be imprisoned, in close custody, not less than six months nor more than two years.

Art. . By foreign Powers, in this chapter, are understood all foreign nations and parties, or sections of such nations, waging war with each other.

Art. . If any citizen of the United States, or any inhabitant thereof, not being a citizen or subject of the Power in whose service he shall engage, shall, within the United States, accept any commission or authority, or enlist or engage to serve in any capacity whatever, on board of any private armed vessel of one belligerent foreign Power to cruize against another with whom the United States shall at that time be at peace, he shall be imprisoned, in close custody, not less than one, nor more than three years.

Art. . If any citizen or inhabitant of the United States, on land, or on any waters out of the limits of the United States, shall, intentionally, commit any illegal act of hostility against a foreign Power with which the United States shall then be at peace, its citizens or subjects, which does not amount to piracy, he shall be fined not exceeding four thousand dollars, or imprisoned not exceeding two years, in close custody, or both ; and, if the act is attended by homicide or other act, which, if committed in a place under the exclusive jurisdiction of the United States, would be punished as a CRIME, the punishment shall be imprisonment in the Penitentiary for the same term that would have been incurred had the act been done in such place.

COROLLARIES from the last preceding article.

Cor. 1. All subjects or citizens of foreign Powers, and their property, as well as the public property of such Powers, while within the United States, are protected by the municipal laws : Therefore, offences against such persons or property, which are there committed with the intent only of injuring the person or appropriating or injuring the property, are not acts of hostility, but private offences.

Cor. 2. An act done by order of a superior military officer, or by instructions from the President of the United States, is not an offence described by this article.

Cor. 3. An act of hostility, within the meaning of this article, must be an attack upon person or property, or an invasion of territory directed against a foreign Power, or some local division of its territory, and the citizens and inhabitants thereof, aggregately ; or against designated individuals or societies belonging to such foreign Power, or their property, under the pretence of asserting national right or punishing or avenging national wrong; or of making reprisals or procuring redress for real or supposed national or individual injuries.

Cor. 4. An act of private aggression against person or property in a foreign country is not an act of hostility within the meaning of this article.

Cor. 5. An act of hostility, otherwise within the description of this article, is not within its meaning if done by a military or naval officer, in consequence of a bonâ fide misunderstanding of his instructions.

Cor. 6. A capture or detention of a neutral ship, when the United States shall be at war, on a bonâ fide suspicion of any circumstance that would justify such capture by the law of nations, is not a hostile act.

Art. . If any citizen or inhabitant of the United States shall go, or procure another to go, into the territory of any foreign Power with which the United States is at peace, with the design to commit, and shall there actually commit, any such injury to person or property, as would be punishable by this Code if committed in a place under the exclusive jurisdiction of the United States, he shall be punished in the same manner as if the said act had been done in such place.

Art. . But if the proper authority of the foreign Power, whose citizens or subjects shall have been injured, do not, after reasonable request made by the Executive of the United States, cause the witnesses, as well for the prosecution as for the defence, who may reside within its dominion, to attend at the time and place of trial, the accused shall be discharged.

Art. . If any one shall, within the limits of the United States, fit out, or arm, or begin the fitting out, or arming, any vessel, with the intent that it shall be employed in the service of a foreign Power, to commit hostilities against another foreign Power with which the United States are at peace, he shall be punished by fine, not more than five thousand dollars, and imprisonment, in close custody, not exceeding three years.

Art. . Whoever shall, within the United States, augment the force of any armed vessel belonging to a foreign Power then at war with another Power with which the United States is at peace, by any equipment solely applicable to war, such vessel being designed to be employed against the Powers with whom the United States is so at peace, shall be punished by fine, not exceeding one thousand dollars, and imprisonment, in close custody, not exceeding one year.

Art. . In all cases, vessels fitted out and armed, or begun to be fitted out and armed, contrary to the provisions of this chapter, shall be forfeited to the use of the informers.

Art. . Whoever shall within the jurisdiction of the United States, begin, or set on foot, or provide, or prepare, the means for any military expedition, to be carried on from thence against the territory of any foreign Power with which the United States are at peace, shall be fined not more than three thousand dollars, or imprisoned in close custody, not more than three years.

Art. . If any citizen or inhabitant of the United States, on the *sea*, shall commit, against any citizen or subject of a foreign Power with which the United States are at peace, any act described as an offence in either of the two several titles of this Code, entitled " Of offences affecting the person," and " Of offences affecting property," he shall be tried, in a court of competent jurisdiction of the United States and be subject to the same punishment as if the offence had been committed in a place within the exclusive jurisdiction of the United States.

CHAPTER IV.

Of offences against the law of nations affecting the diplomatic agents of foreign powers.

Art. . All the acts declared by this code to be LOCAL OFFENCES, affecting reputation, person, or property, are hereby delared to be GENERAL OFFENCES against the law of nations, when committed against a public minister or consul of a foreign Power, and shall be punishable in the same manner as is designated in this Code for the said offences, respectively, unless such offence be committed against a public minister ; in which case, if the offence be a misdemeanor, the punishment shall be fine, at the discretion of the court, and imprisonment, in close custody, not exceeding three years ; but, if the offence be a crime, the punishment assigned for such offence, when committed against an individual, shall be doubled.

Art. . By public minister, in this Code, is meant any person, generally or specially, appointed by a foreign Power to represent the same in its national transactions with the United States, whether under the denomination of ambassador, minister plenipotentiary, minister resident, chargé d'affaires, or any other denomination.

Art. . The term consul includes all persons accredited by a foreign Power to the Government of the United States, and by it received and acknowledged, for the superintendence of the commercial rights of its citizens or subjects, by the title of consuls-general, consuls, vice-consuls, commercial agents, or other equivalent denomination.

Art. . If any of the offences referred to in the first article shall be committed against the wife or child of a public minister, the secretary of legation, or any person whose name shall be registered in the manner hereinafter directed, as attached to the legation, or employed by the minister as a domestic in his family, the offenders shall incur the punishment directed by the first article.

Art.   . No judicial writ or process shall be issued, levied, or executed, against the person or property of any public minister, or of any of the persons enumerated or described in the last preceding article. And any person issuing such writ or process, or procuring it to be done, or executing the same, shall be punished by fine at the discretion of the court, and imprisoned not exceeding three years; and all such writs, process, or orders, shall be void.

Art.   . The last preceding article shall not protect citizens or inhabitants of the United States from the payment of debts contracted prior to their entering into the service of such public minister ; nor shall it exempt such citizen or inhabitant from being arrested and punished for offences before committed ; nor shall any one be punished for any offence under this section committed against any person attached to the legation, or employed as a domestic servant of such minister, unless the name of such person, with the quality in which he shall be employed, shall be transmitted, by such public minister, to the Secretary of State ; whose duty it is to register the same, and immediately to transmit a copy of such register to the marshal of the district in which Congress shall sit ; to be by him affixed in some public place in his office, whereto all persons may resort and take copies without any reward.

Art.   . If any one shall intentionally destroy, or intercept and conceal, any letter or despatch addressed to, or sent from, any public minister of a foreign Power, relating to the business of his mission, knowing it to be so addressed or sent ; or shall intentionally stop or delay any messenger charged with such letter or despatch, for the purpose of retarding or preventing the delivery thereof ; or shall commit any of the offences (in relation to the correspondence of such minister) that are described in the section of this Code entitled " Of the violation of Epistolary Correspondence," he shall be punished by fine at the discretion of the court, and imprisonment, in close custody, not exceeding two years.

CHAPTER IV.

Forms of charges in indictments for GENERAL OFFENCES.

SECTION I.

Forms of charges in indictments for offences against the sovereign power.

Art. . Form of charge for conspiracy against the United States.

"That A. B., C. D., [and others to the said jurors unknown,] on the   day of   in the year   , at the city of Philadelphia, in the eastern district of Pennsylvania, did conspire together and agree to make an insurrection against the United States, by meeting together and promising others to meet with them in the said district for the purpose [of opposing, by force, the execution of a certain law of the United States, entitled ' An act,' &c. in its general operation,] or [for the purpose of committing treason by separating the State of Pennsylvania from the United States, and, by force, making the said State independent of the Union.]"

Art. . Form of charge for insurrection.

"That A. B., C. D., and others, to the said jurors unknown, to the number of one hundred and more, did, on the   day of   in the year   assemble and meet together at a place called   in the district of   with the intent [of opposing, by force, the execution of a law of the United States, entitled ' An act,' &c. in its general operation on the citizens of the United States,] or [with the intent of committing treason against the United States, by levying war against them for the purpose of procuring, by force, the repeal of

a certain act, entitled, ' An act,' &c.] and, so the said
jurors say, that the said A. B. and C. D. are guilty of
insurrection against the United States."

Art.   . Charge for giving aid to the enemies of the
United States.

" That A. B. on the   day of   in the
year   at   in the district of   he
then being a citizen of the United States, did, in the
course of trade, supply sundry subjects of the king of
          with whom the United States then were at
open war, with certain naval stores, that is to say, one
thousand barrels of pitch, &c., contrary to the laws of the
United States."

Art.   . Charge for treason in the lower degree, by a
levy of war.

" That A. B. being a citizen of the United States, or
[being within the United States, enjoying the protection
of its Government,] on the   day of   in
the district of   did, with many other persons to
the said jurors unknown, for the purpose of preventing
the execution of a law of the United States, entitled,
' An act,' &c. in its general operation upon the citizens
of the United States, levy war upon the United States,
by [making a hostile attack on the military force of the
United States, who were legally called out, in aid of the
civil power, to enforce the execution of the said law,] or
[by making a hostile resistance to the troops (or militia)
of the United States who were, &c.] or [did levy war
upon the United States, by making a hostile attack upon
[or resistance to] the military force of the United States,
after it had been legally called in aid of the civil power
to secure the State of   against domestic violence :]
whereupon, the said jurors say, that the said A. B. is
guilty of treason in the lower degree."

Art.   . Charge of treason in the higher degree, by a
levy of war.

" That A. B. [being a citizen of the United States,] or
[being within the United States and enjoying the protection of its Government,] together with many other

persons, on the   day of   at   in the
district of   for the purpose of dissolving the union
of the United States, by making the State of
independent of the government of the said States, did
levy war upon the said United States, [by forcibly seizing
upon a fort belonging to them, called   and
making prisoners of the garrison;] wherefore, the said
jurors say that the said A. B. is guilty of treason in the
higher degree against the United States."

Art. . Charge of treason in the higher degree, by
adhering to the enemies of the United States, giving
them aid and comfort.

"That A. B., [being a citizen,] &c. or [enjoying, &c.]
on the   day of   at   in the district
of   , a public war then existing between the king
of   and the United States, did adhere to the
troops of the said king, they being enemies of the United
States, and did give them aid and comfort, by then and
there giving to the commanding officer of the said troops,
intelligence of the state of the army of the United States,
and advising him in what manner they might be attacked
to advantage, with intent that the army of the United
States should be destroyed or taken prisoners : wherefore, the said jurors say, that the said A. B. is guilty of
treason in the higher degree against the said United
States."

SECTION II.

Forms of charges in indictments for offences against the law of nations
which affect public enemies.

Art. . The forms of indictments for offences against
the persons or property of prisoners of war, and other
alien enemies enumerated in the first article of first
chapter of the second title of the second book of the

Penal Code, shall be in the same form as is prescribed for indictments for the same offences against citizens.

Art. . Charge for making a hostile incursion into an enemy's country without authority.

"That A. B. and several other persons to the jurors unknown on the day of   , in the year   , not being commissioned by the United States, and having no authority or command from any one so commissioned, did make a hostile incursion into the province of Upper Canada, a place belonging to the dominions of the King of Great Britain, with whom the United States were then at war, and did then and there [attack and plunder sundry inhabitants of the said province] contrary to the laws in such case provided."

Art. . Charge for destroying property in an enemy's country.

"That A. B., being a military officer of the United States, on the   day of   in the year   , did wantonly, and without deeming the same necessary for the purposes of war, burn and destroy a house belonging to C. D., a subject of the King of Great Britain, situate in the province of Upper Canada, a country belonging to the said king, with whom the United States were then at open war."

Art. . Charge for assassinating an enemy.

"That A. B., on the   day of   , in the year   , at   in the district of   , did assassinate and murder C. D., an officer in the army of the king of   , with whom the United States were then at open war, after he the said A. B. had placed himself under the protection of the said C. D., [as the bearer of a flag of truce] or [by pretending to be a deserter, &c.]"

Art. . Charge in indictment for a breach of truce.

"That, on the   day of   , in the year   , J. S., then commanding the army of the United States at   , in the district of   , concluded with the commanding officer of the army of the king of   , with whom the United States were then at open war, an agreement for a cessation of hostilities for the space of one day, and that A. B. then and there, well knowing that the said agreement had been made, violated the same by firing upon a sentinel of the army of the said king of Great Britain contrary to public faith, and to the laws in such case provided."

Art. . Charge for mutilating the dead body of an enemy.

"That C. D., on the   day of   , in the year   , at   , in the district of   , did mutilate and treat with indignity the dead body of an Indian belonging to the nation of   , with which the United States were then at war, by [tearing off the scalp from the head of the said dead body] contrary to the laws in such case made and provided."

SECTION III.

Charges in indictments for offences against the laws of nations committed on the sea.

Art. . Charge in an indictment for piracy.

"That A. B., on the   day of   , on the sea, at [or about the latitude of ten degrees north and   degrees west from the meridian of London] did commit the crime of piracy [by fraudulently and by violence attacking and taking a certain schooner called the Gnat, he, the said A. B., being then on board of, and having the command, of a schooner called the Fly, and appropriating the said schooner, called the Gnat, to his own use.]"

Art. . For corruptly surrendering a vessel to pirates.

"That A. B., being the master of [a brig or vessel belonging to citizens of the United States, called the New York,] did, on the seas, [about one league east of

Sandy Hook,] on the   day of   , in the year   , voluntarily and corruptly surrender the said brig to pirates, who seized and captured the same, contrary to the laws in such case made and provided."

Art. . For preventing an officer from defending his vessel against pirates.

"That A. B., being a seaman on board a vessel of the United States, called the Boston, on the sea, at, &c. on the   day of   , did designedly, and by force, prevent C. D., the commander of the said vessel, from defending the same against certain pirates who had then attacked the said vessel."

Art. . For making a revolt.

"That A. B., being a seaman, &c. as in the last article, did combine with others of the crew of the said vessel, to the jurors unknown, to disobey the orders of C. D., the master of the said vessel, and did, in consequence of such combination, actually refuse to perform the lawful commands of the said master, whereby the said jurors say that the said A. B. did then and there make a revolt on board the said vessel, contrary," &c.

Art. . Combination to commit piracy.

"That A. B., C. D., and E. F., at the city of   , in the district of   , on the   day of   , did conspire and agree to commit the crime of piracy, [by seizing or capturing a certain vessel then about to sail from the said port], or [by fitting out a vessel in the said port of   , for the purpose of robbing and taking other vessels on the sea], or [by some other act (specifying it) that would be piracy.]"

Art. . For providing arms necessary for the commission of piracy.

"That A. B., &c., at, &c., on, &c., did provide [three six-pound cannon with their carriages,] for the purpose and with the intent that the same should be employed in committing an act of piracy."

Art. . For concealing property taken by pirates.

"That A. B., at, &c., on, &c., did receive and conceal five boxes of tea, which had been taken from persons unknown to the jurors, [or from C. D.], by pirates, he, the said A. B., knowing that the said boxes of tea had been so piratically taken."

Art.   . All other offences against person or property, committed on the sea, shall be charged in the indictment in the same manner as is directed for such offences when committed on the land, except that the offence shall be specially alleged to have been committed on the sea.

SECTION IV.

Forms of charges in indictments for offences against the laws of nations, committed by citizens or inhabitants of the United States against nations with whom they are at peace.

Art.   . Form of charge against a citizen and resident, for engaging in foreign military service, the United States being neutral.

"That, on the   day of   , in the year   , war then existing between the King of Spain and the Republic of Colombia, A. B., a citizen of the United States, residing therein, at   , in the District of New York, enlisted himself as a soldier, to serve in the army of the said King against the said Republic, the United States being neutral between the said belligerent powers."

Art.   . Charge against a *resident* for entering a foreign privateer, the United States being neutral.

"That, on the   day of   , in the year   , war then existing between the Emperor of Brazil and the Republic of Buenos Ayres, and the United States being neutral, A. B., a resident of the said United States, did, at Baltimore, in the District of Maryland, accept a commission from the said Emperor, to cruize against the said Republic and its citizens, on board of a private armed ship called the Don Pedro."

Art.   . For hostile attacks upon a power with which the United States are at peace.

"That, on the   day of   , in the year   , the United States being then at peace with the Republic of Mexico, A. B., a [citizen or resident, as the case may be], of the United States, and divers other persons, to the jurors unknown, intentionally, under pretence of [making reprisals], illegally committed an act of hostility against the said Republic, by entering the territories thereof, from the United States, with an armed force, and [taking and holding possession of a fort, in the said territory, called St. Maria, or other act of hostility, as the case may be.]"

Art.   . Form of charge against a citizen or resident of the United States for going into a foreign country with intent to commit an offence, &c.

"That, on the   day of   , in the year   , the Republic of Mexico and the United States being at peace, A. B., being a resident of the United States, at New Orleans, in the District of Louisiana, went from the said District to St. Antonio, in the territories of the said Republic, with the design to [murder one C. D., an inhabitant of St. Antonio afore-said,] and, on the   day of   , in the same year, did then and there [describe the murder or other offence in the manner prescribed by this Code.]"

Art.   . For fitting out and arming a vessel with intent to cruize against a power with whom the United States is at peace.

"That A. B., on, &c., at, &c., within the limits of the United States, did [fit out] or [arm, or begin to fit out, or begin to arm, as the case may be,] a vessel, with intent that it should be employed in the service of the Emperor of Brazil, a foreign Power, to commit hostilities against the Republic of Buenos Ayres, another foreign Power, with which the United States were then at peace."

Art.   . For augmenting the force of a foreign ship of war.

"That A. B., on the   day, &c., at, &c., did

augment the force of a certain ship of war [called the
Mars, belonging to the King of France, by putting on
board of the said ship, and mounting there, five pieces
of cannon, the said King of France being then actually
at war with the King of the United Kingdom, &c., with
whom the United States were at peace, and such vessel
being designed to be employed against the said King of
the United Kingdom, &c.]"

A BOOK OF DEFINITIONS.

TITLE I.

GENERAL PROVISIONS.

Art. 1. These definitions are intended to show the sense in which the words defined are employed in the system of Penal Law, not to denote or fix their general signification in the language.

Art. 2. The words printed in small capitals in the body of this system, are alphabetically arranged in this Book, with the definition annexed.

Art. 3. Generally the definitions that are incorporated in the other parts of the work are not repeated in this Book; but this rule is departed from when the general use of the term, in other parts of the System than that in which the definition is contained, renders a reference to the explanation necessary.

Art. 4. Corollaries, illustrations, and developments, are used in several instances to fix the attention more strongly to particular parts of the definition: but the omission to employ them, in other cases, is not to be considered as giving any latitude for the construction of any word in a definition beyond the plain import of its meaning in connexion with the context.

TITLE II.

DEFINITIONS.

ACCIDENT, in this System, means an event happening without the concurrence of the will of the person by whose agency it was caused. It differs from MISTAKE, because the latter always supposes the operation of the human will in producing the event, although that will is caused by erroneous impressions on the mind.—See MISTAKE.

ACT—when applied to a written instrument, is a term used to show the connexion between the instrument and the party who has given it validity by his signature or by his legal assent: when thus perfected, the instrument becomes the ACT of the parties who have signed or assented to it in a form required by law.

ADVANTAGE, applied in different parts of the system to that which is to be gained or lost, means whatever, in the estimation of mankind, causes pleasure by its possession or enjoyment, or uneasiness by its loss or cessation.

AFFIDAVIT—a written declaration, sanctioned by the oath of the declarant administered by a person or court duly authorized for that purpose. The administration of the oath must be duly certified by the official SIGNATURE of the person, or the clerk of the court, before whom it was taken; and the declaration must be SIGNED by the declarant; or it must be certified by the person administering the oath that the declarant cannot sign.

AFFINITY—a connexion formed by marriage, which places the husband in the same degree of nominal propinquity to the relations of the wife as that in which she herself stands towards them, and gives to the wife the same reciprocal connexion with the relations of the husband. It is used in contradistinction to CONSANGUINITY, which is the relationship that exists between several persons who derive their descent in the same or different degrees of propinquity from an ancestor common to all.

AFFIRMATION and OATH. An affirmation is a solemn declaration, made before a person or court authorized to receive it, attesting the truth of a statement already made or about to be made by the affirmant, or the truth or sincerity of a promise made by him. An oath is a similar declaration, accompanied by a religious invocation to the Supreme Being to bear witness to the truth of the declaration or the sincerity of the promise, and by a renunciation of the blessing of God and the respect of man if the engagement should be violated. Vide the Chapter of the Code of Procedure, "Of Oaths and Affirmations." The term "oath," whenever used in this System, as to its effects and consequences and all penalties attending its breach or falsity, includes affirmations, unless the contrary appears from the context.

AMICABLE COMPOUNDER. An arbitrator with extensive equitable powers.

TO APPROPRIATE, in relation to property, is to possess, and to make such use or disposition of it as none but the owner, or some one legally authorized by him, could do; and, with respect to rights, to do such acts in relation to them as none but the person entitled to them, or his representatives, could lawfully do.

Appropriations are legal or fraudulent. No appropriations are fraudulent but such as come within the definition of fraud in this book.

Corollaries.—I. If the property be destroyed but not possessed, or if the possession be for the purpose of destruction, or be such a possession only as is necessary for effecting the destruction, it is not an appropriation.

II. If the property be taken possession of and transferred, although it be afterwards destroyed, it is an appropriation.

ARBITRATOR—any one appointed by the parties in any litigated question, either of law or fact, to decide it between them. In this system it is used to include REFEREES, UMPIRES, and AMICABLE COMPOUNDERS, whether they are named by the court, in cases where they are authorized to do so, or by the parties.

ATTEMPT. An attempt to commit an offence, in this system, means an endeavour to accomplish it, which has failed from some other cause than the voluntary relinquishment of the design.

BAILABLE OF RIGHT. Those offences, on a charge for which the magistrate must admit to bail, if good security be offered, are bailable of right. The constitution provides, that bail must be taken for all offences, except those which were punished capitally at the time of its adoption: these were, murder, rape, exciting insurrection, and stabbing, or shooting, or poisoning with intent to murder. All other offences, therefore, are bailable of right. The offences above enumerated, are also bailable, when the proof is not evident nor the presumption great.

BREACH OF THE PEACE—any offence against public tranquillity, or against person or property, when accompanied by violence.

BRIBE. The gift or promise which is accepted : of some ADVANTAGE, as the inducement for an illegal act or omission ; or of some illegal EMOLUMENT, as a consideration, for preferring one person to another in the performance of a legal act.

TO BRIBE—to make such gift or promise which is received. If it be not received, it is an OFFER TO BRIBE.

TO RECEIVE A BRIBE, is to accept the gift or promise, and either expressly or impliedly consent to do the act, or be guilty of the omission required. Whatever would be proof of consent in cases of contract, according to the rules of evidence, would show an acceptance in this case.

Corollaries and Illustrations.—I. The gift or the promise required by the definition need not be direct : although the gift be clothed in the form of a sale for an inadequate price, or of the payment of a debt ; or the promise be made colourably for some other consideration ; or a wager, or any other device, be used to cover the true intent of the parties, it is a bribe.

II. The gift or the promise must be the inducement for the act or omission ; it must, therefore, precede or accompany such act or omission. If the act be first performed, uninfluenced by any such promise, it is not bribery.

III. When the act or omission is illegal, the promise or gift of any ADVANTAGE, as the consideration, is bribery. If a magistrate should discharge, without bail, a person legally accused of a crime, on the promise of that person's influence with the governor for an appointment, this would be bribery ; because, although the inducement, that is to say, the influence with the governor, is only an ADVANTAGE, not an EMOLUMENT, yet the act, that is to say, the discharge without bail, being illegal, it comes within the definition.

IV. But when the act is legal, but the impropriety consists in the undue preference given to the person offering the inducement, that inducement, to constitute the offence, must not only be an advantage, but an emolument. If an officer of justice were to promise a magistrate to recommend his friend for an employment, as an inducement for the magistrate to employ him in preference to any other in the business of his office, this would not be bribery; although it would, if the inducement had been a sum of money or any other emolument.

V. The emolument, when that is required to constitute the offence, must be illegal, that is to say, either not allowed or more than is allowed by law. If two persons should apply to a notary, each to have an act of sale drawn, and he should give the preference to the one who paid him double fees, this would come within the definition; but if he took no more than the tariff allows, the preference would be no offence.

VI. No acts of bribery, or offer to bribe, are punishable as such, but those which are designated by express law.

VII. Whenever by the Penal Code bribery, or an offer to bribe, is made punishable, in relation to officers of a particular description, or to persons exercising certain duties, powers, or privileges, it is intended to extend to all official acts and omissions of such officers, and to all acts and omissions of such other persons as relate to their duties, privileges, or powers; but not to include any other.

BUILDING—anything erected by art and fixed upon or in the soil, composed of different pieces, connected together, and designed for permanent use in the position in which it is so fixed.

Corollaries.—I. A single piece of timber, although fixed in the ground, is not a building.

II. A fence or enclosure is a building.

III. A heap of stones, although some of them may be fixed on the earth, is not a building.

IV. Every building comes under the description of real estate.

COLOUR. Doing an act under colour of an office, or other legal power, means the doing it under the false pretence that it is authorized by the duties of such office, or by the due exercise of such legal powers.

CONDITION of a Person—a situation in civil society which creates certain relations between the individual, to whom it is applied, and one or more others, from which mutual rights and obligations arise. Thus the situation arising from marriage give rise to the CONDITIONS of husband and wife; that from paternity to the CONDITIONS of father and child.

COROLLARY, in this system, is used not so much to designate the just consequence that, according to strict reasoning, ought to be drawn from any proposition, as the consequence which is established by law as resulting from the definition or proposition to which it refers. Those who are to execute or interpret the law, therefore, are forbidden to modify or reject any such consequence under the pretence that it is not a just dedction.

CORPORATION, is an incorporeal being, created, and capable of acting only in the manner prescribed by law. It is composed of one or more persons having a common name and uninterrupted succession. It may hold property, and for certain purposes specified by law is considered as an individual.

Corollaries.—I. As a corporation, by this definition, is capable of acting only in the manner prescribed by law, no act done in any other manner or form, can be the act of the corporation. It cannot, therefore, commit an offence. All such acts, although done under the colour of being corporate acts, are those of the individual members who perform them, and they alone are criminally liable.

II. Acts which are offences against the property and rights of individuals, are also offences when committed against the property of corporations, and such rights as are vested in them by law.

III. Corporations are of two kinds: Public, also called Political Corporations, and Private Corporations. PUBLIC CORPORATIONS are those to which are confided certain police powers in a designated portion of the state. PRIVATE CORPORATIONS are all such as are not public.

CORRUPTLY. This adverb is applied to the doing of acts with the intent of gaining some ADVANTAGE inconsistent with official duty or the rights of others.

Corollaries.—I. Corruption includes bribery, but is more comprehensive. An act may be corruptly done, though the advantage to be derived from it be not offered by another.

II. It is not corruption to do an official act from an expectation of ADVANTAGE, if the act be not contrary to official duty, or does not injure the rights of another.

III. The corruption is not measured by the nature or amount of the ADVANTAGE.

COUNTERFEIT—to make something false in the semblance of that which is true. Whenever this word is used, in this system, it implies fraudulent intent.

COURT—COURT OF JUSTICE. These terms, in this system, are synonymous. A court is an incorporeal political being, which requires for its existence, the presence of the judge and clerk at the time during which, and at the place where, it is by law authorized to be held; and the performance of some public act, indicative of the design to perform the functions of a court.

Corollaries.—1. There can be no court without a clerk or some one authorized to perform the duties of a clerk.

II. Executive officers are not essential to the existence of a court.

III. The judge is not the court.

IV. The court cannot exist before the time at which, by law, it is authorized to hold its sessions; nor after the time to which its sitting is limited.

V. All acts done by the persons composing the court, importing to be acts of the court, at any other place than that authorized by law, are not the acts of a court.

VI. A justice of the peace, or any other magistrate authorized to perform judicial duties, without a clerk to record his proceedings, does not constitute a court; but courts may order certain executive acts to be performed at other times and places, such as the issuing of writs and filing of papers.

CRIME, is an offence the punishment of which, in the whole or in part, may be the forfeiture of any civil or political right, or hard labour, or for which hard labour is an alternative, to be inflicted at the discretion of the court.

DAY, given as the period of a notice, prescribed as a necessary interval between two acts or events, excludes the day of the notice and the day the act is to be performed; or of the first and second act or event; so that the full number of days prescribed shall intervene, unless there be a contrary provision in the law.

DAY, used as a period of time, means the period of twenty-four hours, beginning at the expiration of the twelfth hour at night.

DAY, or DAY-TIME, used in contradistinction to night, means the period beginning at half an hour before the rising of the sun, and ending half an hour after its setting.

DEADLY WEAPON—any instrument which, when offensively used against the person, will probably produce death.

DEMUR, is to admit the truth of a fact stated, but to deny the legal consequence for the establishment of which it was alleged. The only case in which a formal demurrer is admitted, in this system, is that of a demurrer to a challenge to the panel of jurors.

DESIGNATED PERSON, is a term used to express one who is either known by name, or by person, or station, or office, or dwelling-place, or in any other way that may designate him to be the person referred to.

DISCRETION—the exercise of sound judgment, directed by what may be supposed would have been the will of the legislature, applied to the case in which the discretion is to be used, had the circumstances of that case been legislated upon: for a development of this definition—See the Code of Procedure, chapter " Of the Judgment."

DISCUSSION of Property, means the using the means prescribed by law for rendering it available to the payment of a debt.

DOMESTIC ANIMALS, means only animals of that kind that are usually employed in hunting, or in husbandry, or which are raised for the purpose of food.

EMOLUMENT—anything that forms an increase of property.

ESTATE, is used as synonymous with property. See PROPERTY.

EVIDENCE, is that which brings the mind to a just conviction of the truth or falsehood of any substantive proposition which is asserted or denied.

Illustrations and Developments of the different Parts of this Definition.—

I. A conviction produced by evidence which ought not, according to the rules of true reason, to have that effect, is not a just conviction: the law, therefore, declares what effect different species of evidence ought to have in producing such conviction; and that evidence, in its different degrees, is called LEGAL EVIDENCE.

II. Evidence being different according to the different degrees of effect which it ought to produce; those degrees, therefore, receive different denominations, indicative of the operation they each ought to have on the mind. These denominations are—presumptive evidence, direct evidence, and conclusive evidence; all of which are hereafter defined.

III. The word "substantive," in the definition, is intended to exclude all such abstract propositions as can be demonstrated to be true or false by the reasoning power, without having recourse to the establishment of other facts. The propositions intended by the definition are either of *fact* or of *law*. What is evidence of law, will be shown in the Code of Evidence. The three kinds of evidence enumerated, apply only to propositions of fact.

EVIDENCE (presumptive). Presumptive evidence is that which, by directly establishing the existence of one fact, renders the existence of another probable.

EVIDENCE (direct). Direct evidence is that which, if true, conclusively establishes or destroys the proposition in question.

EVIDENCE (conclusive). Conclusive evidence is that which, by law, is declared to be such proof of that which it asserts, as cannot, while it exists, be contradicted by other testimony.

EXCITE—to offer any persuasion or inducement.

EXTORT, is to obtain some illegal EMOLUMENT or advantage from another, under colour of, or as the consideration for, some official act.

FORCE—VIOLENCE. These terms mean the exertion of physical power, and when unqualified by any thing in the context, the idea of the illegal exercise of such powers is intended to be conveyed.

Corollaries.—I. No words, whatever may be their inport, can constitute force or violence.

II. Gestures, indicating an intent to apply physical power to the object intended to be affected, when such object is within the reach of the exercise of such power, do amount to force or violence.

III. The exercise of physical power amounts to *force* or *violence*, although it may be insufficient to carry the intent into effect.

IV. Violence and force are, in some instances, considered as offences merely by the intent with which they are used—as in assault, and assault and battery. Sometimes they do not amount to the offence described, unless they are sufficient to carry the intent into effect—as in the offence of violently obstructing the proceedings of a court of justice; in which case the offence is not complete, unless the violence has produced the obstruction.

FRAUD—TO DEFRAUD—unlawfully, designedly, and knowingly, to appropriate the property of another.

Illustrations.—I. Every appropriation of the right of property of another, is not fraud. It must be unlawful; that is to say, such an appropriation as is not permitted by law. Property loaned may, during the time of the loan, be appropriated to the use of the borrower. This is not fraud, because it is permitted by law.

II. The appropriation must be, not only unlawful, but it must be made with a knowledge that the property belongs to another, and with the design to deprive him of the same.   It is unlawful to take the property of another; but if it be done with a design of preserving it for the owners, or if it be taken by mistake, it is not done designedly or knowingly, and, therefore, does not come within the definition of fraud.

III.   Every species of unlawful appropriation enters into this definition when designedly made with a knowledge that the property is another's; therefore, such an appropriation, intended either for the use of another or for the benefit of the offender himself, is comprehended by the term.

IV.   Fraud, however immoral or illegal, is not, in itself, an offence. It only becomes such in the cases specially provided by law.

HABITUALLY—so frequently as to show a design of repeating the same act.

HOUSEHOLDER—one who occupies a house, or part of one, in which he habitually dwells.

Corollaries.—I.   It is not necessary that the dwelling-place should either be owned or hired; an occupant at sufferance, or in his own wrong, comes within the definition.

II.   By employing the word " dwells," in the definition, it is intended to exclude a sojourner or guest.   The occupant must be provided for at his own table, not board at that of another.

III.   The dwelling must be so habitual as to show an intent of continuance.   The quality of householder cannot be assumed, merely for the purpose of using it, in order to do some act for the performance of which that character is required by law, with the intent of relinquishing it when the purpose is attained.

HOUSE—any edifice, which being so built as to come within the definition of REAL PROPERTY, as defined, is closed in on all sides, and has the area, which is enclosed by the sides, covered by a roof.

HOUSE (dwelling).   A dwelling house is one in which some person habitually sleeps or eats his meals; or one that is built and intended for that purpose; although not actually inhabited.

INDUCEMENT—the object, whether of advantage to be obtained or evil to be avoided, which brings the mind to determine on any act or omission.

INFANT—a minor, who has not yet obtained the age which usually gives physical and mental power to avoid the ordinary dangers, or without aid to use the ordinary means of sustaining life when they are provided for him.

INJURY, is used in its most enlarged signification, meaning whatever causes evil or detriment, or renders the object of less value.   When it is intended to be used in the restricted sense of an evil or detriment, caused contrary to law, it is called illegal injury, or some other qualifying epithet is annexed to show such intent.

INSANITY—a malady operating on the perceptive or on the reasoning faculties of the mind, which either prevents the person affected from receiving true impressions through his senses, or from drawing just conclusions from what is truly perceived; and existing in such a degre.

as to render him incapable of performing the usual duties or transacting the ordinary affairs of life.

JUDGE—a public officer, appointed to decide litigated questions. This term, with exceptions that are specially made, is used to designate only such officers as preside in COURTS, and who are designated by that title in their appointments.

Exceptions and Illustrations.—I. Jurors, although they are judges of fact—and ARBITRATORS, although they are private judges, chosen by the parties, and in some cases assigned by the court—are, in this system, not included in the term, unless specially named.

II. When used in relation to a power to be exercised, or a duty to be performed, in a court having more than one judge, the power or duty is given to or imposed on all the judges, or so many as are necessary for the constitution of the court. When the term judge is used in relation to a duty or power to be performed or exercised out of court, it is intended to impose the duty or confer the power on any one judge where there are several.

III. A justice of the peace is included in the term judge in the first two chapters of the title of the Penal Code, " of Offences against the Judiciary Powers."

JUST REASON—to fear—to think—to believe—to doubt—such cause as would produce these effects by their operation on the apprehension or mind of a man of ordinary understanding in the common occurrences of life. The definition does not call for the exertion of very extraordinary courage, or an unusual degree of intellect.

LAW, as used in this system. This word signifies all those rules established by the people of the state in their constitution, or necessarily governing them as a member of the Union, or adopted or made by the legislature in conformity with the powers given by the constitution, and according to the forms it prescribes.

Corollaries, Developments, and Illustrations.—I. The laws in force in this state are the following, each having a controlling force over the others in the order in which they are enumerated :

1. The constitution of the United States, because it was adopted by the people of the state as paramount to their own constitution.

2. The laws and treaties of the United States, made in conformity with the constitution.

3. The law of nations, so far as the same has been recognised by the United States.

4. The constitution of the state.

5. The state laws, passed in conformity with the powers granted by the constitution, and according to the forms prescribed by it.

6. The laws in force in this state, at the time its constitution was adopted, and which have not been since repealed.

II. No other laws or authority for making laws are recognised as having any force to bind the people of this state.

III. No act of the legislature of the United States is law which is not warranted by some power given to them by the constitution of the United States, and which is not made according to the forms it prescribes.

IV. No act of the legislature of this state is law which is not warranted by the powers given to them by the constitution of the state, and is not made according to the forms it prescribes, or which contravenes the constitution of the United States, or laws, or treaties, constitutionally passed or made by the government of the United States.

V. If any provision in the constitution of the State should be found to contravene the constitution of the United States, or any constitutional laws or treaties made under it—the latter must prevail.

VI. Rules, ordinances, and by-laws, made by any court, corporation, body politic, or society, pursuant to powers legally vested in them by the legislature, have the force of law to the extent of those powers, as respects the rights of persons, or property, submitted to their operation.

LAW (penal). A penal law is one having for its immediate object the enforcement of civil or political duties, and the preservation of correspondent rights. It must command certain acts to be done or omitted, and must impose a PENALTY to be enforced in the name of the state for a breach of its provisions.

Corollaries.—I. A law which forbids or commands, but without declaring any penalty for disobedience, is not a penal law.

II. Laws authorizing courts to impose fines, or to imprison, for defaults occurring in the administration of justice, or for disobedience to its rules for the maintenance of order, or authorizing corporations or other collective bodies to impose fines on their members, are not penal laws.

III. Ordinances or by-laws of PUBLIC or PRIVATE CORPORATIONS, are not penal laws, although they should impose penalties.

IV. Laws declaring contracts or acts, which want certain formalities, or which are not conformable to the provisions of such laws, to be void, are not penal laws.

V. Laws which impose forfeitures, or pecuniary penalties to be sued for in their own name, and for their own use, or for the joint benefit of the prosecutor and the state, are not penal laws.

LAW (military). Military laws are regulations for the government of the military force; and although they contain penalties, they are not considered as penal laws, because their immediate object is not the enforcement of civil or political duties.

LAWS (of Nations,) are those rules which, by the general consent of nations, govern them in their intercourse with each other in their national capacity. Offences against those laws, not being cognizable in the courts of this state, they are not detailed in this system.

LAW (civil). Every law which does not come within the description of penal, military, or national law, is, for the purpose of these Codes, called CIVIL LAW.

LAWFUL. Nothing is lawful that contravenes any of the laws in force in this state. All acts or omissions are lawful which are not forbidden by some written law or by the laws of nations.

LYING-IN-WAIT—waiting in or near a place where the property or person of another is expected to come or be brought, for the purpose of committing an offence which shall affect such person or property.

MAGISTRATE. This term means all judges, including justices of the peace.

MAGISTRATE (competent)—one whose legal official powers are sufficient for the execution of the duty required.

MALICE—a malignant design to cause INJURY.

MANIFEST—whatever is apparent of itself, and is not made so by other evidence or by induction.

Illustration.—In the chapter of the Penal Code, concerning offences against decency, there is a provision forbidding the exhibition of any work MANIFESTLY designed to corrupt the morals of youth. If this term had not been introduced, the design might be inferred from expressions or figures usually and innocently employed in works of art or science, but at which overstrained delicacy or puritanism might take offence.

MAY—when employed to confer a power, is intended to render the exercise of it discretionary.

MINOR—any person under the age of twenty-one years. All the rules and provisions of penal law, with respect to minors, apply to them, although they may be emancipated.

MISDEMEANOR—any OFFENCE less in degree than a crime.

MISTAKE—a belief in the being of that which does not exist, or in the truth of a conclusion that is false.

Mistakes are REAL or INTELLECTUAL. In this system MISTAKE, when not qualified by the context, means exclusively a real mistake, as the same is here defined.

REAL MISTAKES relate to facts, and are caused either by the erroneous operation of the senses, or when the impression on the senses having been true, other circumstances produce a false conclusion in the mind.

INTELLECTUAL MISTAKES are such as are caused wholly by a defective operation of the reasoning faculty, either by drawing false conclusions from true principles, or by adopting false principles, and reasoning either correctly or falsely from them.

Illustrations and Corollaries.—I. If one, intending to shoot an animal in the wood, should fire at a fur cap, and kill the man who wore it, thinking it to be the animal he was hunting, this would be a REAL MISTAKE, produced by a false impression on the organ of sight. If the same event should be produced by supposing the rush and tread of the man through the bushes to be those of the animal, this would be a mistake of the same description, arising from a false impression on another sense, that of hearing.

II. One who shoots an innocent but unknown man, believing him to be a robber equally unknown, of whose attempt he has been apprised, gives an example of mistake arising from other circumstances, without any error of the senses. There was no error in perceiving the man; both men were equally unknown; therefore, the error did not arise from the sight;

but the information of the intended robbery, and the entry by night at the time he was expected, were the circumstances from which the erroneous conclusion was drawn, that the innocent man was the robber.

III.   If one should establish in his own mind, the erroneous principle that no human law can rightfully control his revenge for an injury, and from thence deduce a right to challenge and kill the man who has offended him, this is an intellectual mistake, by drawing true conclusions from the establishment of false principles unconnected with the fact.

IV.   If a curator should believe that because he has a right to administer the real property of his ward, he has also that of disposing of it at his pleasure, he commits an intellectual mistake, by drawing a false conclusion from true principles.

V. In those cases in which the law declares that an act which would otherwise be an offence is not punishable, or is punishable in a less degree when done by mistake, it does not intend intellectual mistakes.

VI.   All mistakes, as to the tenor or the construction of law, are intellectual mistakes.

VII.   No mistake of law can excuse or palliate an offence.

MONTH, in this system—by the term month, a calendar month is always intended.

TO OBSTRUCT, as applied to any proceeding or course of action — means, not only to stop altogether, and to interrupt for a time, but to render inconvenient, or to turn out of the usual legal course.

OFFENCE, is the doing what a PENAL LAW forbids to be done, or omitting to do what it commands.   In most cases the contravention must be voluntary to constitute the offence ; but there are exceptions to this part of the definition to be found in the description of different offences in the Penal Code.

Developments.—I.   Penal law here is not used synonymously with penal statute.   If a penal statute should contain any prohibition not SANCTIONED by a penalty, the breach of that part of the statute would not be an offence.

II.   An act, or omission, in contravention of a penal law, is not an offence in any one who does not come within the purview of the law.

OFFICE, is a delegation, either mediately, or immediately, from the state, of powers to perform certain duties ; either for carrying the operations of government in some one of its branches, which is called a PUBLIC OFFICE, for performing some duty in relation to some designated individuals, or their property, which is denominated a PRIVATE OFFICE, or for exercising certain functions unconnected with the state government in a public or private corporation, which is designated as a CORPORATE OFFICE.   In relation to the functions they require, offices are divided into CIVIL and MILITARY ; and civil offices are either LEGISLATIVE, JUDICIAL, or EXECUTIVE.

OFFICER (civil).   Any one who fills a legislative, executive, or judicial office of the state.   No one is an officer until he has received the evidence designated by law of his election or appointment, and (where they are required by law) unless he has taken the oath of office and given security for its faithful performance. But any one performing the functions of an office without being thus qualified, is liable to all the penalties imposed by law for any misconduct of which he may be guilty in the exercise of such office.

OFFICER (military). One who fills an office in the army, or navy, or militia; the last are considered as military officers only when doing military duty.

OFFICERS (legislative). The members of the general assembly are legislative officers. The governor or person acting as such is an executive officer : but performs legislative functions in exercising his right of sending back bills to the general assembly for reconsideration.

OFFICERS (judicial). All those officers whose legal functions are the decision of litigated questions either of law or of fact. Judges, or those who are exclusively employed in the administration of justice, justices of the peace, clerks, and other officers of courts are judicial officers.—ARBITRATORS and jurors are not officers.

OFFICERS (executive). Every PUBLIC OFFICER comes under this description, whose duties are neither military, legislative, nor judicial.

ORDINARY CARE—ORDINARY ATTENTION. These terms signify that degree of attention and care which a man of common prudence and activity employs in his daily occupations ; they exclude that deliberation and solicitude which is shown by men of extraordinary circumspection and diligence in common affairs, or which concerns of more than ordinary interest excite in all.

PANEL, is the list formed, according to law, of the names of the grand or petit jurors summoned to attend a court.

PERSONATE—to pretend to be another, either by assuming his name, his addition, designation of office, occupation or place of abode, with an intent to injure or defraud.

POISON—any substance which, by some inherent quality, causes death, when applied to, or received in the human body.

POISONING—the act of administering poison. It is effected by any of the means by which the poisonous substance may operate, whether by swallowing, by respiration, by incision, or by any other mode of application.

Corollaries from the two last definitions.—I. Death caused by the deprivation of respirable air, is not poisoning.

II. To suffocate by smoke or steam, or to kill by any of the gaseous fluids, which cause death by stopping respiration, is not poisoning.

III. Death caused by the inhaling of any gaseous fluid, which, by some deleterious quality it possesses, causes death when brought into contact with the organs of respiration, is poisoning.

IV. The deadly quality must be inherent in, not adventitious to, the substance. Death occasioned by the administration of a substance, which disorders the functions of the body, but does not usually produce death in the quantity in which it was administered, is not poisoning ; but may be murder, or a less offence, according to the intent.

V.   The deleterious effect may be supplied by the quantity.   A sub·stance which, given in small quantities, may have no deadly effect, may come under the description of poison, if administered in a quantity that usually causes death.

PROPERTY.   This term conveys a compound idea, composed of that which is its subject, and of the right to be exercised over it.   In relation to its object, property is CORPOREAL or INCORPOREAL ; the other part of the definition, the right connected with the object, is that of possessing and using, with respect to corporeal property, or of enforcing or transferring, with respect to that which is incorporeal.

PROPERTY (corporeal).   Is that property which is material in the physical sense of the word, or which may be perceived by any of the corporeal senses.

PROPERTY (incorporeal).   Means the right to enjoy either at the present, or any future time, some species of corporeal property not in the possession of the person having the right ; and for this reason in common parlance, and frequently in this system, it is called a RIGHT.

PROPERTY (real).   Is land, and everything naturally rooted or growing therein, or artificially and permanently erected on, or affixed to the soil.

Corollaries, Illustrations, and Developments.—I.   By land or soil is meant not only ground capable of cultivation, but every other matter composing the globe, while it forms a part thereof ; therefore rocks and minerals, while they are yet in the quarry or mine, enter into this definition, but cease to form a part of the land when they are dug out or detached.

II.   Trees and all other vegetable matters, while they are rooted in the soil, whether produced by nature alone, or by nature aided by cultivation, and their fruits, while they are attached to them, are real property : but the plants cease to be real property when they are rooted out or cut down, as do the fruits after they are separated from the plants which produced them.

III.   Land covered with water, and the water standing in or upon or flowing over the soil, is real property.

IV.   Every thing that is constructed upon the land by art, which is not by its construction calculated and intended for locomotion, and all things permanently fixed to such erections as parts thereof, are real property. Therefore, a BUILDING erected on a foundation of wood or stone, or on posts, is real property ; but one resting on wheels or slides, and intended to be moved from place to place, is not real, but personal property, as are also all furniture, ornaments, or implements of trade which are usually moved, although they may be fastened to the soil or the building.

V.   The rents of real property reserved to the proprietor, while they are unpaid, whether such rent be reserved in money or other things, is real property.

PROPERTY (personal).   Every species of property which is not real property, comes under this description.

Corollaries.—I.   Money, bank bills, and public securities, are personal property.

II.   Credits, or the right of demanding or sueing for money or other personal property, and the evidence of such debts, are personal property, whether the same be debts of a personal nature or secured on land.

III. Rents, or annuities charged on land, payable to any one but the proprietor of the land, are personal property.

IV. The title deeds of real property, are personal property.

V. Shares in any banking, commercial, or manufacturing corporations or societies, and the certificates and other evidences of ownership thereof, are personal property, although such society or corporation may own real estate.

PUBLIC PRISON—the building designated by law, or used by the sheriff, in each parish, for the confinement of those whose persons are judicially ordered to be kept in custody.

If the prison designated by law should be destroyed, or if none should be provided, the sheriff must find some place for the imprisonment of those who are committed to his custody; and this place is then a PUBLIC PRISON, although it may be a private house.

PUBLIC PROSECUTOR—the attorney-general, the district attorneys in their respective districts, any person legally performing the duties of either of these officers, and any other officer who may be hereafter appointed by law to prosecute offenders on the part of the state.

PUBLIC RECORD—a written memorial made by a public officer authorized by law to perform that function, and intended to serve as evidence of something written, said, or done.

Corollaries.—I. Every statement in writing, made by a public officer, is not a public record. It must be one which that officer is specially authorized by law to make and record.

II. It must be memorial; by which is meant a written statement, intended to preserve the remembrance of what it contains.

III. It must also be intended to serve as legal evidence, the force of which is provided for in the Code of Evidence.

PUBLISHING, as applied to libels and violations of epistolary correspondence, means the mechanical operation of engraving, copying, painting, printing, or writing, from the dictation or reading of another; and CIRCULATING is the selling, giving, distributing, reading, or exhibiting it to others.

TO RECEIVE—voluntarily to take from another what is voluntarily offered.

RECOGNIZANCE, is an engagement in writing to pay a penalty therein expressed, if the person making the engagement, or some other designated person, shall not do a specified act required by law, or shall not abstain from doing other specified acts.

REPUTATION (general)—estimation for those qualities, the possession of which is essential to happiness in society, not those which render one more agreeable in it.

RIGHT, is in one sense synonymous with INCORPOREAL PROPERTY. In the other and more enlarged sense, it signifies every ADVANTAGE that man ought to enjoy according to the laws of nature, which are called NATURAL RIGHTS; or, according to law, which are called LEGAL RIGHTS.

RIGHTS (political). Political rights form one of the divisions of legal rights. They are those which are given by the constitution or by law of electing, or being elected, or appointed, to fill any PUBLIC OFFICE, or to perform any functions in any branch of the government.

RIGHTS (civil). Civil rights are those which every free person is authorized, by law, to exercise for the preservation either of his own person, property, or reputation; or of the persons, property, or reputation, of certain designated individuals, by virtue of some authority conferred by law, given by consent, or vested in him by the powers annexed to some PRIVATE or CORPORATE OFFICE.

SCHOOL-MASTER, is a person employed for the education of youth, of either sex, in the arts or sciences.

Corollary and additional Provision.—I. This definition includes private teachers of any art or science, and professors and tutors in universities, colleges, and academies, as well as in schools.

II. The right of restraint and correction given by the Code to school-masters, may be modified by agreement with their employers.

SECURITIES FOR MONEY, mean the written evidence of the existence of a debt.

SIGNATURE, when used in relation to an instrument in writing, means a name, a firm, or a mark, affixed thereto, in order to give it validity as the act of the party whose name, firm, or mark, is so affixed. The name of a witness, subscribed to an instrument, is also a signature; but it is always, when mentioned in this system, distinguishable by the context from the signature of the party.

TO SIGN, means to affix a signature.

THREAT. When this word occurs without any qualifying expression to show the nature of the evil that is threatened, it means a menace of great and illegal injury to person, property, or reputation.

TO UTTER, as applied to a false or forged instrument, means not only the declaring it, in words, to be true, but the saying or doing with, or in relation to it, any thing that shows a design, to cause another to believe that the instrument is true.

VERBAL PROCESS, is a written account of any proceeding or operation required by law, signed by the person commissioned to perform the duty, and attested by the signature of witnesses.

WARRANT, is the written order of a magistrate, attested by his signature, authorizing the person or officer to whom it is directed to perform certain duties of executive justice therein specified.

WORDS FOLLOWING. This expression, used in relation to the recital of an instrument in writing, includes all numerical figures, or other written signs, or marks, contained in the instrument to which they relate.

WRIT, is a like order, issued by a court, under its seal.

WRITING. Whenever the contrary does not appear from the context, this word means, not only words traced with a pen, or stamped but printed, or engraved, or made legible by any other device.

YEAR. The year intended in this system is the calendar year.

ADDITIONAL DEFINITIONS.

These Definitions relate to terms found printed in SMALL CAPITALS *in the " Extracts from a System of Penal Law for the United States."*

TO APPROPRIATE, in relation to property, is to possess, and to make such use or disposition of it, as none but the owner, or some one legally authorized by him, could of right do; and, with respect to rights, to do such acts in relation to them as none but the person entitled to them, or his representatives, could lawfully do. Appropriations are legal or fraudulent. No appropriations are fraudulent, but such as come within the definition of fraud in this book.

ATTEMPT. An attempt to commit an offence, in this system, means an endeavour to accomplish it, which has failed from some other cause than the voluntary relinquishment of the design.

CRIME is an offence, the punishment of which, in the whole or in part, may be the forfeiture of any civil or political right, or penitentiary imprisonment, or for which such imprisonment is an alternative, to be inflicted at the discretion of the court.

FORCE—VIOLENCE. These terms mean the exertion of physical power, and, when unqualified by anything in the context, the idea of the illegal exercise of such powers is intended to be conveyed.

FRAUD—TO DEFRAUD—unlawfully, designedly, and knowingly, to appropriate the property of another.

OFFENCE, is the doing what a PENAL LAW forbids to be done, or omitting to do what it commands. In most cases the contravention must be voluntary to constitute the offence; but there are exceptions to this part of the definition, to be found in the description of different offences in the Penal Code.

OFFENCES (general) are such as arise from contraventions of those laws of the United States which are made in their Federative capacity, and which operate upon the citizens and inhabitants of the whole Union, as contradistinguished from those passed for the government of districts or places over which they have the power of exclusive legislation.

OFFENCES (local) are such as arise from the breaches of laws passed by the United States, to have force only in places over which they have exclusive power of exclusive legislation.

DATE DUE